Shakespeare's
Earliest Tragedy

Shakespeare's Earliest Tragedy

Studies in *Titus Andronicus*

G. Harold Metz

Madison • Teaneck
Fairleigh Dickinson University Press
London: Associated University Presses

Associated University Presses
440 Forsgate Drive
Cranbury, NJ 08512

Associated University Presses
16 Barter Street
London WC1A 2AH, England

Associated University Presses
P.O. Box 338, Port Credit
Mississauga, Ontario
Canada L5G 4L8

The paper used in this publication meets the requirements
of the American National Standard for Permanence of Paper
for Printed Library Materials Z39.48-1984.

Library of Congress Cataloging-in-Publication Data

Metz, G. Harold (George Harold), 1917–
  Shakespeare's earliest tragedy : studies in Titus Andronicus / G. Harold Metz.
    p. cm.
  Includes bibliographical references and index.
  ISBN 0-8386-3653-5 (alk. paper)
  1. Shakespeare, William, 1564–1616. Titus Andronicus. 2. Titus Andronicus (Legendary character) in literature. 3. Shakespeare, William, 1564–1616—Authorship. 4. Generals in literature. 5. Rome—In literature. 6. Tragedy. I. Title.
PR2835.M48   1996
822.3'3—dc20   95-52067
                                                                      CIP

To Mary

and to the memory of
Matthew W. Black

Contents

List of Illustrations   9

Preface   11

1. Authorship   17

2. Twentieth-Century Criticism   45

3. Revision in *Titus Andronicus*   111

4. The Text   125

5. Sources, Origins, Influences   150

6. Date of Composition   190

7. Stage History: 1970–1994   199

8. The Longleat Manuscript   233

9. Nashe's *Unfortunate Traveller* and *Titus Andronicus*   248

10. Music in *Titus Andronicus*   255

Notes   262

Bibliography   299

Index   307

Illustrations

The title page of the First Quarto, 1594.   16

The title page of the Second Quarto, 1600.   44

The title page of the Third Quarto, 1611.   110

The title page of *The History of Titus Andronicus, The Renowned Roman General,* ca. 1536–64.   149

"A Stage for *Titus Andronicus,*" drawn by C. Walter Hodges, 1968.   198

The Longleat drawing of *Titus Andronicus,* ca. 1595.   232

Preface

SHAKESPEARE'S *Most Lamentable Romaine Tragedie of Titus Androni-cus* was one of his most popular plays during his lifetime. Ben Jonson, a scholar and a critic as well as a dramatist, was not easily impressed by the literary quality of the work of his fellow playwrights. In the induction to his *Bartholomew Fair,* which is cast in the form of a quasi-legal Agreement between "the spectators . . . and the author," the conduct of the audience is defined, including its right to censure the play, though not capriciously. The opinion of each member of the audience should "be fixed and settled in his censure, that what he approves or not approves today, he will do the same tomorrow . . ."

> He that will swear Jeronimo [The Spanish Tragedy] or *Andronicus are the best plays yet, shall pass unexcepted at here as a man whose judgment shows it is constant, and hath stood still this five and twenty, or thirty years. Though it be an ignorance, it is a virtuous and staid ignorance, and next to truth, a confirmed error does well; such a one the author knows where to find him.*

The proposed Articles of Agreement are dated precisely, as a legal document should be, on "the one and thirtieth day of October, 1614." Manifestly, Jonson does not approve of the audience's attachment to the two old plays, but in the course of his criticism he tells us, almost inadvertently, what the people in attendance clearly already know: that *Titus Andronicus* had at least a twenty-five year history of stage performance by 1614.

Although the play continued to be popular with theatrical habitués, scholars and critics were less enthusiastic. They were supported in this by a comment from Edward Ravenscroft, who in 1678 adapted Shakespeare's play for the stage and in 1687 published his version. In his address To the Reader he tells us that

> I have been told by some anciently conversant with the Stage, that it was not originally his [Shakespeare's], but brought by a private Author to be Acted, and he only gave some Master-Touches to one or two of the Principal Parts or Characters.

Even though he was promptly contradicted by Langbaine in 1691, who cites Ravenscroft's own original prologue in which he acknowledges that

11

"he but winnow'd Shakespear's Corn," critics of the eighteenth and nine-teenth centuries, with a few exceptions, were inclined to accept the tale. It is generally thought that this was so because they were repelled by the brutal quality of *Titus,* and credited Ravenscroft because he provided a rationale for neglecting the play, which they generally did. Bradley in the Introduction to his monumental *Shakespearean Tragedy* (1904) gives us his reasons for limiting the application of his title to *Hamlet, Othello, King Lear,* and *Macbeth.* He explains that he decided to omit eight other tragedies and historical tragedies, and says of *Titus Andronicus:* "I shall leave [it] out of account, because, even if Shakespeare wrote the whole of it, he did so before he had either a style of his own or any characteristic tragic conception." In the course of his book Bradley comments on *Titus* now and then as he does other tragedies, saying on one occasion: "hardly anyone doubts that he had a hand in it;" and on another designating it as "that horrible play." His assessment epitomizes the prevalent opinion at the time he wrote.

But at that moment, the critical tide had begun to turn, even though barely perceptibly. In the same year that Bradley's book was published, the original Arden edition was issued, edited by H. Bellyse Baildon, who treated the play as serious tragedy and presented a perceptive critical evaluation of its worth. Three years later G. P. Baker, in his *Development of Shakespeare as a Dramatist,* set forth his view that Shakespeare had transformed melodrama into something much finer. There followed a pause punctuated by Eliot's damning criticism (1927), Bolton's inquiry into structural deficiencies (1933), and Howard Baker's doubting investi-gation of the play's Senecanism (1939). Next came a decade of crosscur-rents, exemplified on the one hand in a largely successful effort by Price to understand and to highlight the play's Shakespearean values, particu-larly the structure, and Tillyard's appreciation of the characterization and the play's political implications; and on the other hand by Harbage's emphasis on what he perceives as "the incongruity of matter and man-ner," and by Charlton's finding of the play's deficiencies in the art of tragic drama.

The pace of the publication of *Titus* criticism quickened in the decade of the 1950s, during which significant comment was offered by M. C. Bradbrook, Clemen, Harrison, T. J. B. Spencer, Spivak, Gardner, and Waith (whose informative presentation of the importance of Ovid's poetry to *Titus* was the critical highlight of the period). The number of commen-taries doubled during the 1960s, followed by an unprecedented surge in critical activity with some eighty essays presented in the twenty-year span from 1970 to 1990; and the interest in the play on the part of scholars and critics seems to be continuing. Less than a century after Brad-ley's dismissal of *Titus* from serious consideration as a true Shakespearean tragedy the critical community has reestablished its Elizabethan reputation.

A parallel development took place in the theater. After a long production drought extending from the adaptation performed by the American black actor Ira Aldridge between 1849 and 1860 in Britain and on the Continent, the Old Vic presented a production by Robert Atkins and Lilian Bayliss in 1923 that ran for nine performances. It was well received, in general, as part of a cycle of all Shakespearean plays, an achievement that, according to Harcourt Williams, had never been attempted before. There followed a lull until 1951, when a group of Yale University students presented it, followed by a series of productions that had brief runs, culminating in the much admired and justifiably acclaimed Peter Brook–Laurence Olivier Stratford Memorial presentation of 1955–57.

Following that there were half a hundred productions over a nearly forty-year span, of which three have been hailed by scholarly and press reviewers as being worthy of favorable comparison with the Olivier–Brook presentation. These were the Joseph Papp–Gerald Freedman production in the New York Shakespeare Festival of 1967; the 1978–80 Brian Bedford presentation in the Stratford, Ontario Festival; and the Deborah Warner Royal Shakespeare Company 1987–89 mounting of the play. Warner's production exceeded, by a wide margin, all others in the number of performances, totaling, altogether, 163 at Stratford, Newcastle, in the Pit at Barbican, at London's Riverside Studios, and in Madrid, Paris, Copenhagen, and Aarhus, Denmark.

Thus, in the twentieth century both the critics in their studies and the theatrical producers on their stages have endorsed the many values of Shakespeare's earliest tragedy, and enhanced its reputation. *Titus Andronicus* has, in the last half-century, been reestablished in the Shakespeare canon and has seen its theatrical values vindicated. This is in the nature of a cultural revolution that is worthy of being recorded.

Anyone embarking on a study such as this will inevitably incur obligations to other members of the scholarly community who have generously given of their time and freely imparted their knowledge—and permitted citation of unpublished material—in response to not-infrequently importunate inquiries. For such indulgences and favors I wish to thank the late Giles E. Dawson, Stanley Wells, Gary Taylor, Trevor H. Howard-Hill, Maurice Charney, James L. Sanderson, William B. Long, Marga Munkelt, Alan C. Dessen, Ernst Haublein, John W. Velz, Richard Hosley, Letitia Yeandle, Joseph H. Stodder, and Margaret M. Tocci.

I also wish to express my thanks to the Marquess of Bath for granting permission to reproduce the famed Longleat drawing; to the Folger Shakespeare Library for consenting to the reproduction of the title page of the only surviving copy of the first quarto of *Titus*, and of the title page of the third quarto; and of the title page of *The History of Titus Andronicus;* to Oxford University Press and C. Walter Hodges for permission to reproduce his drawing of "A Stage for *Titus Andronicus;*" and to the Huntington Library and Art Gallery for allowing me to reproduce the title page of the second quarto of *Titus,* one of only two extant copies of that print. The American Philosophical Society, Philadelphia, generously awarded a grant to facilitate the collection of bibliographical materials relating to the texts of *Titus Andronicus,* for which I wish to express my gratitude. An earlier, shorter version of the Chapter on Date of Composition was initially published in *Notes and Queries* (223 [1978], 111–17). I appreciate the permission of the editors to print it here in revised and expanded form.

This book is, in the first place, dedicated to my wife, whose unfailing exhibition of "devotion, patience, courage, and fortitude" during the course of its preparation has been remarkable; and in the second place to the late Professor Matthew Black who was, to at least one graduate student, both a mentor and a friend.

Shakespeare's
Earliest Tragedy

THE
MOST LA-
mentable Romaine
Tragedie of Titus Andronicus:

As it was Plaide by the Right Ho-
nourable the Earle of *Darbie*, Earle of *Pembrooke*,
and Earle of *Suffex* their Seruants.

LONDON,
Printed by Iohn Danter, and are
to be fold by *Edward White* & *Thomas Millington*,
at the little North doore of Paules at the
figne of the Gunne.
1594.

Title page, First Quarto of *Titus Andronicus*, 1594. Reproduced by permission of the Folger Shakespeare Library.

1

Authorship

SHAKESPEARE'S authorship of *Titus Andronicus* has been debated for three centuries. A doubt about the authenticity of the play on the basis of purported stage gossip was raised in 1687 by Ravenscroft, whose report was promptly and vigorously attacked by Langbaine in 1691, and ever since the question has been much contested. Commentators of every persuasion since Ravenscroft and Langbaine joined the issue have uttered pronouncements ranging across a broad spectrum, opinion shading into opinion in great diversity.

As a play, *Titus* has been judged by many scholars to be deficient. Theme, verse, and diction are thought to be uncharacteristic of Shakespeare. The perceived lack of an informing idea, the seeming absence of or deficiency in an ethical stance, the relatively static nature of the action, and the emblematic quality of the characters mark the play, in the judgment of many critics, as one that is measurably inferior to his other works. It is sometimes said to be unworthy of Shakespeare. The manifest disparity in style between that of the long first scene and that of the rest of the play, and the stylistic peculiarities of the play as a whole are disturbing to those who believe that while Shakespeare's writing may have varied in quality there is a certain level below which it could not have fallen. Inconsistencies discerned in the characterization; insufficient, or what is sometimes called nonexistent, motivation; the inadequate dynamics of some scenes; weaknesses in the plot; the mechanisms employed to distance the horrors; the horrors themselves—all these, for many critics, raise authenticity questions. Contemplating these perceived flaws, and others identified by diligent seekers after defect, has caused many students of *Titus* over the years to experience strong doubts on aesthetic grounds concerning the attribution of the play to Shakespeare. However, in this century there has been a distinct trend toward rehabilitation of its canonical standing.

Scholarly judgments, although widely varied, may be grouped into a half-dozen categories. A few critics have denied that Shakespeare wrote any part of the play. Some think with Ravenscroft that he lightly revised the work of another writer. Others speculate that, as a beginner in writing plays, he collaborated with a more experienced dramatist, or was one contributor to a collaboration involving several poets. Still others believe it is a thorough-going revision of an earlier version of the Titus story. Then there are scholars who accept the play as entirely or substantially Shakespeare's, some without reservation, others continuing to entertain doubts particularly about Act 1. A minority consider it possible that it is early Shakespeare revised by another hand. Finally, there are a few critics who seem to conclude that the authorship problem is insoluble.

Two items of external evidence attest to the authenticity of *Titus:* its attribution to Shakespeare by Meres in his *Palladis Tamia Wits Treasvry,* published in 1598; and inclusion in the First Folio of 1623. Heminges and Condell, who brought together the plays and prepared them for publication, were close associates of Shakespeare's in the Lord Chamberlain's–King's Men from 1594, and perhaps a little earlier, until at least 1613, when Shakespeare seems to have begun to limit his active participation in the affairs of the company. He remembers them, along with Richard Burbage, in his will, calling them "my fellows."[1] They surely were working closely with him while he was writing all except possibly his very earliest plays and they were undoubtedly present while he "instructed" the players, including themselves, in their parts when his plays were first produced. No doubt they also had a hand in mounting revivals. Their inclusion of *Titus* among the collection of *Mr. William Shakespeares Comedies, Histories, & Tragedies* is strong *prima facie* evidence for Shakespeare's authorship because it has never been successfully maintained that any play in the First Folio was not at least substantially his. None of them, including *Titus*—unlike some plays included in the Beaumont and Fletcher Folio of 1647—was challenged at the time of publication.[2] Meres also appears to have been reliable. Of the dozen comedies and tragedies he attributes to Shakespeare, ten are solidly within the canon; one, *Loue labours wonne,* is not extant;[3] the twelfth is *Titus Andronicus.*

Ravenscroft cast doubt on the authenticity of the play in an address "To the Reader" in the prolegomena to his printed "Alter'd" version entitled *Titus Andronicus, or the Rape of Lavinia,* 1687. He says, in part,

> I think it a greater theft to Rob the dead of their Praise then the Living of their Money: That I may not appear Guilty of such a Crime, 'tis necessary I should acquaint you, that there is a Play in Mr. Shakespears Volume under the name of *Titus Andronicus,* from whence I drew part of this. I have been told by some anciently conversant with the Stage, that it was not Originally his, but brought by a private Author to be Acted, and he only gave some Mastertouches to one or two of the Principal Parts or Characters; this I am apt to believe, because

'tis the most incorrect and indigested piece in all his Works; It seems rather a heap of Rubbish then a Structure.[4]

Langbaine controverts Ravenscroft's story by quoting his original prologue to the 1678 production, which Ravenscroft claims "In the Hurry of those distracted times . . . [was] lost," and was therefore unavailable to be printed. Langbaine says:

> I will here furnish him with part of his Prologue, which he has lost; and if he desire it, send him the whole.
>
> *To day the Poet does not fear your Rage,*
> *Shakespear by him reviv'd now treads the Stage:*
> *Under his sacred Lawrels he sits down*
> *Safe, from the blast of any Criticks Frown.*
> *Like other Poets, he'll not proudly scorn*
> *To own, that he but winnow'd Shakespear's Corn;*
> *So far he was from robbing him of 's Treasure,*
> *That he did add his own, to make full Measure.[5]*

Ravenscroft's report of the stage tradition, if in fact there ever was one, is of doubtful value as evidence in view of his own earlier prologue. There may have been some such story circulating in theatrical circles in the late seventeenth century as there were many others; and, like virtually all of those, Ravenscroft's is unlikely to be true. Nevertheless, later commentators on *Titus,* probably because the play's brutal events repelled them, experienced doubts concerning its authenticity, and accorded Ravenscroft's tale serious consideration and, in many cases, credence.

Most critics from the time of Rowe until well into the nineteenth century tended to approach the problem of authenticity as an aesthetic question. They concentrated their critical faculties on qualities of style, "manner," versification, and diction, which they thought exhibited distinctive personal characteristics by which the author could be identified. In the case particularly of *Titus Andronicus,* the matter of taste is frequently discussed, usually as an argument against Shakespeare's participation because it was commonly believed that gentle Shakespeare could not have been the author of the horrors. Pope says:

> If I may judge from all the distinguishing marks of his style, and his manner of thinking and writing, I make no doubt to declare that those wretched plays [that were added in the second issue of the Third Folio] cannot be admitted as his. And I should conjecture of some of the others, (particularly *Love's Labour Lost, The Winter's Tale,* and *Titus Andronicus*) that only some characters, single scenes, or perhaps a few particular passages, were of his hand. It is very probable what occasion'd some Plays to be supposed *Shakespear's* was only this; that they were pieces produced by unknown authors, or fitted up for the Theatre while it was under his administration: and no owner claiming them, they were adjudged to him.

Theobald writes: "This is one of those plays which I have always thought, with the better judges, ought not to be acknowledged in the list of Shakespeare's genuine pieces . . . That he . . . introduced it a-new on the stage, with the addition of his own masterly touches is incontestable." Johnson tells us: "All the editors and criticks agree with Mr. *Theobald* in supposing this play spurious. I see no reason for differing from them; for the colour of the stile is wholly different from that of the other plays, and there is an attempt at regular versification, and artificial closes, not always inelegant, yet seldom pleasing. The barbarity of the spectacles, and the general massacre which are here exhibited, can scarcely be conceived tolerable to any audience; yet we are told by *Johnson* [i.e., Ben Jonson], that they were not borne but praised. That *Shakespear* wrote any part, though *Theobald* declares it *incontestable,* I see no reason for believing." Percy comments: "There is reason to conclude that this play was rather improved by Shakespeare with a few fine touches of his pen than originally writ by him; . . . the style is less figurative than his others generally are."[6]

Capell discusses some considerations other than those that are aesthetic, such as Shakespeare's professionalism as a theater poet, and attacks the impressionistic judgments of other critics:

> We are now come to . . . 'Titus Andronicus:' commentators, editors, every one (in short) who has had to do with SHAKESPEARE, unite all in condemning it,—as a very bundle of horrors, totally unfit for the stage, and unlike the Poet's manner, and even the style of his other pieces; all of which allegations are extreamly true, and we readily admit of them, but can not admit the conclusion—that, therefore, it is not his . . . for though a work of imitation, and conforming itself to models truly execrable throughout, yet the genius of its Author breaks forth in some places, and, to the editor's eye, SHAKESPEARE stands confess'd.[7]

Malone, in his study of Shakespearean chronology, classifies *Titus* with *Pericles* and the other apocryphal plays of the Third Folio as spurious. Regarding *Titus,* he gives as his reasons: "The high antiquity of the piece, its entry on the Stationers' books without the name of the writer, the regularity of the versification, the dissimilitude of the style from that of those plays which are undoubtedly composed by our author, and the tradition mentioned by Ravenscroft, at a period when some of his contemporaries [John Lowin, Joseph Taylor, and Sir William D'Avenant] had not long been dead render it highly improbable that this play should have been the composition of Shakspeare." The minor reservation in his closing words seems to have been resolved against Shakespeare's authorship by the time of his 1790 edition of the plays. Finally, Malone, in the 1821 Variorum, after reiterating substantially the same considerations, cites in addition "the whole colour of the composition, [and] its resemblance to several of our most ancient dramas . . . all these circumstances combined, prove with irresistable force that the play of *Titus Andronicus* has been erroneously ascribed to Shakspeare."[8]

Hanmer, Steevens, Ritson, Boswell, Farmer, Hallam, Dyce, Dowden, and Swinburne, although expressing their views with differences of emphasis, substantially agree, on the basis of the same grounds, with the judgments of Pope, Theobald, Johnson, and Malone. Other commentators who conclude, whether or not accepting Ravenscroft's story, that Shakespeare merely lightly revised the play are Warburton, Coleridge, Collier, Furnivall, Symons, and Lee. Critics who arrived at the same opinion as Capell, that *Titus* is entirely or substantially Shakespeare's, include Tyrwitt, Schlegel, Knight, Ulrici, Verplanck, Delius, Elze, Boas, and Raleigh. Boas expresses his judgment directly: "External evidence ascribed the play to Shakespeare, and the conjecture that he merely added revising touches to it finds no support in the character of the work. For, whatever its demerits are, it has an unmistakeable stamp of unity."[9]

Halliwell-Phillipps, after having had doubts about the authenticity of *Titus Andronicus* in his edition of Shakespeare, gives us his mature opinion in 1898:

> [His] theatrical success was neither the result of a devotion to art, nor of a solicitude for the eulogy of readers, but of his unrivalled power of characterization, of his intimate knowledge of stage business, and of a fidelity to mental nature that touched the hearts of all. These qualities, although less prominently developed in *Titus Andronicus* than in many other of his plays, are yet to be observed in that inferior work. Even amidst its display of barbarous and abandoned personages, neither sternness nor profligacy is permitted to altogether extinguish the natural emotions, while, at the same time, the unities of character are well sustained. It is by tests such as these . . . that the authenticity of Shakespeare's earliest tragedy should be determined . . . The external testimonies to the reality of [*Titus*] . . . as the work of Shakespeare are irrefutable. [In addition to the determination of Hemings and Condell there is] the evidence of Meres, which is not only that of an accomplished scholar giving his voluntary opinion within five years from the appearance of *Titus Andronicus,* but also that of one who has faithfully recorded so many other literary facts, ought to satisfy us that there is no alternative but to receive that drama as one of the genuine works of Shakespeare.[10]

An effort to establish more objective bases for judgments of internal evidence bearing on questions of chronology and authenticity, employing analytical and statistical techniques, coincided with the activities of the New Shakspere Society (established 1873). The results of such studies by Furnivall, Ingram, Pulling, and, most notably, Fleay, who made the major contribution to the development of metrical tests, were published in the Society's *Transactions* (1874–85). Most of these tests were based upon counts of the total number of lines in a play, the number of lines of prose and blank verse, of verse features such as couplets, alternating rhymes, short lines, run-on lines, and the calculation of percentages of each observed phenomenon to the total number of lines. The data are then analyzed to develop a means of identifying and quantifying characteristics of style peculiar to an individual playwright, and, within his writings, identifying trends of development that would assist in solving questions of chronology as well as authorship. In the case of Shakespeare it was possible to show that the proportion of run-on lines, short-line speech endings and verses with feminine, light, or weak endings to the total number of lines in a play exhibit a generally progressive increase from the plays known from external evidence to be earlier to those that are later. Internal evidence of this type can sometimes be useful as an aid in assigning dates to plays when no external evidence exists. Its use in developing answers to questions of authenticity is less reliable, as Chambers pointed out.[11] Fleay employed such tests freely in attempts at solving authorship puzzles. His frequent changes of opinion, which is admittedly a personal characteristic, may also be reflective of an important limitation of the early metrical and stylistic tests, namely their susceptibility to divergent interpretation, not only by different critics, but also by the same critic at different times. In 1874 Fleay says that, on the basis of an interpretation of a set of metrical tables, "*Taming of the Shrew, Henry VI,* and *Titus Andronicus* are not Shakspere's in the main bulk; they are productions of what I call the Greene and Marlowe School." He next expressed substantially the same opinion in 1876, but renaming the "school" as "Lodge, Peele, and Marlowe." He reworked his statistical tables from time to time, and one such revision was published in 1881 in a book by Ingleby, where his comment on *Titus* is: "Begun by Marlow and Peele 1592–3; finished by Peele 6th February 1594, for Sussex' Players." In 1886 his finding is: "That this play is not by Shakespeare is pretty certain from internal evidence." His evidence at this point consists of Latin quotations, classical allusions, versification (but he does not specifically mention verse tests), and the introduction of rape as dramatic material. He says:

> That it was written by Marlowe I incline to think. What other mind but the author of *The Jew of Malta* could have conceived Aaron the Moor? . . . Nevertheless I think the opinion that Kyd wrote this play of *Andronicus* worth the examination, although, with such evidence as has yet been adduced Marlowe has certainly the better claim. Shakespeare probably never touched this play unless by inserting iii.2 which is possible.

In his final word on the authenticity question he confesses mystification (1891).

The authorship of this play will, I fear, long remain a puzzle to critics. How such a play came to be produced by Sussex' men [of whom he has a low opinion] . . . is a mystery. I cannot believe that either Kyd or Marlow would have written for these strollers . . . The more likely view is that the author was dead, and they got the play cheap in some exceptional fashion. Again, the absence of any trace of allegorical personages or Induction militates against its being Kyd's work. I fear it is Marlow's.[12]

Vocabulary tests in a variety of forms were devised in an effort to develop a quantified evaluation of the presence of rare words in Shakespeare. Richard Simpson compiled and published a "Table of Shakspere's Once-Used Words" covering the canonical thirty-seven plays. "The table . . . will show, [he notes], the futility of any attempt to prove that *Titus Andronicus* . . . is not Shakspere's." The mere averages are adverse to such an argument.[13] These efforts came more nearly to fruition in a comprehensive study by Sarrazin of words used throughout the canon only two or three times. He developed his tests to try to provide an objective means of determining chronology with only a secondary interest in authenticity. He makes no direct comment on *Titus,* but includes it in his statistics, and the tables themselves exhibit no aberration setting it apart from other early plays.[14] Hubbard studies forms of repetition (use of the same word in the same or succeeding lines) and parallelism (use of the same form of expression in the same or succeeding lines) in some thirty Elizabethan plays, of which five are Shakespeare's. He does not offer a conclusion about the authorship of *Titus,* but one of his tables shows that the frequency and distribution of occurrences of these forms in the three *Henry VI* plays and *Richard III* approximate that in *Titus Andronicus.* Grosart devised a test employing parallel passages and drew up a comparison of *Selimus* and *Titus Andronicus.* He also takes into account similarities and classical allusions in the two plays, of vocabulary, of structure, and of horrors. *Titus* is substantially assigned to Greene, but Grosart acknowledges that there are things in the play not unworthy of Shakespeare, especially in the later acts. His hypothesis is somewhat vitiated, since neither Grosart nor anyone else has successfully established Greene's authorship of *Selimus.*[15] Fuller analyses and compares the incidents in *Titus* with those in the somehow related Dutch *Aran en Titus* and the German *Eine sehr klägliche Tragödie von Tito Andronico und der hoffertigen Kayserin.* He concludes that the two Continental texts, manifestly shortened, descend from different English originals, which he identifies as Henslowe's *Titus and Vespasia* and *Titus and Ondronicus.* The surviving English text is a free and superior adaptation of the two earlier plays, the structure and diction of which are characteristic of Shakespeare. He "believe[s] Shakspere to be the author of practically every line of *Titus,*" and that it belongs to the year 1594. Baker supports

Shakespeare's authorship: the play "shows that by 1594 Shakespeare was a competent dramatist."[16]

Starting with Root in 1903, a few scholars have studied mythological allusions as a clue to authorship. Root finds three factors that bear on the question. The count of the number of mythological allusions is high for Shakespeare in any period but especially in contrast to other earlier plays. Of greater significance is a series of four allusions that seem to show an acquaintance with Greek drama, which it is presumed Shakespeare did not have. These, plus the mention of six mythological names that do not occur in Shakespeare's acknowledged plays, leads Root to conclude that "the evidence becomes strong that Shakespeare is not the author." Law traces fourteen of the Roman names that occur in *Titus Andronicus* and some of the incidents in the play associated with the names, to the *Aeneid, The Breviary of Eutropius,* and especially to Plutarch's *Life of Scipio Africanus.* He points out that "the play is a curious composition of crime and revenge borrowed from Roman lore, chiefly in Seneca and Ovid, joined together by the young Shakespeare . . . If this study is soundly based, I think there can be no serious doubt that Shakespeare is the sole author of the play." Highet, as part of a general study of the classical tradition in European literature, assesses Shakespeare's knowledge of Greek and Latin writers, particularly Ovid, Seneca, and Plutarch, who are "Shakespeare's chief classical sources." Highet does not directly address the question of the authorship of *Titus Andronicus* but he considers the play to be of "doubtful" authenticity, apparently on the authority of Shakespearean scholars. Nevertheless, he shows that the use of classical sources conforms to that in the acknowledged plays. Thomson, covering somewhat similar ground, assumes as a working hypothesis that *Titus* is wholly the work of Shakespeare because the evidence, both external and internal, for authenticity "is almost irresistible." He examines in detail the Latin passages in the play and the classical allusions that the author was well-grounded in Seneca, Horace, and Ovid, and knew some Virgil and Cicero, though not necessarily in the original of any of these writers because there are a few signs that he used translations. There are also passages drawn, directly or indirectly, from other classical authors such as Herodotus and Livy. The sum of this suggests "a considerably wider range of classical reading than is discoverable in the plays that are Shakespeare's own." He cites two passages that may reflect a knowledge of *Hecuba* of Euripedes and the *Ajax* of Sophocles, notes that they occur in almost immediate succession in Act 1, but elects to leave the evaluation of this "to the experts." He finds that "the classical allusions which occur most frequently in Shakespeare's other plays are most evident in the second act of *Titus.*" In two studies of classical influence, more specifically focused, Mowat and West find nothing in the mythological and classical elements of *Titus* inconsistent with an assumption of Shakespeare's authorship.[17] Robertson was a disintegrationist who wrote a book-length attack on the authenticity of *Titus*. He makes use of metrical and vocabulary tests developed by others, but he relies most heavily on parallels. By means of them, he identifies significant parts of the play as the work of poets other than Shakespeare, including Peele, Greene, Marlowe, Kyd, Lodge, and Chapman. His multitudinous parallels are of varying value, cogent ones being rare, the majority of them showing only vague, distant, or incidental relationships. One fairly representative example compares a line from *Titus* with two from Peele's *David and Bethsabe:*

My sons sweet blood will make it shame and blush

(3.1.15)

With blood that blusheth for his conscience guilt

(David and Bethsabe, 3.3)

And makes her fields blush with her children's blood

(David and Bethsabe, 3.5)

Most of Robertson's parallels are of approximately equivalent evidentiary value. In the Summary of his position in the second version of his book he decides that the external evidence of the authenticity of *Titus* is inconclusive. He says Meres was repeating playhouse gossip and Heminges and Condell were defending ownership of the play by the Chamberlain's Men. The quartos, published without attribution to Shakespeare, and Jonson's gibe in *Bartholomew Fair,* tell strongly against authenticity. Greene and Kyd, and possibly Peele, collaborated to produce *Titus and Vespasian,* which Peele recast as *Titus Andronicus* in 1593. Marlowe "worked at the later stage." Alleged internal evidence of Shakespeare's authorship, Robertson says, breaks down at nearly every point. "The case is thus proved against his authorship independently of the extremely strong presumption that the most coarsely repulsive play in the entire Elizabethan drama cannot have been the work of the greatest and most subtle of all the dramatists of the age."[18]

Greg was early persuaded by such means. He says that he is in general agreement with Robertson, but that he fails to discover any clear internal evidence of Shakespeare having touched the play at all, though there are a few lines whose Shakespearean authorship is not impossible. The testimony of Meres and the First Folio editors present a difficulty and he devises a complex explanation of two original versions of *Titus Andronicus,* one of which was revised by Shakespeare but perished in the Globe fire, leaving only the non-Shakespearean text. He reasserts this hypothesis later, saying that "no trace of his [Shakespeare's] hand was discoverable in the extant text." This becomes, even later, in one of his Clark Lectures: "I find no evidence of more than one hand . . . The search for Ravenscroft's 'master touches' has proved futile . . . On the other hand, the addition to the Clown's speech certainly has a Shakespearian flavour." In his definitive work on the First Folio, Greg reiterates his attribution of the Clown's lines to Shakespeare, but offers no further discussion of authorship. It appears possible that he may have continued to doubt Shakespeare's authorship of the play.[19]

Among the vestiges of Robertson's disintegrationist influence is Eliot's frequently-cited comment that the play is "one of the stupidest and most uninspired plays ever written, a play in which it is incredible that Shakespeare had any hand at all, a play in which the best passages would be too highly honored by the signature of Peele." Other commentators, influenced at least in part and in varying degrees by Robertson, include Adams, Fripp, Van Doren, and Bowers.[20]

Parrott posits a Pembroke's ur-*Titus* that the company sold to Henslowe in 1593. It was revised at the instigation of Alleyn, who presumably took the part of Aaron. We know that the reviser was Shakespeare because Meres and Heminges and Condell regarded the play as his, but the revision was hasty and superficial and confined to certain scenes, an inference supported by Ravenscroft. By means of a test of the incidence of feminine endings, Shakespeare's hand can be detected, then confirmed by parallels of thought and diction. The steadily increasing use of feminine endings over Shakespeare's career marks a steadily increasing mastery of blank verse. The findings of the test divide *Titus* neatly in half. Seven scenes show a low proportion while the other seven have a much higher proportion. Parallels of vocabulary and content confirm the relatively thoroughgoing revision of half of the scenes. Shakespeare did not revise the whole structure of his source. He merely retouched certain scenes, as in his revision of the *Henry VI* plays.[21]

Neilson and Thorndike bring together the metrical statistics of Fleay, König, and Ingram, primarily for purposes of chronology. However, the tests also show an affinity in such characteristics as the frequency of rhyme, feminine endings, run-on lines, short lines, and light and weak endings of *Titus* with the *Henry VI* plays and *Romeo*. Henry Gray, in a related chronology study, conflated some of the same sets of statistics. He thinks that the low averaged percentages seen in *Titus* and *1 Henry VI* "will be attributed by most critics to their composite authorship." Wentersdorf, once more linking metrical tests and chronology, tells us that the play "bears many signs of painstaking if inexperienced literary effort, and the trend of modern criticism . . . is to regard the tragedy, on the basis of imagery and other stylistic features, as a genuine but very juvenile work."[22]

Concurrent with the rejection of the authenticity of *Titus Andronicus* by critics ranging from Fleay (1891) to Robertson, Parrott, and Gray (1931) there was a less-prominent tide running in the opposite direction. Saintsbury, for example, says "*Titus Andronicus* as we have it has been denied to Shakespeare, but this denial really passes the bounds of all rational literary criticism . . . the genuinely Shakespearian character of Aaron and the genuinely Shakespearian poetry . . . joined to the external [evidence] . . . is simply irresistible."[23] This trend found its culmination in Chambers's British Academy Shakespeare Lecture, in which he effectively discredited Robertson's anti-Stratfordian proposition. He exposes the numerous weaknesses in Robertson's argument, his lack of scholarly rigor in presenting his evidence, his overevaluation of parallel passages of doubtful significance, his abuse of metrical tests, his ignorance of many aspects of theatrical conditions in Shakespeare's day, and his failure to accord due weight to the external evidence. Chambers, step-by-thoughtful-step, dismembers Robertson's thesis and redirects the trend of Shakespearean authenticity studies toward an emphasis on objective evidence. In a more general treatment, he notes that Shakespeare's original authorship of *Titus* has been generally doubted from the days of Malone on stylistic grounds and because of Ravenscroft's stage tradition. There are in the play some parallels to Peele's *Edward I* and *The Honour of the Garter,* but other Peelean qualities, such as long pedestrian passages and rhyme, are absent. Henslowe's "ne" of 24 January 1594, the earlier *Titus and Vespasian,* the German and Dutch versions of *Titus Andronicus,* and the allusion in *A Knack to Know a Knave* are crosscurrents of evidence that are difficult to harmonize. He thinks the ballad rests on the play, and perhaps that the *History of Titus Andronicus* may also. Greg's tentatively-offered theory of two versions of *Titus* is reviewed, but Chambers rejects it as too complex to be likely. If the play was originally written in 1592 or 1589, the stylistic case against Shakespeare as an original writer is weakened. Chambers apologizes for being inconclusive, saying "the complicated *data* are themselves so."[24]

Alexander advocates the authenticity of *Titus Andronicus,* citing the external evidence, reasserting the integrity of Heminges, Condell, and Meres, and the reliability of their evidence. He also calls attention to the links to *Venus* and *Lucrece* and argues that, in view of Shakespeare's stint as a schoolmaster in the country, the classical content and the Latin phrases point to his authorship.

Timberlake studies the feminine ending in the blank verse of every important Elizabethan playwright and in many anonymous plays of the period as a means of solving problems of date and authorship. He offers two counts expressed as percentages of feminine endings to total blank-verse lines, one designated "total feminine endings" and the other "strict feminine endings." To arrive at the "strict" category, he eliminates contextual phenomena such as proper names with light final syllables. The incidence of feminine endings in *Titus* is analyzed scene by scene. He evaluates four theories of authorship: all Shakespeare's; not Shakespeares; Shakepeare's revised by others; and a Shakespearean revision of an earlier play, again reviewing the play scene by scene because "in a play which is so certainly not by one hand, the percentage of feminine endings for the whole is not significant, and we must consider the variation of individual scenes." On this basis he assigns three scenes to Shakespeare, five to Kyd or Shakespeare, and four to Peele or Greene or possibly Marlowe, leaving two scenes that he considers too brief to provide adequate material for a test. The data show that a considerable part of the extant text exhibits a level of feminine endings characteristic of Shakespeare. Therefore he concludes "that *Titus* is not entirely the work of Shakespeare, that it does contain considerable Shakespearean matter; and that the appearance of this matter in widely separated parts marks a thorough revision by him of all but the first act."[25]

Sampley analyzes the plot structure of Peele's acknowledged plays. He finds as characteristic of Peele's plotting a discursive, haphazard, chronicle type of structure, incoherent plot development, useless incidents, and a weak and straggling conclusion. "A serious and fundamental lack of unity is characteristic of every play known to be by Peele." He notes that *Titus Andronicus* is "well constructed" and concludes that it is hard to understand how Peele could have been responsible for the structure of the play. In an earlier essay on Peele's lexical preferences, Sampley had arrived at the same judgment. Maxwell, in his edition, cites Sampley's 1936 study favorably and agrees that the structure suggests Shakespeare. The Shakespearean structural qualities are noted by a number of scholars, not always by specific reference to Peele. Price sees Shakespeare's hand in the plot and Talbert concurs: "A basic structural precision and a unifying control is at work in *Titus Andronicus*," qualities that he considers to be Shakespearean and among the reasons for the popularity of the play.[26]

Kittredge rejects Ravenscroft and his story, branding him "irresponsible" and his stage tradition "idle gossip which he reports (or invents)" and says it "cannot weigh against the positive assertion of Meres." Critics doubt Shakespeare's authorship of *Titus Andronicus* because they feel it is too horrible to be his, but Shakespeare was always prone to try experiments, and it would be strange if he did not write a tragedy of blood that Kyd had shown could appeal to playgoers. Kittredge finds that the highly successful interweaving of classical themes exhibits Shakespeare's hand.

"Distaste for horrors ought not to make one regardless of the skilful construction of the play, of its dramatic power, and of the magnificence of many poetical passages. With all its faults, it is far beyond the abilities of either Peele or Greene. Shakespeare must have the credit as well as the discredit of its authorship."[27]

Price thinks that on grounds of style, character, theme, plot, and structure the play could have been written only by Shakespeare. He draws attention to the presence in *Titus* of the Renaissance practice of imitation: "It simply will not do to say that Peele, Greene, or Marlowe wrote any particular part of *Titus* that happens to resemble their work. It is all the less possible as Shakespeare imitated freely till the end of his days. At the time when *Titus* was written, he was a conscientious student of other men's work." Discussing the vocabulary tests and parallels deployed by Robertson, he cites first the three types of words that Robertson says are common both to *Titus* and to Peele, but Price denies that they are special to Peele. "All three classes are good common Elizabethan . . . frequent in Shakespeare . . . There is nothing about any of these three classes which would point to Peele rather than Shakespeare." He evaluates with precision Robertson's parallels, and his tests of meter and finds that they as readily support Shakespeare's authorship of the play as Peele's. It has been asserted that the prevalence of classical allusions, and the fact that some are recondite, argues for a university education on the part of the dramatist, but Price finds that the familiarity with classical literature exhibited in the play is the result of wide though probably casual reading rather than deep study. The classical allusions are employed as "so much local color," used solely for their dramatic values. "I submit that the 'pattern' of the classical learning points to Shakespeare as the author of *Titus Andronicus*." Price believes that the best test of authorship is construction.

Phrases may be borrowed here and there, but construction refers to the planning of the work as a whole. It is the most intimate expression of the author's meaning. The carriage of the plot and the weaving together of many motifs to form unity require a particular kind of skill without which all outside aid is futile . . . the only parallel to the plot of *Titus* is to be found in the other works of Shakespeare. Construction, characterization, intensity of conflict, exuberance, the power to give variety with unity—these demand qualities that no playwright can transfer from another man's drama to his own. As it is in these things that *Titus* closely resembles Shakespeare's work and differs widely from anything written by Marlowe, Greene, or Peele, we must conclude, however regretfully, that Shakespeare was the author of *Titus Andronicus*.

Price also studies certain types of spellings that occur in *Titus* and in the quartos of seven other Shakespearean plays. None of the texts resembles the general pattern in every detail, but he finds enough general likeness to support the theory that these texts all belong to one family. *Titus* exhibits the same types of spellings because it was "printed from the same kind of copy which was a manuscript written by Shakespeare himself."[28] Dover Wilson believes that the solution to the puzzle of authorship of *Titus Andronicus* is that the play "may be of mixed parentage, that is to say, a production for which Shakespeare is only in part responsible." Assuming that Shakespeare was revising an earlier text, in part, at least, by Peele, he analyzes the fourteen scenes. "The whole [of Act 1] . . . is Peele's . . . 'Act 2, with all its faults and outrages is . . . mainly from the hand of Sh[akespeare].'" Of Act 3, the first scene is Peele, "pretty thoroughly rewritten: scene 2 "seems . . . to be" Shakespeare's. Act 4 exhibits "a substratum of Peele . . . while . . . Sh[akespeare's] hand seems evident" in places. Of Act 5 "the whole [first] sc[ene] may well be Sh[akespeare]'s"; scene 2 is Shakespeare based on "An orig[inal] sc[ene which has been] re-written . . . with care; [and he] seems to have revised . . . scene [3] rather thoroughly." In the introduction to his edition, he includes a comprehensive discussion of authorship, in the course of which he offers two specific judgments: "All the evidence points to Peele as the man solely responsible for the basic play." And that it is a "fact that Shakespeare was deeply involved in the received text." Nineteen years later, without explanation, Wilson revises his conclusion: "Though there is little doubt that the play owes much to the influence of Peele, Greene, etc., I no longer believe that the author, after the first Act, was anyone but Shakespeare throughout."[29] Stauffer finds that "the maker of *Titus Andronicus*—so the play tells us—was a writer who could turn out smooth blank verse; who had read around enthusiastically in the Latin storytellers Ovid, Vergil, and the tragic Seneca; who was somewhat naively proud that he knew the Latin poets in the original, and who was so much at home with birds and animals and country scenes that he almost makes his bloody Roman city into rustic village . . . The play is a storehouse of themes and episodes and attitudes and images and situations which Shakespeare was later to develop. It is much easier to assume that Shakespeare wrote it than to explain how so many of his later preoccupations got into a play written by someone else." Feuillerat identifies three authors in the verse, style, and mannerisms of *Titus*. It "is an old play, written by author A (traces of his versification and style are found in practically all the scenes), first touched up by author B to give it a Marlovian flavor, and finally revised in an important way (as the mannerisms and images show) by Shakespeare . . . *Titus Andronicus* must be composed of passages in which the old text has been preserved word for word, of mixed passages reproducing part of the old text more or less modified, and of passages entirely Shakespearean." Thus Meres was not entirely wrong when he included *Titus* among Shakespeare's tragedies, nor was Ravenscroft's theatrical tradition far from the truth.[30]

Maxwell points out that "the early establishment of an orthodox opinion hostile to the Folio attribution is notable." Several dramatists have been thought to have had a share in the writing of the play, but Peele is now the only serious candidate for such participation. There is much better evidence of his presence in Act 1 than in the rest of the play, the evidence being primarily stylistic: verbal parallels, a tendency to mechanical repetition, and a syntactic trick of style frequently used by Peele. "The case (from internal evidence) against [Peele] rests on considerations of structure . . . [which] suggests Shakespeare rather than Peele." Perhaps Price is right in assigning the whole play to Shakespeare, but Maxwell "can never quite believe it *while* reading Act 1. At the same time, the alternative to which I find myself driven is not a very plausible one, since it involves holding that as early as 1589–90 Peele, already a well-established dramatist, acted as a very subordinate collaborator with a writer a number of years his junior in both age and experience." Similarly indecisive conclusions are expressed by McManaway, Munro, and Cross.[31]

Sisson has no reservations. He vigorously attacks disintegrationist hypotheses. "External evidence is decisive for Shakespeare's authorship . . . it will not do to take refuge against the [external] evidence in complex theories of revision, improvement, or even deliberate parody by Shakespeare of an old manner of writing. The doubtful evidence of parallel passages, so much used as proof of the authorship of Peele, is in fact strongest in support of Shakespeare's own authorship, if fairly handled." Editors and critics who have recently accepted *Titus* as entirely Shakespeare's, more or less whole-heartedly in the manner of Sisson, include Brooke, Oppel, Barnet, Schoenbaum, Bevington, Wells and Schlösser (who offers a discussion of the various scholarly opinions, but with quintessential directness tells us at the beginning of his discussion: "Shakespeare ist der Verfasser").[32]

Hill, comparing the rhetorical elements of eleven early Shakespearean plays, views the authorship question in a different way. "The discovery of certain [rhetorical] eccentricities in the style of *Titus* leads to the conclusion that it is either Shakespeare's first play, an alternative to which I incline, or else the work of more than one author."

Baldwin studies the extant versions of the story of Titus Andronicus and posits an *Old Titus* that "ran in much the same fashion as the *Titus* of 1594," and may have been the *Titus and Vespasion* first noted in Henslowe's *Diary* on 11 April 1592. Since "*titus & ondronicus*" is noted as "ne" by Henslowe on 24 January 1594 and "*tittus & vespacia*" as "ne" on 11 April 1592, there were therefore two revisions. The casting pattern of the surviving play supports this because it is that of the Admiral's Men before 1590, reflecting the *Old Titus*. Since Peele appears to have been the inventor in June 1593 of the word *palliament,* and because two consecutive lines in *Titus* are combined from two separate lines in Peele's *Edward I,* therefore Peele must have revised the *Old Titus* about the end of 1593. Other evidence, such as the "double hunt" (one on earth and the echo in the skies) in *Titus, Venus,* and *Midsummer Night's Dream* probably indicates "that Shakspere did some work upon *Titus* in 1593–94. This should mean that Shakspere and Peele were co-writers or co-revisers for the version which appeared in Henslowe's Diary as 'new' January 24, 1594." Hamilton appraises the "technical . . . mastery of stage resources [exhibited in *Titus* as] an accomplishment that is distinctively Shakespearean." The conception "reveals Shakespeare's architectonic skill . . . It foreshadows the later tragedies because it is their archetype." Those qualities, such as the horrors and the decorative verse, are not defects, but excesses flowing from Shakespeare's effort to outdo not only Kyd but even Ovid and Seneca. Hamilton interprets Jonson's gibe in *Bartholomew Fair* as indicating that it is Shakespeare's most popular play. "It deserves to be approached as a central and seminal play in the canon of Shakespeare's works." Ashley, persuaded by Dover Wilson's solution to the authenticity problem, thinks that Shakespeare is the reviser of an earlier "potboiler by Peele . . . [that] has a status rather like that of *The Raigne of King Edward the Third* . . . Peele may have been the original author in both cases."[33]

Braekman identifies significant differences that exist among the three extant dramatic versions of the story of Titus Andronicus: the Dutch *Aran en Titus* (designated D), the German *Tito Andronico* (G), both of which survive in acting texts, and *Titus Andronicus.* Most plot elements are common to all three, but there are some incidents common to *Titus* and G but not in D; others common to *Titus* and D but not in G; others occur in D and G but not in *Titus;* and there are many incidents in *Titus* that either do not occur in D or G or are fundamentally different. The most important of these are the stabbing death of Mutius, the means by which Lavinia's assailants are identified, and Lucius's banishment. There are several others of lesser significance. Braekman believes these disparities can be explained only by hypothesizing an *Old Titus* that contained all the incidents in the three plays. The deviations from the old text are attributable to several causes. Some may be ascribed to the relatively limited resources of the Continental stages and playing companies of the time. Others are traceable to the different objectives of those who prepared the texts. G is a report probably by Frederick Menius, a professor at the University of Dorpat, and some of the alterations, particularly the name changes, are a consequence of his classical education. The author of D, Jan Vos, reshaped the old play to conform more closely to the dramatic unities, to enhance the Senecan elements, and to provide more balance and contrast. The incidents in *Titus Andronicus,* absent from or different in D and G, resulted from Shakespeare's thorough revision of the *Old Titus.* Braekman acknowledges but does not explain the presence of Shakespearean elements in D and G. Kermode takes note of the arguments for and against Peele's part in the play—elements of style seem to favor Peele, but the structure appears to reject his participation—and concludes: "These difficulties seem indeterminable. The main possibilities are (1) sole Shakespearean authorship and an early date; (2) sole Shakespearean authorship, 1593–94; (3) collaboration between Shakespeare and Peele, 1593–94; (4) early composition by Peele, revision in 1593–94 by Shakespeare, or by Peele and Shakespeare. The fourth, or some slight variant upon it, is the most probable in the present state of the evidence." Kermode does not give his reasons, nor does he attempt to identify the parts attributable to the two playwrights in the posited revision of collaboration. Waith, placing emphasis on the strong external evidence for Shakespeare and the absence of any such evidence indicating the involvement of any other playwright, dismisses Ravenscroft's tale, the arguments based on an evaluation of the style of *Titus* as being significantly inferior to that of Shakespeare's accepted plays, and those founded on parallel passages. The perceived resemblances to Peele's style and vocabulary especially in Act 1, even if credited, do not prove that Peele is the author. It may have been Shakespeare writing under the older playwright's influence. One of the most convincing arguments against Peele is structural, especially the fundamental lack of unity in his plays. His conclusion is that the play "is entirely by Shakespeare . . . no compelling evidence associates any other playwright with it."[34]

Three recent studies concerning the authorship of *Titus Andronicus* employ new or updated techniques, two linguistic, the other stylometric, all statistically based. Slater, in the course of an analysis of the vocabulary of *A Lover's Complaint,* compares the occurrence of rare words in the poem, in the canonical plays, and in *Venus* and *Adonis* and *The Rape of Lucrece.* "It will be seen that both *Venus* and *Lucrece* are associated by these [rare] word links with the earliest plays . . . The strongest association of all is with *Titus.*" In summation he says that "the results appear to provide weighty evidence that *A Lover's Complaint* is an authentic work of Shakespeare. As a by-product of the inquiry, the same can be said for the authenticity of *Titus Andronicus.*" Jackson devotes a section of a monograph primarily on Middleton to a discussion of *Titus* in which he preliminarily separates the play into two parts based on Parrott's counts of feminine endings. Part A (1.1, 2.1 and 4.1) exhibits a comparatively low frequency of feminine endings (3.6 percent, 2.3 percent, and

2.4 percent respectively) while in Part B (the rest of the play except for Act 2 Scene 2, which Jackson omits from consideration because it is short) the frequency is considerably higher (ranging from 5.5 percent to 20.7 percent). He notes that Hart's vocabulary studies and Feuillerat's study of images supports this division. Jackson then applies a newly devised "vocabulary index" of his own derived from Sarrazin's counts of rare words in Shakespeare. This test shows that Part A has links to Shakespeare's very earliest writing (about 1588–89 in Wentersdorf's chronology), while Part B, though early, is linked to plays of about 1591–92. He "think[s] that this evidence supports the view that there are two strata in *Titus Andronicus,* but it is not easy to decide what these two strata represent. My inclination would be to suppose that Part A is very early Shakespeare, the bulk of Part B belonging to a later date." He does not reject outright the possibility that Peele wrote Part A but notes that the division of the play into two parts "is not sharply defined . . . The possibility remains . . . that the two strata in *Titus* are both Shakespearean and belong to the same period but that Shakespeare consciously treated different material in different ways or that his imagination was more deeply engaged in the writing of some parts of the play than in the writing of others." A team of three members of the Computer Science Department of the University of Edinburgh, led by Morton, studied the text of *Titus* employing a computer-assisted method of stylometry originally developed for the study of the Pauline epistles. The system concentrates on the analysis of frequently used functional words and collocations of such words that tend to fall into compositional habits common to all writers of a given time or tradition but are employed by different writers at different characteristic rates. By this means it may be possible to identify the different authors in a collaborative text. The study indicates that all of the play is the work of a single playwright. A comparison of the compositional habits exhibited in *Titus* with those in *Julius Caesar,* the authenticity of which is well established, leads to the conclusion that both plays are from the hand of the same dramatist. A similar comparison with Peele's style exhibited in his *Arraignment of Paris* and *David and Bethsabe* shows that his habits of composition are fundamentally different from those exhibited in *Titus* and therefore Peele could not have collaborated with Shakespeare.[35]

Taylor evaluates the various forms of internal evidence that may be indicative of authorship, such as, among others, the tendency of writers to drop biographical hints, to repeat themselves predictably and idiosyncratically, to use actors' names for characters in the plays, and to coin new words. These may be clues to a playwright's presence in the work in question. Taylor systematically surveys many kinds of internal evidence under a comprehensive list of headings such as biographical, palaeographical, theatrical, chronological, vocabulary, oaths and exclamations, imagery and image clusters, verbal parallels, structure, metrics, linguistics, stage directions, and stylometry. In the course of his examination of the question of the authorship of *Titus Andronicus,* Taylor finds that "the external evidence strongly supports the play's authenticity . . . [but] Nevertheless, a number of stylistic anomalies have suggested that the play may be a collaboration between Shakespeare and another writer . . . Suspicion has in recent years concentrated upon Act I." He takes note of studies of irregularities of style by Hill and Jackson, of Timberlake's investigation of feminine endings, and Maxwell's inquiry into an unusual grammatical construction of which Peele made frequent use. Each of these, as Taylor shows, has a measure of validity as an element in the determination of the authorship of the play, but, as a body, they do not appear to be sufficiently cogent to offset the evidence in favor of Shakespeare's authorship. He acknowledges the persuasiveness of the argument that in regard to Act 1 the author may be Shakespeare writing under the influence of Peele, thus producing parallels that "suggest that the first scene was written by either Peele or an imitator of Peele; but the rest of the play seems to have been written by neither."[36]

As can be seen in the above discussion, many who favor a solution to the authorship question that envisions Shakespeare working with a single collaborator settle on Peele. Mincoff addresses this hypothesis in some depth. He begins by conceding that "many of Peele's more obvious mannerisms do appear with considerable frequency, especially in the first act." But the fundamental style lacks Peele's "typical sentence structure with its relative clauses and appositional phrases often piled three deep. And besides the mannerisms extend, often enough, into passages that are obviously Shakespeare's, and it is impossible to divide the play sharply between two utterly different styles." He grants that the first act is formal—"stilted"—but points out convincingly that it is a "sort of throne scene with every one on his public behaviour, and full of set speeches and orations." The quality of the style is partly because of the formality of the first act and partly because "it *is* the first act, and one would expect the effort to maintain a strange style to be kept up most consistently there. The play is not by Peele, but by someone who had many of Peele's more marked cadences running through his mind, and it is by one hand throughout." In Shakespeare's "work as a whole it represents something of a blind alley, but that is no reason for denying it to him." In other early plays he can be seen "making various false starts, as with the extended simile, and swerving off in directions that were soon abandoned again, even within the same play. And here too the extreme swerve in the direction of the style of the first act is soon modified into something that, though distinctly different from the [early] history plays, is nevertheless plainly Shakespearian." Structurally, *Titus* is a "mature piece of work . . . The play . . . shows every sign of having been planned by Shakespeare."[37]

Separate from the question of the general authenticity of *Titus Andronicus,* there has been some scholarly discussion of the authorship of 3.2, a scene absent from the quartos, initially printed in the First Folio. The original Cambridge editors think that the scene agrees "too closely in style with the main portion of the play to allow of the supposition that it was due to a different author." Lee and Pollard consider the scene to be stylistically of the same origin as the rest of the play without specific ascription to Shakespeare. Chambers has doubts: "If iii.2 was not added to this [Jacobean] or an earlier revival, it must have been in some way recovered from the original text, in which a mark of deletion may have excluded it from Q1. This seems less likely. The scene does not advance the action. The earlier part, no doubt, is not unlike the rest of the play. I have sometimes fancied that the fly episode might be Webster's. I see no clear signs of Shakespeare." Wilson has no such reservations. He describes it as "one of the finest in this highly popular play," and says it is certainly Shakespeare's. Price classifies 3.2 as a "mirror-scene," one that is symbolic rather than dramatic and employed to express an informing idea, to intensify a mood, to enlarge the audience's knowledge of the play's central problem, or to concentrate significant events into a symbol. Such scenes are episodic and detachable, and he notes examples of them in twenty Shakespearean plays. He also finds that the mention of an alphabet in 3.2 leads up to Lavinia's writing in the sand in 4.1, and the reference by Aaron to killing a fly in 5.1 constitutes another link. These together convince him that "III, ii was in the play from the first." Maxwell says that "In my 1953 edition, I dismissed too hastily the possibility that this scene is a later addition . . . The date of the scene remains very much an open question—it would be convenient, but hazardous, to make its addition the justification for Henslowe's 'ne' of 24 January 1594—and, if so, its authorship must also be uncertain. There is no positive reason to deny it to Shakespeare." Greg believes that "For this, there must of course have been a manuscript, but it is not certain whether the scene formed part of the play as written or was a later addition . . . The scene differs appreciably from the rest in manner, and several critics have recognized this manner as later—an opinion with which I am disposed to agree." Cross considers it to be a piece with the rest of the play. Kermode thinks that in spite of certain small puzzles it is probably by Shakespeare. Kramer, on the other hand, judges "the banquet-scene . . . bathetic in its conceits, textually remote from the rest of the play, and dramatically inept . . . an excrescence." He says it is late and questions Shakespeare's authorship but offers no other candidate. Waith thinks that "Those who have argued for Shakespearian authorship seem to me to

have made the stronger case." Taylor discerns metrically more license
than in the rest of the play, "suggesting a somewhat later period of composition. Given the scene's brevity, its authorship may be indeterminable
upon purely stylistic evidence: it seems safest to assign it to Shakespeare."[38] Although a few commentators have reservations, the consensus seems to be that 3.2 is Shakespeare's.

All of the proposed solutions to the problem of the authenticity of *Titus
Andronicus* face difficulties. Those who hold that Shakespeare had no
hand in the play must confront the external evidence of its inclusion in
Meres's list of Shakespearean tragedies and its presence in the First Folio.
Unlike many critics who simply ignore this evidence, Robertson attacks
it head-on, but his arguments that Meres and Heminges and Condell are
unreliable because Meres repeats only gossip and Heminges and Condell
are protecting rights in the text do not shake the objective testimony. In
other respects Meres is a reliable witness and, as Chambers has pointed
out, there were no property rights in the play that Heminges and Condell
could have protected by publication. The earlier printing had already
made the text available for use by rival companies, the prevention of
which would have been an important objective of the King's Men, if it
had been possible.[39]

Scholars who accept Ravenscroft's stage tradition must explain the
apparent contradiction of it in his prologue to the original production of
Titus Andronicus, or the Rape of Lavinia. None have done so and indeed
few have attempted it. Neither have they addressed themselves to an-
swering the oft-repeated assertion that Ravenscroft's tale is merely a way
of excusing his adaptation and helping to promote—with considerable
success—this stage version.[40] Nor have they been able effectively to
counter the attacks by such critics as Langbaine, Knight, and Halliwell-
Phillipps. Parrott says of the tale: "The reference to the supposed 'private
author' is a genuine Restoration touch. Ravenscroft evidently supposes
that counterparts of the Restoration mob of 'gentlemen who wrote with
ease' existed in Shakespeare's day." Robertson, the leading disintegrator,
rejects the tradition: "On the face of the case, such late and loose testimony in itself counts for nothing, and it was used by Malone merely as
confirming a disbelief which was already so strong as not to need fresh
justification . . . In reality it is valueless, save as testifying to a current
doubt, in 1677, of Shakespeare's authorship." Kittredge calls Ravenscroft
"irresponsible" and his stage tradition "idle gossip."[41] Hazleton Spencer
offers a detailed discussion: "The disintegrators find aid and comfort in
an unsupported allegation by the popular playwright Edward Ravenscroft
. . . [whose] statement is worth very little. He is out to minimize his
indebtedness, and this address 'To the Reader' is not remarkable for
candor. He boasts:

> Compare the Old Play with this, you'l finde that none in all that Authors Works ever receiv'd greater Alterations or Additions, the Language not only refin'd, but many Scenes entirely New; Besides most of the principal Characters Heighten'd, and the Plot much encreas'd.

This single sentence contains five misstatements of fact. Fourteen plays of Shakespeare had received more extensive alterations or additions; the language of Ravenscroft's version is comparatively little refined; only two scenes are really new; characterization is virtually unchanged; the increase in plot consists of a few unimportant variations and a piling up of horrors in the final scene . . . The doubt Ravenscroft casts on the original authorship is probably no more reliable." Spencer concludes by pointing out that Ravenscroft's phrase—"this I am apt to believe"—which immediately follows the story of the Master-touches, is an "admission of uncertainty."[42]

Maxwell somewhat equivocally tells us "There is no evidence that Ravenscroft had any good authority, and (though it seems unlikely that he simply invented the whole story) his chief motive may well have been to justify his own rewriting of the play."[43] Velz calls attention to the fact that the traditional view of Ravenscroft's assertion—that it is *sui generis* literary criticism, the earliest attempt to expel from the canon "what does not appeal aesthetically"—may in fact be mere literary commonplace. Building on a brief essay by Brooks in an appendix to Maxwell's edition, Velz traces the origin of the "image of the heap of rubbish and [of] the concept of disintegration" to the preface to Dryden's version of *Troilus* (1679), thence to the preface to Abraham Cowley's *Poems* (1656), then to Ovid's *"rudis indigestaque moles"* in Book 1 of the *Metamorphoses*. Ravenscroft's architectural metaphor is lacking from Ovid but Velz locates it in Horace's third book of *Odes*. The well-known topos of poetry as a monument occurs in Webster's address "To the Reader" in his *White Devil* (1612), in the prolegomena to the First Folio, and in Milton's epitaph in the Second Folio. Ironically, Velz notes, "sluttish time has dealt most unkindly with Ravenscroft's pretensions." He is remembered not for having improved Shakespeare's play "but only for the preface in which he claimed to have done so."[44] While a number of critics to the end of the nineteenth century accepted Ravenscroft's tale, it is worthy of note that recently most scholars—of every shade of persuasion as to Shakespeare's authorship of *Titus Andronicus*—have rejected it.

Believers in Shakespeare as a reviser of another dramatist's work, whether "light" or otherwise, must explain away not only the external evidence of the First Folio per se but also the fact of the presence of *Titus* while *Pericles* and *Two Noble Kinsmen* are absent. Suggestions that *Pericles* survives only in a corrupt text and was for that reason excluded, and that *Two Noble Kinsmen* was thought to be principally Fletchers's and therefore not included, may or may not be true, but whether or not these explanations are valid, it is clear that *Titus* is more soundly within the purview of the canon than these other two not-exactly-negligible plays.

Critics who hold that the play as we have it is a more or less comprehensive Shakespearean recension of an earlier text by another dramatist or by a collaboration of playwrights, possibly including Shakespeare as one of the original contributors, must account for the consistent and palpable Shakespearean qualities of *Titus*. This is exhibited in the numerous parallels of diction, theme, imagery, and thought with the poems and the canonical plays that are pointed out by almost every critic and editor; in the firmness of the structure completely unlike the plotting of other plays of the '80s and early '90s, especially Peele's, but very much like that of the acknowledged Shakespearean plays; and in the characters, particularly Titus, Tamora, and Aaron, that adumbrate later, greater roles unquestionably Shakespearean. The explanation that a thorough rewriting explains the Shakespearean quality of the play is insufficient in view of the play's pervasive structural cohesion, the links in fine details to the poems and the other plays, and the lack of any convincing evidence of the existence of an earlier play on the Andronican theme. The arguments put forth in support of claims that *Titus and Vespasian* is the predecessor play are slight and, in view of the fact that it is not extant, highly speculative.[45]

Scholars who favor the conclusion that Shakespeare wrote the play originally and in its entirety must explain the manifest difference in style and diction between Act 1 and Acts 2–5. Resemblances between the style of Act 1 and that of Peele's poems and plays—the mechanical use of repetition; the occurrence in Act 1 and in Peele's poem *The Honour of the Garter* of the rare word *palliament;* the syntactical trick of employing a possessive adjective or pronoun as antecedent to a relative clause, which occurs much more frequently in Act 1 than in the rest of the play and at about the same rate as it occurs in Peele's known writings; and the stiffness of the verse in certain passages, which is judged to be unlike Shakespeare's verse—are taken to reveal Peele's hand. The theories that the classical allusions and the horrors argue against Shakespearean authorship and thus support the presence of another playwright, making it likely that Peele wrote at least part of the play, are no longer credited. Scholars favoring Shakespeare's authorship have put forth some counterarguments. While there are in *Titus* some resemblances to Peele's writing, there are more pervasive and closer resemblances to Shakespeare's writing. There is no conclusive evidence that the word *palliament* was coined by Peele nor that its first occurrence is in the *Garter* poem. It could have been a Shakespearean neologism that Peele appropriated, especially if an early date of composition of 1589 or 1590 is accepted for *Titus*. Some critics think the word is used incorrectly by Peele.

As to the uncommon grammatical construction, Maxwell points out that while it is unusually prevalent in Act 1 and in Peele and is not very common anywhere, it is seldom entirely absent. The construction is six or seven times as frequent in Act 1 as in the rest of *Titus*. In Peele's plays, the incidence varies widely from only one occurrence in *The Old Wives' Tale* to an average of once in 140 lines in *David and Bethsabe*. It is employed in seven other early Shakespearean plays, including *King John*, in which it is about as common as in Peele's *Edward I*. It also occurs in plays by other dramatists, some, such as Kyd's *Cornelia*, showing a high incidence. In Greene's *James IV*, as in *John*, the occurrences are concentrated in the early scenes, a warning, as Maxwell says, "against being too confident about the significance of the variations within *Titus*." Counts of anonymous plays also show considerable variations. Maxwell acknowledges that his evidence is ragged and inconclusive but thinks that, in view of the variation in frequency of occurrence, it is significant that a strikingly high frequency is found "only in Peele's poems, in his one reasonably well-preserved late play, and in the first act of *Titus Andronicus*."[46] He does not discuss the statistical basis of his test, but merely by inspection of his counts it seems possible that employing any one of several standard statistical techniques used to reduce the effect of aberrant phenomena might show that the central tendencies in both Peele's plays and Shakespeare's do not materially differ. At the beginning of his essay, Maxwell says that the grammatical construction "is not likely to be imitated by one author from another," thus discarding at the outset, and without supporting argument, a likely alternative explanation for its occurrence in *Titus*, namely that Shakespeare was intentionally imitating this characteristic, among others, of Peele's style. The repetitions and the formality of the verse in Act 1 may have also been the result of a conscious effort by Shakespeare to adapt to his purpose some of the qualities of the verse of an older, notably successful playwright. However, the case for Peele fails fatally on the point of structure. The firmness of construction evident in Acts 2–5 is equally apparent in the significantly complex first act, and is completely unlike the diffuse, rambling form of Peele's plays, which some scholars conclude can scarcely be called a structure at all. The construction of *Titus* is consistent throughout the play and is a strong argument in favor of a single author.

The denial of Shakespeare's authorship of *Titus Andronicus* by the early editors and critics is grounded largely on aesthetic considerations. They were repelled by its horrors and what some perceived as bad taste.

Others could not bring themselves to believe that Shakespeare was responsible for the overly formal verse and the repetitions in Act 1. But many of the horrors are paralleled in his later plays—notably the onstage blinding of Gloucester in *Lear*—and at other times in his career he experimented in the manner of his contemporaries. Most of the various kinds of statistical tests, so much in vogue during the past century, have been shown to be susceptible of interpretation that supports as readily as it denies the authenticity of *Titus*.

The theories of collaboration, particularly those set forth by Fleay, Robertson, Wilson, Feuillerat, and Baldwin, are too complex to be accorded belief. There is no reliable contemporary external evidence indicating that *Titus* is a collaboration, as there is in the cases of the lost *Cardenio* (a *Stationers' Register* entrance) and *The Two Noble Kinsmen* (a *SR* entrance and, in addition, the title page of the 1634 quarto). These generally accepted instances of joint composition cannot be cited in support of a posited parallel, though much earlier, Shakespearean collaboration because it seems clear that they were undertaken in prospect of a reduced level of dramatic activity on the part of Shakespeare toward the end of his active career. Out of respect to his colleagues and his interest in the future of the King's Men, he may be thought to have consented to work in tandem on these two plays, and *Henry VIII*, with a younger dramatist of promise who in fact became his successor as the company's regular poet.[47] There is some internal evidence that Shakespeare may have, as a beginner in writing plays, been willing to work with other playwrights. This may be a possibility in the case of *Edward III*, in which four scenes appear to be notably Shakespearean (1.2, 2.1, 2.2, and 4.4) while the bulk of the play is considered doubtful. In the instance of *Sir Thomas More*, it is thought that Shakespeare contributed two passages, the more important and extensive of which is viewed as an effort to meet the objections of the stage censor, Edmund Tilney. The structure of *Edward III* could support a contention that the play is a Shakespearean collaboration. In *Sir Thomas More*, the Shakespearean elements amount to an interpolation, and he appears not to be fully aware of the preceding text. His revision of the insurrection scene (Addition IIc) exhibits signs that he does not know the names of some of the key characters, designating them as "other," "oth," and even simply "o." The scholarly consensus is that it is probable that Shakespeare collaborated with Fletcher at the end of his career, that he might possibly have done so in the very early *Edward III;* that he made a contribution to *Sir Thomas More* but did not write in close coordination with the other playwrights involved.[48]

Taylor, of currently active scholars, is unusually open-minded to consideration of Shakespearean collaboration. He is prepared to entertain the possibility throughout the dramatist's career as an instance of a recognized phenomenon of Elizabethan play writing, whereas other critics judge it to be likely only under special circumstances. In addition to *Timon of Athens,* which has been noted, and the manifest case of *Sir Thomas More,* he evaluates the evidence in regard to *Pericles, Cardenio, All is True (Henry VIII),* and *The Two Noble Kinsmen* as pretty clear proof of collaboration. Of the early plays, he also finds it likely that Shakespeare worked with other playwrights. His conclusions in regard to the *Henry VI* sequence are of special interest particularly because of the dates of composition he assigns. *The First Part of the Contention (2 Henry VI)* and *Richard Duke of York (3 Henry VI)* are dated 1591; *1 Henry VI* is dated 1592, as is *Titus Andronicus.* In regard to the two earlier *Henry VI* plays he finds some evidence pointing to multiple authorship but concludes in both instances that, pending further and more comprehensive investigation, the question of authorship must remain open. In the case of *1 Henry VI* he cites evidence of "a variety of linguistic and verse tests" and certain stylistic peculiarities that "all indicate the presence of more than one author." Shakespeare's collaborators cannot be confidently identified, "but Thomas Nashe probably wrote most of Act 1 (Sc. 1–8); more conjecturally, there are a number of links between *Locrine . . .* and the author of Act 3 and the bulk of Act 5." Concerning the authorship of *Titus,* Taylor sets aside Ravenscroft's tale as self-serving and unlikely to be true: "his late testimony in any case cannot challenge Meres's early attribution of the play to Shakespeare in a list which contains no other item which can be seriously doubted." He does not consider it evidence of collaboration. Following a review of an array of tests of various kinds, mostly stylistic and structural, Taylor decides that "As yet, the internal evidence mustered in defence of single authorship is inconclusive or unreliable. The matter merits further investigation."

Taylor's summation on the question of collaboration is unexceptionable, but it is also inconclusive. He says, cogently, that Morton's stylometric results "If anything weigh against Peele, as a particular alternative, more successfully than they support Shakespeare," and that "the changes of plan evident in the first scene (discussed at length by Wells, *Re-Editing)* [may] result from Shakespeare tidying up and improving the work of his collaborator; the apparently late addition of the Mutius material, for instance, contributes strongly to the structural patterning which critics have praised as characteristically Shakespearian."[49] After balancing all the scholarly pros and cons, the net result of the debate on collaboration is that there is insufficient evidence to support a hypothesis portraying Shakespeare as having worked with Peele or anyone else on *Titus Andronicus.* The firmness of the structure, unrivaled at the time the play was written, and the skillful interweaving of the elements of the plot appear persuasively to eliminate consideration of a collaborator, whether

Peele or another of the dramatists active around 1590. If then *Titus* is not the fruit of a collaboration, but the work of a single playwright, it seems most unlikely that it could be the work of any poet other than Shakespeare. The external evidence, never successfully challenged, solidly supports the attribution. We are then left with the conclusion so unambiguously stated by Schlösser: Shakespeare *is* the author.

The moſt lamenta-
ble Romaine Tragedie of *Titus*
Andronicus.

As it hath ſundry times beene playde by the
Right Honourable the Earle of Pembrooke, the
Earle of Darbie, the Earle of Suſſex, and the
Lorde Chamberlaine theyr
Seruants.

AT LONDON,
Printed by I. R. for Edward White
and are to bee ſolde at his ſhoppe, at the little
North doore of Paules, at the ſigne of
the Gun. 1600.

2

Twentieth-Century Criticism

Pʀɪoʀ to this century, comment on *Titus Andronicus* included little that could be viewed as true criticism. Most of the discussion of the play, such as it was, concerned itself with the question of authenticity accompanied by collateral and usually brief comment on such matters as staging and diction in the context of influence on the dramatist of the interests of the educated members of the Elizabethan audience in classical tags and of the groundlings in gory theatrical outrages. Appreciative evaluation is sparse, scattered, and not infrequently casual. Little value was perceived by early scholars in the serious appraisal of a work that may have been the product of a third-rate playwright.

Almost all of the early critics either rejected or seriously doubted Shakespeare's authorship or, at the most, accepted Edward Ravenscroft's story that "he only gave some Master-touches to one or two of the principal Parts or Characters" (see the previous chapter). Consequently, from the days of Ravenscroft to those of Malone the aspects of Shakespeare's other plays, which were customarily critically examined and elucidated, particularly by the eminent eighteenth-century editors, were almost completely neglected as far as *Titus* is concerned. It was not until the emergence toward the end of the first decade of the nineteenth century of British and, notably, German Romantic commentators that anything approaching true criticism was generated. The methods of these critics, particularly those of what is known as the biographical school of Romantic criticism, had limitations, sometimes severe. With the possible exception of Charles Knight—and in his case only in part—bona fide scholarly appraisal of *Titus Andronicus* for its own sake without the intrusion of other, no doubt valid but generally noncritical considerations, only became possible in the twentieth century. Even then, the critical landscape was not completely reordered until mid-century. As late as 1948 the redoubtable but nonetheless respected Dover Wilson m.ıde an attempt at recurring to the custom of the preceding century, in which doubts of authenticity shaped scholarly response and inhibited pure criticism. Upon his limited recantation—

> Though there is little doubt that the play owes much to the influence of Peele, Greene, etc., I no longer believe that the author after the first Act, was anyone but Shakespeare throughout;

which came in the 1968 reprint of his 1948 edition—the last of such stumbling blocks effectively was removed. Critics who had already begun to appraise *Titus* as a tragedy seized the opportunity to view the play clearly, without the distraction of a question of authenticity.[1]

The earliest significant effort to cast off nineteenth-century critical preconceptions was made by Frederick S. Boas in his *Shakspere and his Predecessors* in 1896. In this he was only partially successful. Elements of the earlier biographical criticism are intermingled in his largely historical account of "Shakspere's Dramatic Apprenticeship." H. Bellyse Baildon, the editor of the original Arden *Titus Andronicus* (1904), has virtually no element of the alloy of the old school in his generally truly critical appraisal of the play. Nevertheless, his introduction was considered "diffuse and wayward" by his Arden successor, J. C. Maxwell.[2] Following Baildon came G. P. Baker, J. S. G. Bolton, Fredson Bowers, Howard Baker, William T. Hastings, Hereward T. Price, and E. M. W. Tillyard, collectively representing the dawn of historical flowering of perceptive and revealing criticism of *Titus*. It is with these scholars that we will begin our account of the twentieth-century critical appreciation of *Titus Andronicus*.[3]

"Creative power," says Baildon, "and in particular the power of creating characters," is the first essential to the making of a great author of fiction whether narrative or dramatic. "In *Titus Andronicus* we find a series of powerful, and even exaggerated, studies for the great characters that peopled his later tragedies." He refers primarily to Tamora, Titus, and Aaron, but he also includes Lavinia. In Titus, Baildon discerns prefigured

> three of the great male characters in his acknowledged masterpieces, . . . Lear, Coriolanus, and Hamlet . . . Titus has the Empire of Rome within his grasp, and like Lear, feeling some of the languor of age coming over him, he declines, as Lear wishes to resign, the burden of power. But they both deceive themselves, they do not wish *really* to resign their *power itself,* but merely its burdens and toils. Titus's resemblance to Coriolanus is simpler. They have the same military qualities, the same immense pride, the same inordinate claim on the gratitude of their countrymen. His similarity to Hamlet is in his real or feigned madness. That it is, like Hamlet's, mainly assumed, I think there can be no doubt; for whenever he chooses he is not only sane, but capable . . . In the character of Aaron, Shakespeare seems to have made a great, if only partially successful, attempt to humanise the ordinary stage villain or monster . . . Shakespeare aimed obviously, not at whitewashing his villains, as a modern author might do . . . but at humanising them, which is . . . quite another thing.

Baildon compares Lavinia to Cordelia, noting that they "both have a share of the family failings, and both exemplify . . . that there is nearly always about virtue an element of harshness."

Titus Andronicus, Baildon tells us, is Shakespeare's first essay in tragedy. It is the work of an apprentice playwright "copying too closely his
predecessors . . . unsure of himself, and still unconscious of his superior
powers . . . he exhibits his power of distinctive characterisation, his working to a certain moral balance . . . his gift of humanising grotesque types
of wickedness, his interest in psychologic and moral problems . . . He
has already command of a noble poetic rhetoric, and the beginnings at
least of fine versification . . . " The dramatist who wrote *Titus* "had undoubtedly . . . ample psychologic acumen and dramatic genius to have
written in his maturity all the masterpieces associated with the name of
Shakespeare."[4]

G. P. Baker studies the dramaturgy of *Titus Andronicus.* He finds
Shakespeare transforming melodramatic material into something much
finer, raising the level by means of "convincing characterization . . . consistent motivation" and by indulging his "poetic instincts," to something
approximating tragedy. Baker cites particularly "the extremely large
amount of incident, the constant use of suspense, the strong feeling for
climax, and the relative unity of the plot." He also notes the careful
concern for motivation of later events in Act I, and "the swift, climactic
exposition . . . which grips the attention from start to finish." The play
demonstrates that "by 1594 Shakespear was a competent dramatist . . .
in melodrama."[5]

A poet and notable critic has, in this century, enunciated most memorably an opinion regarding *Titus,* if we may judge by the frequency with
which his censure has been cited since 1927. In an introduction to a
reprint of a 1581 volume of Seneca's tragedies in English, T. S. Eliot
expressed the view that the taste for horrors exhibited by Elizabethan
audiences "developed only after it had received Senecan license . . . But
it must be admitted that the greater number of the horrors are such as
Seneca himself would not have tolerated. In one of the worst offenders,
indeed one of the stupidest and most uninspired plays ever written, a
play in which it is incredible that Shakespeare had any hand at all, a play
in which the best passages would be too highly honoured by the signature
of Peele—in *Titus Andronicus*—there is nothing really Senecan at all.
There is a wantoness, an irrelevance, about the crime of which Seneca
would never have been guilty. Seneca's Oedipus has the traditional justification for blinding himself . . . In *Titus,* the hero cuts off his own hand
[*sic*] in view of the audience, who can also testify to the mutilation of the
hands and tongue of Lavinia . . . There is nothing like this in Seneca."
Eliot attributes the "spectacular and sensational elements of Drama" to
Italian Senecanism. "The Tragedy of Blood is very little Senecan, in
short, though it made much use of Senecan machinery; it is very largely
Italian; and it added an ingenuity of plot which is native."[6]

Bolton directs attention to structural deficiencies in *Titus* that reflect themselves in unsatisfactory characterization. He finds the shortcoming most evident in the shifting significance, as the action proceeds, of Tamora and Aaron. In the middle three acts Aaron is the engine that drives the retribution against the Andronici for the sacrifice of Alarbus, while "the queen shows herself to be little more than an emotional onlooker." Toward the end of Act 4 she "comes again into actual prominence," while the part of Aaron fades in consequence. This "irregularity in the structure of *Titus Andronicus*" is a noteworthy weakness in dramatic design that Bolton attributes to a Shakespearean revision of an earlier play that was perfunctory in the first and final acts.

Bowers also reviews the construction of the play, finding that it is structurally and otherwise based on Kyd's *Spanish Tragedy* and on an earlier version of *Titus* as exemplified in the German and Dutch texts, with elements adapted from the plot of Kyd's ur-*Hamlet*. He notes that Titus has no plan for revenge until Tamora in the disguising scene presents him with an opportunity. Another plot weakness is the "blurring" of motivation by the domination of the action in the middle part of the play by Aaron, diverting attention from the motive of blood revenge for the death of Alarbus. *Titus* "must be considered . . . experimental . . . uniting in an imperfect form two wholly dissimilar methods of plotting and theories of tragedy." Bowers's exposition of the defects in the design of the play depend in part on an ur-*Hamlet*, of which no text survives, and on a posited early version of *Titus Andronicus* as reflected in the Continental versions of the story, which are now accepted as shortened traveling texts of Shakespeare's play.[7]

Baker argues persuasively for the presence of native tragic strains in *Titus Andronicus* equal at least in significance to the classical elements. The latter derive in part from Seneca's tragedies but Seneca is of no greater importance than Virgil and of even less consequence than Ovid, whose *Metamorphoses*, specifically the tale of Tereus and Philomela, is the dominant classical influence. The English components he identifies as those developing out of nondramatic metrical tragedies, the morality and mystery plays and the poetry of Wyatt, Surrey, Sackville, Spencer, and Sidney—and more remotely Chaucer and Gower. The ghost, the chorus, and the *nuntius*, which Baker points out as specific examples, were as frequently present in the native drama of the earlier sixteenth century as in the classical plays: "*Andronicus* shows traits of classical-medieval narrative art." Since his objective is to demonstrate the limited influence of Senecanism, he has some tendency to overload his argument for the greater significance of native and of non-Senecan classical influences. He does show that although Senecanism influenced Kyd and Shakespeare it is not dominant in the conceptions of the playwrights but in actuality is

only one component among several that they inherited from their predecessors. Hunter restates and more ably argues in favor of the conception
of the limited nature of Senecan influence on Elizabethan revenge tragedy. Vernacular tragedy "was already a theatrical tradition . . . The arts
of spectacle, of emblematic presentation, of dumb show, of multilevel
statement, of pictorial metaphor . . . go forward from the miracle plays
and the interludes as a continuous tradition." Mowat accepts Ovid as the
predominant influence on the play but argues with considerable persuasiveness that the story of the revenge of Hecuba, "into which the Philomela myth [is] embedded, [is] the larger, shaping myth."[8]

Hastings sets out to show that the low opinion of the dramaturgy of
Titus expressed by other critics is not justified. Elizabethan plays exhibit
"a strong tendency to observe conventions in character portrayal, to deal
in types." The more exactly the character conforms to type, "the more
credible . . . The world of the play is a Renaissance world without nu-
ances . . . the moral code is that of complete self-sacrifice, of intense
devotion, of unlimited revenge." Hastings notes that the code did not
conform to life "but a great art may employ such simplification . . . If
Titus Andronicus were not hidden away under the mantle of the gentle
Shakespeare . . . it would be hailed as a perfect example of Renaissance
sophisticated brutality . . . It is a fine example of youthful power unleashed, even if taking a wayward direction alien to that of its later happy
development."[9]

The most comprehensive and effective assessment of the construction
of *Titus Andronicus* is that by Price. He draws attention to "the planning
of the work as a whole. It is the most intimate expression of the author's
meaning . . . The carriage of the plot and the weaving together of many
motifs require a particular kind of skill," which can be found in the plot
of *Lear,* but not in the work of Greene, Peele, or Marlowe. Some find the
structure of *Titus* weak "because the leadership of the 'bad' party varies
. . . I do not think this criticism has any force, since this variation does
nothing to impede the sweep and rush of the play . . . The only parallel
to the plot of *Titus* is to be found in the other works of Shakespeare . . .
in that it is built upon the principle of contrast [which] dominates the
play and informs every scene of it . . . He uses contrast to heighten
incident and situation as well as character." The structure is superior in
"its quick succession of closely knit incidents, enlivened by many sudden
turns and surprises, by its intricacy, in that the fates of so many persons
are involved in it and yet the thread is never lost, and by the skill with
which all the different threads are bound up into one knot and untied at
once in the fifth act. Intricacy with clearness, a firm hand on the story,
a swift succession of effective situations logically leading out of what
precedes and on to what follows, these are qualities lacking" in other

dramatists. Shakespeare wrote a complete Senecan tragedy, an experiment of unity in harshness and gross cruelty. Price then points out that there "is no convincing parallel to the character of Titus outside the works of Shakespeare. He owes, indeed, a few hints to . . . Kyd's Hieronimo [in that] he is an old man angry, seeking revenge for murder, but in the essentials of characterization he is quite different. Titus, like the typical Shakespearean hero, falls by a mixture of good and bad qualities." In his "blunders . . . we see the corruption of the best turned to the worst, qualities fine in themselves, producing disaster because of Titus's devotion to a false ideal." His loyalty and probity make him vulnerable. Thus "he is a mixture of virtues and weaknesses, and by a strange irony his virtues are the more devastating," a quality Price finds particularly Shakespearean. Aaron "is the obvious villain, black like the devil, lustful, cunning, cruel, a consummate dissembler and hypocrite, admiring himself for his superiority in evil, and taking a childlike pleasure in contemplating his villainies." But Aaron is a varied personality. He speaks romantic poetry, delights in magnificent dress and "suddenly at the end of the play . . . He is a devoted father . . . Shakespeare does not make the mistake of softening Aaron . . . He remains a killer . . . It is his many-sidedness that makes Aaron unique. There is a fire, a vigor, and a concentration . . . [that] no Elizabethan villain in the early nineties had displayed." When it comes to style, Price finds that Shakespeare is writing in the rhetorical manner of Seneca, but his style, though rhetorical, is not therefore undramatic. He took great pains to differentiate among the various speakers. "The play on its merits . . . [is] an excellent piece of stagecraft . . . not unworthy of the young Shakespeare."[10]

Although Tillyard's focus is not specifically aesthetic criticism, he does not completely neglect such considerations. He notes that Ovid's poetry is as important an influence on *Titus Andronicus* as Seneca's dramas, and he considers the play "academic, ambitious, and masterfully plotted . . . The very violences are exquisitely proportioned . . . Aaron is "a magnificent comic villain." The play is rich in political material, including the question of succession much on the minds of Elizabethan audiences. Shakespeare's handling of the contention for the imperial crown is stiff, "the work of a young man being solemn beyond the capacity of his years," but interested in and "minding about his politics."[11]

To Harbage "It is not merely the exciting quality of Shakespeare's language that transforms his source materials. . . The changes he makes in the outline . . . are crucial . . . That *Titus Andronicus* was not Shakespeare's in conception . . . is suggested by the presence of episodes [he] habitually eliminated from all other plays: rape . . . adulterous relationship[s] . . . a mother disposed toward infanticide, a father slaying first a son and then a daughter . . . a parent encouraging . . . acts of lust and murder, a victim cruelly maimed . . . In a word the incongruity of matter and manner is absolute." The results, he says, "can be described only as disastrous."[12]

In the course of a comprehensive discussion of the symbolic association of Queen Elizabeth with Astraea in both her manifestations as goddess of Justice and the zodiacal Virgo, Yates notes allusions to this identification by several poets, including Shakespeare. Astraea is mentioned twice in the plays, once in *1 Henry VI*, where the reference is to Joan of Arc, "Astraea's daughter," and again in *Titus Andronicus*, in which the painfully stricken Titus pleads for divine retribution on Saturninus and Tamora. The goddess is not to be found, and he cries, quoting Ovid, "Terras Astraea reliquit." She has ascended to the firmament, where she has become the astrological Virgo. Titus arranges for his family to shoot arrows into the heavens, one of which hits Virgo, bringing her down to earth. "The apotheosis of Lucius at the end of the play . . . perhaps represents the Return of the Virgin—the return of the just empire and the golden age."[13]

Charlton, an adherent of the critical tenets of A. C. Bradley ("I am a devout Bradleyite"), attacks the tendency of some modern critics, including T. S. Eliot, to slight character development as a major concern in Shakespearean studies. Following Bradley, Charlton's discussion of *Titus Andronicus* focuses on representation of human action through the play's characters. He finds the play deficient in all the "deeper reaches of the art of tragic drama." He believes that *Titus* "is melodrama, the crudest of Shakespeare's tragedies, magnificent only in this, that its language is always adequate to its own dramatic and theatrical demands, crude or low, spectacular or sentimental, as on varying occasion they may be. But as drama it can never disguise its own quality. It is a rudimentary type of tragedy."[14]

Noting that *Titus* is "well and powerfully written . . . and well constructed," Craig draws attention to the fact that the first act is so organized that it "make[s] a Senecan tragedy out of the crude story" as related in the chapbook. Titus makes the "fatal decision between the imperial claimants [Saturninus and Bassianus] . . . and in this tragical blunder provides for his own ultimate downfall." He also "exacts the sacrifice of [Alarbus] . . . thus instituting a motive of revenge." Bassianus then bears off and marries Lavinia, whom Saturninus had chosen as his Empress, an offense the Emperor does not forgive. "The tragedy unfolds in perfect Senecan order from these causes selected or invented by Shakespeare." This is "expert plot management" worthy of the dramatist. "The bloody and violent action of the plot [in the chapbook] is shoved back into the second and third acts, and one may say that Shakespeare has provided both a political and a personal setting for the tragedy." The play is "theoretically—in intent and structure—a very great tragedy [but] practically it is not. In spite of Shakespeare's masterly motivation in his re-arrangement of scenes, and in spite of excellent invention and noble rhet-oric, *Titus Andronicus* remains a relatively unpleasing work."[15]

Dover Wilson advances a hypothesis that the play as published in the first quarto is a burlesque based upon an earlier version, now lost, written by George Peele. Wilson theorizes that Shakespeare was induced to re-vise Peel's text, but he found the task distasteful and he purposefully produced a parody "knowing it for what it was." This can be clearly seen by comparing pairs of passages from *Lucrece* and *Titus* that are close in manner, diction, and theme. The comparison demonstrates "a world of difference in tone or spirit." The verses from *Lucrece* are "the unques-tionable product of a serious artistic impulse . . . [those from *Titus* are] a bundle of ill-matched conceits held together by sticky sentimentalism . . . Shakespeare is drawing upon imagery already put to serious use in *Lucrece* in order to disport himself with the ridiculous *Titus*."[16]

Early Elizabethan tragedy, Bradbrook notes, was modeled "from ac-cepted designs . . . *Titus* is largely a dramatic lament [and] . . . the other parent-stock from which [it] derives" is the early revenge play. About all the characters of *Titus* "there is an emblematic or heraldic quality." For-mal groupings occur throughout the play, beginning with the first scene. Murders, rapes, mutilations, and other atrocities remain mere moral her-aldry with no more sense of physical embodiment than if all the charac-ters had been given such [symbolic] names." *Titus* is more like a pageant than a play, a first attempt to portray an experience that Shakespeare was to embody only at a later state.[17]

As Clemen reads *Titus Andronicus,* he has the impression that tremen-dous events have taken place, but the frightful deeds lack logical motiva-tion and consequently are not convincing. This is in part due to a quality of the imagery that is not organically related to the framework of the play. The desire for effective expression is greater than that which is to be expressed. The frequency of similies is noteworthy. It is clear that such images are simply additions, "dove-tailed into the context, appended to what has already been said as flourish and decoration." Clemens cites several examples of "absurd contrast between occasion and image [but] the best example" is Marcus's speech upon encountering the mutilated Lavinia (2.4.11–57). The absurdity resides not only in "the idea that a human being at sight of such atrocities can burst forth into a long speech full of images and comparisons which appears so unsuitable and inor-ganic; but it is rather the unconcerned nature of these images, as it were, their almost wanton playfulness which reveals the incongruity." He concludes that the "dialogue in *Titus* only pretends to be dialogue . . .

in reality the characters . . . are delivering pompous orations to the audience."[18]

At the beginning of his career, Harrison tells us, "Shakespeare was an imitator," heavily under the influence, in writing his first tragedy, of Kyd's *Spanish Tragedy* and Seneca's *Theyestes.* "In his [Shakespeare's] early experiments there is a certain lack of high seriousness . . . [he] was making plays as it were rebelliously, as a form of livelihood that was beneath a gentleman's notice. He wrote for money to give the public what it wanted; and if the public thirsted for gore, he would fill them up to the ears." The real defects of *Titus* are not the horrors nor the stale stage tricks nor the elaborate language. The play "lacks a sense of morality, seriousness, and consistency." Shakespeare wrote without feeling, "as a play-maker and not as a dramatist . . . Lavinia's . . . sufferings were good theatre for a hard-boiled audience and an excuse for extravagant lamentation, but no more . . . the characterization is feeble, not one of the persons is consistently imagined . . . Aaron's wickedness [for example] is motiveless and therefore, inhuman and unconvincing . . . It is not likely that in after years Shakespeare was proud of his first tragedy—[it] is little more than an experiment in horror—but it had been a valuable experience."[19]

Spencer addresses the question of Shakespeare's intentions in portraying Rome and its citizens in his Roman plays. In spite of some adverse critical comment and a number of anachronistic details . . . Spencer believes that Shakespeare made "a serious effort at representing the Roman scene as genuinely as he could . . . producing a *mimesis* of the veritable history" of the Roman people in conformity to "the views of Roman history in Shakespeare's time." He traces the extent to which Shakespeare was in step with contemporary thinking. *Titus Andronicus* "is a not untypical piece of Roman history" as Shakespeare's contemporaries knew it. *Titus* would easily be recognized as typical Roman history by a sixteenth-century audience; the claim that it was a 'noble Roman history' was a just one."[20]

Waith elucidates the significance of Ovid to Shakespeare's play more effectively than it had been previously. While he is prepared to allow for somewhat more importance to Senecan influence than most other critics, he reminds us that "however important the Senecan model *(Theyestes)* may have been, Ovid exerted a more direct influence" through the stories of Lucretia, Appius and Virginia, and of Philomela. His central thesis is that there "is a relationship between the violence of *Titus Andronicus* and the style in which it is written," which is essentially Ovidian. This is apparent not only in the story elements themselves but even more significantly in the transformation of Shakespeare's characters who, like Ovid's, "are transported by emotions which rise steadily to the point of obliterating their normal characters." Thus Titus, originally the model of absolute Roman integrity becomes, by the drumfire of horrors visited upon himself and his family, a most bloody and merciless revenger. "Ovid's style reinforces in several ways the effects" of intense emotion and the ensuing metamorphosis. "At the same time, the elegant urbanity of these [Ovid's] narrations implies a considerable detachment . . . The seemingly illogical combination of emotional excitement and psychic distance contributes to the effect of impersonalization . . . The theme of *Titus Andronicus*—the opposition of moral and political disorder to the unifying force of friendship and wise government . . .—is at least consonant with what . . . Ovid" may be supposed to be saying; but the theme is not so important as an organizing principle because Shakespeare is "more interested . . . in portraying the extraordinary pitch of emotion to which a person may be raised by the most violent outrage. The passions of Titus transcend the limits of character . . . and the end in pure frenzy." Character disintegrates and becomes personified emotion. "*Titus Andronicus* is Shakespeare's contribution to a special tragic mode. Its first spectacle is both horrible and pathetic, but above all extraordinary. Ovid more than Seneca or the epic poets was the model for both characterization and style, with the result that Shakespeare's rhetoric of admiration, as seen in such lines as Marcus' description of Lavinia, is more elegantly florid than that of his contemporaries. The hero, in this respect like Tamburlaine or Bussy D'Ambois, is almost beyond praise or blame, an object of admiration."[21]

Aaron, Richard III, Don Juan, and Iago are studied by Spivack as characters exhibiting similar qualities. All four are descended from the Vice appearing in a distinctive type of morality play of the earlier sixteenth century that Spivack calls a "hybrid" type. In these plays, vice and virtue, variously designated, occur with one or more other individualized roles representing Mankind in the eternal psychomachia for possession of the soul. The characteristics setting these four apart from other stage villains are dramatic vitality, self-revelation, love of evil for its own sake, delight in their brutal strategems, a measure of humor, and the total absence of repentance for the crimes they perpetrate. Support for Spivack's hypothesis of Aaron's descent from the morality character is the mumming of Tamora, Chiron, and Demetrius as the abstractions Revenge, Rape, and Murder in 5.2. Spivack concludes that Aaron's heritage from the homiletic Vice is proved by the total absence of conventional motives for evil in his character. The "overwhelming testimony to his lineage" is his "gleefully itemized . . . villanies" in his speech addressed to Lucius (5.2.124–44).[22]

In the course of a lecture devoted primarily to a discussion of *Hamlet*, Gardner points out that, like Hamlet, the revengers in *The Spanish Trag-*

edy, Titus Andronicus and *The Revenger's Tragedy* await an opportunity for vengeance provided by the villain, and then seize the advantage. In *Titus,* Tamora thinks she can outwit the mad hero, and makes the mistake of leaving her sons in his hands. Up to this point, Titus "has done nothing but indulge in wild gestures of grief and distraction." He has waited for his opponent "as if for a signal" and then taken the initiative. The revenger, as in *Hamlet,* is conceived as being committed to counteraction, to responding to events rather than to creating them. The irony is that the villain, "acting as if all were well, invites [the avenger] . . . to destroy him."[23]

In a study of the tragic design of *Titus Andronicus,* Ribner notes that in this aspect of theatrical craftsmanship the play is superior to any play written before it, specifically including *The Spanish Tragedy.* In spite of this, and its surpassing poetry and characterization, it has been thought a failure due to deficiencies in morality, seriousness, and consistency. However, Shakespeare shaped his "unpalatable material" under the influence of Ovid's *Metamorphoses,* "with its emphasis upon the transformation of man into beast through excess of passion. This transformation of Titus is set within a specific moral system which the play in its totality affirms." The most important innovation is in the conception of the principal characters and their relations to one another. Titus towers above the others. He is "the first of Shakespeare's heroic figures whose very virtues are the sources of their sins." Shakespeare tries to place the fall of Titus within a larger framework in which evil is also destroyed. The path Titus could have taken is seen in the reconciliation, when the forces of both good and evil lie dead upon the stage. In the downfall of a noble figure "we have a formula for tragedy which postulates the reality of evil, man's free moral choice in spite of it, and divine justice in a harmonious moral order. " In spite of the crudity of style and the Senecan horrors that alienate modern readers, there is a controlling idea of tragedy behind *Titus Andronicus,* a conception of how evil operates in the world and may cause the destruction of a virtuous man by his own moral choice. In this play, Shakespeare had not yet attained the stature of a great dramatist, "but he had a greater awareness of the potentialities of tragedy than usually has been allowed him."[24]

The character of Aaron is sometimes thought of, Smith tells us, as composed of "two incompatible layers, ill-laminated under the arbitrary pressure of dramaturgic incompetance." First he is the energetic mastermind who implements Tamora's ill-will, then he is the loving father who protects his infant son, even at his own peril. This combination of qualities in a dramatic character is said to be offensive to reason and common sense. But there is empirical evidence in a psychoanalytic analysis of a personality by a criminologist, a summary of which Smith cites, that

describes an analogous case. Therefore, a similar group of personal qualities in Aaron may be as "real," that is, may have "as close a correspondence in objective reality" and he may therefore be credible. The good
and evil in Aaron spring from the circumstances of his being. He becomes
what the people about him think him to be. Objection to his Freudian
qualities as anachronistic is no more reasonable than to presume that
bacterial infection could not have been described before Pasteur. How
much of the Freudian element in Aaron "Shakespeare consciously understood, how much he vaguely sensed, how much he hit upon by sheer
accident we cannot know." Nevertheless, the character "stands . . . erect
from some kind of truth in him." Whether the analysis be accepted or
not, "it must be granted that the character of Aaron roughly parallels the
surface of the character reported by . . . [the criminologist] and therefore
that Aaron is not merely an impossible fabrication beyond the pale of
the species."[25]

Sommers sees, in the strained and luxuriant pathos of the writing of
Titus, "an element of cruelty, or aesthetic sadism" and also "much of
what Wilson Knight has termed 'the comedy of the grotesque.'" The
essential conflict in the drama "is the struggle between Rome, and all
that this signifies . . . and the barbarism of primitive organic nature . . .
constituting a specific reaction from civilization, religion, and humanity
. . . The opposition is stark, and the drama leaves it unresolved." The
ritual murder of Alarbus "releases the whole conflict; it is the source of
the tragedy." The structure of the play "has one important characteristic:
the whole action develops from, depends upon, and in a sense returns
to, the opening situation . . . The split in Rome forms a prelude to the
greater conflict, its opposing forces merging into the main antagonism
. . . Thus the initial juxtaposition links the main conflict with the problem
of Roman integrity." The crown of the plays' idealism is its conception
of justice, a term frequently reiterated. Titus's actions neglect justice,
bringing about a chaos of values. His revenge results in the restoration
of the Roman order indirectly through "the sacrificial tragedy and the
death ritual of the feast . . . The agent and principal victim of the dissolution, [he] is exquisitely conceived, in the mould of later Shakespearean
tragic heroes . . . he cannot be denied tragic status."[26]

Talbert analyzes the theatrical structural and rhetorical aspects of *Titus
Andronicus,* the interrelationships between them, and their effect on characterization and other elements of the drama. The initial conflict "is handled pageantically to utilize the upper stage and opposite entrances
[which] was probably appealing and familiar to any spectator who had
watched open-air pageantry." With the sacrifice of Alarbus and the killing
of Mutius "vigorous action and bloodshed is well under way . . . Six
bloody spectacles . . . develop from the opening situation" followed by "a

nurse's sudden murder . . . a near hanging . . . and the pseudo-allegorical [disguising] . . . Obviously this dramatist was capitalizing upon the popularity of the tragedy of blood." Despite the "display of a bloody multiplicity, a basic structural precision and a unifying control is at work in *Titus Andronicus*." The dialog may have given the impression to an Elizabethan audience of classical speech. Sententious statements appropriate to the Senecan concept of tragedy and related to the ethical situation of *Theyestes;* Ovid's influence, which is constantly apparent; and Horatian verse contribute to this impression. Some situations "are essentially episodic or tangential to the main line of action . . . Although firmly embedded in the basic movement . . . these halting effects appear throughout *Titus* . . . In this respect, the artistry of the play seems purposeful in its consistency . . . [thus] *Titus Andronicus* might well have satisfied a taste for multiplicity in unity. As a result, one can perceive some good reasons for the popularity of this drama." Karr draws attention to the pattern of pleas in the play that "often echo and mirror one another . . . close up their content and placement seem deliberate . . . There are also at times, verbal likenesses." They strengthen the unity of *Titus* and are a source of irony in the changing positions of ascendancy of the two factions (Goths and Romans). Of the six pleas, signified by kneeling or prostration, five implore mercy but in the sixth, Titus, Marcus, Lavinia, and young Lucius kneel for vengeance. It is with this plea that the balance of power shifts to the Andronici.[27]

"At the end of each of Shakespeare's mature tragedies," Hapgood observes, "we hope for a transformation in the life of the community . . . If Shakespeare fully gratified our hopes, the transformation would be so complete as to approach the condition of sacrificial ritual: through the sacrifice of human life, the revelation of truth, and the advent of a savior, the community would be purified, unified, and renewed." Shakespeare confronts such hopes with reality, attaining a balance between hope and disappointment. "His rites are always maimed by reality . . . producing a finale at once numinous and true." Titus is the first Shakespearean tragic hero to undergo the change from cynosure to outcast. His nobility is reduced to madness and blasphemy, and he must himself be purged: the hero becomes scapegoat. In the bloody banquet, he performs a sacrifice that is a kind of "Black Last Supper, the ritual dismemberment through which Shakespeare will shortly seek to produce a new Rome." The play's community never comes sufficiently to life because the horrors and the rhetoric are too schematic. "It is as if Shakespeare had been so intent on making his sacrifice that he neglected to vivify and individualize its participants."[28]

As part of an examination of the treatment in Elizabethan drama of African characters, Jones discusses the character of Aaron and the part he plays in *Titus*. Shakespeare transformed the nameless Moor of *The History of Titus Andronicus* from a mere tool of the Gothic Queen into a many-sided villain. Jones describes Aaron as flamboyant, callous, shamelessly cynical, and "an artist in villainy." When he "discovers" the bag of gold that he had previously buried under a tree, "he is the confident artist delighting in his own sense of timing, tak[ing] a ghoulish pride in his work." He admires wit in himself and others and employs his ingenuity to stage-manage "the villainies in the play rather than executing them himself." In doing so he demonstrates that he is "a brilliant opportunist . . . rather than a deliberate plotter." He uses the quarrel between Demetrius and Chiron over Lavinia to bring about her rape, takes advantage of the murder of Bassianus to incriminate Quintus and Martius, and plays on Titus's vulnerability to cheat him out of his hand. In an effort to explain the character of Aaron, Jones notes "his complete isolation from his surroundings [and a] deeply felt insecurity." His sense of isolation is demonstrated in the "tenacity with which he clings to his child and the lengths he will go to preserve its life. The child . . . extracts the one totally unselfish act from him." He forfeits his own life to protect his son's. Shakespeare "makes Aaron, in spite of his villainy, into a human being, and a better parent than either Titus or Tamora."[29]

To Hamilton, *Titus Andronicus* is an ambitious tragedy. It displays a mastery of stagecraft and comprehensively combines earlier traditions: Seneca, the morality plays, and the poetic heritage from Ovid. This is a "distinctively Shakespearean [accomplishment], both popular and literary, a stage play and a work of literature. The play reveals Shakespeare's architectonic skill . . . it foreshadows the late tragedies because it is their archetype . . . it deserves to be approached as a central and seminal play in the canon of Shakespeare's works." The handling of the story of Lavinia gives tragic form to Ovid's tale of Philomel. She is central to the play, "not merely as the instrument through which Tamora seeks revenge against Titus, but as a tragic symbol." Her mutilated body is the emblem of fallen nature projected by the play. Ovid provides Shakespeare with the pattern for his tragedy. The action reflects the mythical overthrow of Saturn, the end of the classical golden age followed by the departure of Astraea from the earth. "Titus laments: *'Terras Astraea reliquit.'*"

The dramatic high points are Marcus's presentation of the mutilated Lavinia to her father, the return of Titus's severed hand with the heads of his two sons, and the throat-cutting execution of Tamora's two sons. This last scene may appear the crude work of an inexperienced dramatist catering to a debased public taste for the merely horrific. In the dramatic context, however, it is not murder that we witness, not even personal revenge, but a solemn sacrifice. Tamora's sons have offended not alone against the Andronici but also, as we are told, "against Nature herself

. . . [Titus's] victims are no longer Tamora's sons; their disguise reveals them for what they are: Revenge's sons, Murder and Rape."[30]

Prosser finds the play "curious," Titus "puzzling," and his characterization "fuzzy." In the first act he is "rash, headstrong, and self-centered" in his "unwise support of Saturninus, his decision to sacrifice Alarbus, and his unsympathetic killing of Mutius." He "moves through the next three acts in the role of suppressed virtue." He bides his time "relieving his tortured spirit by sending riddling taunts to his enemies." Although showing signs of madness, he is rational in the masking scene and when he murders Demetrius and Chiron; but by gagging them to prevent their pleas he becomes if not a "villain-revenger" at least a "tainted revenger." By sacrificing Lavinia to eliminate his own "shame and sorrow [he] alienate[s] sympathy and has lost all claim to virtue."[31]

In Brooke's view, Titus is an experimental play in which the dramatist employs nondramatic poetic techniques and devices, tries out different kinds of theatrical construction, and tests new means of revealing character. The scene between the mutilated Lavinia and her uncle Marcus exhibits experimental qualities. Its "baroque development of bloodiness" is couched in "elaborate rhetoric [and] formalized language"; the speech is "static, undramatic, not at all the stuff of which stage plays are made, [yet] the verse, however formal, is not frigid. Wilson was right in noting affinities between the play and The Rape of Lucrece, especially in the development of "interpretation and commentary through emblematic elaboration." The use of poetry that Shakespeare is experimenting with in Titus is similar to that in Lucrece; itself derived from Spenser's achievement in The Faerie Queene: formal in structure and tone, relying on emblems to fuse imagery and moral idea, and responding to Ciceronian ideas of decorum in matters of style, related to the form of emblem used. The use of formal, emblematic verse is echoed in a formality of dramatic structure, and in "visual images . . . powerfully effective in establishing emblems of the play's significance." The central theme of Shakespeare's play is the deterioration of men and women, under the stress of revengeful passion, into beasts; and Marcus's speech is to be understood as a thematic statement of the formal concern of the play. Brooke concludes that the play was planned in two main movements, with Act 3 standing between them as a pivot with the central metamorphosis in which "Titus deteriorates into mad beast, while Aaron displays a kind of nobility." There is "tremendous inventiveness" and "an imaginative intelligence which later found the blinding of Gloucester necessary to the tragedy of Lear." The play is experimental "and in many ways it does not succeed, but it is characterized by a remarkable linguistic and dramatic vitality."[32]

The core of the structural unity that Cutts identifies in Titus Andronicus is the pervasive presence throughout the play of the "renaissance topos which frequently finds representation in iconography: the mistaking of the shadow for the substance." The principal character so deluded is Titus, who "in taking 'false shadows as true substances' (3.2.70) . . . is by no means aware that his seeing has all along been at fault and still is." His lack of understanding is at the root of all the horrors endured by his family as well as himself. Lavinia is only Titus's tool, in whom "is mirrored the destruction of Titus's own power." When he sees her mutilated and says had he but seen a picture of her in this plight "it would have maddened him, he is ironically showing he lives and walks with shadows, not with substances . . . [she] represents one part of the image which his own hand shattered." Aaron is the black shadow to everyone's substantive evil ". . . monstrously delighting in the foolishness of Titus [yet] he may well think he is the real substance of the tragedy." At the end the Andronici "project all the family's guilt onto Aaron," thus exonerating themselves at his expense. Shakespeare's use of the shadow-substance topos "not only illuminates the structure of the drama but also demonstrates the unity of that structure . . . [the play] culminates in tragedy because Titus persists throughout" in deluding himself.[33]

Stampfer finds that the "excessive brutalities" of *Titus* are "essentially variations of infanticide." Titus kills Mutius, and twenty-one of his other sons were sacrificed in his military campaigns. Giving the imperial seat to Saturninus brings about the death of Quintus and Martius, and forces Lucius to flee. The Goths have a murderous mother. Defeat in battle leads to the death of Alarbus, and Tamora delivers Demetrius and Chiron to Titus, who slaughters them. The two families come to Rome for destruction, the dark, barbaric family with their witch mother, and the civilized family with their fanatical father. This primitive typology defines a play different from Senecan tragedies. "Seneca maintained an even surface of hysteria and violence, a constancy of sadistic episode on a stream of charged dialog, that suggests an emotional climate of an adult encased in a paranoid universe." In *Titus*, the murders, mutilations, and the cannibal feast have a flavor of fairy tale, not the hysterical sadism and paranoia of adults, but the literal animation of small children. The stylized symmetry of the play, with its fairy tale atmosphere, is the opposite of realistic drama. "In this play Shakespeare's doctrines are . . . too morally stark . . . [The] symmetry of structure suggests . . . an aggressively dialectal mind [that can] grasp the core of his structure . . . assert its polar opposite, and blurt both on stage, side by side, dream and reality, moral structure and lunge of feeling."[34]

Chakravorty discusses the concept of revenge as it is displayed in *Titus Andronicus*, the earliest Shakespearean examination "of the very ethos of violence," deeper than any playwright had previously attempted. The dramatist was interested in revenge, but neither *Titus* nor *Hamlet* is a "revenge play pure and simple." Shakespeare is writing a tragedy. He kills Mutius "to uphold a point of honour just as Brutus kills Caesar to save the Republic." The sacrifice of Alarbus and the killing of his son are both done "in a mood of pride and haughtiness which anticipates Lear." In Ovid, there is mutilation and in Seneca, a cry for revenge, but "in Shakespeare alone even at this early date [there] is an element of conflict posed by the rival demands of honour, justice, and revenge . . . " He took a gruesome story and improved it. The concept that the protagonist, after sustaining repeated brutal blows delivered by his enemies, is "yet so just that he will not revenge" (4.1.127), Chakravorty notes, is "altogether new in Elizabethan drama . . . The old notions of justice and revenge are turned by Shakespeare into a moral issue."[35]

Broude dismisses the importance of political themes in *Titus* and the means by which Romans are differentiated from Goths. Modern readers tend "to assume that Rome represents goodness, civilization, and order, and the Goths evil, barbarism, and chaos." Shakespeare's audiences would have viewed the relationship differently, however. While they admired Rome's accomplishments, they were also well aware of "her vices." They also knew of "the Gothic virtues—vitality, valor, integrity, and love of freedom." English "antagonism toward Rome" was partially religious in origin and partly due to the conception that "the moral and military virtues of the Germans made them more fit protectors of Western civilization than the descendants of the old Romans . . . Shakespeare's depiction of the Romans and Goths is otherwise quite in keeping with informed Renaissance English thought on these peoples. Titus' Rome is Rome as seen by Elizabethans, the familiar Roman virtues mingling with the equally familiar Roman vices. But it is also Rome in a period of crisis and transition, menaced by two of the very problems which the real Rome had had to face and overcome—the replacement of an ailing dynasty and the assimilation of a conquered people into the Roman commonweal." Shakespeare's attitude toward the Goths is neutral. There is generosity in their acceptance of Lucius and valor in their military campaign. The "amalgamation of Goths and Romans under Lucius" is an appropriate resolution of the crisis facing Rome. "For Elizabethans, whose opinion of the Goths was not . . . unflattering" the ending of *Titus* would have seemed "neither puzzling nor forced." In a later essay Broude draws attention to the four forms of vengeance in the play: "human sacrifice, the vendetta, state justice . . . and divine vengeance." The pagan setting "enables Shakespeare to underline the differences between 'non-Christian' and 'Christian' forms of vengeance." Thus, the sacrifice gives rise to the vendetta. State justice and divine vengeance "assume as the norm of human existence a condition of order which crime may temporarily disrupt but which is re-established by the retribution that inevitably follows." The sacrifice of Alarbus to appease the shades of the Andronici killed by the Goths reflects ancient beliefs known to Elizabethans. The vengeance taken for Alarbus's death is blood revenge, which "functions in the interests of families . . . predicated upon the principle of collective responsibility. Elizabethan attitudes toward the vendetta were mixed . . . religious, moral, and political writings treat[ed] blood vengeance . . . [as] 'private revenge,'" therefore pernicious. The sympathy of the Romans with Titus and the advance of Lucius with the Goths causes Tamora to adopt desperate measures against the Andronici. Her disguising and effort to mislead Titus "proves [to be] the instrument of her own undoing." Titus's vengeance is appalling, but "he sees his revenge as a duty prescribed by the gods."[36]

Titus Andronicus can be distinguished from Shakespeare's other Roman plays, according to Ettin, by the fact that the playwright did not "vigorously" develop in the early work "the possibilities for dialectic in the sustained conflict between disparate aspects of the Roman image." He observes that the "numerous allusions to Roman mythology almost invariably stem from the darker, crueler, uncivilized reaches of the Roman mind." The sacrifice of Alarbus and the dialog between Tamora and Titus concerning it constitute a sequence that "makes it difficult for us to regard Rome as the image of civilized humanity." Titus's "'Roman virtues' of piety . . . and pride must be seen in part as faults, though they are also the sources of his personal nobility." The allusive richness of the text "accounts to a large extent for the artificial literary quality that has been noted." Ettin finds the technique undramatic, but he believes Shakespeare "was fully aware that this method was inappropriate to drama." He notes that Marcus's "fountain metaphor . . . must be read as a poetic exornation that purposely contrasts shockingly in tone and meaning with what we see. The actual spectacle becomes merely an occasion for poetic embellishment or fantasy . . . The sudden metamorphosis produces the emotion of astonishment . . . It follows, therefore, that his [Marcus's] 'admiration' should be expressed naturally in formal, basically Ovidian style." Shakespeare in his first tragedy explores the possibilities of classical Roman sources "with uncommon acuity . . . it is typical of Shakespeare to force us to recognize the severe limitations of this framework. Always aware of the richness and complexity of the many traditions which feed his art, he tests here the nature and meaning of the Roman legacy."[37]

The unrealistic, formal, "even stylized" qualities of *Titus* are investigated by Reese, who finds that the "formalization" of the horrors and other characteristics of the play are called for in the text and the stage directions. He directs attention to complex and elaborate "balances and approaches," of the systematic arrangement of characters into "dramati-

cally opposed groups" in which all-except perhaps for Titus and Aaron—
are either "wholly good or wholly bad," to significant repetition of pleas,
supplications, tableaux, "of words, phrases, scenes, and images," all of
which constitute a substratum of formalization that makes the play "more
artificial. The characters become less like human beings and more like
symbols being manipulated in an excessively orderly framework . . .
[they are] dehumanized by their language, their self-conscious posturing,
and their association with a deeply formal and ritualistic environment."
The drama is a "fascinating and partially successful attempt to subdue
the sensationalism of the most shocking material imaginable."[38]

Resolutely setting aside the "antagonism[s]" of other critics against
Titus Andronicus, Shadoian hopes to demonstrate "that the play needs
no apologies." Conceding that elements of melodrama are prominent in
Titus, he nevertheless insists that the question to be addressed is whether
the play is "adequate and effective on its own terms . . . [whether] it is
an artistic success as it stands. It is not without verbal unity and splendor.
However, it is essentially theatrical, immediate, and visceral, more than
thematically substantial or psychologically penetrating. Specific critical
investigations would do well to concentrate on its stagecraft and formal
structure. Although its violence, and a playwright's choice to be so violent, is quite accessible and understandable to a modern audience, it is
still sufficiently removed from contemporary taste in mood, idiom, and
emphasis, to demand careful, calculated production to have any success
. . . Nor is it really 'poetic.' It is more fitting to speak of its verbal resources than its verbal magic. Occasionally, the poet and the dramatist,
language and action, come into conflict, are not perfectly integrated and
seem to vie for momentary supremacy. But all suspicions of ineptitude
are surely unfounded. *Titus Andronicus* is clearly an accomplished work
. . . if the play is in spots youthfully shrill and awkward, it is as a whole
tough, accomplished, coherent, and effective."[39]

Titus Andronicus, Brower tells us, is several different kinds of play,
incorporating tragedy, "Noble Roman History," mystery-revenge, horror
and Grand Guignol, epic travesty and Ovidian fantasy. It is transitional
in character, "being at once distant from the later plays . . . and surprisingly close to them." It looks backward to Kyd, Marlowe, and Senecan
imitations, to medieval complaints and pageants, "more obviously to Ovid
and Virgil, and in some details, to Seneca," and, at the same time, looks
forward to the Roman plays and the tragedies. The play "exhibits the
young ambition typical of many Renaissance writers . . . The surprising
thing is that . . . [it] has more order than disorder . . . intelligible progress
in action . . . large dramatic emphases . . . and at least four distinct and
memorable characters, Titus, Lucius, Tamora, and Aaron." There is frantic killing and cunning villainy, but also noble Roman eloquence and vir-

tue. A serious defect of the play is the failure to bring into contact "the voices of innocence and civility . . [and] the voices of barbarism and chaos." Though Lucius speaks for order, "no dramatic connection is made between political disorder and the disordered mind of Titus." In the play, Shakespeare does not control dramatic direction, nor does he model speech to fit new occasions. "The literary feat of connecting . . . [such] contrasting and conflicting kinds of experience is well beyond the author of *Titus Andronicus*."[40]

Calderwood examines *Titus* as metadrama and finds that "Shakespeare's plays are not only about the various moral, social, political, and other thematic issues with which critics have so long and quite properly been busy but also about Shakespeare's plays . . . [themselves and] dramatic art . . . the metadramatic theme in . . . *Titus Andronicus* is neither single, separate, nor persistent. It can in no way precede or exist apart from the play because its subject is the play." If Shakespeare had wanted to suggest "the poet's sacrifice of verbal autonomy when writing for the theatre, he could hardly have found a better myth to dramatize than that of Philomela . . . whose problem is linguistic and is solved by 'art," and which is reflected in the plight of Lavinia. Calderwood suggests that *Titus* "metadramatically presents us with a rape of language, with the mutilation that the poet's 'tongue' suffers when forced to submit to the rude demands of the theatre." In the postbanquet portion of the last scene, "Lucius-the-light . . . entirely Shakespeare's creation . . . [overcomes] Aaron-the-black . . . [who is the] foul, murderous core of the play." His giving way to the fair Lucius converts revenge tragedy into a political morality in which Rome's recovery is framed by justice and mercy. The poet submits his play to the judgment of his audience. Calderwood finds this no less corruptive than his reliance on Senecanism. "Simultaneously classical and popular, it suffers from both, as Shakespeare seems aware." Nevertheless, it embodies a coherent metadramatic theme, "a mode of autistic meaning in which Shakespeare has played, for the most part ironically, on the goals and frustrations and the sense of loss of the poet exploring the complexities of drama."[41]

Shakespeare in *Titus Andronicus* is "exploiting artifice upon artifice: to a degree greater than in other plays, according to Arthos. The form of his early histories is modified by the poet acting as "a manipulator of . . . a moral idea [as he does] in the two poems" (*Venus* and *Lucrece*). The result is a kind of deadly game in which the basic rule is simple: "every offense calls for violence in retaliation." In this context, Tamora and Aaron arrange and oversee "a whole series of events in . . . single-minded fury." They play the game perfectly, but "just short of the last trick the game is lost." Titus, who is "both the pawn and prize" in the game, divines the techniques employed by his opponents and begins countermoves. As the final success seems to be in their grasp "he reveals to them that they have been trapped and he has inflicted greater losses upon them than they could ever have dreamed of." The audience is interested in the way the game is played. The horror of the crimes visited upon Titus is compounded with sympathy in his suffering so that "we are ready to accept the final killings as not only tolerable but as the only means of satisfying our concern that the wicked shall be punished and the tortured put out of their misery."[42]

Taking as his theme the stranger in Shakespeare—and specifically "The Moor as Stranger"—Fiedler interprets the role of Aaron in *Titus Andronicus*. Aaron represents the dark side of Shakespeare's ambivalence toward the stranger in this Senecan play. The Moor is by no means directly responsible for the horrors but "only, somehow, *symbolic* of them all, an embodiment of the psychic blackness [of the tale of the] blasphemous black man . . . of godless Africa whom Shakespeare intends Aaron to represent, thus suiting the expectations of an audience to whom Moors seemed creatures more diabolical than human." In actuality we see him do "few of the fell deeds of which he boasts." He does stab the nurse and tricks Titus out of his hand, but he "commits no crime which equals in horror Titus's own final atrocity." Titus, however, is portrayed as an equivocal figure, essentially noble though excessive in rage and half mad, while Aaron remains "a villain unqualified, since his evil is established more in speech than action, by the role he plays rather than the atrocities he commits."[43]

Huffman interprets the play in the light of Ovid's concern for change and continuity as set forth in his *Metamorphoses*. He cites Bassianus's first speech, with its emphasis on grace, honor, virtue, justice, and nobility. Most of these themes recur in later ironic contexts to suggest their absence from the Rome of Saturninus and Tamora; yet Bassianus's "prayer of Act One is fulfilled when Lucius [speaks in the final act of] hopes that he may govern so as 'To heal Rome's harms and wipe away her woe.' Natural hope has become natural regeneration." The recurrence of theological associations signals a sacrificial purgation. Ovid's return of Astraea to earth and his restoration of the Golden Age, with its moral values and Christian views, point to "Rome's internal healing . . . [and] provide the resolution of Shakespeare's first Roman tragedy."[44]

Use of emblems contributes to the thematic structure and pictorial ingenuity of *Titus Andronicus* according to Haaker. Although Shakespeare employed the emblematic method in many of his plays, "*Titus* is unique in the concentration of such scenes and passages. In no other play is symbolic spectacle so paramount." The three elements of the emblem—a motto or sententia; a picture, in the play frequently a tableau, or words that suggest a picture; and verses that interpret the emblem or draw a moral or religious lesson—are readily identifiable. Most commonly, "a representative character voices the motto, often a classical tag;" the commentary follows by means of "dialogue and symbolic action—sometimes illuminating, sometimes ironic, but always ambiguous with an intentional double meaning." Haaker identifies and describes three emblems in Act 1 and others throughout the play, and traces a number of them to well-known sixteenth-century emblem books.[45]

Muir finds that in *Titus* "Shakespeare's dramatic skill was only intermittent." There are eloquent passages, and he accomplishes the evocation of the woodland scenes, but characters are portrayed with little effect. Apart from "Aaron, who is splendidly theatrical, Tamora, and Titus, the characterization is not very successful. Perhaps the play is chiefly interesting as a forerunner" to *King Lear.* "Shakespeare seems to have hoped to arouse commiseration . . . [and] admiration by means of effective oratory . . . but the oratory . . . instead of forcing our commiseration, acts as a screen between the horrors and our hearts."[46]

"The extremities of horror and suffering in *Titus Andronicus* seem to stretch the capacities of art to give them adequate embodiment and expression," Palmer says at the beginning of his evocative essay. "Perhaps it was this sense of testing the limits of his poetic and dramatic resources that attracted Shakespeare to the subject at the beginning of his career." As do other critics, Palmer first examines Marcus's speech upon encountering the ravished Lavinia. This lament "is the expression of an effort to realize a sight that taxes to the utmost the powers of understanding and utterance." Marcus dwells upon the figure before him "that is to him both familiar and strange, fair and hideous, living body and object: This is, and is not, Lavinia . . . [her] plight is literally unutterable . . . By realising Lavinia's tragedy, Marcus' formal lament articulates unspeakable woes." In reshaping the narrative of *The History of Titus Andronicus,* Shakespeare related the events to analogs in Roman literature and mythology. He altered the name of the emperor to suggest the astrological aspect of Saturn, in which the god's influence is baleful and malignant. Palmer identifies this influence as of central significance in the play. The play's first two acts represent "the metamorphosis of Roman civilization into Gothic barbarism through a transition from solemn ceremony to wild and brutal sport. So clearly structured is the sequence of action in this opening phase of the play, leading to the violation of Lavinia, that its significance can be followed almost entirely in terms of the strongly defined patterns of stage spectacle and movement. We attend as much to Shakespeare's choreography as to the dialogue, while the shifting tableaux of groups of figures, their physical movements and gestures, create a series of expressive parallels and contrasts in rhythm, emotional pitch, and tone. The tragic issues are here presented in the language of theatrical form."

The central symbol of the tragic action of the play is the devouring mouth, the tomb that receives the dead Andronici; the pit mouth that consumes Bassianus, Quintus, and Martius; Lavinia's mutilated mouth; the need for speech that when attained brings no relief. "The action of the play as a whole seems to turn upon the dual nature of the mouth that utters and devours . . . extremities of horror and suffering seek comfort in utterance, [but] of their very nature they are too dreadful to be named."

Palmer's claim for *Titus* "is not only that it is a highly ordered and elaborately designed work, but that it is also one in which Shakespeare takes some extremely bold yet calculated risks with the resources of his art. Its faults are those of an excessively conscious theatrical and poetic ingenuity rather than those of crude sensationalism. It moves to admiration, in the Elizabethan sense of wonder and amazement, more often than to compassion or sympathy . . . The play is rich in dramatic and stylistic invention, and so full of analogues to its own art that it might be described as Shakespeare's thesis in tragedy, anticipating many of the formal techniques used in the later tragedies."[47]

The interplay of the action pattern of *Titus* with the character pattern is examined by Toole. The central theme of the play is the mutilation of order. The motif of mutilation begins with the sacrificial dismemberment of Alarbus and it is echoed in Marcus's plea to Titus to set a head on headless Rome, "suggesting metaphorically the theme of disorder in the body politic." The motif of revenge is part of this pattern, "which instigates most of the crucial action in the play." Titus begins a learning process that is roughly analogous to that experienced by Lear, but the process is abortive. The drumfire of grief to which he is subjected brings him to the edge of madness, and his thoughts turn to revenge. This represents a gradual movement toward sympathy for Titus because the mutilation for which he was responsible was directed by a principle; the mutilation in response, directed against the Andronici, represented by Lavinia, was prompted by Satanic malice. But the element of horror in Titus's plan of revenge leads to the opposite effect—the patterns of character and action conflict. "Though the themes of madness and poetic or heavenly justice serve, to some extent, to dissociate the character of Titus from the monstrousness of his actions, they are not strong enough to permit the viewer to feel sympathy for the tragic protagonist . . . this is so primarily because of the dramatist's inability to develop the motif of compassion within the protagonist . . . The development of [his] character has been subordinated or sacrificed to the development of sensationalistic action."[48]

Godshalk traces recurrent and linked structural patterns employed in

Titus among other Shakespearean plays to underline continuity of action, to build a scheme of dramatic irony, and to suggest the total dramatic significance of the individual incident. He believes that Shakespeare's ability to unite the diverse elements of a play into a well-knit whole is unique, that his structural competence is seen as both initial and continuing throughout his career and is not developmental or evolutionary, as many critics think. The word "pattern" is aimed at underscoring a particular method of structural analysis. It is inclusive and may comprehend image, theme, action, and characterization, united to form an organic whole. General patterns occur in many plays, an example of which is the polarity of place, meaning that two locales in a play exhibit "contrasting images, ideals, modes, actions, which together create ideological opposites. The poles may be seen as emblematic or symbolic . . . [and may] have origins in the morality play. . . The poles [in *Titus*] are the city of Rome and the forest outside where Lavinia is raped and mutilated; one pole suggests order and continuity, the other disorder and chaos."

In the final scene the confrontation between Saturninus and Lucius echoes the conflict at the opening of the first scene. Another contrasting pattern is in Titus's victorious hand which blessed Lavinia in the initial scene but slays her in the concluding scene. "The play begins and ends with Titus killing one of his children. . . The culmination of the united patterns of dismemberment and eating [is in] the cannibalistic feast. . . And with the deaths of Lavinia, Tamora, Titus, and Saturninus which garnish the feast, the way is clear for the reconstruction of Roman society. . . The reintegration of the body politic and the culmination of the dismemberment pattern are two faces of the same coin. The initial conflicts of the play are resolved."[49]

Nevo presents an illuminating critique of the structure of *Titus Andronicus*, informed by the "Bradleyan tradition," along the classic lines of protasis, epitasis, catastrophe. The protasis, "presents both the peril or evil which can be predicated of the protagonist's circumstances, and that aspect of himself which causes them to constitute, for him a test situation, a plight. This aspect of himself is the heroic attribute. The epitasis is characterized by "the greatest turbulence, a crisis in the hero's fortunes . . . a total reversal of his initial status and situation . . . Titus, savior of the city, becomes 'the woeful'st man that ever liv'd in Rome.'" The tragic action

"comes to an end with the catastrophe . . . The worst of the possibilities inherent in the initial situation has been pressed to its ultimate issue . . . all is revealed and all consummated. Aaron, self-confessed monster, glories to the end in his catalogue of horrible villainies, repudiates 'conscience' with surly contempt even while demanding in its name that Lucius save the child . . . The masque of revenge brings the contest between Titus and the ravenous tiger

Tamora to a climax of double concealment, a game of blind man's bluff in which the over-confident deceiver is herself duped by the shrewd madman. And at the Theyestean banquet which follows, Titus, blind with tears, a Samson come to judgment, brings down the pillars upon Lavinia's, his own, and the Philistines' unholy heads. Justice has not only been done, but has been most indubitably and poetically seen to have been done. Lucius brings healing to Rome . . . [Yet] it is as suffering *pater familias* that the tragic protagonist is finally identified . . . it is upon the theme first played in *Titus Andronicus* that *Lear* is a prodigious variation.[50]

Rothenberg discussed the possibility that Shakespeare was expressing in *Titus Andronicus* "A strong 'pattern of the past' . . . the pre-Oedipal fear of being smothered, buried alive, and eaten by the breast or mouth of a cannibalistic mother." To incorporate such an idea into his play, the dramatist was forced to present characters that are monsters. He motivates Titus's ultimate revenge on Tamora by having her sons mutilate Lavinia. "The shocking fantasies released . . . obviously tap deeply repressed impulses that customarily find more economical artistic expression" in other ways. Shakespeare's preference for metaphor seems to be because it is "only an imaging within an imagining . . . the subjunctive land of 'as if it were.'" By this means he avoids the possibility that "his audience [would] turn away from his plot action, increas[ing] its chances of receptivity."[51]

Danson studies the world of *Titus Andronicus* as one in which "man's words go unheeded and his gestures acknowledged, a world unresponsive to his cries, demands, prayers . . . a nightmare world." In Shakespearean tragedy, man is "not only man speaking, but man trying to speak, trying to create the language that can denote him truly." The image that dominates the play "is of humanity tongueless and limbless, sunk in a world inimical to its fundamental need to be understood, yet still trying by every means to speak." The image of the silenced Lavinia haunts the play. Danson cites the many pleas in *Titus* that are not heard. They are mostly Andronican petitions, but they arise from Titus's deafness to Tamora's entreaty on behalf of Alarbus. The need to find a satisfactory response becomes an overwhelming concern. The imperious demand for relief through expression, which is not met, leads to contemplation of fantastic actions. Titus proposes "some device of further misery To make us wondered at in time to come."

The play contains a series of devices that adumbrate the frustrated need to speak. The central device is the mutilated Lavinia, who is an emblem for the plight of the voiceless Andronici in a now alien Rome. Others are Titus's proposals to weep all day into a fountain and to pass their days in dumb shows. The paradoxical in effectuality of the play's rhetoric derives from powerlessness to take action. Titus's failure to ease his stomach with his bitter tongue (3.1.232) brings him to the edge of madness. "He takes the final step from rhetoric through madness to death . . . Through his extended pursuit of revenge . . . the culminating action that may bring 'wonder' out of rhetoric . . . the tragic hero plays out the ritualization of death," his own as well as that of his enemies.[52]

Hunter elucidates the thematic content of *Titus Andronicus* by comparison, in part, to similar themes in *Romeo and Juliet*. Parallels of structure, social position, dramatic necessity, symbolic significance, and tragic inevitability exhibit the comparability of the two plays that are in other ways palpably disparate. The differences are made manifest by the symbolic reality of the two cities: martial Rome and "cozy" Verona. The similarities exhibit themselves in the functions of family and its implicit need for stability in a threatening world. In these two plays, Shakespeare "mark[s] out the extreme polarities of his tragic range." However, a comparison of *Titus* with *King Lear*—"in some ways a reworking of themes" from the earlier play—shows that while many qualities are shared, notably the tortured father hounded into madness, many are also significantly different. Family hostility in *Titus*, for example, is between the Andronici and the "barbarian outsiders;" in *Lear* "the opposition of good and bad emerges from the matrix of a single family."

The meaning of *Titus Andronicus* "can only be brought to focus inside the walls of its city . . . We are here concerned with self-sacrifice and self-indulgence, rule and disobedience, with suffering and cruelty, with the destructive will to chaos, set against personal commitment to justice as the only meaningful basis for society. Only in Rome, it is implied, can the victory of cosmos or chaos be fully significant."[53]

The Senecan contribution to *Titus* is reasserted by A. L. and M. K. Kistner, particularly in the "stress of content and external form." These include the chorus, the messenger, the nurse, the tyrant; stichomythia, the five-act structure, sensationalism, violence, rhetorical and reflective passages, philosophic ideas expressed in aphorism, and presentiments of coming destruction. There is also a Senecan element of internal form, a pattern in which the protagonist "discovers that whatever means most to him . . . is irrevocably taken from him," leading to despair and then to madness, revenge, or a desire for suicide. Specific influences include the sacrifice of Alarbus derived from the sacrifice of Polixena in Seneca's *Troades* and the cannibal banquet inspired by *Theyestes*. "The non-Senecan background, ample as it is, does not provide the structure Shakespeare is realizing in the actions of his hero." Titus's response to the horrors visited upon his children is despair shortly transformed into a desire for vengeance and symptoms of madness, but no impulse toward suicide. "The Senecan pattern provides the motivation and subsequent course of action for the tragic hero."[54]

Irony as a perspective freed from the dialectal tension between conflicting principals is elucidated by Payne, who employs the term in this sense based on an analysis by Kierkegaard. There are several strains of ironic perspective exhibited in Shakespearean tragedy. That employed in *Titus Andronicus* "relies on the Ovidian myth of the Four Ages of Man and Elizabethan suppositions about Roman history." Before the action of the play begins, there has been a fall from the equivalent of Ovid's Age of Gold, the reign of the previous Emperor, and shortly it is apparent that the Age of Iron has been entered, providing a contrast between a lost world of order and impending chaos. The first contrast is between the dead and the living. A second contrast is between those who seek justice and those who hide their treachery behind a hypocritical concern for justice." Titus, as his cries for justice resounding throughout the play attest, genuinely seeks justice, according to his harsh conception; Saturninus "uses justice only for its rhetorical effect . . . Once he is Emperor . . . justice becomes . . . insignificant . . . the setting . . . is the Iron Age . . . The play's structure . . . could be visualized as a set of concentric circles . . . The largest circle would represent the Ovidian myths of transformation and of the Four Ages of Man; within this would be found the theme of Roman history, with its emphasis on the consequences of civil war in contrast to the order and stability of a prelapsarian Golden Age; and at last within this theme is the mimetic circle enclosing the specific settings, plot, and characters of the play. The ironic structure of *Titus Andronicus,* then, results from the interaction of myth, theme, and mimesis."[55]

The language of *Titus Andronicus* is peculiar in the literalness of its central metaphors, Tricomi points out. "The figurative language, in fact, imitates the gruesome circumstances of the plot, thus revealing that Shakespeare subordinates everything in *Titus,* including metaphor, to that single task of conveying forcefully the Senecan and Ovidian horrors that he has committed himself to portraying." This relationship between language and event is "strange." Metaphor ordinarily extends the imaginative compass of a play by translating its immediate events beyond the limits of the stage. In *Titus,* metaphor "draws its images from the narrower events of plot . . . in an endeavor to render the events of the tragedy more real and painful." The play continually investigates the chasm between the spoken word and the action. The self-conscious didactic use of metaphor is "quite distinctive in Elizabethan drama." The continuing use of certain metaphors amounts to a witty exploration of the relationship between language and event, of the multiple perceptions that are the mark of intellectual comedy. "These gruesomely ironic perceptions are rooted in irrepressible wittiness . . . in this witty competition with Ovid and Seneca, Shakespeare is just what Greene said he was, 'an upstart

Crow' striving to overreach his masters in their own vein." Tricomi emphasizes that in *Titus Andronicus* "we must understand that we are dealing, not with a paucity of imagination, but . . . with a talent untamed . . . we ought to recognize that *Titus* is a uniquely important experiment in drama . . . Shakespeare is exploring the resources inherent in a referential use of metaphor and is trying to integrate the power of the poetic language with the immeasurable potential of dramatic action itself." In a later essay, Tricomi posits and convincingly demonstrates the centrality and pervasive iteration of pastoral imagery throughout the play.[56]

Under the rubric "Civility," the mutual caring of citizens for each other, Zeeveld examines the conduct of the characters in *Titus Andronicus*. The reverse of civility is, of course, barbarity. In the play, Shakespeare presents Goths and Moors, from whom barbarity could have been anticipated, at least initially, as civil; while Rome, "the historic image of civility," is inhabited by characters who, under sufficient provocation, "exhibit the utmost barbarity." By this juxtaposition, "Shakespeare creates a rough but potent irony. Implicit in Shakespeare's thought, even at this early time, is the inexplicable paradox in man's nature that civility and incivility should be so inextricably intermingled." Tamora is the embodiment of the barbarous revenger, but "there is excuse for the revenges she plans." Aaron's blackness, the color of Satan, proclaims his devilishness, "yet, as with Tamora, Aaron is not without human instincts." Titus, the preserver of the Roman civil commonwealth, "finds himself in the irreconcilable role of private revenger, and . . . in the course of his revenges he commits a series of acts which all but obliterate order in the state he sought to preserve." Lucius, shortly to be proclaimed Emperor, vilifies Aaron as barbarous, ravenous, and accursed, yet would hang the Moor's infant son to vex the father's soul. "The paradox of civil barbarity is . . . clear . . . at the close of the action; gentleness has been blotted out by a Roman revenge comparable in its ferocity to that of the most barbarous of races."[57]

Champion analyzes the characterization of Titus as protagonist. He finds that the essence of the role is defined early in the play by two of the seven deadly sins: pride and anger. He is "furiously proud . . . [and] in his wrath [exhibits] monstrous arrogance." The "uncontrolled fury of his pride" leads to "tragic foolishness" and opens the way for the horrific experiences that move him from "wrath to self-pity to madness." His sanity "is the victim of his extreme pride stretched on the rack of ignominy and suffering." Throughout the misery of the repeated blows of adversity, the surrounding characters—Marcus, Lucius, even the wordless Lavinia—maintain the attention on Titus and his reactions to his sufferings. "Demonstrably, Shakespeare has focused the first four and one-half acts on the character of Titus." The proud soldier of the first act is "by degrees broken through pain and madness" and rendered incapable of effective action against his enemies. The conclusion would appear to be either stoic resignation or some form of poetic redress or some carefully devised scheme for a measure of retributive justice. But what "Shakespeare provides is the very conclusion the structure will not support . . . the unanticipated emergence of Titus as a sophisticated revenger outwitting his adversaries at their own game." Furthermore, the scheme does not arise "from the pattern of the plot and [is] in no way consistent with the character of Titus." The central problem of the play is the protagonist. Motivation is defective and there is excessive dependence on "pointer characters" to depict Titus's degeneration.[58]

In the course of a comprehensive scholarly discussion of *Titus*, Mincoff addresses himself to a critical assessment of the play. He notes that structurally, the absence of an induction "seems rather a bold innovation [for its time], suggesting a certain independence of judgment." For a tragedy that includes not only revenge but also the initiating action it is desirable that the audience should feel that the hero is a part "of the ineluctable sequence of events towards which . . . [he] has contributed. To that demand *Titus Andronicus* answers perfectly . . . Titus unwillingly sets off a cycle of evil, of human crimes and horrors but with his death that cycle eventually works itself out."

The appeal of the revenge play must have been largely "in the vicarious satisfaction obtained from the hero's triumph over injustice and oppression." The assumption that revenge was considered reprehensible rests on the supposition that the theater was an extension of the church, but the audience attended plays for enjoyment, not edification. Blood revenge is fitted into what Mincoff considers "the basic structural pattern of Shakespeare's tragedies," and unlike, in form, Kyd's *Spanish Tragedy*, to which he compares *Titus*. The first act is introductory "with its own climax and descent." In the second act, "The turbations of the action proper set in . . . with a series of blows . . . rising step by step up to the exact middle of the play . . . the last blow of all, the banishment of . . . [Lucius, Titus's] one remaining son, introduces at the same time a turn in the direction of the action, and the countermovement is ready to set in . . . Structurally indeed *Titus Andronicus* . . . is one of the most faultlessly plotted tragedies without a superfluous episode, following a line of almost mathematical precision," and the plotting is characteristic of Shakespeare. Mincoff notes, however, the "un-Shakespearian effect of the whole . . . one might, I think, sum up the case against it in a single word—its frigidity." He cites "the prettification of the horrors through the imagery which is no doubt the point that grates most distressingly on modern ears . . . it is perhaps even more the horrors themselves than their treatment, that seem so coldly calculated."

In style, *Titus* is formal. This effect is accomplished by the oratorical language, repetitions, invocations, apostrophes, the use of rhetorical figures, balanced couplets, alliteration, and a persistent "patterning" in diction and imagery. "Behind all this there does seem to be a conscious purpose," that of projecting a stately Roman tragedy.[59]

Knight notes that parallels between *Titus* and *Lear* include the protagonist's yielding of political power, suffering age and irascibility, his sacrifice of a prisoner, and the killing of his own son (Lear rejects Cordelia). Although "somewhat laboured [in *Titus*] . . . the accents of tragic poetry are there . . . it swells and subsides with considerable power." The "rampaging villanies" prompt Titus to appeal for justice by shooting missives on arrows to the gods. "This fantastically conceived extravaganza serves, in a manner characteristic of Shakespearian tragedy, to give the middle-action new life and impetus. It lifts us beyond revenge, and we regard the final horrors as actions of justice . . . Though the play's substances are horrible, the emotional and poetic correspondents are handled in masterly fashion and the artistry is on occasion superb." Aaron is "the main agent of wickedness," but when his infant son is threatened he responds "in accents of courage . . . that arouse our admiration . . . The evil in Aaron is so extreme that it raises metaphysical questions regarding the authority of evil in the universe . . . Can it be that Providence and Nature are, in some moods, malignant? And that human evil has authority behind it?"[60]

The "revolution" in Shakespearean criticism to performance orientation is chronicled by Styan. He observes that the roots of this twentieth-century movement are diverse, and that it is based on the "grand discovery . . . that Shakespeare knew his business as a playwright." In part it represents a reaction against the "circumstantial character analysis of Bradley," and the "elaborate [stage] decorations" of Irving and especially of Beerbohm Tree. More positive in bringing about change were the efforts "of William Poel and the Elizabethan Stage Society . . . to show that Shakespeare should be understood in his own medium"; of Granville-Barker in "His plea . . . for a new school of Shakespeare criticism based upon experiment with the plays in the theater"; of Geoffrey Whitworth and the British Drama League "to encourage . . . the establishment of . . . drama departments in universities"; and of "such apparent eccentrics as Nigel Playfair, Barry Jackson, and Tyrone Guthrie [who] sought repeatedly to give their audiences what they took to be the stuff of the Shakespeare experience."

Some nineteenth-century critics believed that Shakespeare would not be "other than diminished by his association with the stage." Goethe, Coleridge, Lamb, and Hazlitt participated in what Granville-Barker called a "school of metaphysical closet-criticism," whose main interest was in the realization of Shakespeare's gift for creating characters. Bradley fell heir to this movement and he elevated it to preeminence in his treatment of Shakespeare's tragic characters, but his process of "recreating Shakespeare's scenes concealed as much as it revealed [of] Shakespeare's way of working." The advance of "stage-centered criticisms" was facilitated by the rise of numerous dramatic societies throughout Great Britain devoted to "Elizabethanism" in production, "forswearing . . . elaborate staging . . . austerely doubling the parts, [and] keeping monotonous lighting in imitation of the daylight at the Globe."[61]

Links between *Titus Andronicus* and *Cymbeline* brought about through the medium of Ovid's story of Philomela are illuminatingly studied by Thompson. While in *Cymbeline* the dramatist does not make such insistent references to his source as he does in *Titus,* he does go "to the trouble of telling us" that Imogen has "been reading late the tale of Tereus" and Philomel (2.2.44–46). "This scene then is a symbolic rape of Imogen's honour [in Iachimo's theft of a bracelet from her arm] rather than a real one" as in the case of Lavinia. In *Cymbeline,* it is Cloten who is mutilated. Both plays "have a tendency to harp on the themes of mutilation . . . [but while] *Titus* does this very self-consciously and to an almost ridiculous extent . . . The references in *Cymbeline* are less obtrusive." Nevertheless, "the combination of rape with mutilation . . . is what makes the Philomel story appropriate to both plays." The violation of Lavinia is a forceful episode in the accumulation of the woes of the Andronici, but there is little to link it to the denigration of justice or an attack on Rome. The theme is "in fact much more pervasive and central in *Cymbeline.*" *Titus* is more of a family drama, less of a political one. "Both plays are remarkable for the sheer number and range of their classical allusions . . . [They] are alike too in that their method of using classical allusions seems to be of a narrative rather than a dramatic cast." However, in regard to Marcus's speech on encountering the mutilated Lavinia (2.4.11–57), Thompson notes that its effect is "heightening . . . rather . . . than . . . reductive." Imogen's similarly lengthy speech (4.2.293–334) is more fragmented and over-wrought. "The influence of Ovidian narrative is . . . apparent in the leisurely pace . . . and decorative detail."[62]

In an essay making use of explicatory methods derived from psychoanalysis, Willbern discusses the manifest sexual, symbolic, and sadistic elements of *Titus.* His goal is "by observing the central action of rape and the corresponding reaction of revenge . . . and through careful scrutiny of images and metaphors which sustain this interaction, [to present a] more radical disclosure" of the fundamental fabric of the play.

In his examination of *Titus,* Willbern illuminates a recurrent pattern of attack and defense, and specifically—and most pervasively—of sexual attack, either actual or in fantasy, on the female principals, including Mother Rome: "The threat of rape or dishonor or invasion to the maternal figure (Lavinia, Tamora, Rome) requires dutiful vengeance," a form of defense. The misadventures of Quintus and Martius at the loathsome pit emphasizes its symbolic importance as both womb and tomb but most significantly as an engulfing mouth. When Lavinia, the mutilated and ravished bride, appears, "she has accumulated a great deal of symbolic significance. Her lamentable condition is a stark visual reminder of the unconscious proximities of sexuality, rape, death, and dismemberment on which the play builds." This has transformed her into "a kind of Medusa," symbolically blinding her family when they look on her. she also evokes "the all-consuming bloody pit . . . [Thus] to avoid being swallowed up by either grief or future villainy, Titus will have to force the devouring threat to serve his own purpose." While he matures his schemes in Rome, Lucius, at his father's order, has gone over to the enemy. His vengeance is aimed at Saturninus, but also it is "directed against ungrateful Rome as well."

Titus's plans for retaliation are "fiendishly ingenious; he will return the villains [Chiron and Demetrius] to the womb which engendered them, reincorporating them into the dark and dangerous place from which they came. For the womb is also a tomb, like the pie which is a kind of coffin . . . as well as a devouring mouth." Lucius, who has both enacted and repulsed the attack on Rome and killed the Emperor, is welcomed back by the city he has invaded, "but as filial rescuer and not as traitorous aggressor. His revenge . . . is a just retaliation and not an unjust attack . . . [He] has become the ruler and judge of the world of the play."[63]

The performance history of *Titus* reveals that audiences have laughed at moments of brutal violence, notably at the carnage at the end of the play, with its rapid sequence of stabbings, but also, though less frequently, at other horrific events. Brucher studies "comic violence" in the play, darkly comic effects in which "staged atrocities are so outlandish that they seem funny . . . a form of violence which is shocking in its expression of power and evil, and yet so outrageous in its conception and presentation that it causes laughter as it disrupts our sense of order in the world." Shakespeare purposefully made some violence comic "to thwart conventional moral expectations." In its crudest form, comic savagery celebrates barbaric power; and in its witty and complex form, it "reflects an ingenious malevolence which defines its own order in a world of doubtful values." Shakespeare combined the two forms and directs the onslaught against sympathetic victims, testing "assumptions about human values and behavior . . . which cannot comfortably be called tragic . . . Comic violence vividly depicts the dissolution of commonly held values because it implies that there is no sane order in the world to make the violence seem legitimate." Laughter signals audience participation in the disorder. The crimes in *Titus* indicate the collapse of moral order and the absence of justice. The forces of law and order are painfully inadequate. Shakespeare employs extreme effects to convey the experience of an unpredictable world. The action of *Titus* derives from literary sources (Ovid and Seneca), but it denies the reliability of precedents in understanding the heinous events. Comic distortion intensifies the sense of extremity in which conventionally serious responses are disallowed.[64]

Shakespeare's use of discrepant or unequal awareness between characters and between character and audience, "deceptive devices [that] exist in great abundance" in *Titus Andronicus,* is examined by Evans. Unlike the later tragedies, "the unawareness of participants in this play is exploited for passing effects only [as in the comedies] and serves not at all in the determination of outcomes." Evans analyzes a number of such unawarenesses, especially those in which Aaron alone has the advantage over the other characters. These, he finds, provide Aaron with opportunities for "multiple practices and exploitable gaps between awarenesses" that are directed against the Andronici. It is not until Lavinia's revelation of her violators that Titus "for the first time, having taken a step up the ladder of awareness, clearly focuses on his enemies . . . All his raving, therefore, is mere misdirected rant designed to claim our sympathy for the protagonist, [but] the dramatist has failed to convince us that Saturninus even deserves the title of villain." Evans judges that Act 5 "from the point of view of the management of the awarenesses and the fulfilment of dramatic promises is the most garbled and unsatisfactory portion of the tragedy." There are fundamental "structural flaws . . . in the final action . . . It is this final portion that lines up least well with the middle of the play. Shakespeare's first tragedy was meant to exploit Rome's historic reputation as a city of blood and ruthless might . . . But the great fault of the tragedy is that in the actual translation of the theme into action, all the 'ruthless' might of oppressive Rome is reduced to the gratuitous practices of one wicked wretch who is not even a Roman, but a Moor, and all of whose fierceness dissolves in his bizarre concern for a spectacular but essentially irrelevant black baby."[65]

An assessment and interpretation of *Titus* taking into account the "seeming difference between the play as read and the play as seen" is undertaken by Hulse. The action moves early to a setting "in which spoken language sickens and decays, leaving only the mute visual signs of wounds and gashes." The play retreats from civilization to wilderness "through the outlands of crumbling visual symbols and empty social gestures." Visual, oratorical Rome is replaced by the silent woods. Titus's pleading for his condemned sons is unavailing because its setting is "divorced from the fixed world of Roman institutions, [and thus] the plea wanes into futility." The mounting inadequacy of normal speech in the face of violence is signaled by the appearance of the raped and mutilated

Lavinia. In Marcus's reaction to the sight of his ravished niece, classical oratory yields to "a new formal rhetoric in which physical appearance is given symbolic vestments." Titus reacts similarly. The interior grief of the Andronici is no longer distinguishable from the exterior action of their revenge. Titus performs the final murders in a gleeful mood, delighting in his role. The ritual execution of Demetrius and Chiron is a visual recapitulation of both Lavinia's rape and her brothers' deaths. Tamora devours the pasties returning the fiends to her womb and reversing the birth of her black son. Titus slays Lavinia and Tamora, "the pitiful and the pitiless, to signify the depth of his grief and to complete the action of the play." The death of Titus brings about a restoration of Roman order. "If Lucius is the new Aeneas, then Titus becomes a younger Priam, and has melted wholly into the stuff of a legendary past."[66]

The sacrifice of Alarbus is the first of a series of acts of violence that spread "like a blot through Shakespeare's first tragedy" and Slights notes that their dramatic function has been debated for generations. Bassianus's seizing and bearing off Lavinia, who had been promised to Saturninus, and Titus's killing of Mutius in the succeeding melee leads to the dissolution of crucial relationships, such as those between ruler and subjects, and "violations of the primal bonds [of family] that spell disaster" for the house of Andronicus. Aaron's plotting brings about the accusation of Titus's sons for the murder of Bassianus. Titus pleads in vain for their lives, as Tamora did for Alarbus, and "the failure of both petitions for mercy accelerates the process of revenge. The renowned system of Roman jurisprudence has produced a result no more equitable and no less violent than barbaric war, ritualistic sacrifice, and cyclic revenge . . . the distinction between Gothic horde and Roman civilization becomes progressively obliterated." When Titus's severed hand is returned to him with the heads of his executed sons, and Lucius, Rome's noble son, takes the Goths as allies, normal distinctions cease to function, and the sacrificial crisis is nearing its peak." With the approval of the Emperor, Lavinia is sacrificed, then Titus kills Tamora. "The cycle of revenge is complete when Saturninus immediately retaliates by killing Titus . . . His death is not so much just as it is wearily required . . . [it] trigger[s] Lucius's fatal assault on the centre of licensed corruption in Rome, the Emperor himself . . . [whose] assassination goes unrevenged for want of a blood-relation, and the time is ripe for social consolidation . . . But whichever element in the Shakespearean dual closure predominates, the human impulse that begins and ends the tragedies is violence, not justice, order, or charity."[67]

In an essay concerning the significance of the iconography of stage violence in Elizabethan drama, Diehl asks "does a symbolism understood by Renaissance audiences extend violent acts on the stage into moral and

ethical contexts?" Most critical discussions of savagery in drama focus
on theatrical appeal, emotional effect, and the cultural basis of violence,
but Diehl proposes to examine the "possibility that stage violence functions symbolically, reinforces ethical concepts, or is integral to a play's
thematic statement . . . In the visual arts the bloody dagger [for example]
functions this way, as a conventional icon of vengeance . . . Renaissance
playwrights were certainly aware of this iconographical tradition." Early
tragic writers employed such symbols in dumb shows, but later dramatists
incorporate them into the main action, "fusing the actual instrument of
revenge and the larger idea of vengeance." In *Titus,* the metaphor of the
divided body politic is "visually realized in the play's recurring acts of
physical dismemberment which culminate in the horrifying scene when
the mutilated survivors of the ruined Andronici family gather up the am-
putated limbs and severed heads of their dead . . . However repulsive,
dismemberment in *Titus Andronicus* seems to be a thematic motif; it
expresses, in an immediate, physical way the horror and impotency of a
divided state."[68]

The problems confronting dramatists in staging the extremities of grief
and horror are explored by Forker. He analyzes the methods employed
in Elizabethan plays, in which principal characters are subjected to brutal
crimes, to express the crushing emotional burdens borne by the victims,
and notes that the outer reaches of expressibility are represented by two
extremes. "On the one hand, we hear characters *in extremis* venting their
griefs in the most voluble, the most elaborately artificial and rhetorical of
speeches; on the other, we observe them reduced to frenetic irrationality,
disjunctive utterance, or even mute gesture." In *Titus Andronicus,* Lavinia, "the play's visual embodiment of innocence defiled," is patently the
model of the person emotionally and physically mute, driven to indicating
the story of the rape of Philomela in Ovid's *Metamorphoses* and to painfully tracing a few words in sand to convey to her father the sad tale of
her ravishment and mutilation. Titus's intense suffering when his severed
hand and the heads of his two sons are returned to him leads him "to
seek emotional relief in rhetoric so hypertrophic that it totters on the
edge of hysteria." The speech Marcus addresses to the wronged Lavinia
in patterned metaphorical language is "appallingly decorative," but it and
Titus's response upon first seeing his martyred daughter "comprise a
nexus of studied effects and techniques that illustrates the young dramatists's keen awareness of the psychological and dramaturgical difficulties
inherent in his material. However workable or unworkable we may finally
judge his solutions, they at least reflect a clever, even virtuoso, ingenuity."

In a later essay, Forker defines the significance of the different representations of nature in *Titus.* Shakespeare presents the "woodland setting
in a double light—as a place that by virtue of its inherent sweetness and

harmony, should resist violence, and yet that because of its sequestration from civilized influences, actually shelters and encourages it. Shortly after Tamora expatiates so lyrically on the beauties of the forest, she gives us a totally contrasting description of the place, now charging falsely that Bassianus and Lavinia have enticed her to a dangerous place . . . In advance of the horrific deeds that her sons are about to perpetrate, [she] has already transformed the landscape from a pleasance to a jungle, from a place of romance and security into one of horror and bloodshed. After the crimes have been committed, the grief-stricken Titus sees nature in the same depressing light as his enemies." The green world is idealized even as its imperfections are acknowledged. It comprises a "subtext or underworld that allows us to regard the dialectic between good and evil, between hope and despair, as having a basis in the fabric of nature itself. Here, at any rate in theory, the landscape still reflects the order of grace and embodies the moral imperatives of natural law."[69]

"In all drama that really matters," Hibbard tells us, "the interrelationship between plot, character, and dialogue is so close and intimate that they cannot properly be separated from one another." Shakespeare had to learn how to create such closely woven fabric as is exhibited in his mature plays. It is his failure in *Titus Andronicus* to effect that kind of integration that is the most marked feature of the play "and the main reason for the strange and confusing impact which it makes . . . There is still . . . no consensus about whether or not *Titus Andronicus* is a success in its own kind." However, during this century it has come to be viewed as "a most ambitious piece of work." Shakespeare chose Ovid "as a model for the manner of writing to be adopted" as well as for the extraordinary effects of intense passions. Seduced, perhaps, by the many appeals of the Ovidian manner, he "failed to ask himself the all-important question of whether this manner could successfully be applied to a stage presentation in which the audience would actually see . . . the kind of horrors that Ovid describes." Hibbard cites Marcus's speech upon encountering the tormented Lavinia, acknowledging that it is poetic, ornamented with "clever alliterations, picturesque adjectives and . . . a wealth of figures," and that it is connected thematically to the sacrifice of Alarbus, but by contrast to the functionally similar speech by Hieronimo in *The Spanish Tragedy*—a play that Hibbard thinks Shakespeare was attempting to outdo—Marcus's monologue is "blatantly out of character" and unsuccessful. The play suffers from a "lack of logic" in that many speeches are "inappropriate to the occasion" or to the character. "It is true that almost everything that happens in it is motivated by revenge of some kind; but, apart from this blanket notion, adequate and specific reasons to account for and justify the actions that are carried out are extremely hard to find." The only exception to "this broad generalization" is Aaron in his actions and lines in Act 5. He dominates the last two acts because he has excellent reasons for what he does and states them "lucidly and cogently."[70]

As part of a study of the black man in the drama from 1550 to 1688, Tokson notes the Elizabethan philosophical conception that associated inner being with outer appearance, an idea that may have been determinative. If black were considered ugly, then characters with black faces could not be inwardly beautiful. This was shaped in part by a cultural prejudice toward the color black itself because it was the color of evil, and in part by the physical appearance of the black man that would "create in the audience a readiness and an expectation for him to act in certain ways . . . The physical equivalent of sin is blackness . . . Everywhere black skin is held foul, often by the black characters themselves." While Aaron "is not nearly so seethingly labeled diabolic as are some . . . characters [in other, non-Shakespearean, plays] yet he is more fully aware of his essential evil than most." His final speeches in the play constitute an exposition "by a black man of the basic 'truth' of the charge white men would be making. When he has been subdued by his enemies and given the chance to repent his sins, he bitterly proclaims himself not only unrepentant for the crimes he has committed but rather deeply remorseful for those which he did not commit. Furious over the limitations of his evil, he repents in a purely satanic mood only those days void of his villainy. His catalogue of crimes covers the whole range of disaster that can befall some miserable, innocent victim . . . [he] itemizes actions for which the devil is notoriously recognized." Tokson notes that Aaron is under the devilish influence of Saturn as he explicitly says (2.3.30–39). His inclination toward evil appears to be deliberate (3.1.203–4) yet it "need not be a matter of free choice. Nowhere, except in his defense of his black son, one of his own kind, does he choose anything else but the baleful route of evil, and often he is moved by no deeper purpose than to quench his thirst for a revenge that seems unclearly motivated . . . He steadfastly remains demonic in all situations except the scene in which he staunchly defends his child against those who would kill it. In the manner of the pure Machiavellian, Aaron beams over his plans to destroy Titus's sons by accusing them of the murder of Bassianus . . . The whole plot gives him a keen pleasure that he must express . . . Satan-like, he can either use others as his tools of evil or perform a sadistic act himself in which he finds joy." His deception of Titus in inducing him to offer his hand in exchange for his sons' lives is fiendishly brutal and "gives weight to the concept of his satanism. His cruelty and the delight he takes in it . . . [prove him] an active force of evil moving toward its own inevitable fulfillment."[71]

The literary content of *Titus* seems to West to constitute the most notable quality of the play. She points out that all of Shakespeare's characters—the Goths and Aaron as well as the Romans—make a display of their knowledge of Roman poetry. From their reading of the poets they derive learning that however results not in virtue but in barbarity. In this the Andronici are equally as adept as the barbarians. West perceives the frequent literary allusions to be pervasive, artificial, and nondramatic. "Recent inquiries," she notes, "have centered around the disparity between the beautifully polished surface of the language, replete with learned allusion and metaphor, and the gory events of the play." The young dramatist "is trying to adapt the techniques of narrative poetry to drama and does not succeed in creating believable action and dialogue." West understands that the playwright's purpose is to distance the impact of the horrors. "The trouble with this tone, however, is its apparent inappropriateness." Neither the characters nor the action are believable. Shakespeare's accomplishment, as West sees it, is portraying people who speak "through the filter of their literary past . . . His characters emphasize the written word, particularly the written word of their literary past, as a metaphor for the past in general."[72]

Braunmuller surveys the linkage between dramatic language and dramatic character in Shakespeare. Although the prevailing contemporary dramaturgy tended "to make dramatic speech homogeneous rather than individualized," Shakespeare makes use of "a speaker's choice of imagery as a method of characterization . . . language and style may invite the audience to infer an individual cast of mind." In *Titus*, "Shakespeare has given Aaron an ability to move from one register or tone to another, and this quality sets his speeches apart from the rant and lament most characters use." Braunmuller cites Aaron's dialogue with Chiron and Demetrius in 2.1 and, more especially, in his defense of his newborn son in 4.2, as characterizing variants in style. The play exhibits "qualities that lead away from verbal characterization and the larger technique of locating action in character . . . Characters and situations align themselves with preexistent attitudes, values, and events . . . the dramatic need to situate cause in character diminishes, and events gain their meaning through echo, not immediate origin." In another essay, Braunmuller examines other qualities of characterization, such as motivation and expression of emotion, this time by comparison to plays by [other playwrights]. Beginning with Act 4 of *Titus*, the invocation of "allegorical abstractions" (Olympian and infernal deities) is employed by Titus to motivate and direct other characters in their roles in his plan of revenge. "Shakespeare also provides psychological and moral values for the enterprise. Titus'[s] allies and enemies at first accept the inner-play [Tamora's masking] as a method of humouring a crazed, slightly dangerous old man and as a way of achieving their own goals."[73]

Titus Andronicus as a primary text useful in evolving "a theoretical

account of the relationship between the body, signs, speech, and writing,"
and thus to explicate the nature of language, its origins, transformations,
and limits, is analyzed by Fawcett. Although she explores the relationships of language and the body in the cases of Titus, Marcus, Tamora,
and Aaron, her principal concern is with the association of the mutilated
body of Lavinia with the nonverbal language that the rape victim employs
to display words that are "embodied and disembodied throughout" *Titus*.
She "walks through the work challenging both characters and the audience to find some adequate response to her presence . . . she is a text
for . . . interpretation . . . a kind of vortex, a point of intersection between the inner and the outer, a space seeming at once both finite . . .
(delimited by her mutilation) and infinite (in the sense of the value held
within her)." The form of revelation by which she identifies her attackers
is astonishing; her Ovidian Latin "remind[s] us that all language is an
instrumentality, a behavior learned in order to practice upon reality." The
members of the Andronicus family are "the bearers of the language of
the fathers, especially the texts of the fathers." Titus kills Lavinia on a
text from Livy, the story of Virginius and his daughter: "a pattern, precedent, and lively warrant' (5.3.43). If Lavinia should survive after her rape
were known, she might become a competing text.

"As a luminous, beautiful meditation on the relationship between body
and the language, *Titus Andronicus* presents the reader with a wealth of
dreamlike imagery." Two images "resist complete explication but suggest
fascinating implications:" Marcus's description of the mutilated Lavinia
and the victim's tossing the pages of Ovid's *Metamorphoses* with her
stumps. "Both scenes present pictures of utterance, attempts to exter-
nalize values and facts that are internal . . . [they] present simultaneously
several levels of meaning, incorporating expression and interpretation in
the same picture."[74]

Substantial common ground is identified by Miola between *Lucrece*
and *Titus Andronicus*. This is traceable to the pervasive presence in both
the poem and the play of the characteristics of the classical Age of Iron
in which "all modesty, truth, and faith . . . give place to tricks, plots, and
traps, as well as to violence and greed." Civil discord is the mode:
"brother challenges brother for power and wealth, the citizens arrange
themselves into armed factions, the rulers oppose the ruled." Rome under
Saturninus displays many of these qualities: "the ruling family employs
deceits, stratagems, snares, and violence," plots rape, murder, and intrigue, exhibits a "wicked love of gain . . . avarice . . . fraud, and chica-
nery." The origin of Shakespeare's understanding of the Iron Age is
primarily Ovid's *Metamorphoses* and Virgil's *Aeneid* and *Georgics*.
"Rome in *Titus Andronicus* bears strong resemblance to the impious iron
world of Ovid's description. Overwhelmed by the presence of evil in

Rome, Titus takes no constructive action, but resorts to fanciful gesture
. . . Unable to square his former vision of Rome with the sordid reality,
he becomes maniacal and destructive. Lucius, however, provides clear
contrast to Titus. Instead of searching the skies for a banished goddess,
he turns to the Gothic warriors outside the city and organizes an invasion
. . . We note . . . that Lucius, unlike his father, embarks on a direct and
purposeful course of action to combat the evil in the city . . . Lucius has
changed from an impetuous, bloodthirsty youth to a man capable of wise
leadership." After the slayings of Tamora, Titus, and Saturninus, Lucius
emerges as the agent able to reunite Rome. The classical content of the
play is "syncretic in character, variable in application . . . draws upon
the strands of different myths . . . and twists them together for increased
poetic intensity and color."[75]

Aaron erupts in impressive Marlovian rhetoric in his soliloquy at the
beginning of Act 2 of *Titus,* as Charney points out, but this reflection of
Tamburlaine "is not a role in which he can comfortably continue." As
the scene unfolds, Aaron becomes more like Barabas and Ithamore in
Marlowe's *Jew of Malta,* a "witty, sardonic Machiavel delighting in mischief." When he is burying the gold (2.3), Aaron, "like the Vice," justifies
his actions "against any implication of stupidity [and] . . . boasts of his
manipulative cunning." In defending his infant son (4.2), he moves readily
in and out of the Tamburlaine manner of elevated diction and classical
allusions, alternating use of "a more natural, vituperative style, [but] his
grandest histrionic moment in the play" is his boastful confession, in
which he is closer to Ithamore. "Marlowe set Shakespeare a high example
of artful violence, and Aaron shares with Ithamore and Barabas the trans-
gressive delights of being a bad boy." Shakespeare needed Marlowe's
models, by which he was tempted, but mostly he rejected such "super-
human overreachers." The real force of *Titus Andronicus* lies not in
Aaron but in the "tumultuous passions" seen in Titus.

In the course of a book-length discussion of the many challenging aspects of *Titus,* Charney undertakes a scene-by-scene critical analysis of
the play. In the opening chapter ("Introduction") and the final one ("Conclusion"), he sets forth a thoughtful, coherent commentary. He challenges
effectively the still-prevalent belief that Marcus's long speech upon encountering the mutilated Lavinia is static, that it brings the dramatic
action to a complete halt. This overlooks, Charney cogently points out,
"Lavinia's pantomimic role in this oration. She reacts vividly to her uncle's words [though she is unable to speak] and this dramatic context
prevents her reaction from functioning merely as a narrative inset." In
regard to the fly scene, especially when Titus proposes to "insult on" the
fly because he is black like Aaron, Charney points out that the action,
far from being a mere diversion, "has all the elements of tragic farce as

practiced by Marlowe a few years earlier in *The Jew of Malta* . . . Tragic farce," he notes, "is a way of relieving anxiety." The occasional artificiality of the verse in the play "is mitigated in performance, where our literary interests are submerged in the dramatic action." The central issue is the conflict "between Roman values and barbarism." The values of Rome "are oriented to the family, to patriotism, and to basic human and moral considerations." *Titus Andronicus* is therefore a Roman play like *Coriolanus, Caesar,* and *Antony.* "Titus experiences the recognition of a tragic protagonist because he ends the play different from the way he began. He is schooled through his intense suffering . . ." and like Hamlet he is "tainted by revenge and becomes caught in the process that he began as an act of justice. But the revenger is committed to go beyond justice, and he is destroyed by his own fury." That "the revenger cannot escape from the process of revenge . . . is the heart of the ethical dilemma." In a secular world, "we are more ready to accept revenge tragedy in a human and theatrical context that in its ethical and theological implications. *Titus Andronicus* seems to be a play more about suffering than murder. The deaths seem an inevitable consequence of human error."[76]

Shakespeare's ability to manage aural, visual, and kinetic stage effects to attain a desired audience response is studied by Howard. The dramatist realized that his spectators respond not merely to the logic of images of dramatic speech "but to all the elements of a three-dimensional stage event, and that he consciously or intuitively developed strategies and techniques . . . [to] make the greatest emotional and intellectual impact" possible. Each play "is a blueprint for production, an encoding of potential energy waiting to be released by all the sights and sounds of live performance and, above all, by the energies of the living actor." Shakespeare orchestrates "groups of scenes to enhance their cumulative theatrical effect and to parse the theatrical experience into meaningful units for the audience." In the tragedies, "crescendo effects are . . . central to the work's orchestration." Individual scenes progress climatically, as in *Titus* 3.1, which "depends structurally on the repetition of a basic visual and narrative situation: Titus confronted by a messenger bearing bad news." Marcus brings the mutilated Lavinia before her father; Aaron arrives to offer the lives of Titus's sons in exchange for his hand; and a messenger delivers the rejected sacrificed hand and the heads of Quintus and Martius. Shakespeare carefully escalates Titus's emotional rhetoric in response to each horror until the final stroke. At this point Shakespeare uses a device Howard considers especially effective. Titus is seized by a "sudden unexpected silence . . . He has passed beyond the boundary where language or tears can encompass his grief." Spurred by Marcus "to give full voice to grief . . . Titus merely laughs." This scene, Howard notes, shows Shakespeare's skill, in an early play, "in using visual and aural effects to escalate emotional tension."[77]

In his study of Romans in Shakespeare, Platt describes Titus as the epitome of self-abnegation. He lacks the Roman conception of virtue, does not consider the general good paramount, and does not choose wisely. "Wars and especially losing wars are his thing since only losses exhibit self abnegation. He will be more proud of his wounds than his victories . . . A self-abnegator prefers to lose; losses show his virtue, whereas victories would obscure it." He destroys Mutius and Lavinia because he "must practice his virtue against himself and his own." Platt notes some allusions to Christianity and thinks Shakespeare raises the question of whether or not Christian self-abnegation "promotes Rome's decline into barbaric darkness."[78]

Shakespeare's attention in *Titus Andronicus* is, according to Bryant's appraisal, from first to last concentrated on the celebrated general returned from the wars who "once inside the city walls . . . continues to make decisions and set courses of action on the assumption that the civilian world is as uncomplicated as a military exercise . . . with disastrous consequences for himself, the people he loves, and the empire he would loyally support." He included in the play an outsider "who like subsequent Shakespearean outsiders . . . is often said to be at the root of all mischief in his world. In brief, the treatment of Aaron is one of the uniquely Shakespearean things about *Titus Andronicus*." Two subjects are included in the play: the conflict between the Romans and the Goths and the widespread perception of the eroticism and cruelty of Moors. Aaron is cast in Senecan and Machiavellian molds and, like the Vice, delights in mischief. He believes in neither god nor devil, takes pleasure in his wickedness, and relishes recounting his evil deeds. "Shakespeare's world is not . . . Manichaean . . . The villains . . . are not essential villains; all are made . . . rather than born . . . he saw his villains as ordinary people deflected by some accident of birth or society from the normal paths of human intercourse."[79]

The subversion of the political, social, and religious order by the enacting of personal blood vengeance is studied by Jacobs in five plays: *Titus, Hamlet,* Kyd's *Spanish Tragedy,* Marston's *Antonio's Revenge,* and Tourneur's *Revenger's Tragedy.* Specific rituals of various kinds encode and reflect aspects of order of which Jacobs elects to "consider four specific social rituals [that occur] within the drama: plays, banquets, fencing matches, and masques." If the ideological content of such social rituals is granted, then "we are . . . faced with the paradox of systematic [social] perversion and revision that characterizes English revenge tragedy . . . these types of social ritual are distorted and inverted as they become the contexts in which personal blood vengeance is exacted."

Titus presents a notably graphic instance of "the banquet of blood, the perversion of a social ritual into gustatory vengeance . . . The result is the subversion and virtual obliteration of the ideological 'text' normally reflected in a royal fete." Jacobs notes that the Renaissance inherited "the symbolic context in which the banquet of revenge becomes an emblem of perverted ritual *and* ideology." The purpose of the dramatic presentation of the obliteration of traditional social discourse is "to underscore the subversive and radical nature of . . . personal blood vengeance."[80]

"The beginning artist in tragedy [Shakespeare]," Jorgensen points out, "seems to have worked naturally and seriously among the popular Elizabethan designs for the tragedy of blood. For he was, though improvising and experimenting, always aware of his audience and fellow dramatists. More important, he was impelled, with what seems to have been a mixture of studious structure and his conscious anticipation, to use an amazing number of tragic techniques, themes, and characters that inform his later plays." Titus suffers inhuman torments but in some respects improves under these ordeals. Aaron is "meaninglessly evil . . . and yet he is perhaps the most vital character in the play." He is brave and almost human in defense of his infant son. The active evil in the play is 'not cosmic . . . merely distasteful, ugly, and unintelligent." Aaron gives it its only life. "If there is any philosophical theme in the play, it is in the constant pleading to the unresponsive . . . there is no conclusive answer to the most significant questions . . . we are passionately, but not morally, satisfied by the unparalleled revenge of the villains. More in the Shakespearean manner is the union of the few remaining virtuous people at the ending, [which union] comes in the state . . . It is, in the best sense, a political resolution . . . Family and state, though reduced, have survived."[81]

Shakespeare's interest in hunting, the forest, and sacrifice, is examined by Marienstras. The sacrifice of Alarbus corresponds "to what Shakespeare and his audience considered to be Roman custom," necessary so that the "shadows [of Titus's sons] be not unappeased" (1.1.100), but the event is pagan, not Christian, and the audience would not have been sympathetic to Titus. It takes place at a time when the power of Rome is in dispute and is the first of three fatal errors, the others being his refusal of the crown and his sponsorship of Saturninus. "All the horrors that are then perpetrated in the play have these events as their origin . . . Titus later finds himself at the mercy of the woman whose pleas he so implacably rejected. Political authority in Rome falls into the hands of his enemies. There then ensues a reign of injustice, that is to say chaos. Altogether in conformity with habitual cycles of revenge, a chain of reprisals and counter reprisals is set in motion. But the acts of revenge which punctuate the play should not be considered simply as criminal, for here

the atrocities also have a mediating value, similar to that of sacrifice."
When the sequence of personal and family violence comes to an end,
brought about by an alliance of Lucius and the Goths, so do the chaos
and injustice that have ruled in Rome.[82]

Funeral pageantry is defined by Neill as an essential element of Elizabethan tragedy. He reminds us that when the players presented a tragedy,
the stage was hung with black to foster "a sense of funeral as the proper
and expected end of this kind of drama." The stage funeral was "not a
merely neutral piece of action . . . its gestures and decor carried with
them a freight of social and political meanings." The first act of *Titus
Andronicus* "is dominated . . . by the image of the Andronicus family
monument. [Shakespeare] introduces his tragedy with the rites of funeral,
[which, with] the sacrifice of Alarbus and the interment of Titus's sons,
amount both to a symbolic enactment of those traditional Roman values
of piety and order for which Titus stands and an intimation of the latent
barbarity by which this civilization will be consumed." The grisly black
comedy of revenge in *Titus* is carried through a series of "grotesque mock
funerals" that reflect the funeral rite of the first act. The bearing-off in
procession of the severed heads of Quintus and Martius and Titus's hand
is a grim reenactment of the earlier rite, as "is the 'funeral' mockingly
prescribed for the Nurse" who presents Aaron's newborn son to him. In
the closing episode, Lucius defines his new order in part "by setting forth,
with methodical grimness, the funeral arrangements for the victims
and perpetrators of the play's holocaust." The contemptuous treatment
meted out to Tamora and Aaron amounts, in Roman terms, to a form
of damnation.[83]

As an example in dramatic form of the elegy—"a poem of mourning
and consolation"—*Titus Andronicus* is one of the subjects of a study by
Sacks in which he asks how the traditional forms and figures of elegy
relate to the experience of loss and the search for consolation. "When
no consoling substitution is available even in language, the griever will
be unable to avoid responses such as melancholy or revenge . . . the
revenger, like the melancholic, is something of an elegist *manqué*. The
course of his inability to find adequate solace in the mediations of language or law involves a trial of those mediations themselves." *Titus* opens
with a problem of inheritance that is psychologically connected to mourning. Achievement of consolation requires the transmission of a symbol of
power. If the survivors fail to mourn or to acquiesce in the "mourninglike
regulation of their own desires, they subvert the very authority that they
should inherit . . . This cluster of issues . . . is present in *Titus Andronicus.*" Saturninus is nominated by Titus to assume the totemic role of
Emperor and he "immediately asserts his power of sexual choice" by
selecting Lavinia as his Empress. When Bassianus bears off Lavinia,

Saturninus chooses Tamora, thereby "acceding to this contempt for inherited sway." Tamora's sons then repeat the struggle for sexual primacy by raping Lavinia, but in this "grotesque violation of the pastoral world . . . the possible matrix of consolation is itself debauched." The mutilated Lavinia "becomes a frozen emblem of loss." She has the mute stillness of an allegorical figure that leads to "the untroped horror of actual cannibalism." Lucius is the healer of Rome's wounds. The image of his inherited power is speech, "the symbolic organ of renewal," which had been mutilated and "frequently stopped throughout the play." The drama ends with the refusal of burial for Tamora, an instance of "unsuccessful and inadequate mourning . . . one more rejection of the traditional ceremonies, a kind of macabre leftover or remainder of 'non-mourning,' perhaps the essential note of the play."[84]

The theme of Simmons's essay is the different ways Shakespeare treats Roman history in the five "Roman" plays, including *Cymbeline*. The playwright's conception of *Romanitas* "was formed as much by literature, drama, rhetoric, and philosophy as by the Roman historians," and he associated the genre of tragedy with Rome. His informing idea derives ultimately from the biographer and antiquary Suetonius and from the historian and annalist Tacitus. The imperial city of Saturninus is that of Nero, the horrific Rome of Suetonius, while the city of Bassianus loosely suggests a republican image, "an elected monarchy with republican institutions preserved." As Shakespeare shapes it, the play "becomes a commentary on Ovid and Seneca, themselves poets in decline from the golden measure of Vergil and Cicero." Shakespeare's additions to the story "humanize a divided Rome as a city at war with itself, its best and its worst nature inextricable from each other. The hostile fraternity of Saturninus and Bassianus echoes the brotherhood of Romulus and Remus." Lucius is the nemesis figure who restores justice to Rome, the quintessential Roman who, like Coriolanus, with the aid of Rome's enemies will both defeat and restore the city. Simmons, without alluding to the contrary idea held by some scholars of a strong native tradition views Shakespeare's fundamental theme as palpably Senecan, with, of course, a significant Ovidian element. His conclusion is that Shakespeare's "treatment of Roman history [is] throughout his intellectual life . . . clearly that of a Christian humanist."[85]

In an uneven essay entitled "*Titus Andronicus:* Abortive Domestic Tragedy," Barber compares Shakespeare's play unfavorably to *The Spanish Tragedy*. "Designed in obvious imitation of [Kyd's drama], the play is constructed with considerable dramatic skill and written with truly astounding verbal and imaginative energy . . . [but it] fails by contrast with *The Spanish Tragedy* . . . because there is in effect no larger social world" within which the action takes place. "The revenge motive as a struggle for vindication of what is at the core of society is only formally present in *Titus Andronicus* . . . In dramatizing the interplay of individual and national destiny in the English history plays, Shakespeare developed the concept of a hero whose personal fulfillment might also be the consummation of a whole society. In the major tragedies, such concretely felt heroic possibility contributes a crucial part of the substance of tragic loss. *Titus Andronicus* lacks this felt social possibility." Barber finds Aaron's freedom in his villainy "an immense relief after the conflictual constriction we have experienced, and his language is often wonderfully vital." Kyd's play, he sums up, "Seems to me a much better play," despite a lower poetic level because there is "more social experience and meaning in it, until the final rampage of Hieronimo." There is in *Titus* no "larger human and social possibility . . . the play tends to fall into sensationalism and sentimentality."[86]

Both the atmosphere and the narrative of *Titus Andronicus,* according to Barkan, parallel the Ovidian tale of Philomela, Tereus, and Procne, but more is at work than mere parallels. "In a very real sense, the presence of the book of Ovid generates the events of *Titus* . . . it is clear that the characters have read the *Metamorphoses.*" Chiron and Demetrius cut off Lavinia's hands "to improve upon Tereus's crime," about which they had read, as has Marcus, who refers to "a craftier Tereus" when he comes upon his mutilated niece, and Titus, who tells the rapists that he will be revenged "worse than Procne." And of course Lavinia had read the tale of Philomela, because she manages to find it in Ovid's book to reveal the outrage she has suffered. Shakespeare was attracted to the story "because it is centrally concerned with communication [and with] the competition amongst media of communication." As the characters "try to outdo the myth . . . so Shakespeare struggles to find a medium by expanding and exploding other media." *Titus* takes us back to the realm where metamorphosis is fused with perversions of love and family relations, yet it is not such lessons in perversity that Ovid offers to Shakespeare "but a series of paradigms for the act of communication."[87]

In an essay on Renaissance "revenge comedy" devoted chiefly to an exposition of *The Tempest* as an example of that genre, Black discusses by contrast the comedic elements of *Titus Andronicus.* He tests the play by the tenets of tragedy, especially those identified by Thorndike and Bowers, and concludes that it is a true revenge tragedy in both the native and Senecan traditions. In addition he notes that "in the frantic destructive energies—and the indestructibility—of some of the characters [there is an element that] is almost comic," and he singles out Aaron as the prime example. This element has given rise to a critical question as to "just how seriously certain parts of *Titus Andronicus* are to be taken." Black asks "Is *Titus Andronicus* in places a kind of revenge farce?. . .

The mind which neatly parallels the tragedy of Romeo and Juliet . . . with the robust knockabout of 'The most lamentable comedy . . . of Pyramus and Thisbe' is a mind that could have noticed the comic possibilities in Italian stories." Thus, early in his career, Shakespeare "had begun to bring tragedy and comedy close together."[88]

In an effort to discover and divine "a political Shakespeare," Tennenhouse identifies his objective as "to show that, during the Renaissance, political imperatives were also aesthetic imperatives." In Elizabethan times, the system of political meaning included endowing the Queen with two bodies, of which the body politic was enclosed within her natural body. One of the functions of theater was to identify the Queen's body with that of the state: "a drama was never more political than when it turned upon the body of an aristocratic woman . . . [thus] *Titus* plays on the whole notion of the state" as such a body. "The mutilation of Lavinia's body has been written off [by critics] as one of the exuberant excesses of an immature playwright . . . But I would like to consider these sensational features as part of a political iconography which Shakespeare knew as well as anyone else, one which he felt . . . free to exploit for his own dramatic purposes . . . Shakespeare has us see the rape of Lavinia as the definitive instance of dismemberment."[89]

Barthelemy studies the representation of black people in English drama including Shakespeare. Aaron is clearly in the tradition of such representation, notably in the conventional evil significance of blackness, in sharing the reprehensible characteristics of the Vice, and in the concupiscence attributed to blacks. His position of power in *Titus* is the direct result of his sexual domination of Tamora. Aaron's rise in Rome indexes "the rise of chaos and the decline of virtue, justice, and order . . . As he moves through the play Aaron becomes the very symbol of the evil that is loosed upon Rome." The Andronici recognize Aaron as the embodiment of iniquity and his blackness as the outward manifestation of the evil within, but they are not alone: Tamora's faction does also. This becomes clear upon the birth of her black baby, whom the nurse and her sons detest, not because his color signifies the sin of adultery but because it threatens detection. They hate not the sin but "only its signifier, blackness . . . [which] is seen as evil by Aaron's confederates in crime." However, the meaning of "blackness is rendered more complex by Aaron's sense of self-determination. Before he defends blackness [in himself and in his infant son, he] denies the power of blackness to determine his nature; he insists that he chooses to be evil [and is] proud of his villainy." If he is allowed this freedom of will, then there is no inconsistency in his behavior towards his son. "By demonstrating some humanity, Aaron undermines the univocal symbolism of blackness . . . This [is a] chink in the allegory of blackness, however slight . . . Aaron and *Titus* make us feel slightly uncomfortable about stigmatizing this black man."[90]

Shakespeare's tragic heroes, Carducci tells us, search for a mode of eloquence to express their tragic pain; but Titus, unlike the other heroes, tests alternative means of expressing his suffering. His search is not successful: "language becomes ineffectual and confining, a way to hide true feelings behind a mask of rhetoric." Lavinia's dismemberment "represents the whole family's failure to find adequate expression for their overwhelming emotional needs . . . The whole play becomes especially and uniquely concerned with the assertion of gesture; visual images, which replace ineffectual words, are essential to what *Titus* has to say." The fly scene embodies a "brief concord of word, gesture, and feeling [that] enables Titus a fully human response . . . here we seek Shakespeare's early exploration and successful use of the integral relationship between the verbal and nonverbal, a technique that anticipates the psychological depth of his later works."[91]

Garber "explore[s] the ways in which Shakespeare has come to haunt our culture [as explicated in] recent, more subversive theoretical approaches to literature—new historicism, deconstruction, feminism, and psychoanalysis." Her title—*Shakespeare's Ghost Writers*—is multiply referential, alluding to ghosts in the plays, the "missing signifier," and the playwright's comments in which "the text itself becomes a ghost writer [and] takes on a power of its own, supplementing the plot and radically altering it," indeed a ghostly writer. In her discussion of *Titus Andronicus,* she draws attention to "the spectral presence of the 'hand' . . . in connection with a particularly compelling example of authorial fragmentation," Lavinia's handlessness. In spite of her mutilation, Lavinia "is assigned the task of writing *without* hands," which she accomplishes by references to Ovid's *Metamorphoses* and by her inscription on the sandy plot, identifying her attackers. "Lavinia signs her deposition with a missing [ghostly] hand, a hand that is both bloody and invisible." Garber points out, as have others, the insistent presence in the text of the word *hand* and its variants, and the remarkable tendency of critics to employ the word in their comments (e.g., Eliot's "it is incredible that Shakespeare had any hand at all" in the play). The style of *Titus,* "characterized by distortion of scale and perspective, has much in common with the late sixteenth-century expressive style known as Mannerism—a style that traces its etymology to the word 'hand.'" Lavinia's tracing in sand "present[s] women writing as ghosts. Both suggest that women's writing is ghost writing."[92]

The rhetorical context of key events in *Titus* is examined by Hiles, who points out that, according to current rhetorical theory, "the meaning of an utterance emerges from the interplay of its syntactical and semantic elements with situational elements, and that the efficacy of discourse therefore depends upon the exploitation of these linguistic and situational contexts." The plot of *Titus* turns on a series of rhetorical failures. These "occur because characters mistake the context in which they are speaking." Discourse that is at odds with its context or arises from a mistaken sense of context will fail to achieve its purpose. This is "repeatedly the case in *Titus Andronicus,* a drama of language in which offense and revenge . . . are manifested rhetorically." The play moves through a series of distortions to a single self-referential context that marks the reestablishment of Roman control. Lucius's speech of blame and refusal to bury Tamora constitute a curse. "Tamora is . . . consigned to an unrest in the afterlife that corresponds to the unrest that she created in life. Her rhetoric has been defeated, not merely by the power of the language in which the curse is cast, but by the power vested in the context that defines that language and gives it meaning."[93]

Conviviality and conflict at meals in Shakespearean plays, and their structural significance, is assessed by Mahon. Such repasts occur somewhat more frequently in the tragedies than might have been anticipated, perhaps most notably the banquet in *Macbeth* (3.4). The two refections in *Titus Andronicus* serve different functions. The domestic meal in 3.2 "presents a perverse community of revenge" in which Marcus kills an ill-favored black fly that reminds him of Aaron "in anticipation of the revenge to come." Actually Aaron, though sentenced to death, does not die, as the fly does, within the compass of the play. The royal banquet at Titus's house (5.3) is the occasion of the "final horror, an act of cannibalism that defiles the parent-child relationship, that destroys the basic human ceremony of unity, and make[s] a mockery of the laws of hospitality." Appropriately, the concluding hecatomb follows shortly thereafter, leaving Lavinia, Tamora, Titus, and Saturninus dead by the table. "A feast, which should promote harmony and community, becomes a bloodbath. The staged meal is an effective device for the denouement and seems to reflect an effort by Shakespeare to focus the conclusion . . . concisely."[94]

Titus Andronicus seems, on the basis of many characteristic qualities, to be marked "out for certain inclusion in the line of true tragedies of revenge," as Mercer assesses it in a monograph devoted largely to a discussion of *Hamlet.* He cites the "direct borrowing from *Theyestes* . . . the striking re-creation . . . of the Senecan cliche of the haunted grove . . . the debts to Kyd . . . [and] the derangement of Titus." Nonetheless, he points out, following Bowers, "while many of the elements of Senecan revenge are evident here, the structure of the play is significantly different from that of revenge tragedy proper." There is no ghost, the pressure of fate is absent, Titus is not a good man who has been wronged but is the object of revenge because of the sacrifice of Alarbus, and Titus's own revenge comes late in the play relative to the climax. Another structural defect is the "inexorable heaping of injury upon injury . . . [which] make[s] the play seem more a myth of torment than of vengeance." Most important is the distortion arising from the prominence of Aaron, a compelling monster whose busy maneuvering is so prominent that it gravely threatens to transform *Titus* into a "villain play."[95]

Shakespeare presents four major comic elements in *Titus* as points of reference and departure to enhance, in Parker's view, the play's tragic effect. The four are the comic pattern of discord followed by resolution and reconciliation; a romantic comic rural environment; the birth motif, a symbol of new life; and the festive banquet. The playwright uses them "to parody certain comic techniques . . . by employing them in a context in which they would normally be out of place . . . The result of this curious conjunction of conventions is a heightened awareness of *Titus Andronicus's* terrible and trenchant irony."

The first of the comic patterns is parodied in the opening scene, in which the basic comic movement is replicated on three occasions: the dispute over the succession, the discord concerning Lavinia, and the clash between Titus and Mutius, resulting in the latter's death. The scene closes with an apparent reconciliation and two marriages, which symbolize the "formation of a renewed and enlightened society." In some plays, the wood is a retreat from civilization "with its restraints and oppressive social customs . . . [in *Titus*] Shakespeare uses the uncivilized world of the forest not to enhance but rather to pervert the pastoral ideal." The notion of birth "is clearly implied in the marriages with which . . . [Shakespeare's comedies] end and in their final comic visions." But Aaron's and Tamora's child is "a symbol of the perpetuation of evil that the play has dramatized . . . he has been born both in the presence of grotesque deaths and at the expense of other legitimate relationships. Birth . . . in this play . . . is a terrible ugliness, an event which highlights the tragic through its parodic use of the comic." The feast frequently comes at the end of the happy plays, as it does also in *Titus;* "however, rather than serving as a symbol of reconciliation and future new life, it underscores the death and destruction that have been so much a part of the play's action." The conclusion of the first and fifth acts are similar in that in each a conventional comic ending is deceptively proposed by two vengeful characters who "move the play in an opposite direction. A common stock of comic material is brought to the aid of tragedy in order to enhance its effects."[96]

The significance of astrological symbolism in the formation of character and in shaping the plot of *Titus* is inquired into by Jean Richer. The principal characters in the play are equated to the symbolic elements of the zodiacal scheme. Saturninus, Tamora, and Aaron are, for example, linked to Pisces, Cancer, and Scorpio, all, as Richer points out, associated with water; and they exhibit qualities associated with their signs. Shakespeare clearly had the zodiac in mind in writing the play, because he refers in 4.3 (the arrow-shooting scene) to Virgo, Taurus, and Aries. The interplay of the personalities in *Titus,* guided by the qualities determined by their signs, shapes the plot and serves to elucidate the dramatic action. These characteristics in association with the patterned diction and the relatively cool reactions to the horrors distance the effect of the murders and mutilations and impart an atmosphere of unreality. The play presents a nightmare and the audience, in most productions, is spared the gore.[97]

Smidt studies the different levels of allegory and realism, and the discontinuities in the dramatic fabric exhibited in the play. He finds that Titus moves "uneasily" between the two levels because the playwright tends "to characterize by formula rather than observation." After the first scene, the "pace is more empirical, but the characters and action can still be read in allegorical terms . . . Thus Tamora may in turn represent Mother-love, Lust, and Revenge, and Titus Piety, Justice, Revenge and Confusion." At the same time, realistic touches "are constant reminders of a more concrete humanity." Titus is developed from "inflexible observer of custom and principle to abject sufferer and manic avenger." He is a man of blood with a softer side, as may be seen in his love for Lavinia, and he "suffers from a deep-down confusion of mind and conscience." As a consequence of the mixture of allegory and realism, with Titus representing realism and Aaron allegory, "complete adjustment [is] impossible," and character portrayal is "discontinuous on the realistic level." One result is "successive arbitrary transfers of motive and initiative from one character or pair of characters" to another "Bringing about a major change of focus." Aaron, though not fully integrated into the central action, "remains in a sense its presiding spirit." Between the illustration of ideas and themes on the one hand and the exhibiting of character in action on the other, Shakespeare was drawn to the portrayal of individual character and realistic behavior. This tendency clashed with the allegorical preconception of the tragedy," creating discontinuities.[98]

As part of an essay on murder of women in Shakespeare, Frey examines Aaron's murder of his infant son's nurse to prevent the "betraying tongue[s]" revelation of "illicit sex" just as Lavinia's tongue, on which the play centers, was cut out for the same reason. In several of his plays, the dramatists "connects women's tongues with sexual desire, nursing, the snake, the devil, and food-appetite . . . the nurse and bawd who taint motherhood are seen as cursed, devilish, over-appetitive, consumed, or self-consuming . . . Through his murder of the nurse, Aaron connects her to food—'a pig prepared to the spit'" (4.2.146). Shakespeare associates the Moor with hunger and lust. When women "darkly feed on sex, the Moor waits to receive them . . . Call it Shakespeare's racism or merely conventional symbolism for black desire . . . Whatever the sources, Shakespeare's attention to the sex-murderous Moors . . . remains sensational, a palpable ground for his display of foul appetites."[99]

Hunt inquires into the artistic qualities of literary models that attracted Shakespeare's interest in shaping *Titus Andronicus*. Primary among such forms of art are Ovid's *Metamorphoses*, Christian texts, notably the New Testament, and *The Spanish Tragedy*. A noteworthy instance of such modeling is the self-conscious use of the tale of Philomela by Demetrius and Chiron. They "profited devilishly from their exposure" to that story in denying Lavinia the mode of discovery used by Philomela. "In fact, her means of revelation is the very book that originally suggested the nature of her mutilation to the criminals." After the naming of Lavinia's tormentors Marcus, "invoking the Troy story and the legend of Lucrece . . . finds cues for action in literary patterns." Titus's use of art as an agent of vengeance "may spring from his perception that the deity has employed artistic means to reveal truths."[100]

Shakespeare's play, Lamb notes, splits the Ovidian Philomela into two characters: the innocent rape victim Lavinia and the evil revenger Tamora. The pathos of the mute Philomela is preserved in the mutilated Lavinia. The cruel actions of the vengeful Philomela are reflected in the brutality of Tamora directed against Titus and his family. "Her monstrous rage provides a monitory example of women's anger. Lavinia, on the other hand . . . [remains] a dutiful daughter in her role as revenger . . . firmly, comfortably, reassuringly within the bounds of patriarchy. Lavinia's rape and mutilation make of her . . . a piece of soiled goods. In this play . . . [she] is . . . flawed not from her participation in the revenge, but from the loss of her virginity . . . [which] negates a woman's value, justifying her execution."[101]

Under the rubric "tragedy: Noble Weakness" Cox assesses the significance of *Titus Andronicus* as an example of the tragic "high" genre of the Renaissance. Shakespeare experiments with the fashionable form of stoic revenge tragedy that, for the Elizabethans, was identified as Roman. Titus is a true Elizabethan "idealized warrior-aristocrat who is undone by pragmatic, self-serving and power-seeking outsiders and upstarts." Although criticized as barbaric, the sacrifice of Alarbus conversely highlights Titus's "virtuously imperturbable resistance to [Tamora's] emotional appeal when he is faced with patriotic religious obligation." Cox thinks Shakespeare "may well have had in mind" the stoic, archetypal Roman hero Aeneas, who also sacrificed prisoners of war. "Moreover, the consequences of Titus's deed are irrelevant by Roman moral reckoning, for the Stoic sage performs virtuous deeds without regard to [consequences] . . . to do anything else would . . . compromise the deed." The death of Mutius for challenging Titus is of the same pattern, considered in the light of the stoic doctrine of moral rectitude; and the death of Lavinia attests to Titus's "commitment to heroic invulnerability through virtuous action," again without consideration of the outcome. In the light of these events his "mad revenge . . . enhances his admirable nobility." He acts on "potent classical precedent," consistent with the stoic drama of imperial Rome. The Ovidian style of the play has been condemned, but it enhances the portrayal of the stoic sage "who aims to scale heights of virtue that other mortals leave unchallenged." Shakespeare conceived of the ornate style as "a decorous complement to the titanic suffering of his first tragic hero."[102]

Titus, in Green's assessment, is old-fashioned, but both exemplary and memorable. Shakespeare touches the limits of the revenge tragedy genre and exposes its limitations.

> Almost every spectacle, deed, and character is absorbed into the titanic presence of the protagonist." Lavinia, the utter victim, and Tamora, the consummate avenger, challenge Titus's centrality, but they are made to serve "the construction of Titus as patriarch, tragic hero, and . . . central consciousness . . . It is largely through and on the female characters that Titus is constructed and his tragedy inscribed. Tamora . . . illustrates and demarcates the extremes of Titus' character, measures the evil to which this patriarchal avenger has resorted and must resort. Her comment on the barbarity, the 'cruel, irreligious piety,' of Roman religion suggests as much: it inadvertently excuses Titus' error as a product of benighted pagan belief, but also implicates Titus in a whole range of human blindness, imperfection, and crime." Lavinia "is on the other pole of the scale—and the more telling. Her mutilated body 'articulates'

her father's suffering. She must be silenced or she might reveal, in addition to the identity of her attackers, the thoughtlessness of Titus towards her in proposing to unite her "with an unworthy man." She would undermine the design of the play—"the reconstitution of patriarchy under Lucius." The price of this order—"silence and illegibility"—is exacted of women, younger sons, those without power, or those who are otherwise peripheral.[103]

The matching of physical violence with linguistic violence and its rhetorical effect in dismembering what *Titus Andronicus* presents as reality is studied by Kendall. The world of the play "is not simply one of meaningless acts of random violence but rather one in which language engenders violence and violence is done to language through the distance between . . metaphor and what it represents." Words distort the way characters view their world, " and the patterns of previous fictions and myths influence, transform, and mutilate the action of the play." Reality takes vengeance on metaphor: "to lend one's hand is to risk dismemberment." Language disrupts the way the audience perceives imagery, as literal and metaphorical or figurative meanings are mixed. The image of the body politic portraying Rome is no less fragmented than the bodies of the victims. Figurative language obscures possibility. In the central event, Marcus's encounter with his mutilated niece, he decorates his language with figures of speech that impede his ability to recognize the truth of Lavinia's plight. A compromise "between indeterminacy . . . and a perfect correlation between language and meaning" eventually develops: "Titus adapts the tale of Philomela and rewrites old stories with a new alphabet . . . he does not transform the world of *Titus Andronicus,* but he does come to control it." It is a new kind of revenge play, "one in which truth avenges the violence done to it by the conventions of art, and physical reality begins to triumph over the distortions of metaphor." *Titus* is a violent play "but that violence, aside from outdoing any other revenge of blood, is the reflection of a violence inherent in the nature of language."[104]

In the course of showing "how a clear understanding of Shakespeare's exploration and articulation of Roman values . . . [provides] fresh critical insights into the Roman plays'—*Ceasar, Antony,* and *Coriolanus* — Thomas discusses such values in *Titus.*

Clearly, *Titus Andronicus* stands apart from the three plays traditionally categorized as Roman. This early play lacks the rich historical source material which Shakespeare was able to draw on for his mature Roman plays, but it merits more than passing consideration because it reflects so clearly Shakespeare's early awareness of the potency of Roman values in shaping society. Too often dismissed as journeyman work or as an attempt to emulate Kyd's highly successful revenge tragedy, this play provides valuable insights into Shakespeare's exploration of the relationship between the conflicting values of warfare and civilized living.

Shakespeare adopted an independent and iconoclastic standpoint in his Roman plays. In *Titus,* Shakespeare "had, for the first time, to meet the challenge of creating a sense of a highly specific social universe . . . the portrayal of a sense of Rome which would appear impressively authentic to . . . [his] audience . . . Shakespeare very powerfully evokes the sense of a Roman world which is palpable, and reveals that . . . he set himself the highest standards in creating a social and political universe." There is a gradual realization of the fragility of civilized society. The articulation of human values through social and political systems is crucial. The defeat of Tamora and her faction provides Rome with an opportunity to exhibit "a just and coherent institutional framework." At the end "there is a profound sense of the need to establish a humane and durable *political system.* Thus throughout the play, Shakespeare invokes a powerful sense of Rome. The Roman people are appealed to directly at the beginning and end of the play. There is an awareness of officials and social classes such as tribunes and patricians; the physical solidity of Rome, with the Capitol as its symbolic center, is strongly contrasted with the wilderness beyond the walls; its history including the trials and tribulations of wars and its origins in Troy; references to the gods are frequent and Titus appeals directly to them; and finally there is an awareness of a Roman ethos of service, the highest achievement being sacrifice in war."[105]

Kolin points out that the process of "Reading and writing texts is central to the ideas and stage business of *Titus Andronicus;*" that the signifiers . . . books, scrolls, seals, supplications, orations, even a 'grid of steel' regale an audience's sight and hearing. The physical stage itself is transformed into a scroll, a text, that Titus and his kinsmen leave messages on to communicate fear and anger as well as righteous pietas. Shakespeare is engaged in a communal scripting process with the audience through this reflexive stage business emphasizing the performance of writing/reading itself. In Rome, Shakespeare seems to be telling the audience, one must be a careful reader/writer to survive." *Titus* is a palimpsest of classical literature (Seneca, Ovid, Horace, Cicero). The play frequently asks "an audience to recall a classical text," to make the word become flesh, and flesh is transformed "into, or . . . back to, word/text that must be read as any printed source." Titus describes Lavinia's body as if it were a text to be read. "Mutilated stumps and bended knees become texts."

The fourth act of the play especially emphasizes the significance of texts. The first scene underscores the importance of a reading text, specifically Ovid's *Metamorphoses,* the book with which Lavinia begins the process resulting in the identification of her violators. She thus "becomes the family picture album for revenge . . . a text . . . to be read, studied, pitied, and applied in her Roman context . . . The canonized Lavinia is and is not Philomela for the Andronici. In this play Shakespeare makes use of highly patterned action. One of the most provocative patterns in Shakespeare's text is his reification of the idea of text itself through linked stage business and language . . . Shakespeare is exploring and dramatizing a number of significant ideas, now current, about the way text itself is experienced through his literal use of and poetic references to texts. Shakespeare is our contemporary in more ways than were dreamed of by Jan Kott."[106]

The role of an actor's body in conveying meaning in early Shakespearean plays is explored by Gibbons, who finds such nonverbal "signals" necessary and integral rather than optional. Manifestly, it is only "in the theatre that their full importance is recognized." Modern productions of *Titus Andronicus* have presented episodes that focus on Lavinia and Titus in "contrasting ways, [which] helps to bring out the fact that Shakespeare's dramatic style makes effects by deliberate interplay of frankly direct physical spontaneity and balletic stylization." In regard to the latter, he cites Brook's Stratford mounting of 1955 and Freedman's New York version of 1967. In both, understated staging techniques were employed to moderate the effect, for example, of Lavinia's mutilation, but at the same time the actress is called upon to perform actions emphasizing her condition and "implying further physical pain." Employing her handless stumps at a meal and writing in sand with a staff "present . . . graphic stage image[s] expressing Lavinia's estrangement from normal communication . . . this pitiable isolation is heroically overcome . . . [by] great physical effort [that] yields . . . the essential message, and achieves her revenge and cleansing." To the dramatist the "sheer physicality of her suffering is crucially important." In Douglas Seale's 1967 representation at Baltimore, which evoked World War II, "the essentially mixed style Shakespeare uses" was obliterated. Audiences were confused because "With modern weapons technology goes modern medical science," raising the question of "how Lavinia could retain consciousness after such a great loss of blood." Other productions, notably Deborah Warner's of 1987, while not shirking the brutality in Lavinia's situation, nevertheless gave "imposing weight to ceremonious patterns" that presented the "audience with a direct first-hand impression of her mutilated body." Marcus's speech upon encountering her "commemorates a Lavinia who in one sense is no more. Marcus speaks to trace the transformation of the woman's body into an icon of pity," which Shakespeare next has Marcus present to her father, "a monument of tragedy . . . It is intrinsically through the body that Shakespeare focuses such experiences and mediates them." The existential immediacy of Lavinia's "lively body' evokes an instinctive response, but it is not only her body that is significant. Her death in the concluding scene is "shocking, but the spectacle of her motionless body is compelling: finally it is free of agony, mercifully still. Shakespeare ensures that there is no full tragic crisis until the very end of the play."[107]

The process of constructing the female alien in *Titus* is examined by Kehler. Female gender being a locus of Otherness, Tamora may be seen as exemplifying a particularly vicious embodiment of the stereotype soon to become a major presence in Jacobean drama: the lusty widow. Female sexuality—and especially the sexually knowledgeable widow—posed a special problem because of her potential capability of upsetting the balance of power between men and women. The alien Tamora is "engendered out of a misogynistic stereotype . . . [her] desire for vengeance against the Andronici replicates their talionic belief . . . Rome teaches Tamora to unlearn mercy." She becomes a dehumanized Other even as she becomes a Roman. Shakespeare provides Tamora a humanizing event in her pleading for Alarbus but refashions her character in having her address seductive poetry to her paramour, Aaron, on the morning after her wedding to Saturninus. She is subsequently "freighted with such taboo attributes as perversity, hypocrisy, cunning, violence, vengefulness, cruelty, and wilfulness." The playwright's "about-face in characterizing Tamora" may have had biblical origins in the Tamar who, in Genesis, posed as a prostitute and incestuously lay with her father-in-law; or in the Tamar of 2 Samuel who was incestuously raped by her half brother.[108] Kehler points out that by Tamora's encouraging her sons' rape of Lavinia "violence is linked to outlawed sexuality and projected onto the lusty widow, who is accordingly constructed as alien." Nevertheless Tamora hungers for security, notably when she says of Titus "Thy life-blood out . . . Then is all safe, the anchor in port" (4.4.37–8). Kehler notes that "for a moment the mask of the satanic alien drops, and we catch a last glimpse of a wretched, frightened woman, a prize of war, fighting back."[109]

Cunningham draws a parallel between the search for justice in *Titus* and the early English trial by ordeal. In the play, the *locus* that provides the evidence is Lavinia's mutilated body, affording the physical means as in an ordeal to determine that a crime had been committed and reveal the criminal. The determination was accepted as divine judgment, both a mode of inquiry and a mode of punishment. Lavinia is the emblem of a ritual system of justice "in which the bodies of competitors are both the sites and the resolutions of conflict." The problem of "voicing . . . the multiple meanings of Lavinia's body" occupies the central sequence of the play. Her "garrulous flesh . . . remains beyond the taming power of linguistic tropes, her body a reservoir of half-glimpsed truths and insufficient syllables, the dwelling place and the expression of cries for vengeance." If it were possible to "read the signs on Lavinia's body . . . justice would be the inevitable result." The archaic solution to the problem of attaining justice, "like the failed allegory of Revenge enacted by Tamora, is rejected and replaced in the play's final scene by a rhetorical mode that is closely linked to trial by jury."[110]

Bartels directs our attention to the rise in Renaissance England of "cross cultural . . . exchange . . . accompanied by an intensified production and reproduction of visions of 'other' worlds" derived from a variety of sources, including "dramatic and literary conventions." Shakespeare's "contribut[ion] to this discourse" is the production of two Moors: Aaron and Othello, "who are situated in a potentially threatening position very near the 'inside' of authority and power." Shakespeare brings Aaron near the center, "accords him a voice of eloquence and knowledge, and allows his schemes to shape the plot, [but] he concomitantly keeps the Moor on the outside, literally and figuratively, and both answers and promotes the darkest vision of the stereotype" of the vicious outsider. He is "the one character in this play whose malignant differentness is consistently recognized and easily categorized," a situation to which he himself contributes by references to his blackness.

The crisis that descends on Rome is precipitated by the "destablization of legitimating rights," made manifest by the rival claims of Saturninus and Bassianus for the hand of Lavinia. The two brothers "are, in some way, taking their 'own,' depending on what kind of prerogative legitimates possession." Saturninus's subsequent selection of Tamora as Empress is accepted by Titus and his family, as evidenced by the proposal of the hunt in celebration. However, "Saturninus' turn to Tamora signals a fatal alliance with the alien, making his own position finally and absolutely Other," and his rule becomes one of duplicity and dishonor. Aaron gains access to the discourse of Romans and Goths, which integrates him to some degree into the community, yet simultaneously his speech betrays his malign differentness. "For, as he outlines his intentions, he reveals a purposelessness that makes his villainy all the more insidious . . . [In defining himself] Aaron enforces his own alienation . . . What continues to be easily readable is the color of skin, which keeps him and his son . . . from getting too close to the inside."[111]

The opening act of *Titus,* as Breight elucidates it, is a consummate evocation of the political situation in imperial Rome. Shakespeare presents not only the struggle for "empery" between Saturninus and Bassianus but also the marginalization of Titus, who adheres to the values of republican Rome, which "are no longer operative . . . he is a political dinosaur." A principal moving spirit in this process is Lucius, who subtly undertakes "the subversion of Titus' parental authority . . . He is an ambitious figure on the periphery of power who seeks to disrupt a disadvantageous situation through symbolic actions . . . a potential heir whose disenfranchisement renders him vulnerable." On behalf of the common people of Rome, Marcus offers Titus the imperial crown, but he refuses it, and thus "effectively cashiers his eldest son Lucius" as his successor, who, however, assumes thereupon the position of leader of his brothers. "[It] is worth noting," Breight points out, "that he survives while . . . [his] brothers do not." Titus proceeds to set up a "political alliance by supporting Saturninus. This alliance would allow Titus . . . to enjoy an apparently well-deserved retirement after 'ten years' of 'weary wars against the barbarous Goths.' The entire pact is smoothly and cleverly arranged, but it is almost immediately destroyed." Lucius asserts leadership in the matter of the sacrifice of Alarbus. This affords him a strong voice, which he subsequently employs above even that of Marcus in his defense of the seizure of Lavinia. Mutius's outcry to Lucius upon being stabbed by Titus "suggests . . . that Lucius is the leader." This is further enhanced by Lucius's subsequent banishment from Rome, which gains him sympathy and provides the opportunity to approach the Gothic army and to assume the posture, as their leader, of adversary to the Emperor. Aemilius reports to Saturninus that a Gothic army is approaching Rome "under conduct of Lucius" (4.4.64–5), to which the Emperor responds

Is warlike Lucius general of the Goths?
These tidings nip me, and I hang the head

(4.4.68–9)

Breight notes that Lucius's attaining of the generalship of the Gothic army is a "considerable feat" of political skill; and on that he builds as he "improvises beautifully by seizing an opportunity for [the] political murder" of Saturninus in the final scene, thus opening the way for him to attain his cherished goal, the imperial crown.[112]

In an evocative essay, Heather James elucidates cultural disintegration in Titus, with emphasis on the pervasive revenge elements of the play, "but also [on] Shakespeare's curious handling of literary authorities, particularly Vergil and Ovid." His purpose is "in part . . . to 'overgo'" the two Roman poets "as well as the classicizing and violent dramas of Kyd and Marlowe." The turning point from Vergil to Ovid is the rape of Lavinia. "This grisly fulcrum functions logically in the poetics of cultural disintegration, for as Shakespeare knew, Rome was founded on rape," notably those of the Sabine women, of Lucrece, and of Ilia; on "Aeneaes' dynastic marriage to an earlier Lavinia" and the seduction of Dido. James traces parallels between the play and Vergil's Aeneid, beginning with Shakespeare's first act, which she notes produces a storm of rhetorical wit analogous to the storm at the start of Vergil's poem "understood as both political and emotional upheaval . . . Titus Andronicus begins with a political tempest whose passionate storms, thunders, and furies are heard throughout the play. Rome is beleagured not only by the Goths," but also by its own institutions and myths. The choice of Titus for Emperor by the common people and the use for Marcus of the appellation "Pius . . . establishes Titus' spiritual descent from the pius Aeneas." He exhibits the "full rigor of his pietas" [in slaying] Mutius for disobedience." The Aeneid's Dido is figured in Tamora, of whom Saturninus says she "Dost overshine the gallan'st dames of Rome" . . . [a] "compliment [that] alludes" to a passage in Vergil's poem.

Ovid's story of the fate of Philomela is called upon by Marcus "to make some kind of sense of the spectacle [of the ravished Lavinia] and of his own emotions . . . his speech identifies both the Ovidian text that will replace Vergil's as the definitive or shaping myth of this late Roman society, and the violent poetics that separates decorative signifiers from their gruesome referents . . . Shakespeare . . . found in Ovid's Metamorphoses a narrative and critical practice which he assimilated to the semiotics of the pit, which substitutes, inverts, confuses, appropriates, swallows up, and engenders meanings. The most significant difference between Shakespeare's and Ovid's practices of polemical literary conflations is that Shakespeare, in *Titus*, genders and metaphorizes the politics of imitation: the audience is brutally confronted with the art of contamination in the pit and Lavinia's body, both signs of social disorder."

In elucidating the succeeding scenes, James emphasizes their semiotic significance. "Titus insistently focuses his macabre play with literalizing signs on Lavinia's body, which serves as the figurative ground for refashioning his cultural myths, his course of action, and his very identity . . . Her body, inscribed with Philomela's fate, suggests to Titus the course of his revenge and, comically, prepares for the dramatic appearance of the book itself." James's analysis of the concluding scene makes impressively clear the significance of the swift succession of deaths, which is not always appreciated in performance. "Titus knows that if his sorrows die with his daughter's shame, it is only because his revenge guarantees his own death . . . In the concluding move of the play to restore order, Vergil is called upon to perform the last rites." Marcus invokes "our ancestor . . . [and] the Senate places its hope in the healing powers of the *Aeneid*. Shakespeare presents Rome in the late Empire as a state which made a fatally reductive icon of Vergil's poem, and ignored the double meaning of a monument—not just a tribute, but [also] a warning."[113]

Cynthia Marshall explores the enactment in *Titus* of "male terror of female power, conceived primarily in sexual terms. The pathological splitting of affectionate, familial emotions . . . from troubling sexual responses . . . evinces what Freud called 'the universal tendency to debasement in the sphere of love.' Lavinia is idealized, while Tamora . . . is the focus of projected anxieties." Lavinia, though suffering, is silenced and is, "in many respects, unknowable." Titus directs both "anger and dread" toward Tamora. "The play presents the issues of gender, sexuality, and power in dialectal terms . . . women are seen as the source for anxieties about desire, dependence, and death."[114]

Marion Wynne-Davies takes as her "premise the containment and repression of women," and deals with the "tensions and challenges to this convention as dramatic appurtenances." In *Titus*, she finds that the central theme is rape, and that it "seems darkly appropriate that one of the corporal symbols . . . should be the womb." The "wooded valley [of Act 2] includes 'a detested, dark, blood drinking pit' an 'unhallowed and bloodstained hole.' The imagery is blatant, the cave being the vagina, the all-consuming sexual mouth of the feminine earth, which remains outside the patriarchal order of Rome. This is the 'swallowing womb' that links female sexuality to death and damnation . . . The association of hell,

death, and consumption with the womb clearly evokes a concept of
woman's sexuality that is both dangerous and corrupting . . . the cave
. . . 'the swallowing womb' does carry the promise of death, but for men
and not women. Its power is to castrate, not to madden." Wynne-Davies
traces differences in the social role of women as contrasted to men by
reference to the need in a patrilineal society for men to control the womb,
which is essential to guarding the concept of patrilineal descent. When
"this exercise of [male] power failed and women determined their own
sexual appetites regardless of procreation, the social structure was threatened with collapse. This is exactly what happens in *Titus* when Tamora
seeks amorous gratification with Aaron" and bears a black child, bringing
about "stately Rome's disgrace." Thus, the "Roman citadel and state are
envisaged as a headless feminine body, a motif which is repeated at the
end of the play . . . If Rome begins and ends the play as a mutilated
female form, then Titus's resolution of primogeniture can hardly be
adequate."[115]

In the course of a discussion of the role of the moor in English Renaissance drama, D'Amico finds that Aaron "As outcast . . . devotes his energies to the destruction of the commonweal . . . [as a] barbarian [he]
rises to see the state collapse, laughs to see the family dismembered, and
prompts the act of rape and mutilation that strikes at the Roman family,
the state and speech itself . . . When unfolding his devilish plot to Tamora, or coolly manipulating her sons, Aaron seems disposed by nature
to perform deeds society calls evil." The birth of his and Tamora's son
arouses his fatherly instincts and he "sees in his son the image of himself."
He defends the child against the prompting of Tamora and the desire of
her sons to kill the infant, and he thereby "gives himself a soul and creates
a kind of grace. He helps us to understand the change that Shakespeare
saw taking place in the late Roman Empire. Like Machiavelli, Shakespeare recognized that the expansion of Rome eventually destroyed the
state's inner dynamic when productive opposition between classes, medi-
ated by law, was replaced by factionalism and bloodletting. Divided
against itself, the Rome of *Titus Andronicus* collapses back into the disorder from which the state was born. In the midst of this disorder, Shakespeare's Aaron can be seen as a comic figure, not only grimly comic
because of his sardonic distance from human feeling, but also comic in a
higher sense because through him we glimpse a human capacity for survival and renewal." Titus restores the order of his family by the final
hecatomb, including the taking of his own daughter's life, which "can be
justified" only because he thereby "restore[s] civil order."[116]

Joyce Green MacDonald, by concentrating "on representations of
blackness in three texts—Shakespeare's *Titus Andronicus*," and by contrast, the play's "Restoration adaptation by . . . Ravenscroft, and . . .

Jonson's *Masque of Blacknesse*—attempt[s] to identify . . . the historical and cultural contexts out of which the Renaissance constructed these complex representations and [to] . . . help initiate a discussion of its ideological production of blackness as a category of social and moral being . . . [taking as her subject] how they employ the sign of blackness." She examines the early modern relationship between England and Africa. "What was known and knowable about Africa was the scope of its difference from Europe . . . The play understands [Aaron's] blackness as the sign of absolute resistance to incorporation in any system of social or moral order originating outside himself . . . he reserves his one expression of loyalty and affection to the only other creature in the play who resembles him," his son. "Shakespeare's first treatment of blackness allows its subject to proclaim it as a sign of moral character, an integrity directed toward the preservation of a child's life." MacDonald concludes that Shakespeare's play is "fragmented, experimental. It encounters some difficulty deciding whether it is an Elizabethan version of Roman paganism, a revenge drama, a tragedy of state, or some combination of these."[117]

Frederick A. de Armas contrasts *Titus Andronicus* to Calderon's *La Vida es sueno (Life is a Dream)*, and both plays to Seneca's *Thyestes*. He finds that the two modern plays exhibit the Stoic doctrine of metacosmesis, "the periodic destruction and renewal of the cosmos." This is specifically a reflection of the fourth chorus of *Thyestes* cited by Titus when he says:

> *Terras Astraes reliquit:* be you remembered, Marcus,
> She's gone, she's fled.
>
> (4.3.4–5)

de Armas traces other parallels "to show that Shakespeare's play is an attempt to understand the nature of the violence presented by Seneca," and he tells us that *Titus* "is not so much about the triumph of Romans or Goths but is an investigation into the violence that exists within civilization . . . *Titus Andronicus* seeks to reach the end of violence by portraying its extremes."[118]

Charles Wells studies the relationship of *Titus* to Romanitas, which he interprets as "Roman-ness" and "the Roman way;" and notes that "Unfocused and crude it may be, but *Titus Andronicus* conveys powerfully Shakespeare's fascination with the Roman world." He reminds us that the title page designates the play as a "Romaine" tragedy; that the words "Rome" and "Roman" occur in the text 126 times, more frequently than any of his other Roman plays; and that he presents his hero as the embodiment of Roman ideals.[119]

As an element in his general study of Shakespeare's relationships with Ovid, Bate says regarding *Titus,* that 'the play's main structural model is the Ovidian tale of Philomel, Tereus, and Procne . . . [that] *Titus* is also beautified with the feathers of classicism—and with a vengeance . . . [and] precisely because Shakespeare had less formal education than certain other dramatists, his play has more display of learning. He trumps his contemporaries in their own suit. "The play's classical allusiveness is deep, not wide. It relies on sustained involvement with a few sources— Ovid and a little Livy, the most famous part of Virgil, some Plutarch and the odd tag from Seneca that might well be derived at second hand—not on deployment of a Jonsonian range of learning. In what is perhaps the most self-consciously literary moment in all Shakespeare, the play's most significant source is actually brought on stage." Bate appraises *Titus Andronicus* "as a prime exhibit in the case for Shakespeare's artfulness . . . [it] is an archetypal Renaissance humanist text in that it is patterned on the classics . . . The ingenuity of *Titus* is that it is a feigned history . . . based on a series of fabulous and historical exemplars." The play, however is a perversion of a humanist text in that the lessons learned are not virtuous as they should be, but criminal—the identity of a rapist is protected not merely by cutting out the victim's tongue as Tereus did but also by cutting off her hands so she cannot reveal her attackers by writing: "civil virtue breaks down not because the classic texts are neglected, but for the very reason that they are studied and applied selectively. They are evacuated of their wholesomeness and become instead manuals for barbarians. If *Titus* is recognized as one of Shakespeare's most characteristic plays, rather than dismissed as a juvenile aberration, it becomes much easier to see the tragedies as well as the comedies as metamorphic . . . the technique used so extensively in *Titus* of invoking mythological precedents as patterns for tragic structures is sustained throughout Shakespeare's career, with the difference that what was a prominently flaunted mode of composition to the early play became a more inwoven practice in the later ones."[120]

Many of the current "schools" of literary criticism such as deconstruction, feminist, the new historicist, the iconographic, and the psychoanalytic are represented in the current critical approaches to *Titus Andronicus.* These and others attempt to elucidate the significance of the play in the light of the conception scholars have of Shakespearean drama. Some offer an insight into the playwright's cultural formulation of his dramatic plan and manage to define, sometimes impressively, the significance of Shakespearean drama in the contemporary world. Perhaps because the elements of this play are such as they are, psychoanalytical and feminist criticism in the second half of this century has come to the fore. Much of this strain of critical comment serves to illuminate certain aspects of *Titus* that earlier were denigrated as being unacceptable, un-civilized, poor theater, or simply unintelligible, and which sometimes called forth inappropriate audience responses such as laughter at horrific moments. Toward the end of the period, cultural materialist and new historicist critics made an initial effort to move in the direction of a more nearly systematic examination of the canon as in, for example, the symposium entitled *Political Shakespeare*.[121] In that book, to which nine critics contributed, thirty plays are discussed by one or another of them, but *Titus* is accorded only a single brief comment. Stephen Greenblatt, one of the contributors and a leader in the movement, does not discuss the play in his more recent writings, so it appears that we must wait a while longer for a new historicist critique. James Calderwood, our leading metadramatic critic, partly in reaction to T. S. Eliot's dismissive comment on *Titus*, offers a comprehensive—and revealing—analysis of the play as a notable example of metadrama.[122] Almost all the contemporary strains of discourse tend to lead away from a view of Shakespeare's works as literature simply to be read, as the object of, in the words of Sir Edmund Chambers, "leisurely contemplation by [the] fireside [which] often illumi-nates the intention of the dramatists more fully than is possible during the swift progress of a play upon the boards." The conception that a play can only be fully realized in performance has, during this century, been almost universally accepted. "That Shakespeare's mind was permeated by the atmosphere of the stage, in which he lived and moved and had his being, seems [to Chambers] to be indisputable,"[123] and modern critics' minds seem to be similarly infused. Most aspects of the play are ulti-mately associated with Shakespeare's plan for his tragedy, which is, of course theatrical in nature. What is frequently perceived as a disturbing lack of concord in *Titus* between the action and the poetic style—the example most often cited is the scene in which Marcus speaks in elabo-rately patterned language to his brutally mutilated niece (2.4.11–57)—and therefore a defect in design, is in reality a purposefully calculated en-deavor to produce a distancing effect, as a number of commentators have noted. In this it is successful. Another important aspect of the poet's dramatic design that has been the subject of censure is the characteriza-tion, which has been described as wooden and one-dimensional. This perception may perhaps be considered judicious in regard to much of the first act, in which both the action and the verse are ceremonial; but the playwright, having accomplished his purpose in the opening movement, thereafter adopts a significantly less formal mode, as exemplified in Aaron's soliloquy at the beginning of Act 2, and the characters are there-after drawn more realistically. While there still remains a difference of scholarly opinion concerning the quality of the characterization, the ear-lier, emphatically negative judgments have tended to be muted in recent essays, which generally regard it as perhaps less than fully satisfactory, especially as compared to the monumental figures of the later tragedies, but not necessarily defective.

One of the specific aspects of feminist criticism is the effort to portray Tamora as a character who is somewhat less than vicious. This intriguing notion is neatly encapsulated by Kehler who, noting Tamora's "hunger for security' (citing 4.4.37–8), calls her "a wretched, frightened woman . . . fighting back."[124] Another trend currently evident is an unemphatic leaning toward the rehabilitation of Senecan influence on Shakespeare in *Titus Andronicus.*[125]

Above and beyond the importance of any of the critical specifics is the very existence of a significant—in both extent and value—of a body of wide-ranging and insightful criticism that is unrivaled in any comparable earlier period. We may, and should, continue to cite such a luminary as Dr. Johnson on *Titus Andronicus,* but it must be recognized that if he were giving us his thoughts on the play today they, although accepted and heeded, would represent only the voice of one among many. And the trend of the twentieth century gives every evidence of continuing into the twenty-first.[126]

THE
MOST LAMEN-
TABLE TRAGEDIE
of Titus Andronicus.

AS IT HATH SVNDRY
times beene plaide by the Kings
Maiesties Seruants.

LONDON,
Printed for Eedward White, and are to be solde
at his shoppe, nere the little North dore of
Pauls, at the signe of the
Gun. 1611.

Title page, Third Quarto of *Titus Andronicus*, 1611. Reproduced by permission of the Folger Shakespeare Library.

3

Revision in *Titus Andronicus*

In effect, the possibility of textual revision in *Titus Andronicus* has been under discussion since 1687. In that year, Ravenscroft published his adaptation of the play that had been first acted in 1678. In it, he cast doubt on Shakespeare's authorship with his tale of "Master-touches."[1] Thereafter, critics of the eighteenth and nineteenth centuries who studied the play and who were unable to accept the fact that "gentle" Shakespeare had written such a bloody drama had—with the exception of a minority of German scholars—tended to accept Ravenscroft's story. In 1901, Fuller thus assessed the state of scholarly judgment of the play:

> From this cursory history of opinion it will be seen that critics of to-day, with half-a-dozen exceptions, are inclined to believe that Shakespeare had no hand whatever in *Titus Andronicus*, or,—what for our purposes will amount to the same thing,—to hold that he is responsible for only a few scattered passages.[2]

A parallel theory, which received less support and was mostly put forth only tentatively, is that of a Shakespearean revision of a play composed by an earlier dramatist.[3]

Certain abnormalities exist in the texts that have come down to us that may be—and in fact have been—interpreted as evidence of revision, possibly authorial. If these irregularities were to be accepted as proof of alteration then two questions are raised; Who was the reviser? and when were the revisions effected?

The most manifest evidence of revision in *Titus* centers on three and a half lines that occur at the beginning of the first scene in the text of the first quarto (1594) but that are absent from Q2 (1600), Q3 (1611), and the First Folio (1623). Addressing the people and patricians of Rome, Marcus Andronicus says that Titus has spent ten years fighting the Goths and has returned to Rome as he had five times before to lay to rest the bodies of his slain sons, borne in coffins from the field, in the Andronican family tomb

and at this day,

To the Monument of that *Andronicy*

Done sacrifice of expiation,
And slaine the Noblest Prisoner of the *Gothes*.[4]

The unusual *that* in the second line quoted has been explained as a compositorial misinterpretation of y^e for y^t, as it appears it was in the manuscript from which he was working, and should be read as "the *Andronicy*."[5] There have been many attempts to interpret the meaning of the phrase "at this day." Sir Walter Greg suggests that the copy may have read "as this day" and notes that a compositorial "misreading of 'at' for 'as' is easy." The phrase may mean, Greg says, "as he proposes to do," but it could also mean "as he has already done."[6] Bolton would substitute *door* for *day*—another "easy" error—probably alluding to the entrance to a property representing the tomb of the Andronici, or possibly to a stage door fitted up to represent a tomb.[7] A slightly more persuasive suggestion is that offered by Brooks to read the phrase to mean "on the day corresponding to this."[8] However, an interpretation that calls for the minimum of editorial intervention is simply that "at this day" is intended to convey "on this day," meaning that Titus has already sacrificed Alarbus "today."

Although there has been some debate concerning the exact import of the passage, there is little doubt among critics that, in view of the representation of the sacrifice of Alarbus that follows at lines 1.1.96–149,[9] the three and one-half lines were intended to be deleted from the text of Q1, as they were from the later texts. Support for this instance of revision is the absence of Alarbus from the Q1 stage direction for the entrance of the triumphant Titus at 1.1.96.6, although his brothers Chiron and Demetrius are included. This demonstrates that at the original stage of composition Shakespeare intended merely to allude to the sacrifice of the noblest Goth, as he had Marcus do in the lines dropped from the later texts, but not to portray it. Additional evidence of alteration has been detected in the survival of two speeches (1.1.90–95 and 1.1.148–56), by means of which Titus commits the bodies of his dead sons to the tomb. These occur just before and just after the sacrifice of Alarbus and are both eloquent, though the diction varies somewhat. However, they perform the same function, and in that sense they are duplicates. One or the other may have been intended for excision, which was not accomplished.

Another discrepancy pointing to revision due to a second thought is the change in Lucius's initial intention of how to perform the sacrifice. He first asks Titus to

Give us the proudest prisoner of the Goths,
That we may hew his limbs, and on a pile
Ad manes fratrum sacrifice his flesh
Before this earthy prison of their bones

That so the shadows be not unappeased,
Nor we disturbed with prodigies on earth.

(1.1.96–101)

The "earthy prison" is, of course, the tomb of the Andronici, which means that Lucius proposes to carry out the sacrifice on stage, but in fact he does not do so. Instead, he subsequently leads Alarbus offstage to "hew his limbs till they be clean consumed" (1.1.129), and he returns to announce that he and Titus' other surviving sons "have performed our Roman rites" (1.1.142–43). It appears that the reviser neglected to alter 1.1.99 after he had changed his mind concerning the presentation of the sacrifice. Scholars generally are agreed that this array of evidence is equivalent to proof of textual revision. Greg tells us that in the first act "there seems to be clear evidence of expansion . . . [The sacrifice of Alarbus] must be an addition to the scene as originally planned."[10]

Alice Walker raises a question as to the need for the deletion of the three and one-half lines: "Is there as much wrong with these lines as everyone thinks? If 'that' is emended to 'the' in 1.36 can't they mean that on the five previous occasions when he had returned to Rome Titus had sacrificed the noblest prisoner of the Goths to the *manes* of his dead sons? They thus explain that the sacrifice was a ritual and not a piece of wanton butchery and prepare for Lucius' request." The question was directed to McKerrow, but no response is recorded.[11]

A second example in *Titus* of revision accompanied by an apparent failure to delete a superseded passage occurs in the Clown sequence in 4.3. In this instance, evidence of rewriting is the presence of two questions, similarly phrased and of virtually identical significance, asked by Titus of the Clown, with six lines of dialogue intervening:

Tell me, can you deliuer an Oration to the Emperour with a grace?

Sirra, can you with a grace deliuer vp a Supplication?[12]

Critics are agreed that these lines, which appear to be duplicate, and, as Waith observes, "some slight inconsistencies" elsewhere in the passage, are due to revision.[13] Greg points out that "the typographical arrangement [of Q1] at 4.3.89–90 in the same scene suggests that this unquestionably Shakespearian sally ['God forbid I should be so bold to press to heaven in my young days'] was a marginal addition to the Clown's speech as first written."[14] Editors are in disagreement as to the remedy required to attain the text that the reviser intended. Wilson notes that "lines 94–100 and lines 101–7 [of scene 4.3 of his text] seem [to be] alternatives, and the latter to be the later because it is not, like the other, detachable from the text."[15] Maxwell's opinion is that "The lines that could be most easily dispensed with are lines 97–100."[16] Waith omits from the text lines 104a through 104h as designated in his Appendix on "The False Start in 4.3" in consideration of "dialogue shifts from verse to prose . . . and back into verse . . . thus if the prose lines (104a–h) are omitted, the repeated material is eliminated as well as the inconsistencies in terminology, and in the proposed presentation . . . The dialogue, after one passage of prose (lines 80–99) reverts to verse for the remainder of the scene."[17] Wells does not include in his text lines 4.3.94–99 (as numbered by Waith), and prints them as Additional Passage C. to *Titus*. He notes in *A Textual Companion* that "Wilson's arguments . . . [are accepted, adds that] Marcus nowhere speaks prose, and that the Clown's replies to the repeated questions are contradictory."[18] Waith's solution to the tangle in 4.3 is ingenious, while Wells's results in the loss of fewer lines.

In addition of the so-called fly scene (3.2), consisting of some 89 lines, by Hinman's count,[19] which was first printed as part of the play-text in the First Folio but absent from the three quartos, would occupy, as Greg points out, "a single leaf of foolscap."[20] It has been viewed by various scholars as either a revision or a restoration. It is emblematic, does not advance the action and conforms to the characteristics of Price's "mirror scenes."

> The scene has little or nothing to do with the plot: that is to say, if cut, it will not be missed, nor does it add much to those elements of excitement such as hope, suspense, or anxiety which are stimulated by the plot. On the other hand, it enlarges our knowledge of the problem which is at the core of the work, and in this way *Titus* gains in depth and perspective. It brings everything into focus. The chief issues of *Titus* are there, and it may be said to mirror the play. Shakespeare invents such a scene, concentrating significant incidents into a symbol, in order to shed light upon his central thought. Apparently loose detachable scenes, so-called episodes, are frequent in Shakespeare. They vary in function as well as in technique, but certain features tend to recur. Many of them are, as in *Titus,* mirror-scenes, reflecting in one picture either the main theme or some important aspect of the drama. Others offer some kind of contrast to the general run of the action . . . Sometimes, as in *Titus,* he invents a special symbol, arranging around it the more important characters of the play. The symbol often stands for immense forces, cosmic or supernatural, which, according to the mood of the drama may save man or engulf him.

Price describes such scenes in about twenty canonical plays of all types and observes in summation that "III.ii of *Titus* is characteristic of Shakespeare . . . The pregnant dramatic picture that holds the mirror up to nature or that shows the very body of the time is an essential part of Shakespeare's technique . . . [mirror scenes] capture the attention of the audience . . . Their appeal is strengthened by the power of the symbol, by rich revelation of character."[21]

By its very nature as a mirror-scene and because it is largely self-contained, 3.2 does not impact the adjacent text. It is accepted by Taylor as being among "the major examples of such [authorial] revision"[22] in several Shakespearean plays. Wells notes that Shakespeare "appears to have added an entire scene after the play had been on the stage for some time."[23] Price expresses a converse opinion, holding that the scene "is not a later addition. Probably III.ii was marked in the printer's copy to be cut for performance, and the compositor setting up Q1 thought that the marks were an indication to him to omit the scene" which is plausible; but Price, since he does not "wish to discuss . . . bibliography,"[24] fails to take into account the irregular opening stage direction, which designates Titus as *"Andronicus"* followed by *"Marcus,"* apparently without recognizing that Marcus is also entitled to the name *"Andronicus;"* the anomalous speech prefix *"An.,"* employed seven times for Titus, and found nowhere else in the texts; and the variant spelling *Tamira* for Tamora, also unique, all of which argue, as Chambers and Greg pointed out,[25] for a distinct scribal original from Q1, and therefore the scene is unlikely to have been part of the original text. Taken with the variant diction, this evidence indicates a late date for the revision. Kerrigan incisively sums up: "the fly scene . . . fits almost perfectly into the host text. It anticipates the denouement by announcing the motif of the bloody banquet; it subtly develops a number of minor themes, such as handling, storytelling and remembrance; its verse is eloquently Shakespearian; and it features central rather than peripheral characters. That the scene is authorial has never been seriously questioned. What has been suggested, however, is that it slots so neatly into F that it must be considered cut material reinstated rather than new text added. I doubt this."[26] It has been thought that the introduction of the scene into the text may have required a second review of the play by the Master of the Revels and justified Henslowe's "ne" preceding the entry of his *Diary* of 23 January 1594.[27]

Slightly less certainly a revision (merely because there is little textual dislocation to be taken into account as evidence of rewriting) is the Mutius episode. This consists of two segments: the stabbing death of Mutius by his father; and the confrontation between Titus on the one hand, and his brother and his sons on the other, over the entombment of the dead Mutius in the Andronican family monument. The second of these (1.1.341–90) is manifestly self-contained and is clearly separable from the foregoing and the following text. As Wilson pointed out, the subsequent dialogue starting at 1.1.391 can be read "as originally a direct sequel to 1.340," leaving out the entire controversy over admitting Mutius to the tomb. This is demonstrable. The incident of the stabbing of Mutius is textually more closely related to the preceding passage and both the preceding and following action, but it is nevertheless possible to view it as an insertion effected after the play had been originally written. Wilson says; "I suspect that his [Mutius's] death at the hands of Titus has also been added."[28] Waith cites Taylor's suggestion that "these lines presenting the death of Mutius may be additions to a first draft of the scene."[29] Without them, the busy stage action is more readily understandable, especially the withdrawal of Saturninus from the main stage and his retreat to the gallery. If all this is credited and the whole episode accepted as a late, newly written insertion, then it appears that Mutius as a character is a conception of Shakespeare's, which helps to explain his absence from the *History of Titus Andronicus* and the confusion about the number of Titus's sons slain in battle. Wells, in a comprehensive analysis of the staging of the first act of *Titus,* discusses both the Alarbus and the Mutius episodes. That regarding Alarbus he finds to be "the result of a change of plan on Shakespeare's part . . . it is generally agreed that the sacrifice of Alarbus . . . is an addition; Dover Wilson plausibly argued that the later episode of the burial of Mutius is another: and if this is so, then it is not improbable that, as Wilson also suspected . . . the slaying of Mutius, too, is an addition . . . [this] implies revision during, not after composition."[30]

An irregularity in the dialogue of the masking scene (5.2) may point to an intended textual change that appears, however, to have been imperfectly realized. Addressing Tamora disguised as Revenge, who has invited him to talk to her of his woes, Titus bids her to

> Do me some service ere I come to thee.
> Lo by thy side where Rape and Murder stands,
> Now give me some surance that thou art Revenge:
> Stab them or tear them on thy chariot wheels,
> So thou destroy Rapine and Murder there.

But Tamora replies

> These are my ministers, and come with me.

To which Titus responds

> Are they thy ministers? What are they called?

Tamora answers

> Rape and Murder, therefore callèd so
> 'Cause they take vengeance of such kind of men.

(5.2.44–47; 59–63)

Within a compass of fifteen lines Titus twice identifies Tamora's sons as Rape, or Rapine,[31] and Murder then immediately thereafter asks Revenge

"What are they called?" Wilson comments that as "Titus has already named them twice over . . . there is an inconsistency here surely too glaring to be explained as his lunacy;"[32] but one of the distinguishing symptoms of the mentally ill is their denial of their illness and its effects, however manifest. Brooks, in an interpretation of the scene as part of an Appendix to Maxwell's 1961 edition, emphasizes Tamora's designation of her sons as her ministers, not named, but observes that she accommodates "Titus' 'brainsick humours'" and she explains

This closing with him fits his lunacy.

(5.2.70)

Brooks views this line as an effort by Tamora "to humor Titus" by accepting his suggestion of the names.[33] Waith concludes that "Following Titus' previous speech, the question [in line 61] is thoroughly improbable, even though Titus is feigning madness. Maxwell suggests that lines 44–59 were added after the rest of the dialogue was written. If so, this is another instance of Shakespeare's failure to tidy up his final draft."[34] The excision of some part of 5.2.44–59 would certainly tighten up the dialogue and eliminate duplication. The text proceeds satisfactorily thereafter. Brooks disputes the possibility of textual incoherence in the sequence. He denies that the text exhibits corruption and finds "the scene . . . perfectly intelligible."[35]

Greg draws attention to an unusual phenomenon on sig. I2^r of Q1. The usual complement of text lines to the page in Danter's quarto is thirty-five. I2^r (which corresponds to Waith's 5.1.115–40) has only twenty-six lines of text plus four speech prefixes, which, as Greg noted, are anomalously centered and leaded, and accompanied by considerable white space, indicating that, by his count, nine lines of dialogue appear to have been deleted. The next two pages are not quite so unusual, but they show a total of three stage directions of one line each that are centered, as are most stage directions (except for exits and exeunts) throughout the quarto, but they have more than the average amount of white space before and after them. I2^v has twenty-nine lines of text plus two stage directions and I3^r has thirty-one lines of text and one stage direction. All three are centered. The dialogue runs on fairly smoothly through the three pages. It is possible that an original passage, perhaps only on I2^r, was marked to be excised but was nevertheless set in error by the compositor. If he had already set the outer forme of the gathering before the mistake was detected, a decision could have been made by the printer to avoid resetting other pages, and instead to delete the nine unwanted lines and fill up the page by centering the speech prefixes and allocating more than the usual amount of white space. It is likely, though not certain, that the irregularity to be observed on sig. I2^r resulted from authorial revision. It is the third of three and one-third pages of Aaron's defiant confession. The passage is tightly organized and remarkably evocative of character. There may have been some lines embedded in it that were diversionary or perhaps overextended, and Shakespeare decided the confession was more effective without them; or there may have been a passage that alluded to an incident included in Shakespeare's original text but which he subsequently deleted in the process of revision. There are, however, no stigmata—such as manifest incoherencies or duplications in the text— to establish this hypothesis. Greg cautions: "The error may, of course, have had nothing to do with the copy." He does not offer a solution. There is some little additional evidence on I2^v to support a conjecture of rewriting. The first word of 5.1.141—"But" in Q1—is inappropriate. It is emended to "Tut" in Q2, followed by Q3 and F, but this may not be a restoration of the original text since it could have been picked up by the Q2 compositor from 5.1.89. Lucius's abrupt command: "march away" (5.1.165) is not adequately prepared for in the preceding dialogue; and there is no *Exeunt,* as there usually is, to provide for the clearing of the stage throughout most of Q1, marking the conclusion of a scene. These items, though not of great weight, lean toward, rather than away from, a notion of the recasting of the dialogue. On the whole, and in spite of Greg's warning, the state of these pages indicates at least a significant deletion, possibly attendant on textual alteration, the extent of which we can only guess at.[36]

The different alterations recognizable in the text fall into two categories: additions to the original play and deletions from the prototext that were not fully or only minimally effected. The sacrifice of Alarbus, both parts of the Mutius episode, and the fly scene seem clearly to be additions. The Clown incident may be in its entirety an addition, or it may be that it was part of the original in some form and then altered or expanded. In any event it is possible that in the course of rewriting some of the lines were marked to be dropped but were in fact not deleted. The masking segment shows signs of dislocation and probably it was intended that a passage in lines 44–59 was meant to be cut but the mark of deletion was overlooked by the compositor. Sigs. I2^r and perhaps I2^v and I3^r almost certainly indicate a more or less extensive revision accompanied by a deletion, the full extent of which it is impossible to determine. There may have been, elsewhere in the texts, excisions that were so skillfully carried out in the printing house that there are no surviving palpable witnesses to them.

The evidence for revision is manifestly of varying cogency. The matter of the Alarbus incident is quite compelling, and the two segments of the Mutius episode are virtually equally so. Since 3.2 has been generally recognized as Shakespeare's and more mature in style than the rest of the text, it has been accepted by most critics as a late addition.[37] The posited emendation in the disguising scene is a distinct possibility, though not quite as certain as the earlier examples. The anomalous type-setting in the I gathering certainly indicates that there was some change, but that it was attendant on a revision is not unquestionably clear. In connection with the possibility of authorial revision in *Titus Andronicus*, it should be noted that there has been in recent years a growing conviction among a significant body of students of the canon that at least in some of his plays Shakespeare revised his own original texts. The rewriting was done in some cases before they were first acted, perhaps as a result of his own second thoughts or on the acceptance of suggestions offered by his acting colleagues; or the revision came after having experienced audience response to an early presentation; or it may have occurred on the occasion of a revival; or as a consequence of having to shorten the play-text for performance while in the provinces. "No one doubts," observes Wells, "that Shakespeare, like the rest of us, made revisions as he wrote . . . Play scripts evolve in various ways, and may reach print at various stages in this process . . . the very concept of 'the final version of a play' is one that may be questioned . . . it is impossible to believe that he himself regarded such a text [as one that had just been completed] as anything other than provisional . . . the evidence suggests [in some cases] that Shakespeare's mind was changed during rehearsals," and he cites the example of the list of entertainments in 5.1 of *Midsummer's Night Dream*, the arrangement of which was altered in the Folio text from that in the quarto. Certain features, such as the assignment of names to characters, were perhaps left unresolved in the original and their resolution represents "not so much revisions as clarifications" that may occur between first composition and performance.[38] Other Shakespearean plays exhibit palpable traces of revision similar in kind and extent, and in some cases even more pervasive, to those found in *Titus*. Taylor notes that in addition to *King Lear* "there are nine other plays which survive in two texts each, one from foul papers and the other from a good theatrical manuscript (including several in which critics have discerned authorial second thoughts)."[39] Editors have traditionally solved the textual problem thus presented by a process of editorial conflation. Wells believes that such eclectic texts, which represent neither Shakespeare's original nor his revised version, should be replaced by his final intention; that is, the versions of the revised plays that were, or that he anticipated would be, performed in the theater, to the extent it is possible to recover them. "Performance is the end to which they were created, and in the new Oxford edition we have devoted our efforts to recovering and presenting texts of Shakespeare's own plays as they were acted in the London play-houses which stood at the centre of his professional life."[40]

There is, of course, no external evidence that the revising hand in *Titus* is that of Shakespeare. The internal evidence is nevertheless well-founded, although here and there it falls a little short of being convincing to the doubters. However few latter-day scholars express skepticism, and no other candidate for the role of reviser has been effectively put forth. The quality of the revisions clearly points to an outstanding dramatist with abilities beyond those of Peele, for example, whose cause was champ-pioned by Dover Wilson in his edition, although even he seems to express some doubt in a postscript to his introduction in the 1968 issue. Assuming that the play is of an early date, which is the opinion of nearly all commen-tators, the only other playwright who might be the reviser is Marlowe. Since the stylistic evidence does not, except for one or two passages, point to him, the preponderance of possibilities indicates that all of the revisions in *Titus* as described above were almost certainly carried out by Shakespeare on his own original text.

The purposes of the various revisions differ. The reason for acting out the sacrifice of Alarbus was to enhance the importance of the act of expiation and to provide for Tamora a solid motivational foundation for her drive for revenge on *Titus* and his family. It has been argued by some critics that, even as the received text now stands, Aaron must be viewed not as an aide to Tamora in her attack on the Andronici but as an inde-pendent agent dedicated to the "vengeance [that] is in my heart" (2.3.38). This has not been generally accepted, but the conception may provide a clue to the need perceived by Shakespeare for revision. There is reason to believe that Aaron, a mute in the long opening scene, captured Shake-speare's imagination as he proceeded with the play. His vivid monologue at the opening of 2.1 points to this, and it is followed by his deft counseling of Demetrius and Chiron to rape Lavinia, and his clever plot to implicate Titus's sons Quintus and Martius in the murder of Bassianus. His cam-paign of creative villainy proceeds in the cheating of Titus of his hand in a vain attempt to redeem his sons; in his decisive action to protect his son and dispose of the nurse; and culminates in his defiant revelation of his brutal deeds in his confession to Lucius (5.1.87–144). Looking back on the play after he had completed his initial draft, the playwright may have found Aaron overdominant and identified a need to redress the bal-ance between Tamora and Aaron by raising the intensity of Tamora's need for vengeance. He may then have decided to revise the opening segment and to act out the sacrifice of Alarbus rather than merely allude to it. We may even speculate that Shakespeare purposefully took Aaron offstage early in 2.3, although he originated the plot against Lavinia and Bassianus, so that Tamora could play a central role in the fatal scheme

(2.3.55–191). He reenters only after Bassianus has been stabbed to death and Lavinia has been dragged off to be raped.

The possibility of the Clown sequence being an insertion into the text may be best explained as a revision after first performance rather than a pre-theatrical textual alteration. The dialogue has a theatrical tone and the segment is manifestly detachable as it now stands. In discussing the part of the Fool in *King Lear*, Kerrigan comments that "Time and again we have seen adapters amplify jesting and clownage . . . [and] Authors sometimes worked like adapters." He points out that, in addition to *Lear*, comedic enlargements can be identified in *Doctor Faustus, Locrine, Mucedorus*, and *The Malcontent*.[41] If the incident in *Titus* reflects the antics of Will Kempe, then we may here see Shakespeare writing dialogue that expands an opportunity for Kempe's admired clowning. The brief passage of some thirty-four lines (4.3.77–110) is analogous to the porter scene in *Macbeth* and serves the same dramatic function of lowering the tension momentarily before continuing the tragic sequence.

The fly scene appears to have been designed to intensify the audience's perception of the almost unbearable burden of afflictions that have been visited on Titus and his family. The episode presents an advance towards the impending breakdown of his mental and psychological condition begun in the preceding scene with his prostrating himself in the public street in supplication to his sons' judges, with the shock of Marcus's bringing the ravished and mutilated Lavinia before him, followed by the sacrifice of his hand to try to redeem his sons and the brutal return of his severed hand with the heads of his executed sons, concluded by his irrational laughter. After all that, his "insult[ing] on" the fly is a pattern of action as unavailing as it is senseless. Marcus correctly observes that Titus "takes false shadows for true substances" (3.2.79). The action was probably designed to prepare for the ultimate catastrophe.

The two linked parts of the Mutius incident could have been an addition (or, perhaps, two separate additions) by the dramatist to demonstrate the effect of Titus's stern Roman character on his own family as a parallel and balance to his insistence on the ritual sacrifice of Alarbus. His stubborn refusal to entomb the body of Mutius, who had, in company with his brothers and his uncle, Marcus, wounded Titus's honor by, in his words, striking upon his crest (1.1.364), is only mitigated by the bitter comment:

Well, bury him, and bury me the next.

(1.1.386)

By this means, the dramatist exhibits in his protagonist the Roman quality of austere civic virtue so much admired by his Elizabethan contemporaries.

It seems clear that the principal purpose in the change in the text of the masking scene, if indeed there was one, would have been to sharpen the contrast between Titus' manifest derangement and his assertions on two occasions that he is sane:

I am not mad; I know thee well enough:

I knew them all, though they supposed me mad,

(5.2.21 and 142)

If there is an inconsistency between these two avowals and his conduct in the scene itself, especially the latter portion, in which he threatens to cut the throats of Tamora's two sons who raped and mutilated his only daughter, and

to make two pasties of your shameful heads,

(5.2.189)

and then actually does so, it clearly inheres not in any aspect of the text as such but in the character of Titus. As Brooks sums up: "He is sane enough to see through Tamora, to play up to her belief that he is a lunatic, and to organize his (surely not altogether sane) revenge."[42]

What the purpose may have been for the deletion of the passage of somewhere between nine and sixteen lines on the three pages I2^r, I2^v, and I3^r—assuming that lines were cut—we must be content not to know, because the excision left no evidence except the patent waste of space.

To the questions raised early in this essay as to who the reviser was and when the rewriting was accomplished, the following are my answers: some, but not all, of the revisions were made *currente calamo* by Shakespeare working on his own original text, which I date in 1589; some resulted from experience in performance and were accomplished shortly after the play's premier; and others were made subsequently, late in 1593, perhaps including the insertion of the fly scene, although the style it exhibits seems to indicate an even later date. At least one small emendation—the substitution in the Folio text of "Out you whore" for "Zounds ye whore" as it is in the quarto (4.2.71)—is most unlikely to have been made before the *Act to Restrain the Abuses of Players*, which was promulgated on 27 May 1606. However, since Q3 (1611) retains the oath, the probabilities are that someone other than Shakespeare made the change after that year and, of course, before 1623. In fact, it is likely that it was altered by whoever marked up the copy of Q3 from which the F text was set.[43]

There are three or four other textual discrepancies that may or may not indicate revision. After Bassianus bears off Lavinia, Saturninus accuses Titus of complicity.

> Full well, Andronicus,
> Agree these deeds with that proud brag of thine,
> That saidst I begged the empire at thy hands.
>
> (1.1.305–7)

No such boast is in the surviving text, but it could have been deleted in the course of the significant revisions in Act 1.

During the flyting in which Bassianus and Lavinia engage Tamora in the "barren detested vale," they accuse her of "sport[ing]" with Aaron and threaten to give notice of it to the "King" because, Lavinia says,

> these slips have made him noted long.
>
> (2.3.86)

Since Saturninus married Tamora only the preceding day—earlier he refers to both Tamora and Lavinia as "new-married ladies" (2.2.15)—he could not have been noted (notorious) long. This passage may be no more than an exaggeration by Lavinia.

In the scene in which young Lucius presents Titus's gifts to Chiron and Demetrius, they engage in self-congratulatory comments that a great Roman lord should "basely insinuate" to obtain their favor. Aaron pretends ironically, to join in, celebrating their happy situation and adds

> It did me good before the palace gate
> To brave the tribune in his brother's hearing.
>
> (4.2.35–36)

The tribune of whom he speaks can only be Marcus, and of course the brother is Titus, but there is no such incident in the play. It may have been deleted, or we may conjecture with Waith that the lines refer "to something that happened shortly before their entrance."[44]

A catchword—"But"—on sig. G4^v is not followed on the first line of the next page, as it normally would. The first word on sig. H1^r is "Ioine," indicating a gap in the text, but we have no evidence showing how many lines are missing. Every editor since Kittredge either assumes or states that only one line was lost. Maxwell suggests that "join" is an infinitive and that the missing line contained the words "let us."[45]

Contemplating Titus's irrational behavior in shooting arrows into the court, Tamora celebrates her success, saying

But, Titus, I have touched thee to the quick;
Thy life-blood out, if Aaron now be wise,
Then is all safe, the anchor in port.

(4.4.36–38)

The reference to Aaron seems to indicate that she had counseled with him concerning some course of action, but, if so, it does not appear to be identifiable in the text. As in some of the other similar instances the reference might be to an excised incident.

Not all of these constitute in themselves compelling evidence of recasting, but taken with the more substantial examples of textual alteration, they support the probability of significant revision in *Titus Andronicus*.[46]

4

The Text

THE text of *Titus Andronicus* has come down to us in the form of four exemplars: three quartos published during Shakespeare's lifetime and the Folio text of 1623. The first quarto was dated 1594; the second 1600; and the third 1611 (see plates of title pages). Q1 survives in a single copy, which came to light in 1904 among the books of a Swedish postal employee and is now in the Folger Shakespeare Library in Washington. A photographic facsimile was published in 1936 by Joseph Quincy Adams, who was at that time the Director of the Folger Library. It includes an illuminating introduction.[1] Of Q2 we have two copies, one preserved in the University of Edinburgh Library and the other in the Huntington Library, San Marino, Calif. This latter copy presents the cleaner text of the two. Of the third quarto there exist seventeen copies, six located in the United Kingdom, ten in the United States, and one in the Bibliotheca Bodmeriana, Geneva. These copies are all of about the same quality. They exhibit numerous compositor's errors, some poor printing, and a number of variant readings, but they present no extraordinary difficulties.[2] The text of the First Folio exhibits some unusual characteristics which are discussed below. It is the repository of the many accumulated defects of the earlier prints, and includes scene 3.2, which is not in any of the quartos. Modern editors are agreed in adopting the first quarto text of *Titus Andronicus* (1594) as being closest to Shakespeare's original intention, to which is added scene 3.2.[3]

The copy from which the first quarto was set is generally accepted as having been Shakespeare's original draft. The print exhibits a number of qualities that are considered characteristic of dramatists' "foul papers," that is, papers not reworked to improve legibility. Speech prefixes in a dramatist's initial version have been found to vary according to whether the playwright is thinking of the character as an individual or as a type. In Q1 the speech prefixes for the principal characters, such as, for example, Saturninus, exhibit considerable variety. His full name occurs most frequently, but there are a number of abbreviations, such as Saturnine, Saturni, Saturn, Satur, and Sat. Some of these may be traceable to compositional adjustments caused by typographical constraints, but not all. King and Emperour are also used as speech prefixes and, in addition, there are half a dozen uses of Emperour in stage directions. Prefixes for Aron are divided about equally between that form and Moore and there is the same division between the two in stage directions. In addition, there are three occasions when just the letter A is employed. There is a greater degree of consistency in the speech prefixes for other characters. For Titus, that form of prefix is predominant, varied only twice to Tit. and once to the letter T. For Tamora, who has almost as many speeches as Titus, the prefix is shortened only a few times to Tam.; and on two occasions she is designated Queene.

Another characteristic of the copy usually accepted as being indicative of foul papers is the descriptive and sometimes petitory quality of the stage directions. The triumphant initial entrance of Titus with his entourage (Adams ed. sigs. A4^r and ^{v}), which lists eleven characters, not including Alarbus, and then adds "and others as many as can be," is a good example. Similarly, the stage direction for the simultaneous entries of Saturninus and Bassianus from two different stage doors (sig. C1^v) lists seven characters and concludes "with others." Indefinite though clearly plural expressions also occur, such as "and their Attendants" (sig. D1^r), "Enter the Iudges and Senatours" (sig. E3^r), "with Tribunes and others" (sig. K2^r), and the gloriously extravagant "Enter Lucius with an Armie of Gothes with Drums and Souldiers" (sig. H4^r). Scholars generally agree that a text that had been worked through by the acting company's "bookkeeper," who usually served as prompter and was responsible for getting the right actors onto the stage at the right moment, would have made the stage directions more specific and complete, more functional. No doubt he would have provided, among other things, an entrance for Alarbus among the Goths brought to Rome to "beautifie"—in Tamora's phrase—Titus's triumph (sig. B1^r).

A further indication of foul papers copy is the failure to have deleted lines that were superseded by a change in the plan of the play. Especially noteworthy is the passage consisting of three and one-half lines on A3^v of Q1, which most critics agree speaks of the sacrifice of Alarbus as having already been accomplished but which is shortly thereafter actually carried out (A4^v–B1^v).[4] Neither the playwright nor the playhouse personnel excised the superseded verses. There are a number of other characteristics of the text, such as incompletely deleted repetitions, that may point to additional revisions (see chapter on Revision) and which are indicative of foul papers.

Haggard studies the composition and printing of Q1 and concludes on the basis of bibliographic evidence (mainly damaged types) that it was set by forme, except for Sheet A, by a single compositor from a single type case; that this compositor was not a very careful workman; and that Q1 is "more corrupt than any other, indeed perhaps most other, good quartos." He discusses the absence of the line "Yes and will Nobly his remunerate" from Q1 and the subsequent quartos but which appears in F1 (TLN 443), and inclines to the opinion that the compositor of Q1 omitted it deliberately rather than in error because there is sufficient space at the top of C1^v to fit it in. Possibly he did so to conform to the practice, evident elsewhere in the text, of providing white space before and after multiline stage directions. He also thinks the printing generally proceeded in an orderly fashion except for a delay during the machining of sheet I.[5]

In the course of his review of Waith's edition, Jackson notes that in Q1 "do/doe/doo variants differentiate sheets A–E from sheets F–K and there are some suggestive shifts in the spelling of O/Oh." This might indicate the presence of two compositors. Throughout the text the doe forms are predominant but the do/doo variants are distinctly more common in the early gatherings than the later. Similarly the Oh form is the more common in all segments of the text but there is a noteworthy sequence of O forms in sheets F and G. These phenomena may very well support Jackson's question in regard to a single compositor. He sums up: "The Quarto remains a potential subject for bibliographical investigation," a determination in which many students of the play will concur.[6]

It has been generally accepted that the second quarto was printed from a copy of Q1. Spelling and punctuation, with some occasional exceptions, are the same in both texts, including unusual or deviant spellings. Q2 readings that are different from Q1 are rare. Duplicated mistakes and the carrying over of passages no longer appropriate confirm this hypothesis. Noteworthy of this type is the copying in Q2 of the head-title of Q1 citing the three acting companies that had earlier presented the play—"the Earle of Darbie, Earle of Pembrooke, and Earle of Suffex theyr Seruants—"but failing to include the fourth troupe listed on its own title page "the Lorde Chamberlaine['s]." Adams notes that "The compositor [of Q2] preserved many of the typographical peculiarities of his copy, including its unusual and wasteful centering of the speech prefixes on A3 recto, A4 recto, and I2 recto,"[7] and there are quite a few more such peculiarities. The most significant Q2 deviations from Q1 are the deletion of the three and one-half lines that mention the ritual sacrifice of a noble prisoner and the substitution for the erroneous phrase "as Tytus Raies on earth" the expression "as Tytans raies on earth" (1.1.226, Waith ed.). Surely the reference is not to Titus but to the sun. However, the Q1 reading may, of course, be merely one turned letter and the omission of a second letter. The Q2 readings appear in Q3 and F.

The third quarto was composed from a copy of Q2 and in this case the page arrangement of Q2 was duplicated. Again the head-title was copied verbatim from the copy text, ignoring the notation on the Q3 title page, which reads simply "*AS IT HATH SVNDRY times beene plaide by the King* Maieſ ties Ser*u*ants." Bolton, who compared Q3 to both Q2 and Q1, says that "in all cases but one . . . in which a choice between Q1 and Q2 is possible, the Q2 forms are followed [by Q3]," and that "three . . . manifest errors of the Q2 text are corrected in neither Q3 or F1."[8] One passage in Q3 corrects the two earlier texts. It reads (at 2.2.1, Waith ed.): "the morne is bright and gray" where the predecessor texts have "the Moone is bright and gray."

The First Folio text of *Titus* follows Q3, but it adds scene 3.2, consisting of eighty-nine lines (by Hinman's count), comprising eighty-six lines of dialogue and three of stage directions (TLN 1451–1539).[9] As in the cases of Q2 and Q3, F1 corrects some of the errors of the predecessor text and commits its own quota of new ones. The play was composed in the First Folio, except for the first page, by a workman who was identified by Hinman, and designated in an article published in 1957 as Compositor E. His discussion of E and his characteristics was extended and corrected in his *Printing and Proof-Reading of the First Folio of Shakespeare.*[10] Hinman adduced evidence that the pages set by E were proofread in the printing house more carefully than those set by other compositors, and he also concluded that, except for the short "Bnaket" scene of *Titus* (3.2), E was not assigned to compose from manuscript. He worked almost exclusively from printed copy, and even then he was not permitted to set the first pages of *Titus* and *Romeo*. Hinman thinks it is possible that "the initial page of a play [in the First Folio], a kind of title page, might well be regarded by the Folio printers as more important than other pages," and he cites in support of this the four different stages of correction to which the first page of *The Tempest* was subjected. He concludes on the basis of this and other evidence that E must therefore have been an inexperienced compositor, probably a "Prentice Hand."[11]

Cairncross, perhaps led to do so by remarks of Hinman's that certain characteristics of compositor B were reflected by E, studied the work of the two and reassigned large blocks of what had been previously accepted as B's work to E.[12] These reassignments were examined with some rigor by Howard-Hill who, as a result, found that "the evidence adduced by Mr. Cairncross to reattribute pages from B to E is inadequate for that purpose, and that the individual attributions he makes rest on no sure ground." He concludes that "No evidence has been found to suggest that compositor E's share in the setting of the Folio is materially different from Mr. Hinman's description of it."[13]

The copy of Q3 from which E worked had been collated most probably with the acting company's prompt-book. Scene 3.2 had not been printed in any of the quartos, and therefore, as Greg notes, "For this there must of course have been a manuscript."[14] Strong evidence of collation with the "book can be seen in F1 in the many stage directions altered, expanded, or added, of which there are almost a score. The Folio printer's copy may have been the manuscript prompt-book itself; or it may have been based on a copy of Q3 marked up by reference to the prompt-book; or, as Greg reasoned, it may have been a copy of Q3 so marked up from a copy of Q2 that was being used as the prompt-book.[15]

Convincing evidence that E was working from a copy of Q3 can be seen in the many readings in F1 that agree with Q3 when that text varies from Q2, or from both Q1 and Q2 where they are different. There are some 300 occurrences of this phenomenon, of which 180 are variant spellings, 76 are differences in punctuation, and, most important, 52 exhibit some divergence in meaning from that in Q1 and Q2. A selection of the more significant of these follows:[16]

	Q1, Q2	Q3, F
1.1.447; 497	ſupplant you	ſupplant vs
2.1.22; 576	this Nymph	this Queene
2.2.1; 701	Moone	morne
2.3.56; 795	her well-beseeming	our well-beseeming
2.3.60; 799	of my private	of our private
2.3.64; 803	upon thy	upon his
2.3.78; 817	Accompanied but with	Accompanied with
2.3.160; 905	thy deafe yeares	thy deafe eares
2.3.204; 956	diſmallſt obiect hurt	diſmallſt obiect
2.3.220; 974	who it is	how it is
2.3.256; 1011	left them there	left him there
2.4.38; 1111	Philomela, why ſhe but	Philomela ſhe but
3.1.59; 1196	Q1: aged eies	noble eyes
	Q2: aged eyes	
3.1.115; 1258	knowes them	knowes him
4.1.21; 1564	ran mad for	ran mad through
4.1.100; 1649	let alone	let it alone
4.1.105; 1654	Q1: our lesson	your lesson
	Q2: you lesson	
4.2.27; 1706	ſends them weapons	ſends the weapons
4.3.8; 1874	catch her	finde her
4.3.76; 1942	his Lordſhip	your Lordſhip
5.1.43; 2155	her burning luſt	his burning luſt
5.1.68; 2179	in my death	by my death
5.1.133; 2249	Q1: hay ſtalks	Q3: hayſtackes
	Q2: hayſtakes	F: Hayſtackes
5.3.7; 2503	Empreſe face	Emperours face
5.3.195; 2700	mourning weede	mournefull weeds

Most telling in this list are the instances in which E takes over unchanged into the Folio text manifest errors from Q3. "Queene" instead of "Nymph," for example, is a repetition by the compositor of Q3 from the preceding line of his copy; and "noble eyes" is an anticipation of "noble" from the next succeeding line. "your Lordship" is an example of an alteration, in error, of the correct reading of Q1–Q2 as the context makes clear; and the substitution of "Emperours face" for "Empresse face" is the same type of mistake. "Mournefull weeds" is another example of anticipation, in this case of the expression "mournefull bell" in the next line. Somewhat more unusual is the reading in Q3 of "finde her," referring to Astraea, for the "catch her" of Q1 and Q2. None of the editors has commented on it. It may be that this variant is simply a case of E misreading or misremembering his copy; but it may be the result of proof correction in the copy of Q2 that the compositor of Q3 was working from but that was not effected in the two copies of Q2 that survive. Bolton sums up the relationships of the four texts:

> One can without difficulty trace the evolution of the accepted text. That the first quarto stood copy for the second, the second for the third, and the third for the First Folio, is evident from the consistent repetition of variants throughout successive editions, from the successful correction of only the more obvious of the earlier errors, and from the progressive variations traceable in a few striking instances.[17]

The variants between Q1 and Q2, between Q2 and Q3, and between Q3 and F1 are fairly numerous. The most substantial and justly famed is the alternate ending of the play, which first appeared in Q2 and was the only one known until the unique copy of the first quarto came to light in 1904. It has been reasonably postulated that the specific copy of Q1 from which Q2 was set was badly damaged at the foot of each of the last three leaves of sheet K—K2, K3, and K4. This conception was first put forward by Bolton in 1929 in what Adams described as a "Brilliant deduction, for he was not able to examine the First Quarto," but yet arrived at the correct solution. McKerrow, unaware of Bolton's paper but, as Adams says, "with photostats of the First Quarto before him," in 1934 independently suggested the same explanation.[18] Adams canvasses possible causes of the damage:

> It may be that the entire lower portion of leaf K4, an outside lower corner of leaf K3, and a narrow outer section near the bottom of leaf K2 were torn away; or that a very heavy wet stain at the foot of the last leaf obliterated the printing with decreasing seriousness through the three final leaves; or that a burn completely destroyed the lower portion of the last leaf, and affected portions of the two preceding leaves. On the whole, the last explanation seems the most plausible,

a determination generally accepted. The solution to the problem of the loss of the author's lines from the final three leaves was apparently worked out by someone in the printing house who "supplied in whole or in part twenty-three lines, of which fourteen are textually incorrect and nine have no rightful place in the tragedy."[19]

The variants begin in the last three lines at the bottom of sig. K2ʳ of Q1.

Q1   *Trumpets ſounding, Enter* Titus *like a Cooke, placing the diſhes, and* Lauinia *with a vaile ouer her face.*

         Titus. VVelcome my Lord, welcome dread Queene,

Q2   *Sound trumpets, enter* Titus *like a Cooke, placing the meate on the table, and* Lauinia *with a vaile ouer her face.*

         Titus. Welcom my gracious Lord, welcom dread Queene,

Q3   [same as Q2 except *Table*]

F1   *Hoboyes.*
                      A Table brought in.
          Enter Titus *like a Cooke, placing the meat on the* Table, *and* Lauinia *with a vale ouer her face.*

         Titus. Welcome my gracious Lord,
         Welcome Dread Queene,

Manifestly the damage to this page of the copy of Q1 from which Q2 was set was relatively slight. The texts vary even less significantly in the lines at the bottom of K2ᵛ of Q1.

Q1   *King,* Goe fetch them hither to vs preſsently.

         Titus. VVhy there they are both baked in this Pie.

Q2,   *King.* Goe fetch them hether to vs preſently,
Q3
         Titus. Why there they are both, baked in that pie,

F1   *Satu.* Go fetch them hither to vs preſently.
         Tit. Why there they are both, baked in that Pie,

At the bottom of K3ʳ of Q1, the damage was somewhat more extensive. The speaker is designated *Romane Lord* in Q1; as *Roman Lord* in Q2 and Q3; and as *Goth* in F, but editors generally assign the lines to Marcus.

Q1   And force you to commiſeration,
         Her's Romes young Captaine let him tell the tale,
         While I stand by and weepe to heare him speake.

         Lucius. Then gratious auditorie be it knowne to you,
         That *Chiron* and the damn'd *Demetrius,*

Q2   Lending your kind commiſeration,
            Heere is a Captaine, let him tell the tale,
            Your harts will throb and weepe to hear him ſpeake.

            Lucius. Then noble auditory be it knowne to you,
            That curſed *Chiron* and *Demetrius*

Q3   [same as Q2 except no comma after "Captaine"]

F1   Lending your kind hand Commiſeration
            Heere is a Captaine, let him tell the tale,
            Your hearts will throb and weepe to hear him speak.

            Luc. This Noble Auditory, be it knowne to you
            That curſed *Chiron* and *Demetrius*

Each of these five lines as they survive in the unique copy of Q1, but which must have been absent from the exemplar used in setting Q2, is mended in that quarto and is closely followed by Q3. However F, in the first of these lines, adds the word "hand," and altered the first word of the fourth of these lines from "Then," as it is in Qq, to "This." These emandations work no improvement. Also of some interest is the capitalizing of the initial letters of the next two words in the same line to "Noble Auditory" (where Qq employ lower case), a persistent habit of Compositor E in the First Folio.

The deviant reading at the foot of K3ᵛ is limited to five words.

Q1   And from the place where you behold vs pleading,
            The poore remainder of *Andronicie,*
            VVill hand in hand, all headlong hurle our ſelues,
            And on the ragged ſtones beat forth our ſoules,

Q2,   And from the place where you behold vs now
Q3   The poore remainder of *Andronicie*
            Will hand in hand all headlong caſt vs downe,
            And on the ragged ſtones beat forth our braines,

F1   [same as Q3 except for a comma after "now" and a spelling change
            to "Andronici"]

The first of the six lines that we have at the bottom of K4ʳ of the Q1 text is slightly altered, but the other five are completely different in Q2, Q3, and F, and F capitalizes the initial letters of seven words that are not capitalized in Q2 and Q3.

Q1   Many a ſtorie hath he told to thee,
            And bid thee bare his prettie tales in minde,

And talk of them when he was dead and gone.

(lips,
Marcus. How manie thouſand times hath theſe poore
VVhen they were liuing warmd themselves on thine,
Oh now ſweete boy giue them their lateſt kiſſe,

Q2   Many a matter hath he told to thee,
Meete and agreeing with thine infancie,
In that respect then, like a louing child.
Shed yet ſome ſmall drops from thy tender ſpring,
Because kind nature doth require it ſo,
Friends ſhould aſſociate friends in griefe and woe.

Q3   [same except for reading "childe," and "kinde"]

F1   Many a matter hath he told to thee,
Meete, and agreeing with thine Infancie:
In that reſpect then, like a louing Childe
Shed yet ſome ſmall drops from thy tender Spring,
Because kinde Nature doth require it ſo:
Friends, ſhould aſſociate Friends, in Greefe and Wo.

The text of the conclusion of the play as it is on K4ᵛ of Q1, deviates in the other three texts in only six words of the final line; but to the Q1 text the others agree in adding four lines of no authority and in truncating the Finis. Q1 and Q2 also omit the *Exeunt.*

Q1   And being dead let birds on her take pittie.

Exeunt.

Finis the Tragedie of Titus Andronicus.

Q2   And being ſo ſhall haue like want of pitty.
See iuſtice done on *Aron* that damn'd Moore,
By whom our heauie haps had their beginning:
Than afterwards to order well the ſtate,
That like euents may nere it ruinate.

F I N I S

Q3   And being ſo ſhall haue like want of pitty.
See iuſtice done on *Aron* that dambd *Moore,*
By whom our heauy haps had their beginning:
Then afterwards to order well the ſtate,
That like events may ner'e it ruinate.

F I N I S

F1   And being ſo ſhall haue like want of pitty.
            See Iuſtice done on *Aaron* that damn'd Moore,
            From whom, our heauy happes had their beginning:
            Then afterwards, to Order well the State,
            That like Euents, may ne'er it Ruinate. *Exeunt omnes.*

F I N I S .

[ornament]

Maxwell points out that an injury similar to that suffered by leaves K2–K4 could have occurred on I2[r] and I2[v] of the copy of Q1 from which Q2 was set, situated in the same position on the two pages and giving rise to the following variants:

	Q1		Q2
I4[r]	1. 1 braine-ſicke humors	I3[v]	1. 5 braine-ſicke fits
I4[v]	1. 1 VVell ſhalt thou	I4[r]	1. 6 Well maiſt thou[20]

An almost equally notable textual crux involves sig. E3[v] of Q1 (3.1.33–37, Waith ed.). The four texts read as follows:

Q1   *Titus.* VVhy tis no matter man, if they did heare
            They would not marke me, if they did marke,
            They would not pittie me, yet pleade I muſt,
            And bottleſſe vnto them.
            Therefore I tell my ſorrowes to the ſtones,

Q2   *Titus.* Why tis no matter man, if they did heare
            They would not marke me, or if they did marke
            They would not pitty me, yet pleade I muſt,
            And bootleſſe vnto them.
            Therefore I tell my ſorrowes to the ſtones,

Q3   *Titus.* Why tis no matter man, if they did heare
            They would not marke me, or if they did marke,
            All bottleſſe vnto them.
            Therefore I tell my ſorrowes bootles to the ſtones,

F1   *Ti.* Why 'tis no matter man, if they did heare
            They would not marke me: oh if they did heare
            They would not pitty me.
            Therefore I tell my ſorrowes bootles to the ſtones.

The first of these lines is close to being invariant in all four readings. The speech prefix of Q1 has a roman capital T with the remainder of the name in italic. In Q2 and Q3 the prefix is all italic. F1 reduces the prefix to *Ti.*, in the event unnecessarily, since the line affords enough room so that the full prefix could have been fitted in. The "W" of the first word of dialogue in Q1 is set as "VV," as it frequently is throughout the quarto, attesting, as does the occasional initial lower case form of the letter in the first word of a line, to a shortage of upper case roman "W" in this font in Danter's printing house. The other texts have a standard "W." The second word—"tis"—is spelled thus in the quartos but "'tis" in F1, reflecting a habit of Compositor E. The second line is identical in Q2 and Q3, but in Q1 after "marke me" there is no "or" as there is in Q2 and Q3. At that location F1 reads "oh." Since the "or" makes sense in the context, the deviation in F1 can be put down as a compositor's error.

Line three of this passage reads the same in Q1 and Q2 except for a single spelling difference: "pittie" in Q1; "pitty" in Q2. Q3 omits the line entirely, which is most likely a compositorial oversight. F1 prints the first half of the full line as it appears in Q1 and Q2, employing the spelling "pitty," and the presence of this half line in F1 is a puzzle. It has been accepted by scholars that Q3 provided the copy for F1, as it was succinctly expressed by Bolton in 1929 and endorsed since by many, including, most recently, by Waith and by Wells.[21] The evidence set forth above documents these findings. However, the half line in F1 (TLN 1171): "They would not pitty me," is half of the line as it appears in Q1 and Q2, but the entire line is missing from Q3. Possibly it is an invention of Compositor E, but if so it is remarkable that it should exactly reproduce the passage in Q2 even to the spelling "pitty," but no other comparable trace of Q2 appears in the Folio text in contrast to the many reflections of Q3. Possibly E, taking note of the discontinuous transition in Q3:

> or if they did marke,
> All bottleſe vnto them.

sought help and perhaps was shown a copy of Q2 from which he set the half line. This is, at best, not very likely, but if it did happen why did he not set the whole line from Q2? Dover Wilson calls this a "typical Sh[akespeare] tangle," and notes that "If 'And bootless unto them . . .' be deleted as was prob[ably] intended, all is well." Maxwell designates the same line as

Probably a false start which Shakespeare omitted to delete . . . Q3 and F get into curious tangles of which the only interest is that F restores part of a line omitted altogether in Q3, and must therefore have consulted some other source of information, presumably the prompt-copy, which would in all probability have eliminated the unsatisfactory "And . . . them." But why should "yet . . . must" not have been in the prompt-copy? And is it any more than coincidence that F should here introduce two new errors, "oh" for "or" and "heare" (from the previous line) for "marke"? It is worth nothing that "or" (though almost certainly correct does not go back to Q1, and "oh" may be an alternative

> prompt-book reading, independent of the later Quartos . . . the whole passage raises problems which I cannot solve.

Sisson finds the F version "corrupt and incomplete," and says that the only difficulty in Q is a broken line, otherwise "the sense seems clear and logical." Greg finds that "F" had recourse to some authority besides Q3." It could have been the prompt-book, though "there is a trifle of evidence to indicate that the prompt-book was not the source on which F relied," but he then somewhat lamely notes that "The 'or' might of course have been accidently omitted in Q1." Waith thinks that the word "or" may have been in the original manuscript, that the compositor's eye skipped the third line in Q2 and altered slightly the next line ("all" in place of "And") and then "inadvertently repeated 'bootless' in the following line." He finds the Folio text hardest to explain. Part of the tangle he charges to the "editor" who marked up the copy of Q3 by reference to the prompt-book, and part he lays at the door of Compositor E. Wells surveys the crux and the editorial attempts to resolve it and seems inclined to accept Maxwell's solution, but concludes by deleting "or" in the second of these lines and "And bootless unto them."[22]

Another passage perplexing to scholars is 3.1.280 (Waith ed.), which in Q1 reads

> And *Lauinia* thou ſhalt be imployde in theſe Armes,

Q2 varies only in that the name is all italic; Q3 concurs except for the spelling "imployd;" F1 emends:

> And *Lauinia* thou ſhalt be employd in theſe things:

Waith sums up the earlier efforts to make sense of the line:

> The Q1 reading . . . has seemed wrong . . . [generally]. The F correction. . . makes tolerable sense but leaves the line metrically very irregular. Lettson's conjecture, adopted by Hudson, and later by Dover Wilson, improves the metre. Hudson also dropped "And" from the beginning of the line on the assumption that it "crept in by mistake from the line above." W. A. Wright (Cambridge edition) made the ingenious suggestion that the line in the manuscript copy ended at "employed;" that someone had written "arms" over "teeth" in the following line as a possible alternative to a ludicrous piece of business, but failed to cross out "teeth;" and that the Q1 compositor, taking "Armes" for part of 1. 280, filled the gap with "in these." A variant of this suggestion is one made by Bolton that the line originally read as in this text, and that the compositor substituted "these" for "this." The comparative lengths of the two lines make either of these suggestions plausible.

Maxwell prints the verse, between obeli, as

And, Lavinia, thou shalt be employ'd in these arms:

and notes that "I leave this line as hopelessly corrupt." He is joined in this judgment by other modern editors. Sisson suggests "charms" for "Armes," the result of the compositor misreading "if he guessed at a capital *A* of a well-known shape in a *ch* with the descender of the *h* missing or illegible." This explanation might possibly be doubted except that he tells us such a misreading "is an error I have actually made in reading such a manuscript," i.e., a damaged one written in the secretary hand. Bolton's conjecture, though it results in pedestrian verse, seems likely, and is the one accepted by Wilson and Waith, though not by Wells, who adapts the Cambridge editors' solution.[23]

The line

My Lords you know the mightfull Gods,

(Waith, ed., 4.4.5), a verse that reads the same in Qq and F1, is metrically deficient. Editors since Rowe have patched it by adding two syllables. Wilson cites Rowe's insertion of "as do" after "know," although he himself adopts the reading of the Cambridge edition:

My Lords, you know, as know the mightful gods,

and is followed by Maxwell without comment. Waith explains:

This conjectural addition by the Cambridge editors . . . makes sense of the line and brings it to normal length; it is highly plausible, since the repetition of "know" could easily lead the printer to skip two words,

and Wells concurs.[24]

The invariant reference in the four texts to "the Romaine Hector's hope" at 4.1.87 (Waith ed.) has puzzled critics. The expression is accepted as meaning the principal defender of Rome, just as Hector was the warrior who defended Troy. It was a tradition ultimately based on Virgil, that Rome was founded by Aeneas of Troy as it was a British tradition that London was founded by Trojans. The reference in *Titus* does not make clear who is the Roman Hector. It is perhaps surprising that neither Dover Wilson nor Maxwell comment on this passage. Barnet, Cross, and Ribner[25] identify him as Titus. Kermode, Bevington, and Waith[26] designate Lucius. A moderately convincing case can be made for Titus, who certainly had, before the play begins, championed and defended Rome. However, he speaks of his "feeble knee" (2.3.288) and is addressed as "old Titus" (3.1.152), and presumably lacked the vigor to be a champion any longer. Lucius, at the beginning of the play, is only one of four of Titus's sons who accompany him in his triumphant return to Rome, but he does take a leading role in the sacrifice of Alarbus, and in the Mutius incident. By the time of the reference in 4.1, he is Titus's only surviving son and has in the immediately preceding scene, at his father's urging, gone off to raise a Gothic army with the objective of attacking Saturninus. On balance, then, it would appear that the "Roman Hector" is meant to designate Lucius and his "hope" in his son, young Lucius.

Other passages in the texts of the play are thought to call for some resolution or at least explanation, but those noted above are fairly representative and are probably the most important. There has been debate across the generations among editors and textual critics about some verse tangles that are perhaps best left alone. One example is allusive passage at 4.4.23–26 (Waith ed.) in which a reference to "justice" is interpreted by some to mean Astraea, the goddess of justice. This then requires tinkering with later personal pronouns, as Wilson and Maxwell do; but Sisson observes that the "want of immediate clarity is not sufficient evidence of textual corruption. The thought and its expression are clear enough." Waith rejects the emendations.[27]

The textual variants among the quarto texts are many, but the differences between the various copies of Q2 and Q3 are few. The single surviving copy of Q1—being unique—it, in the words of Thomas Berger, "resists collation."[28] Adams lists the following variants in the two surviving copies of Q2 in the introduction to his facsimile edition of Q1.

	EDINBURGH	HUNTINGTON
D2 *verso*, 1.20	wodt	word
I2 *verso*, 1.18	Thon hast	Thou hast
I2 *verso*, 1.21	Wi nes this	Witnes this
I2 *verso*, 1.22	trenchers	trenches
I2 *verso*, 1.25	Empressee	Empresse
I2 *verso*, 1.31	vengeane	vengeance
I3 *verso*, 1.10	thine	mine
I4 *verso*, 1.19	Tnt	Tut

He notes in discussing possible variants that "the Edinburgh copy has long diagonal tears extending across the lower halves of leaves C3 and C4 that have been so crudely mended as to obliterate some letters on the four pages involved."[29] He does not list two other readings in which the two copies differ.

	EDINBURGH	HUNTINGTON
C3 *recto*, 1.18	*Rom*	*Rome*,
C3 *recto*, 1.23	propo	propoſe,

possibly because they are not true variants but merely failures in the Edinburgh copy to print the final letters.

The third quarto has even fewer variants—for certain only two, but possibly two others. The first occurs on F1ᵛ 1.12 (3.1.216, Waith ed.) and reads in the uncorrected state:

Then be my paſſios bottomleſſe with them.

Thirteen copies of Q3, out of the total of seventeen, read thus, and four have the corrected state: "paſſions."[30] The second of these variants is found on sig. G3ᵛ 1.6 (4.2.160),

To calme this tempeſt whiling in the Court,

Only one surviving copy has this reading; sixteen are corrected to: "whirling."[31] The third reading, possibly a variant, occurs on K2ᵛ 1.17 (5.3.63),

Empe. Die frantike wretch for this accurſed deed

The final word appears to be variant, the presumed corrected copies reading

. . .accurſed deede.

Three copies have the uncorrected state, fourteen appear to be corrected. But this may not constitute a textual variant; it may be simply a failure to print the final "e" and the period in the "uncorrected" copies. Some support for this view may be seen in that the final "d" of the line did not fully register at the right edge in two of the three "uncorrected" copies.[32]

The fourth and even more doubtful variant is found on sig. E4ᵛ 1.15 (3.1.158):

Did euer Ranenſing ſo like a Larke,

The first "n" in "Ranen" is manifestly the letter "u" accidentally set in an inverted position by the compositor. The word appears as "Ranen" in fifteen copies. In one of the other two copies the error has been corrected so that the word reads "Rauen." In the second, the letter is not so clearly linked and it appears partially open at both the top and the bottom.[33]

Titus in the First Folio, is based on Q3 but is variant in a number of ways. There are two major differences—the division of the text into five acts, whereas the quartos are divided only into scenes, and the addition of the whole scene 3.2. Other variants occur because Compositor E was following a copy of Q3 marked up by reference to the Jacobean version of the King's Men's prompt-book. Evidence of this has been set forth above. Greg hesitated to endorse this determination, but scholars succeeding him, having credentials in modern bibliography and textual analysis, do accept it. However, though E followed the text of Q3 with a measure of faithfulness, F still evidences significant change. The most ubiquitous divergence is the very liberal use of initial capitals by E as compared to the compositor of Q3. In F Act 1 of *Titus* alone, I have counted over four hundred occurrences of such capital letters other than the first letter of the lines of verse. Most of the words, internal to the lines, so capitalized, are nouns, but approximately 10 percent are other parts of speech—adjectives, verbs, and a few adverbs.[34] Other deviations in F as compared to the Q3 text are also fairly numerous. Following is a list of substantive variants, from which are excluded differences limited to spelling and punctuation.[35]

F1 variants from text of Q3 of *Titus Andronicus*

	Q3	F1
1.1.5; 11	I am his first	I was the first
1.1.73; 81	From where	From whence
1.1.99; 121	earthy	earthly
1.1.109; 130	ſonne	ſonnes
1.1.122; 144	their brethren	the Brethren
1.1.134; 157	looke	lookes
1.1.174; 203	are alike in all	are all alike in all
1.1.217; 247	peoples Tribunes	Noble Tribunes
1.1.223; 253	ſute	ſure
1.1.252; 283	thy feete	my feete
1.1.391; 436	dririe	ſudden
2.1.14; 568	triumph	ttriumph
2.1.91; 651	Saturnine[36]	*Saturnius*
2.1.122; 684	vengeance	vengance
2.1.136; 696	*Sit fas*	*Sij fas*
2.1.136; 696	streame	streames
2.3.20; 755	yellowing	yelping
2.3.210; 963	vnhollow	vnhallow'd
2.4.41; 1114	haſt thou met	haſt thou met withall[37]
3.1.33–37; 1169–72[38]		
3.1.121; 1264	ſigne	ſignes

3.1.134; 1277	miſsery[39]	miſeries
3.1.169; 1314	Wrighting	Writing
3.1.192; 1341	my hand	me hand
3.1.254; 1404	warlike hand	warlike hands
3.1.255; 1405	ſonne	ſonnes
3.1.280; 1430	theſe Armes	theſe things
4.1.9; 1552	Feare her not	Feare not
4.1.40; 1584	for reuenge	to reuenge
4.1.44; 1589	Perhaps	Perhahs
4.1.62; 1607	erſt	erſts
4.2.71; 1755	Zounds ye whore[40]	Out you whore
4.2.155; 1798	ignomie	ignominie
4.4.92; 2088	feede	foode
4.4.112; 2107	plead to	plead for
5.1.13; 2123	Be bolde	behold
5.1.93; 2208	cut her hands, and	cut her hands off, and
5.2.18; 2302	to giue that accord[41]	to giue it action
5.2.31; 2317	thy minde	the mind
5.2.32; 2318	on thy foes	on my Foes
5.2.80; 2366	ply	play
5.2.97; 2383	I will be	Ile be
5.2.150; 2437	But[42]	Tut
5.3.17; 2515	moe ſunnes[43]	more Suns
5.3.48; 2552	mabe me dlind[44]	made me blind
5.3.92; 2597	kind commiſeration[45]	kind hand Commiſeration
5.3.95; 2600	Then noble[46]	This Noble
5.3.108; 2613	and I am the turned[47]	And I am turned
5.3.170; 2675	Doe them that	Do him that
5.3.170; 2675	leaue of them	leaue of him
5.3.189; 2694	ſonle	Soule
5.3.197; 2702	birds to prey	Birds of prey
5.3.198; 2703	beaſtly	Beaſt-like
2706	By whom[48]	From whom

Most of these deviant readings can be put down to compositorial error: dittography (TLN 203); anticipation (TLN 436); misspellings (TLN 568, 651, 684, 696); foul case (TLN 253, 1341, 1589); mistaken attempts at emendation (TLN 1114, 2613); and others that are inexplicable, as in TLN 2597 and the banal TLN 1607. A few variants may however be authorial changes, either initiated by the dramatist or accepted by him in the course of performances, such as TLN 121, 2302, and 2703; and possible TLN 755, though it is perhaps a compositorial sophistication to substitute "yelping" for "yellowing." The change at TLN 1755 is clearly to be traced to censorship. In addition to these variants, F1 also adds and omits a few verse lines. Two such lines, not in any of the Qq, are added:

| 1.1.398; 443 | Yes, and will Nobly him remunerate. |
| 4.1.36–37; 1580 | What booke? |

The first of these lines two is accepted as authentically Shakespearean, and modern editors since the original Cambridge edition have included it in their texts. Many have assigned it to Marcus as an appropriate response to Titus's question in the immediately preceding two lines. Others—Wilson, Maxwell, and Waith—have followed F1 in treating it as Titus's own response to his presumably rhetorical question. The anomolous "What booke?" has generally been excluded by editors on the reasonable assumption that it represents an anticipation of the same expression in 4.1.41; 1585 and is inappropriate following 4.1.36; 1579.

Eight lines or part-lines that occur in one or more of Qq are not found in F1. These lines are cited from Q3, or, when absent from that text, from Q2:

2.1.102; omitted after 663	That both ſhould ſpeede?
3.1.35; omitted from 1171	yet pleade I muſt. (Q2)
3.1.36; omitted after 1171	All bootleſſ vnto them.
4.2.8; omitted after 1687	*Puer.* That you are both decipherd, that's the newes,
4.2.76; omitted after 1759	*Aron.* Villaine, I haue done thy mother.
4.4.102; omitted after 2097	Euen at his *Fathers* houſe the old *Andronicus.* (Q2)
5.2.161; omitted after 2448	And ſtop their mouthes if they begin to cry.
5.3.51; omitted after 2554	To doe this outrage, and it is now done.

Q1 and Q2 have "it now is done," the reading preferred by modern editors.

In the above comparison of readings from Qq with the corresponding passages in F1, the latter is represented by Hinman's facsimile edition. In that edition he set out to reproduce "an ideal copy" of F1, one in which "every page . . . represents the latest or most fully corrected state of the text . . . to give concrete representation to what has hitherto been only a theoretical entity, an abstraction." As part of his monumental study of the collection of Folios in the Folger Shakespeare Library, he comprehensively examined the proofreading and correction of each of the plays in "fifty-odd copies of the Folio throughout and about seventy-five copies through certain parts of the volume." Not all F1 pages were originally proofread by any means, and in some cases the F1 proofreader overlooked compositorial errors. The resulting corrections did not always actually "correct" the text that was proofed, sometimes resulting in a more egregious and even impenetrable reading than in the uncorrected state. It is evident that the objective of the proofreader was to find and have corrected manifest typographical infelicities such as inverted letters and inked quads, and that he was "largely indifferent to the accuracy of his text" as a reflection of what Shakespeare had actually written. Fortunately for students of *Titus Andronicus*, Hinman found that "the proofreading that was done for the Folio was in a considerable measure confined to some six or eight plays [including *Titus*] in one section of the book [the Tragedies], and especially to material set by a particular compositor," the error-prone apprentice Compositor E.

As in general, in the particular case of *Titus* not all 22 Folio pages were proofread. The first page was set by the experienced Compositor B. Of the remaining twenty-one pages, all set by Compositor E, there is clear evidence that eleven were proofread and Hinman records seventy-three variants, a relatively high total. He points out that:

> Compositor E . . . made a great many simple literal errors. He made, indeed, errors of all kinds; and he made mistakes in correcting as well as in setting. But he would appear on the evidence to have been especially given to inversions and transpositions, to single-letter omissions, and to errors in spacing and pointing.[49]

Notes of various kinds appear in certain of the quarto copies. Adams lists about a dozen written in what he designates as "a sixteenth—or early seventeenth century hand" in Q1, varying from the minimal correction of single letters not cleanly printed, or not printed at all, to the substitution on B1^v of "exequies" for "obsequies"; the correction of "alter" on D3^r to "after"; the correction on H3^v of "mrlodie" to "melodie"; and the emendation on D4^v of the phrase "bereaud in blood" to "heere reav'd of lyfe."[50]

On the flyleaf of the Malone copy of Q3 (Barlett and Pollard no. 1191) now in the Bodleian Library, is written the following in what seems to be Malone's own hand.

> Langbaine appears to have possessed an edition of this play printed in 4to in 1594. "This play (says he) was first printed 4to Lond[on] 1594 and acted by the Earls of Darby Pembroke and *Essex*, their servants." Doubtless he had it before him.[51] The description of the Companies by whom it was plaid, is different both from the enumeration of the edit. in 1600 and that at the head of A2 1611. In the year 1800, a copy of this play, printed in 1600, was discovered in the Duke of Bridgewater's Library at Ashridge, which has been since removed to London. I have collated the present copy with it, and the variations are set downe [at the foot of the pages in which they occur].[52] No other copy of the edition of 1600, except this of the D. of B's, is known to exist; nor was it ever seen by any of the editors of Shakespeare before 1800. The title of the edition of 1600, which is in 4to, is as follows:

and he copies the title page of Q2. On [A1^v] is noted the following:

In the year 1800 a copy of this p

The folio copy of this play, 1623, was
printed from this edition of 1611; as
appears from a line in Signat. E2: 1.2

A craftier Tereus hast thou met—

which in the folio copy is followed.
    The word which is necessary to com-
plete the metre (cousin) was inad-
vertantly omitted by the compositor
in this edition of 1611, but is found
in that of 1600.
    A craftier Tereus, *cozen,* has thou
                                                met.

The title page of the Kemble-Devonshire-Huntington copy (Bartlett and
Pollard no. 1199) now in the Folger Library bears this notation:

Collated
    &
Perfect.
J.P.K. 1798.
The M. S. variations
in the margins of
this play are from
the Rev.^d Mr. Todd's
collation with the
Duke of Bridge
water's copy *4to*
1600, which was
lately found in
his Grace's library
at Ashridge.
        J.P.K. 1803.[53]

In the Huntington (Sotheby-Church) copy of Q3 (Bartlett and Pollard
no. 1201) on sig. [A1^v], there is a partial dramatis personae, listing in a
seventeenth-century hand the thirteen principal characters.
    On the title page of the National Library of Scotland copy of Q3 (Bart-
lett and Pollard no. 1196) is written, in what may be Steevens's hand, the
single word "Shakespear." On sig. A2^r in the opening stage direction the
word "Trumpet" is underlined and in the margin is noted "Colours,"
which is the reading of the stage direction in F. Following the comma
after "Capitoll" (1.1.12, Waith ed.), a caret has been inserted and, in the
margin, following another caret is a colon, which is the punctuation of F.

Another caret is inserted in the next line after the "o" in "approach," the spelling of Qq, and in the margin is noted the letter "a," which indicates the F spelling: "approach." There is also a dash and a comma in the margin opposite the next line (1.1.14). The dash seems to be intended to refer to the poorly inked "e" in "The," the first word of the line; and the comma to the lower element of a possible semicolon following the word "vertue." The upper element is a clear period, but neither element is as bold as the commas and periods elsewhere on the page. On adjacent pages there are other likely inked and similarly shaped commas, but the nearest semicolon (on sig. B2ᵛ) exhibits a light upper element and a heavily inked comma. On sig. A2ᵛ there is a caret before a letter "o" in the margin, and a similar caret within the adjacent line after the letter "i" in *Pius* (1.1.23). F reads *Pious*.

On the margin of sig. A3ʳ, there are four notations. Opposite the word "waid" (1.1.55), is noted "weigh'd"; before the Q1 stage direction (1.1.63.1) there is a caret and in the margin "Flouriſh"; and in the next stage direction (1.1.69.2) "and then" is underlined and in the margin is noted "after them", all three of which follow the F text, where it differs from Qq. The fourth notation on this page is the letter "u" in the margin opposite the underlined letter in "Demetrius." The two terminal letters are defectively inked, and the "u" in Demetrius resembles an "n" in this particular copy of Q3, though not in the other copies. On A3ᵛ in the margin opposite the word "earthy" (1.1.99) which is underlined, is written "eathly" *(sic)*. Though misspelled, there can be little doubt that "earthly," which is the reading of F, was the word intended. On A4ʳ in the margin is noted the letter "o" opposite the word "conquerer" (1.1.104), which reflects F's "Conqueror"; and four lines later the letter "s" appears in the margin opposite a caret after the word "ſonne" in the text. Qq reads "ſonne"; F has "ſonnes." All of the notations in this copy of Q3 are made in ink in simulated printing in a hand that does not appear to be Steevens's.

The annotator clearly was collating this quarto with a copy of the Folio, but only in these first five pages. There are no similar notations anywhere else in this copy of Q3. On the title page of the copy in the Bibliotheca Bodmeriana is the signature of George Steevens. Bartlett and Pollard record this copy (no. 1204) as originally belonging to him, and authenticate the signature. There are no signs of collation with the other texts. A few other copies of Q3 have modern notations on preliminary pages—notably the Newberry copy (Bartlett and Pollard no. 1195), but they have no textual significance.

There are a number of events in the play concerning which scholars have raised questions and that some, notably Wilson, have determined to be insufficiently motivated or dramatically defective in one way or another. One such is the sacrifice of Alarbus, which is clearly presented by Titus as religious. Some commentators find this incredible, even though it has a warrant in ancient Greek literature. Another is Titus's nomination of Saturnius to be elected Emperor, rather than Bassianus, who is portrayed as being a better candidate. Critics have viewed this as an error on the part of Titus and consider it a flaw in the play. But Elizabethans would probably have recognized his selection as a legitimate exercise in primogeniture. Barnet, in his edition of the play, finds Titus's action "reasonable."[54] Lavinia's almost wordless acceptance of Saturnius's offer to make her his Empress has been called into question, but it should be noted that she is merely being a dutiful daughter, since her father, to whom the proposal was directed, has expressed himself as being pleased and highly honored, although he must have known she was engaged to Bassianus. She is similarly submissive when her betrothed bears her off in defiance of the Emperor and Titus.[55] Titus's stabbing of Mutius is found hard to accept, but many far-less-proud and even permissive fathers have considered it necessary to discipline their sons by subjecting them to physical punishment. Titus manifestly demands ungrudging acquiescence on the part of his family in his acceptance of Saturnius's offer, and any holding back is to him not merely disobedience but close to treason. He in fact calls his sons traitors (1.1.349, Waith ed.), says his honor has been wounded, and when he finally reluctantly consents to Mutius's interment in the family tomb, he says bitterly

> The dismall'st day is this that e'er I saw,
> To be dishonoured by my sons in Rome.
> Well, bury him, and bury me the next.

> (1.1.384–86)

Given Titus's concept of honor, his action, though extreme, seems adequately motivated.

Dover Wilson considers it an anomaly that "though Tamora is Queen of the defeated Goths, it is to the Goths that Lucius son of Titus repairs to enlist help and raise an army against her and the emperor her husband."[56] Titus directs Lucius to turn to the Gothic army for help presumably because Saturnius controls the Roman forces; and the Gothic princes accept Lucius probably because his knowledge of Rome and its defenses will be an asset to their expedition. It seems clear that they have disowned Tamora because she has gone over to the enemy. One Goth aspires to "be avenged on cursed Tamora" (5.1.16, Waith ed.). Both parties are prepared to make adjustments to enhance their chances of victory. None of this is seriously anomalous.

In regard to Tamora's speech as a response to Saturninus's diatribe against Titus's having shot arrows to heaven for redress of his grievances

(4.4.1–38, Waith ed.), in which she first attempts to calm her husband and later speaks a revealing aside, Wilson queries: "Why pretend thus to Sat.? What relation has all this . . . to Aaron's flight to the Goths? . . . The speech seems to refer to some lost thread of the plot."[57] There is no lost thread. Her remarks at the end of the speech, indicated as an aside in F1, and followed by editors, makes clear her intent. She says:

> Why thus it shall become
> High-witted Tamora to glose with all;
> But, Titus I have touched thee to the quick;
> Thy life-blood out, if Aaron now be wise,
> Then is all safe, the anchor in the port.
>
> (4.4.34–38

She will "glose" (use fair words) to attain her objectives "with all," including, without compunction, Saturninus, over whom she wants to maintain her dominance. She has mortally wounded Titus, yet she plans to

> enchant the old Andronicus,
> With words more sweet and yet more dangerous
> Than baits to fish, or honey-stalks to sheep,
>
> (4.4.88–90)

And after having dispatched Aemilius as an emissary to Lucius and the Goths, she resolves

> Now will I to that old Andronicus,
> And temper him with all the art I have,
> To pluck proud Lucius from the warlike Goths.
>
> (4.4.107–9)

Once Titus's lifeblood is out, then everything is as Tamora would with it, "if Aaron now be wise." She has good reason to be concerned about Aaron's wisdom. Saturnius does not know of her part in the killing of Bassianus, and she is of course anxious that it should not be revealed. She knows Aaron and would not be surprised at his confession to Lucius in an effort to protect their illegitimate son. She is aware that, in the intensity of his feeling, he might disclose too much, which, in the event, he does, telling of her share in the responsibility for the ravishing of Lavinia by her sons:

> That codding spirit had they from their mother,
> As sure a card as ever won the set;
>
> (5.1.99–100)

Unfortunately for Tamora, the anchor is not in the port. But she proceeds on the basis of that assumption to approach Titus disguised as Revenge, accompanied by Chiron and Demetrius as her ministers, Rape and Murder. Their collective attempt to deceive Titus and persuade him to neutralize Lucius's military effort is unavailing. Despite the doubts of critics, Titus is, as he says, not mad—quite the contrary. He is very ingenious in leading Tamora on to believe that, as she desires, he is credulous, until she tries to take her sons with her when she proposes to return to Saturnius "about thy (i.e., Titus's) business," at which point he unequivocally responds:

> Nay, nay, let Rape and Murder stay with me,
> Or else I'll call my brother back again,
> And cleave to no revenge but Lucius.

(5.2.134–36)

Tamora and her sons agree to this, leading directly to the play's catastrophe, the Theyestean banquet.

THE
HISTORY
OF
TITUS ANDRONICUS,

The Renowned Roman General.

Who, after he had faved *Rome* by his Valour from being deftroyed by the barbarous *Goths*, and loft two-and-twenty of his valiant Sons in ten Years War, was, upon the Emperor's marrying the Queen of the *Goths*, put to Difgrace, and banifh'd; but being recall'd, the Emperor's Son by a firft Wife was murder'd by the Emprefs's Sons and a bloody Moor, and how charging it upon *Andronicus*'s Sons, tho' he cut off his Hand to redeem their Lives, they were murder'd in Prifon. How his fair Daughter *Lavinia* being ravifh'd by the Emprefs's Sons, they cut out her Tongue, and Hands off, &c. How *Andronicus* flew them, made Pyes of their Flefh, and prefented them to the Emperor and Emprefs; and then flew them alfo. With the miferable Death he put the wicked *Moor* to; then at her Requeft flew his Daughter and himfelf to avoid Torments.

Newly Tranflated from the *Italian* Copy printed at *Rome*.

London: Printed and Sold by C. *Dicey* in *Bow* Church-Yard, and at his Wholefale Warehoufe in *Northampton*.

Title page, chapbook, ca. 1536−64, entitled *The History of Titus Andronicus, The Renowned Roman General*. Reproduced by permission of the Folger Shakespeare Library.

5

Sources, Origins, Influences

Scholarly investigations of the underlying background of *Titus Andronicus* until the twentieth century were generally limited to the identification and elucidation of the many classical references in the play. Some effort was made to trace the origin of the story in early history, but no single source of the plot nor of the major incidents was identified. This is so in spite of the fact that at least two eminent literary commentators knew of the existence of the prose *History of Titus Andronicus, the Renowned Roman General;* and of the ballad entitled *The Lamentable and Tragical History of Titus Andronicus.* Richard Farmer, apparently alluding to the prose *History,* says: "I have seen in an old catalogue of Tales &c. the history of Titus Andronicus." Possibly the catalogue to which Farmer refers was the one printed in 1764 by Cluer Dicey and Richard Marshall. It includes a section headed "A Catalogue of Histories," one of which was *Titus Andronicus.* The histories listed were those that Dicey and Marshall had printed and that they offered for sale "in Aldermary Church-Yard, London."[1] Halliwell-Phillipps, in the course of a discussion of "the publishing evidences" bearing on the play, mentions "an excessively rare chap-book in my possession entitled, 'The History of Titus Andronicus, the Renowned Roman General . . . Newly Translated from the Italian copy printed at Rome,' 12 mo. Northhampton, n.d." He also notes that the ballad is in the chapbook and that it "was often reprinted."[2] The earliest surviving print of the ballad is in Richard Johnson's *Golden Garden of Princely Pleasures and Delicate Delights* (1620). It is included in Percy's *Reliques* (1765) and in other early volumes of ballads.[3] Both Farmer and Halliwell-Phillipps seem to regard the *History* as in the nature of an analog to the play, and neither makes an attempt to link the *History* to the play as source. Scholarly discussion of sources following that of Halliwell-Phillipps until the publication of Adams's facsimile is concerned mostly with speculations about the lost play *Titus and Vespacia,* ten performances of which are recorded in Henslowe's *Diary;* about the German *Tragoedia von Tito Andronico* and the Duth *Aran en Titus;* and possible Roman and Byzantine origins of the story of Titus.[4]

Adams first designated the *History* as the principal source of Shakespeare's play in his Introduction to the facsimile (1936) of the only extant copy of the first quarto in the Folger Shakespeare Library. Seemingly unaware of the fact that Halliwell-Phillipps had had a copy of the chapbook, he notes that "The source of *Titus Andronicus*—presumably some obscure pseudo-historical romance—has hitherto escaped the most painstaking search of scholars. However, I am now able to point to an early English rendering of that source in a unique chapbook entitled: 'The History of Titus Andronicus, The Renowned Roman General' . . . To this work is appended the well-known ballad headed: 'The Lamentable and Tragical History of Titus Andronicus' . . . The prose story [is] told as veracious history . . . The appended ballad, mainly based on the prose history even to the extent of verbal borrowings, shows unmistakable familiarity with the play, which it follows in important variations."[5]

The prose *History of Titus Andronicus* has been considered late Medieval pseudohistory. Traces of its Medieval origin may be seen in references in chapter 4 to a demand for combat against accusers and to a tournament of jousting. In the opening sentence of the tale, it is said that the events took place in the time of Theodosius, but Bullough tells us that a comparison of the incidents in the tale with those of the reign of Theodosius the Great (A.D. 379–95), and with those of his grandsons Theodosius II (A.D. 401–50), shows that the prose history has little correspondence with actual historical events. Nevertheless he thinks the *History* and its personages bear some resemblance to historical people and events scattered throughout late Roman history. Andronicus Comnenus, who was Emperor at Byzantium (1183–85), was a tyrant against whom the people rebelled, and before executing him they cut off his right hand. Bullough also believes that the Titus of the prose history "has something in common with Stilicho (early fifth century), who kept the barbarians at bay for many years and in the end was barbarously treated by the Emperor (Honorius) and others whom he had protected." He speculates that the tale may ultimately derive "from some semi-fictitious chronicle." The general impression is one of an amalgam of sensational historical events assembled from divergent sources.[6]

The concluding portion of the *History* (Chapters 5 and 6) is adapted from Ovid's story of Philomela as told in *Metamorphoses*, with some influence from Seneca's revenge tragedy *Thyestes*. The author took from Ovid the rape of Philomela by Tereus, altering some important elements to serve the needs of his own tale. In the *History*, as contrasted to the *Metamorphoses*, there are two ravishers who are abetted by a villainous Moor, and Lavinia not only loses her tongue, as does Philomela, but her hands are also cut off. She is freed by her attackers rather than being released from confinement by a member of her family and reveals the names of her tormentors by writing in sand, in comparison to Philomela's weaving. There are other differences of detail, but the general story line follows closely that in *Metamorphoses*. The vengeful banquet in which a parent is victimized by being made to eat the flesh of its own offspring of course occurs in Ovid's tale, but there are sufficient differences so that some scholars have leaned toward the opinion that the *History's* source may have been the somewhat similar incident in Seneca's play. No direct reference is made in the prose tale to either *Thyestes* or *Metamorphoses*. The cruel Moor is not in either of these identifiable sources of the *History*. He may well have been in the Italian original, if it existed, but in any event derives from a prevalent European tradition. According to Bullough, similar characters appear in Italian and French stories emphasizing the eroticism and cruelty of Moors, and versions were published in England in story and ballad form. In Bandello's *Novelle* (1554), there is a story of a cruel Moor that exhibits some affinities with the prose tale.[7]

The ballad printed with the *History* consists of thirty stanzas in the form of rhymed quatrains. It follows ballad traditions: for example, it has a military setting. The ghost of Titus tells the story beginning with the ten years' war against the Goths and ending with his own suicide at the Thyestean banquet. Adams, as cited above, concluded that the source of the ballad was the prose *History* with some influence from the play but in regard to this there is some disagreement among scholars. The relationships among the prose tale, *Titus Andronicus,* and the ballad are in fact not completely settled, and the question of the precise nature of those relationships is not yet finally determined to the satisfaction of all scholars. We can, however, arrive at answers that have a high degree of probability.

There are no incidents in the ballad that are not in either the *History* or the play, while the ballad exhibits important omissions. The early part of the prose tale, which relates the lifting of the siege of Rome as told in Chapters 1 and 2, excepting only the capture of the Queen of the Goths, is not in the ballad. The political content of Act 5 of the play is absent. These may possibly be considered prunings in the interest of compression, but there are also incidents within the framework of the story included in the *History* and *Titus Andronicus* that are not in the ballad. Lavinia's solitary wanderings in the forest in lamentation because of the loss of her betrothed, which in the *History* led to her undoing, is omitted, as is Aaron's spirited defense of his infant in the play. When the same incident occurs in both the tale and the play, the ballad sometimes parallels the *History* and sometimes the play.

It is evident that the relationships of the ballad to the *History* and the play are anomalous. It is in theory possible, though unlikely, that it stood intermediate between the prose tale and *Titus Andronicus;* or it may have been an amalgam of the other two versions. Sargent, who first systematically studied the prose tale and compared it to *Titus,* decides that the *History* was the original form of the story, which Shakespeare adapted in his play, and that the ballad, third in order, generally follows the *History* with a single minimal alteration under the influence of the play. According to his hypothesis, the alteration consists in a rearrangement in the ballad of the *History's* sequence of events in the plot against Bassianus and Lavinia so that the rape of Lavinia occurs after Bassianus's murder but before the execution of Titus's sons, which is the way the play proceeds. In the prose tale, the sons are executed before the rape. Sargent says that this result could have been achieved by changing the position of three quatrains. If those that are now twenty-first, twenty-second, and twenty-third were inserted between stanzas twelve and thirteen, this would make the ballad sequence agree with that in the prose tale without requiring any other alteration. Therefore, the opposite change could have occurred, placing them in their present position, which has the effect of making events in the ballad conform to the play. This he accepts as evidence of some influence of the play on the ballad. Sargent determines that

> the editor or printer of this edition had only to rearrange the pertinent stanzas in order to make the episodes proceed as in the play. At the conclusion of the ballad, where conformity with the play could not be achieved without rewriting the stanzas, the deaths occur exactly in the manner of the prose history, not as in the play. The status of the ballad is thus clear. Except for the relocation of some three quatrains in the present version it owes nothing to Shakespeare's play. The ballad is no more than a metrical compression of the prose history.[8]

This is much too sweeping. There are in fact a number of instances in which the ballad conforms to *Titus Andronicus* when the play differs from the prose story. The very killings at the Thyestean feast, which Sargent says occur in the ballad as in the *History* are, in fact quite different and are closer to the play than to the prose tale. The sequence of the deaths and the agent by whom they are accomplished differ. In the *History,* the Emperor and Empress are killed by Titus's friends after they have dispatched the Emperor's guards; and then they set the Moor "in the Ground to the middle alive, smeered him over with Honey, and so between the stinging of Bees and wasps and starving, he miserably ended his wretched Days." Titus kills Lavinia at her request to prevent the torments they expected and falls on his sword. In the ballad, Titus is the executioner, killing Lavinia first, then the Empress, the Emperor, and himself, and after his death the Moor is dealt with ("Alive they set him half into the Ground."). In the play, Titus stabs Lavinia and then the Empress, but the Emperor kills Titus and is in turn killed by Lucius. Aaron is then by Lucius's order "set . . . breast-deep in earth."

Not only the order of the deaths but also the avenger in the ballad varies significantly from the *History*—in the tale it is Titus's friends, in the ballad it is Titus himself—and while the sequence of the deaths in the ballad is not exactly the same as in the play, nevertheless it is significantly closer to the play than to the *History*.

Furthermore, the manner of the Moor's death in the ballad differs from that in the *History* but is identical to the death of Aaron in *Titus*. In all three versions the Moor is buried breast deep in the earth to starve, but in the prose tale he is in addition smeared with honey to be stung by bees and wasps, a feature in neither the ballad nor the play.

There are other instances in which the ballad follows the play. There is no direct reference in the *History* to the story of Philomela, and in fact the only literary allusion in connection with the rape of Lavinia is to the Biblical story of Suzanna and the elders. The Moor in the *History* counsels the Empress's sons "to make all sure . . . by cutting out her Tongue to hinder her telling Tales, and her Hands off to prevent her writing a Discovery." The fourteenth and fifteenth quatrains of the ballad reflect this passage, but an echo of the Philomela story is introduced in the fifteenth stanza:

Then both her Hands they basely cut off quite,
Whereby their Wickedness she could not write,
Nor with her Needle on her Sampler sow
The bloody Workers of her dismal Woe.

In the prose *History,* no mention is made of a sampler, nor is that specific term used for the weaving Philomela did to reveal Tereus's crime to Procne in Golding's *Metamorphosis.*[9] The word does occur in *Titus* when Marcus, finding the ravished and mutilated Lavinia, exclaims:

Fair Philomela, why, she but lost her tongue,
And in a tedious sampler sew'd her mind:

(12.4.38–39)

It is probable that the ballad writer took it from the play.

One of the most notable incidents in *Titus* is the masking scene, 5.2, in which Tamora visits Titus disguised as Revenge accompanied by her sons as her ministers, identified by Titus and later by Tamora as Rape and Murder. Although he recognized all three of them, Titus leads Tamora on, seeking an opportunity for vengeance. The ballad relates this incident thus:

The Empress thinking then that I was mad,
Like Furies she and both her Sons were glad,
So nam'd Revenge, and Rape, and Murder, they
To undermine and hear what I would say.

I fed their foolish Veins a little space,
Until my Friends did find a secret Place,
Where both her Sons unto a Post were bound,
Where just Revenge in cruel Sort I Found.[10]

There is no comparable incident in the *History*, nor even any mention of masking.

In the prose tale, after the murder of the Bassianus figure, his body is thrown into a pit previously prepared for that purpose. Two of Titus's sons fall into the pit and are found there, which is taken to be evidence of their responsibility for the crime. Their falling into the pit is an unhappy accident: "unluckily coming in the Way where the Pit was digged, they fell both in upon the dead Body, and could not by reason of the great Depth, get out." In the play, Aaron leads the two sons to the pit by promising to show them a sleeping panther. The ballad, concurring with the play, reads:

The cruel Moor did come that way as then
With my three *(sic)* Sons who fell into the Den

Subsequently, at Aaron's bidding, Titus sends his severed right hand to the Emperor to ransom his sons. The *History* says that

whilst he was rejoicing with the Hopes of their Delivery, a Hearse came to his Door with Guards, which made his aged Heart to tremble. The first Thing they presented him was his Hand, which they said would not be accepted; and the next was his three Sons beheaded. At this woful Sight, overcome with Grief, he fainted away on the dead Bodies.

In the play, his sons' heads, not their bodies are returned with Titus's hand (3.1.232–40). Except as to the number of sons, the ballad agrees with the play:

But as my Life did linger thus in vain,
They sent to me my bootless Hand again,
And therewithal the Heads of my three Sons.

In the *History*, Lavinia reveals the identity of her tormentors by writing in sand using a "wand." The play and the ballad both use the word "staff." The influence of the play on the ballad thus can be seen to be significant. Adams's conclusion that the ballad "shows unmistakable familiarity with the play" is amply justified.

A comparison of the *History* and *Titus Andronicus* shows that they share a good deal of common ground. Generally, the play lacks only the early incidents related in the *History*. Shakespeare does not employ any

of the events in Chapter 1 of the tale. Of Chapter 2 the play has only
the bringing of the Gothic prisoners to Rome. The sequence of Titus's
banishment and the uprising of the common people of Rome, forcing the
Emperor to recall him, which forms the first half of Chapter 2, is absent
from the play. From the middle of Chapter 3, commencing with the marriage of the Emperor to the Gothic queen and the Gothic plot to murder
the Emperor's son (in the play it is Bassianus, the Emperor's brother),
the play and the *History* run together. Of some thirty-five incidents comprising the last three and one-half chapters of the *History,* the play has
all but three. The exceptions are Titus's banishment and recall; Aaron's
banishment on the birth of Attava's black baby; and Lavinia's distracted
wanderings in the forests. All of the other incidents in the *History*—
including all those of significance to the essential action—are in the play.
This close incident-by-incident correspondence would appear to leave
little room for doubt that an assumed early print of the *History* was the
primary source from which Shakespeare developed his play (see
Appendix).

The events of the prose tale are freely adapted by the playwright to
his theatrical purpose. Incidents are transposed, changing the order of
events; motivations are altered; new incidents are introduced, such as
the sacrifice of Alarbus; and events are compressed. At the beginning of
the play, and again at the end, the playwright introduces political themes
different from those in the prose story. These changes are fairly typical
of Shakespeare's handling of source material. While both the play and
the *History* are tragedies in the Medieval sense, *Titus* is dramatic, while
the prose tale is clearly not in any sense. Nevertheless, the setting, the
principal narrative elements of the story, all of the most important characters, and some of the minor ones are already present in the *History.* The
fusion of the Ovidian story of Philomela with Thyestean elements had
already been accomplished by the writer of the *History.* Shakespeare
recognized these elements, enhanced and adapted them to his play,
molded them to his theatrical needs, adorned them with decorative, emblematic verse and numerous classical references, and transformed them
from narrative to drama.

It might seem from the discussion above that *The History of Titus
Andronicus* in a sixteenth-century form has been accepted as the primary
source of the play, but in fact scholars are not in agreement. The principal
students of Shakespeare's sources in the twentieth century adopt distinctly different points of view. Bullough designates the *History* as a
"Probable Source" and in his analysis says it "may well represent a major
source." He notes in regard to the first act that the dramatist rearranged
the incidents and supplemented them from other sources, which 'greatly
enriched the tale."[11] Muir, on the other hand, is studiedly agnostic, saying

"there is the difficulty of knowing whether *The History of Titus Andronicus,* published in the eighteenth century, was derived from, and was substantially the same as, Shakespeare's main source . . . [and adds that]
There is no trace of Elizabethan phraseology in the chapbook tale," a
statement that is at odds with the general opinion. He thinks "there may
well have been an Elizabethan version which served as Shakespeare's
source. But we cannot know whether the chapbook was contaminated by
memories of Shakespeare's play, or to what extent the Elizabethan version differed from its eighteenth-century successor."[12] In a book devoted
to a comprehensive study of the humanist cultural setting within which
Shakespeare worked, "the wide range of intellectual materials and opportunities open to him" and, specifically in regard to *Titus Andronicus,* to
the origins of "Shakespeare's over-all conception of tragic form," Jones
also examine the immediate sources of Shakespeare's plays. Concerning
the relationship of *Titus Andronicus* to the *History* he tells us that "the
chap-book . . . probably contains a version of the chief narrative source
. . . The tale throws valuable light on Shakespeare's aims and methods
in this early tragedy."[13] His conceptions of dramatic sources are discussed below.

Most editors of the play since Adams's facsimile edition and Sargent's
study have accepted the *History* in the form in which it has survived
as representing the most important source. Maxwell finds that "all the
differences between the prose story and the play are compatible with the
hypothesis that the former is substantially identical with the source of
the latter."[14] Barnet thinks it "likely" that the prose tale is the play's
source. He points out that if the *History* were indebted to the play it
would surely—in the eighteenth century—have made reference to Shakespeare; and more characters—Aaron for example—would have been
mentioned by name. He concludes that the surviving chapbook is a reprint of a much older piece that Shakespeare dramatized. Ribner says
that Sargent's conclusion is "now shared by most scholars," and Kermode
notes that "it is generally agreed that an ancestor of this chapbook was
the source of *Titus Andronicus.*" Munro, Cross, Bevington, and Waith
concur. Stanley Wells expresses some reservations. He notes that the
story is fictitious, and "Whether Shakespeare invented it is an open question: the same tale is told in both a ballad and chap-book which survive
only in eighteenth-century versions but which could derive from pre-
Shakespearian originals. Even if Shakespeare knew these works they
could have supplied only a skeletal narrative," and he notes that the play
"owe[s] much" to Ovid and "something" to Seneca.[15]

Commentators, other than editors and source students who have examined the play since Sargent, generally allude only briefly to the *History*
as source, sometimes in the context of directing attention to the way in

which the play differs from the tale. Spencer, noting that *Titus* presents what was "intended to be a faithful picture of Roman civilization" by sixteenth-century standards, rejects the idea that the play derives from authentic Roman historical accounts. Although he does not specifically cite the *History,* he notes that the play's "sources probably belong to medieval legend." Baldwin analyzes the chapbook version of the Titus story and compares it to the play. He concludes that "there can be no question that the chapbook represents the source." He also says that its "pseudo-historical setting" indicates that it is earlier than *Titus Andronicus.* Oppel, with some words of caution, accepts the "Prosa-Version" as a representative of Shakespeare's source although he believes that Shakespeare independently drew upon Seneca, Ovid, Plutarch, and Virgil. In his book-length examination of the relationship between the German *Tito Andronico* and Shakespeare's play, Braekman indicates that the *History* "is now generally recognized as representing the direct or, more likely, the indirect main source of the plot of *T[itus] A[ndronicus].*" Tricomi, contemplating the aesthetics of the mutilation of Lavinia, comments that her means of revelation of the names of the rapists derives from "a prose narrative, which in all probability Shakespeare knew." He finds "convincing" Sargent's evidence identifying the *History* as a source. Forker notes that the "eighteenth-century chap-book . . . is our closest analogue to the lost narrative from which . . . [Shakespeare's] tragedy derives." West does not overtly agree, but her citations of the tale in illumination of the text imply acceptance. In an essay on Shakespeare's use of Roman history, Simmons states that the *History* "is now believed to be a bibliographical recapitulation of Shakespeare's source." In assessing the contribution of the *History* to the composition of *Titus,* he finds that the tale "is independent of Shakespeare's play and yet affords a more cohesive source for its elements than the farrago of Ovid, Seneca, and Plutarch hitherto suggested." The prose work, he notes, evokes Tacitus and Suetonius showing corrupt imperial Rome in decline, a pessimistic view of the effete city in moral collapse. The alliance between Lucius and the Goths echoes Tacitus's account of Claudius's accommodation with the Gauls, which underlies Shakespeare's "affirmative restoration that at the denouement rises out of the tragic mangle."[16]

The *History,* though almost certainly the primary source of Shakespeare's play, is not the sole source. The classical content of *Titus Andronicus*—chiefly Latin though possibly (in at least two instances) Greek—is pervasive and varied, as has been pointed out by numerous commentators.[17] It is so extensive that it could not have been derived from the *History* alone; includes elements not in the prose tale; occurs continuously throughout the play; and takes many forms, including Latin quotations, elaborate allusion, casual reference, direct borrowing, paraphrase, the bringing of Ovid's *Metamorphoses* onto the stage, and a comment by Chiron that a verse just quoted is from Horace—he knows it well because he "read it in a grammar long ago" (4.2.22–23).[18] The origins of certain plot elements and classical ornamentation correspondingly differ. Thomson identifies Ovid's *Metamorphoses;* Seneca's *Thyestes, Phaedra,* and *Troades;* Virgil's *Aeneid* and maybe his *Georgics;* Horace's *Odes;* Plutarch's *Lives,* Cicero, Herodotus, Livy, possibly derived indirectly from encyclopedic synopses; and perhaps Euripides' *Hecuba* and Sophocles' *Ajax.*[19] Of these diverse origins the Ovidian and Senecan elements are of the greatest significance, but the precise degree of influence of Ovid and Seneca on *Titus* has been the subject of some debate. It seems probable that Shakespeare, having recognized the fusion of Ovidian and Senecan components in the *History,* returned to those sources, either by memory or by direct reference. He drew "Senecan" elements of his design from the plays and from *the History of Titus Andronicus,* perhaps from Plutrach, and possibly from the two Greek plays. He wrote *Titus Andronicus* in emulation of the most successful drama of its type then on the boards *(The Spanish Tragedy),* and though it bears the distinctive Shakespearean stamp, it is nevertheless conceptually indebted to Kyd's play.[20] Some of the well-known conventions observed in Seneca's plays are evident in *Titus,* such as the role of the confidant to the protagonist that Marcus Andronicus plays from time to time, and that of the Messenger. Most significant is the simple choice of the dramatist to write a revenge tragedy on a popular model that reflects Senecan drama.

Many scholars have accepted the validity of the Senecan source for *Titus Andronicus,* but a few evaluate Seneca's influence as of minor, or at least secondary, importance. Baker argues, partly in reaction to Cunliffe's position, that Shakespeare's play is in many important ways not Senecan at all. In an extended discussion of *Titus Andronicus, The Spanish Tragedy,* and Senecanism in drama, he develops the point by closely reasoned argument that many of the so-called "Senecan" qualities of *Titus* are drawn from English dramatic moralities and mysteries and from Medieval metrical tragedy. Discussing first the structure, Baker says: "The five acts, chorus, messenger . . . and ghost are, as I think it has been shown, either historically independent of Seneca or dependent upon enormously complicated influences. The most significant of the structural principles in the great English tragedy seem to be developed fairly directly from Medieval metrical tragedy." He then examines the essential qualities of Shakespeare's play in the light of the nondramatic tragic tradition and concludes that Medieval tragedy

> was meant to illustrate the essential horror of life and [to give] the reasons for a Contempt of the World morality. . . with this fundamental tradition as to the

nature of the tragic, it follows that any story of lavish violence could provide the crude stuff of drama, and that the violence enacted on the Elizabethan stage springs first of all from the adaptation of narrative stuffs to the needs of actors . . . The conception of the nature and form of tragedy was inherited from non-dramatic literature, while some incidental technique was borrowed from the older drama. To these principles, the contribution of Seneca, which I think was insignificant, must in any event have been secondary, as also the probably more important contribution of the contemporary French and Italian tragedy, itself subject in its classicism to modification by those same principles. It is, for example, primarily the medieval conception of what was tragic that motivates the slaughter at the end of *The Spanish Tragedy* . . . *Titus Andronicus* and *Hamlet*.[21]

Henry Wells examines Baker's assertions as well as Cunliffe's and concludes that neither has precisely assessed the influence of the Roman dramatist. He accepts Baker's conception that much of the supposedly "Senecan" element of *Titus* is drawn from Medieval sources rather than, as Cunliffe proposes, directly from Seneca's plays; but he also discerns unmediated Senecan influence in such matters as the philosophical attitudes in *Titus* and in the character of the protagonist.[22] It is clear that there is more than a little of Seneca in Shakespeare's play. Even though the earlier notion that the Elizabethan revenge tragedy had its roots substantially in Seneca has been effectively questioned, the contribution of the Roman playwright to the classical element of *Titus Andronicus* is nevertheless of some importance.

Shakespeare's debt to Seneca in *Titus* is, however, manifestly of less consequence than his obligation to Ovid. Thomson, a classical scholar, has demonstrated in his analyses of the content of the individual Shakespearean plays that Ovid's influence in several of his plays is of the first importance. He believes that Shakespeare knew the *Metamorphoses* in the original Latin as well as in Golding's translation. "Undoubtedly, he read a certain amount, perhaps a good deal, of Ovid in Ovid's own words."[23] That he was especially attracted to the *Metamorphoses* is evident in a number of his plays, but nowhere more explicitly than in *Titus*. In consideration of the Ovidian content in *The History of Titus Andronicus*, there can be no surprise that he repeatedly refers in the play to the tale of Philomela and Procne, mentioning Philomela specifically by name on six occasions, Tereus three times, and Procne once. Thomson concludes that Shakespeare "knows the *Metamorphoses* from end to end and clearly delights in its innumerable stories."[24]

Baker counts the many allusions to classical story in *Titus Andronicus* in an effort to determine the relative importance of the several Latin and Greek poets as sources:

allusions . . . furnish an excellent means of reconstructing the reading of—indeed the literary influences upon—the dramatist, and of checking upon a specific problem like that of the influence of Seneca. According to my count the distribution of fairly clear classical allusions is this: Ovid, sixteen (excluding the repeated references to Philomel); Virgil, fifteen; Livy-Painter, four; Horace, two (from Lyly's grammar); Seneca, two (both are short Latin tags from *Hippolytus*); and perhaps one or two from Homer, Sophocles, Euripides, Herodotus or Plutarch, and Cicero. This list reads, both in point of names and proportionate importance, remarkably like an Elizabethan pre-University curriculum; possibly it suggests as accurately as anything can the degree of the influence of Seneca on a typical [*sic*] author of a tragedy of blood . . . The tragedy . . . is to be understood as (and only as, I think) a purely Elizabethan transformation of the Philomela story.[25]

In this judgment, Baker fails to recognize that in the circumstances of the cannibal banquet in Act 5 there are as Maxwell notes, citing Brandl, points in which *Titus* is closer to *Thyestes*.

The summoning of Revenge from below (4.iii.38; 5.ii.3) recalls Seneca's apparitions from the underworld; two sons are served up at the banquet in both Seneca and *Titus*, and one has been guilty of ambition, whereas in Ovid there is one—innocent—victim; the mother is not the slayer either in Seneca or in *Titus*, as she is in Ovid. In Seneca as in *Titus*, there are elaborate preparations for the killing, the killer is also the cook (this is at most implied in Ovid), the feast is public, and the head is not shown.[26]

While Baker's fundamental hypothesis inhibits him from acknowledging the extent of Seneca's influence on *Titus*, he is nonetheless essentially right in his determination that Ovid is the more important of the two.[27]

As noted above, in the case of two allusions, Thomson discerns the influence of Euripedes and Sophocles. The first is a reference to the revenge taken by Hecuba on "the Thracian tyrant [Polymestor] in his tent" (1.1.136–38). Ovid retells the story but does not mention a tent. Thomson thinks Shakespeare therefore knew Euripides' *Hecuba*, possibly in a Latin translation. The second is an allusion to Ajax and "wise Laertes' son" [Ulysses] (1.1.379–81) derived from the *Ajax* of Sophocles. According to Thomson, it could not have come from *Metamorphoses* because Ovid depicts Ulysses as a villain, not as a chivalrous opponent.[28]

In comment upon Kittredge's discussion of the sources,[29] Law notes that there are a number of elements in the play for which Kittredge does not account. He includes the names of many of the *dramatis personae* and the political content, particularly of the first act. The source of Lavinia's name is identified by Law as Virgil's *Aenied;* that of the names Saturninus, Bassianus, and Demetrius is *The Breviary of Eutropius* possibly by way of some such intermediary as Nicolas Haward or Holinshed; and the names Titus, Marcus, Lucius, Martius, Quintus, Caius, Aemilies, Publius, and Sempronius come from "The Life of Scipio Africanus" in North's translation of Plutarch's *Parallel Lives*.[30] The name Mutius occurs in "The Life of Tiberius." In addition, Law lists a number of parallels of incident between Plutarch's "Life of Scipio" and *Titus,* mostly military and political, and notes the reference in the play to Coriolanus that he also links to *the Parallel Lives.* He directs attention to the description of the vale of Ampsanctus in the *Aeneid,* which is "analogous" to Tamora's "barren detested vale" in 2.3; and to a passage in *Thyestes* that describes the disarrangement of the zodiacal signs upon the occasion of Atreus's murder of his brother's sons (the passage also includes the name Chiron) that he thinks inspired the incident of a similar disorder described in the arrow shooting scene in *Titus* (4.3.65–72). He sums up that "we must add to the . . . classical sources suggested by Kittredge two others," the *Aeneid* and Plutarch's "Life of Scipio Africanus."[31]

Jones identifies a structural parallel between *Titus Andronicus* and Euripedes's *Hecuba.* Each play "falls into two clearly marked movements" In both, the early action depicts "a series of stages marked by increasing pain and suffering," reaching a climax of woe, at which point there is a pause followed by an abrupt change of direction. The principals—Titus and Hecuba—alter their stance from one of tragic yet passive grief to one of active search for the means of revenge. Jones compares the development of the plot to the swing of a pendulum, moving first toward a climacteric of grief succeeded by a slow reverse in direction accelerating toward the relief of revenge accomplished, followed by a slowing detachment. There are intermediate similarities in event such as the sacrifices of Alarbus and Polyxena, the deaths of Lavinia and Polydorus, the madness of Titus and Hecuba, and the revenge taken on Tamora and Polymestor. Jones is aware of the prevailing critical opinion that Shakespeare knew little or nothing of Greek tragedy at first hand, but he reminds us that *Hecuba* was frequently translated into Latin, and Shakespeare's "small Latine" was sufficient for him to have read one of the translations, and not necessarily in the version by Seneca. Shakespeare may have been led to Euripides's play by Sir Philip Sidney's discussion of the myth in his *Apology for Poetry* (published in 1595, but "Shakespeare may have had access to it in manuscript"); or he may have been directed to it if he had a copy of Ovid's *Metamorphoses* with notes by Raphael Regius, one of which cites "Euripidis Hecuba." Jones believes it likely that Shakespeare read *Hecuba* at school in Erasmus's translation and, in support, he points out that an Erasmian proverb that occurs in both his *Adagia* and *The Praise of Folly* "is quoted in the last scene of *Titus Andronicus*" (5.3.117). Both plays have

> an action divisible into two parts, the first dominated by grief, the second by revenge, in both the transition from first to second part being similarly rapid and decisive. Moreover, the *relation* between the two parts is also very similar,

for the Euripidean theme of 'the growing of sorrow into hatred and of lamentation into a desire for revenge' finds a strong echo in Shakespeare.

Jones notes that conclusive evidence that Shakespeare, in writing *Titus Andronicus,* made use of Euripides's original does not exist; but he may have seen it, or a version of it, acted. Shakespeare's play, although "Roman," may have been perceived by at least some of his audience as 'Greek," in fact Thracian—"Thrace was a land of wild passions and fierce inhuman cruelty." Human sacrifice is Greek, not Roman. In support of his hypothesis, he points out that *Julius Caesar* also exhibits "Euripidean influence" in the quarrel scene between Brutus and Cassius, a reflection of a similar quarrel between Menelaus and Agamemnon in *Iphigenia in Aulis.* Perhaps a comment by Dover Wilson may serve to place in context these classical sources and potential sources: "There are at least two scenes in *Titus* which only a classical scholar could fully understand . . . 4.2 and 4.3."[32]

In addition to *The Spanish Tragedy,* several other contemporary dramatic sources have been suggested. One is Marlowe's *Jew of Malta,* primarily in the general conception of the character of Shakespeare's Aaron, but also specifically in the catalog of horrors Aaron committed, including his boast (5.1.135–40) that he set up dead men before their friends' doors, an incident that, Kirschbaum reminds us, occurs on stage in Marlowe's play. Charney identifies some minor reflections of *Tamburlaine* in Aaron but even more significant influences of Barabas and, especially, Ithamore, on Shakespeare's Moor.[33] Ettin conjectures that there is a Marlovian link between Titus's killing of Mutius and Tamburlaine's slaying of his son Calyphas.[34] Harvey, while acknowledging that Seneca's *Troades* is probably the source of the sacrifice of Alarbus, demonstrates that the pattern of action in *Titus* is extraordinarily similar to the structural pattern of the slaughter of the Innocents in the Shearman and Taylor's play of the Coventry cycle.[35] The lost play that Henslowe, in his *diary,* variously designates "tittus & vespacia," "titus & vespacia," "titvs", "tittus," and "titus," was performed at the Rose ten times by Strange's Men between 11 April 1592, when it was marked "ne" (probably for *new),* and 25 January 1593. The last performance is dated almost exactly one year before the first recorded presentation of "titus & ondronicus" by Sussex's Men on 23 January 1594.[36] There was much speculation among early critics that the first play, the correct title of which is accepted to be *Titus and Vespasian,* was a predecessor of *Titus Andronicus,* the latter thought to be the result of a recast, possibly by Shakespeare, or by a collaboration including him. The most important arguments put forth in support of this conjecture are the common ground of the titles, especially since Lucius in the German version is named Vespasianus; the example of Shakespearean rewriting of earlier texts as in *King John, Hamlet* and *King Lear;* and the palpable disparity in style between Act 1 and the rest of the play, taken to be evidence that that act was only lightly revised from the original as compared to the other acts, which are assumed to have been more comprehensively rewritten. The argument from *King John* has been rejected by some students of the play. *The Troublesome Reign of King John* is considered to be either a bad quarto version of an authentic text or a "derivative play" rather than a source; but this has been disputed. In the case of the earlier *Hamlet,* the text is lost and cannot be studied. Therefore, its relationship to Shakespeare's play is indeterminable. No one denies the connection between the extant *King Leir* and Shakespeare's tragedy: he worked from the earlier play. However, the *Leir-Lear* situation at most shows that *Titus Andronicus could* have been based on *Titus and Vespasian,* but not that it was. In fact, since *Titus and Vespasian* has not come down to us, the *Hamlet* parallel is more apt than that to *Lear* and raises the same questions.[37]

Scholarly opinion began running against the *Titus and Vespasian* hypothesis in the early years of this century. Greg says that the assumption that *Titus and Vespasian* "was an earlier version of *Titus Andronicus* . . . is open to doubt. It is difficult to believe that the title could have been given to any play not connected with the siege of Jerusalem . . . the German play is never called *Titus and Vespasian* . . . [and] the part of Vespasianus (Lucius) is quite subordinate."[38] However, Chambers points out that Strange's men already had a play—now lost—entitled *Jerusalem,* which was presented twice in 1592 at about the same time that *Titus and Vespasian* was being performed. Although its subject is, of course, unknown except for what might be deduced from the title, it tends to reflect adversely on Greg's line of argument. Furthermore, Chambers continues, "the appearance of a *Titus and Vespasian* [referring to *Titus Andronicus*] in a Revels list of plays about 1619 . . . gives some confirmation to the view that the titles are equivalent . . . [but] the theory of a play written . . . in 1592, and then revised in 1594, is not without its own difficulties. It is a short interval for a play to become out of date in." Adams also finds it "difficult to believe that Strange's *Titus and Vespasian* did not dramatize the very popular story of that name relating to the destruction of Jerusalem by Vespasian and his famous son Titus."[39] Dover Wilson characterizes the identification as "the tiresome business of the lost play *Titus and Vespasian.*" Maxwell considers it to be a Mare's nest . . . In spite of all the ink that has been spilt on the subject I can see no reason to reject the obvious explanation that *Titus and Vaspasian* . . . was a play about the two Flavian emperors, probably dealing with the destruction of Jerusalem." The level of interest on the part of most recent editors in the conception of a linkage between *Titus and Vespasian* and

Titus Andronicus may be gauged by the fact that Ribner, Cross, Bevington, and Stanley Wells do not even mention the earlier play; Kermode thinks that the "evidence is probably worthless"; and Waith notes that *Titus and Vespasian* "is more likely to have been about the two Roman emperors who were the subject of a romance with that name."[40] Proudfoot finds that a line spoken by Barabas in *The Jew of Malta*—"Till Titus and Vespasian conquer'd vs"—reveals that the Rose audience was familiar with the story of the Flavian conquest of Jerusalem, which they may have known from the play designated by Henslowe simply as *Jerusalem,* that was "about the emperor Vespasian and his son Titus," and not about the story of Titus Andronicus.[41] The stylistic anomaly of Act 1 has been explained as an effort by Shakespeare to employ a formal, ceremonial diction perhaps in emulation of Peele.

In the introduction to his edition of the anonymous play *Edmund Ironside,* extant in an undated manuscript, Sams makes an attempt to establish Shakespeare as the author. In this it is judged that he is not successful, but he does demonstrate some potential and previously unexplained affinities between *Ironside* and *Titus.* At one point he states that "either Shakespeare plagiarized *Ironside* or he wrote it;" and again, "*Titus* is perhaps, in some sense, a rewriting of *Ironside.*"[42] These assertions are based on a comprehensive examination of similar incidents in the two plays; likenesses in staging, in style, and in rhetorical devices; correspondences of phrasing, of which Sams lists half a hundred, a few identical, though mostly commonplace, others lightly variant ("Causeless flight"–"fly, causeless"), and miscellaneous resemblances. Although Sams attempts to infuse into his presentation a favorable comparison to the example of R. W. Chambers's work on *Sir Thomas More,* most of his examples are not as striking as those of Chambers and can be readily explained in ways other than assuming that Shakespeare in *Titus* rewrote *Ironside.* His reasoning in regard to the relative dates of the two plays rests on a series of assumptions. He cites an earlier conclusion of Everitt that "the brawling scene [in *Ironside*] between the two archbishops . . . could not have passed the licensers after November 12, 1589 when the privy Council instructed the Archbishop of Canterbury to join the Lord Mayor of London and the Master of the Revels to scrutinize all books and plays then being used by the players."[43] The inference is that the action recommended by the Council was initiated immediately, but, in spite of the Council's expressed wish that it be done "with some speed," there is no evidence that it was or that they really wanted it to be. The Council may have been trying to placate the City in response to their plea for control of the theaters without actually acceding to the request, as they seem to have done on other occasions. Nevertheless, this leads Sams to the further assumption that *Ironside* "could hardly have been

. . . written or even contemplated by any practising playwright at any time between November 1589 and June 1594 . . . we must look for it in or before 1589." Hence, such elements shared by *Ironside* and *Titus Andronicus* must have originated with *Ironside*. This series of deductions is patently weak. The truth is that we do not have conclusive evidence as to which of the two plays is the earlier, and therefore which may be presumed to be the borrower and which the lender. However, Foster, a thoughtful critic who reviewed Sams's edition of *Ironside* and engaged in a subsequent exchange of correspondence with him, says that "it seems likely that *Ironside* is indeed the source" and that "Fragments of *Ironside* source-material appear in *Titus*." He concludes that "the pattern of borrowing in this case indicates quite clearly that *Ironside* was a direct source for *Titus Andronicus*." He does not, however, attempt to support his conclusions with argument.[44]

Mincoff put forth in 1971 a novel theory concerning the relationships among *Titus Andronicus,* the *History,* and the ballad. "Since . . . Sargent's article," he says, "it has generally been accepted—with excessive credulity—that the source of Shakespeare's first tragedy is preserved in the chapbook . . . prose 'history.'" Starting from the *Stationers' Register* entry by John Danter, which Mincoff thinks may have been intended to cover all three versions, he weaves an argument that the sequence of composition began with the play first, the story of which was apparently invented by Shakespeare. As with other plays it inspired the ballad— "the author of the ballad knew the play well." This was followed by the *History,* which was composed last as a "re-expansion from the ballad made by someone unfamiliar with the play . . . a companion piece to the ballad, to be published together with it in order to fill in the gaps left by the rather allusive ballad style." Concerning the true source of the play he notes that "it has yet to be found, though I suspect one need seek no further than *the Spanish Tragedy,* with a hint or two from Bandello."

In support of his conjectural construction of the order of the texts, Mincoff adduces some evidence, most notably as set forth in his statement that "there is not one single point beyond what is contained in the ballad that clearly connects Shakespeare's play with the history." This innovative hypothesis, otherwise unknown in Shakespearean studies, seemed worthy of examination. In studying it, I came to the conclusion that it was vulnerable in several ways but especially in Mincoff's assertion that the *History* and the play were unconnected. It proved possible to show that in seven instances of significance (Waith later added an eighth) there are elements common to *Titus* and the *History* that are absent from the ballad, so that the ballad therefore could not possibly have served as the source of the *History*. His less-prominent but in reality more-important conception—that the play is the original and the *History* derivative—also fails under scrutiny. It is clear that the *History* is not a re-expansion of the ballad because the *History* includes important story elements missing from the ballad; that the latter, exhibiting the influence of both the play and the tale, is tertiary in the sequence; and that the *History*, which exhibits no familiarity with Shakespeare's version, nor manifestly with the ballad, must have preceded the other two. The true order of the texts is therefore *History*—play—ballad.[45] Seconding Mincoff's supposition of the sequence of the texts, Hunter joined in the debate in the 1983 paper[46] that concentrates on the seven story elements to which I had drawn attention and that are common to the tale and the play but absent from the ballad. Hunter's method is to raise objections to specific items of language; to debate small collocations; to emphasize the significance of the allusive tradition of ballad writing, which tends to leave important matters unstated for the reader to infer; to explain away significant points as merely *topoi;* to question whether a confession (Aaron's) is a true confession or a process of self-glorification; and to excuse the absence of a plot element from the ballad as something that anyone could readily deduce. He finds it necessary to acknowledge the validity of four of my seven points, couched in a "yes, but" mode, which leaves the main thrust of my argument unaffected. In the course of a response published in 1988, each of Hunter's challenges is taken up in order, and, I believe, adequately answered.[47]

In a more considerable essay,[48] the last portion of which is genuinely illuminating on the underlying origins (as distinguished from the immediate sources) of *Titus Andronicus* in Roman history and literature, Hunter again champions, this time more comprehensively, Mincoff's theory of the sequence of the texts. In his exordium, he sets forth a series of propositions apparently designed to set the reader's mind to be receptive to what he intends to purvey. "The belief that Shakespeare preferred to 'borrow' his plots instead of 'inventing' them . . . might seem difficult to sustain in the face of the complex picture of adaptation and refashioning we find . . . in Muir's *Shakespeare's Sources*" and other studies. Nevertheless, a preference persists for "a Shakespeare with a passive relationship to the cultural context within which he worked." Hunter cites the comment of Fuller (in 1901) to the effect that while no explicit source for the play had been found, it was probably some "novel of Titus Andronicus;" and he notes the subsequent citation of the *History* by Adams, which was later studied by Sargent. "The so-called 'prose history' of Titus Andronicus . . . thus appears," says Hunter, "as a kind of Messiah, an answer to a mythic need. It behooves the rational mind to examine such fulfilments of prophecy with the utmost scepticism . . . I take for granted," he continues, that there is "no hard evidence" that the extant prose tale represents the source. "Mincoff's alternative . . . has at least as much probability, even if less mythic resonance." A number of broad-side ballads were based on Shakespearean plays, and the Titus ballad was probably written "to cash in on the [popularity of the] play." Such ephem-era conform to the requirements of a different genre and do lack motiva-tion and connections between events, but these characteristics "cannot be used to point to a particular position in a chain of sources." What is essential in the ballad "is our grasp on Titus's emotional state," and the genre requires everything else to be subordinate. The *History* "is clearly enough organizing the focus to procure a different kind of unity . . . The generic focus that seems most relevant is that of history in a narrow or scholarly sense . . . this is a work with its own rationale, not simply a link in a chain of versions." Hunter reviews the "historical" element of the prose tale, drawing attention to the reflection in the chapbook version of actual recorded events and favorably comparing certain passages to similar descriptions in Gibbon to exhibit the degree of detailed historical knowledge the author of the *History* possessed. This attainment was "a rare commodity in the Elizabethan period and the odds seem to me to lie against a chapbook writer having access to them in the years before the publication of *Titus Andronicus.*" He also notes the authors' historical attitude "as he substitutes for the impressive bareness of the ballad a system of explanations, a set of political and prudential motives, and a careful sequential ordering." The prose historian provides motivation in place of ballad inconsequence, "show[ing] that the bizarre story in the ballad is as capable of explanation as other bizarre episodes that histori-ans (such as Gibbon) deal with." At the end of the second part of his paper, Hunter concludes that while the mode of the play is "undoubtedly spectacular . . . [nevertheless it]

> reveals a mind not simply seeking spectacle but everywhere using the spectacu-lar to indicate the general lesson of Roman history and, even further, the rela-tionship of primitive and decadent, whenever and wherever they occur. That this was a task whose achievement was entirely worthy of Shakespeare's inven-tive powers seems to me not to be open to doubt.

Some elements of Hunter's argument are unexceptionable—for exam-ple, his estimate of Shakespeare's dramatic capability and inventive pow-ers—but it is difficult to see how such generalized statements serve to advance Mincoff's conjectures about the source of *Titus Andronicus.* Other artfully worded comments are manifestly designed to prejudice the reader against the *History* as source. His evocation of the genre differ-ences between the ballad and the prose tale are fairly presented and supported by a considerable display of erudition. This might have been persuasive (except for Hunter's enviable intimacy with the thinking of the anonymous "ballad writer" and the equally anonymous "prose historian") were it not for the fact that the posited foundation—that there is no evidence of a connection between the *History* and the play—is, in spite of what he says about taking it for granted, most unlikely to be allowed to him (see appendix). In effect, lacking evidence to support Mincoff's sequence, Hunter assumes it and then shows how it *could* have come about. This is a far cry from an acceptable probability, let alone proof. It fails for the same reason as his earlier paper did. Hunter has neither proved Mincoff's theory nor disproved the findings of Adams and Sargent.

Wells, in a review of the Hibbard festschrift, finds Hunter's proposition an exercise in disdain: "Hunter somewhat haughtily dismisses the theory that an earlier printing of the eighteenth-century chapbook on *Titus Andronicus* was the source of Shakespeare's play as wishful thinking on the part of most scholars.[49]

In his edition of the play, Waith reviews both theories as to the order of the texts.[50] He says in summary that Hunter shows that "some of . . . [my seven plot] elements are indeed in the ballad, some are standard *topoi,* and some do not constitute genuine connections . . . the omission in the ballad of Titus' invitation to the Emperor and Empress proves nothing about indebtedness." Waith then reviews directly the sequences of events in each of the three versions, their differences and similarities, and comes to some conclusions. In the instance of the plot against the Andronici, the play is tightly woven, whereas the *History* is diffuse. "It is much easier to imagine Shakespeare improving on this story than the history-writer disassembling the tightly-knotted strands of Shakespeare's plot . . . The combination in the ballad of resemblances to both the play and the prose history is most easily explained by the assumption that the ballad writer knew both . . . if the author of the history knew the play, he omitted the telling episode of Aaron's defense of his child," and substituted a "fantastic" explanation. Therefore, he probably did not know the play. In the matter of the confusion in all three versions of the number of Titus's surviving sons, the "careless inconsistency [of the *History*] could have led to the two versions of the ballad, and the prominent 'Loss of two and twenty of his valiant sons' in the heading of Chapter 2 would initially have fixed that figure in Shakespeare's mind. Once again it is easier to see Shakespeare improving on the plot of the history than to understand what the history-writer would have thought to gain by altering these details. My conclusion is that the most probable order is history-play-ballad," which is indeed the determination of all but a few students of the sources of Shakespeare's earliest tragedy.[51]

The most significant of the influences on *Titus Andronicus,* as distinct from sources and origins, is the Vice of Medieval and early Renaissance drama whose personification in the play is Aaron. Numerous critics have pointed out this possibility,[52] but the most comprehensive discussion of the Vice in Shakespeare is that by Spivack.[53] He analyzes four exemplars of a specific type of Vice in the plays; Aaron, Richard III, Don John in *Much Ado,* and Iago. Spivack's book concentrates, as may have been expected, on Iago, but Aaron is fully treated. The character developed from Medieval allegory, "Especially that central type of Christian allegory known as the Psychoamachia, in which the personified forces of good and evil contend for possession of the human soul." The moral play developed from the allegory and "for two centuries provided a type of drama whose purpose and method were homiletic," in a broad sense. In these plays the "sardonic intriguer," who brought about "the spiritual and physical ruin of frail humanity" was known by such names as "Envy, Avarice, Sensual Suggestion, and Ill-Report . . . [all] enveloped within his generic title of *The Vice.*" Shakespeare's characters of this kind are difficult to understand, Spivack tells us, because they exhibit the qualities of the dramatic villain, motivated by human considerations, by passionate causes, and moral accommodations; but in addition they also exhibit motives and actions of the Vice, which are totally evil, the intrigue of agents of damnation against the human soul. The morality play persisted until the middle of the sixteenth century and then gradually died out, but "its most significant and vital personage did not." In the case of these four of Shakespeare's characters (Aaron, Richard, Don John and Iago),

> we are aware of an inexplicable disjunction between the passional implications of their expressed incentives and their inextinguishable vivacity and hilarity. Their one real emotion is an effervescent zest in the possibilities of mischief and a jubilant savoring of success therein . . . Their essential relationship to their crimes and to their victims is not moral but *artistic.* . . . They are, then, first of all great artists, and if, incidentally, they are also great criminals, that is because the traditional expression of their talent moved from its origin in one dramatic convention, where they were full of meaning in their artistic amorality, into another, where they were no longer viable without a surface accommodation, at least, to moral values.

These characters Spivack designates as hybrids[54]—a mingling of the villain and the vice, the one doing evil for human considerations, the other for the pure joy of it. A comparison of Aaron with Tamora exhibits the difference. Spivack finds her villainous but "perfectly credible," set in motion by revenge. "Her actions, moreover, are organic to the plot, not a stylized performance based on premises outside it." In nothing does Aaron's

> heritage reveal itself more clearly than in its liquidation of the conventional motives that naturalize him to the play as Aaron the moor, follower and lover of evil Tamora as well as a criminal in his own right . . . The conventional

ambition that appears in his adjuration to himself .t;.t;. and the conventional vengeance in his vague rhetoric to her about "Blood and revenge . . . hammering in my head" not only have neither coherence with his behavior nor even verbal endurance in his utterance, they are sunk fathoms deep by the mood and method of villainy for the sake of homiletic display. In the archaic stratum of his performance his wickedness is neither acquisitive nor retaliatory; it is demonstrative—a serial exhibition perpetuating the veteran stage image of almost two centuries. His behavior has its absolute meaning in his self-proclaimed villainy . . . his stratagems exist, not as instruments of practical purpose, but as illustrations of a talent in villainous deceit that, by his traditional intimacy with them, he invites the audience to acknowledge.

He recites his *"moral pedigree"* in the final act, in a "long speech of evil application which universalizes and immortalizes the Vice." Spivack finds that the opening words of *Richard III*, though better, "duplicate the cadence and sentiment" of Aaron's first speech, and the morality features of Aaron survive in Richard. Iago, unable "to say as much [as did Aaron] by way of valediction (5.3.183–89), says nothing."[55]

The efforts of the few critics to deny the presence of *Titus* of any significant Senecan influence have been discussed above. These commentators either question or make an effort to dilute a possible contribution by Seneca to the Elizabethan "Tragedy of Blood' almost as though it would not be possible to establish the viability of the native tragic tradition unless Seneca is totally removed from consideration.

Since we are here concentrating our attention on Shakespeare's first tragedy, perhaps it may appear that this one play alone shows evidence of his interest in Seneca, that only a relatively youthful playwright would have looked to the Roman dramatist for inspiration. But such is not the case. Senecan elements have been recognized in a number of his plays, early and late. The students particularly of the sources perceive this clearly. They have identified such elements in *3 Henry VI, Richard III, King John, Hamlet,* and *Macbeth* in addition to *Titus.* Thomson finds *Richard III* "markedly Senecan" and tells us that "Shakespeare had Seneca in mind when he was writing *Macbeth*." Bullough agrees, and, in addition, he notes Senecan rhetoric in *King John;* sees his ideas in *3 Henry VI;* and detects "Senecan undertones in *Hamlet,* derived specifically from *Agamemnon* and *Troades.*[56] Muir designates *Richard III* "the most Senecan of Shakespeare's plays," and thinks that "Shakespeare reread Seneca's plays with the intention of writing a more classical play" in composing *Macbeth.*[57]

Jones, in an appendix entitled "Shakespeare and Seneca," points out the use by Seneca of certain common terms (in Latin, of course) as motifs, the English equivalents of which are to be found in certain of Shakespeare's plays. Also in *King John* "the tragic figure of Constance . . . recalls Andromache; an exchange between Goneril and Albany in *Lear* echoes a similar exchange in *Octavia;* Leontes in *Winter's Tale* acts "like a tyrant" in pushing Paulina, who is holding his new-born infant, off the stage, a vivid stage effect, "remembered perhaps from a play of Seneca's—*Agamemnon.*" Beatrice in *Much Ado* abruptly demands the death of Claudio in a manner reminiscent of Medea. Jones observes that "we need to allow that Shakespeare's use of Seneca . . . may be more oblique and audacious than is often supposed—more a matter of glancingly rapid effects than of a laborious working-out of correspondences."[58]

Scholars, other than those whose chief interest is in the sources of the play, have recently taken up the challenge of reestablishing the presence of a Senecan influence on *Titus.* The Kistners conclude an essay on Seneca, *The Spanish Tragedy,* and *Titus* with the direct statement; "the hero's motivations and actions in *Titus Andronicus* are governed by the Senecan pattern."[59] Lever points out that "those who attempt to minimize the importance of Seneca in English tragedy generally direct their arguments toward phrases . . . But the widespread concurrence of Senecan motifs, images, and direct quotations or paraphrases in Kyd, Shakespeare, Marston, Chapman, and others, against a European background of frankly admitted indebtedness, cannot be thus dismissed. More important than particular borrowings is the resemblance in spiritual orientation, outlook on life, and conception of tragic experience."[60]

The Martindales tell us that while "[t]he battle over the question of Seneca's influence on English Renaissance tragedy continues to rage [and] for some time the anti-Senecans have held the field, [now] there are signs that their opponents are regrouping and beginning a counter-attack." They cite Hunter's comment that much of Elizabethan literature was only superficially classical but, as they point out, this made Seneca "more assimilable." Also they detect a scholarly "dissatisfaction with the single influence of Seneca . . . compounded by the narrow and prescriptive attitude . . . towards him . . . But a liking for Seneca needs no apology; he had a restricted but powerful genius."[61]

In tracing the rise of Latin tragedy in England in the sixteenth century and its influence on the popular theater, Smith points out that many "superficial features" mark *Titus* as a "classical play." He cites specifically its "Roman subject matter . . . its borrowing of plot motifs like Thyestes' banquet . . . its . . . Latin sententiae (including one quotation from Seneca's *Hippolytus*) . . . [and] its characterization of Titus as a hero who suffers with the Stoic patience of Seneca's Oedipus—until he turns into an implacable revenger like Seneca's Tantalus." From a philosophical point of view "an inimical universe like that in *Titus Andronicus* is Seneca's most important contribution to Elizabethan tragedy." Though flawed, *Titus* refuses to reduce life to "a simple formula," as did "[m]ost academic productions . . . Only in the public theatre was Seneca's dark world" depicted. In conclusion, Smith notes that the ancient Greek and Latin dramatists, including Seneca, "challenged Christian assumptions" and that "Out of that dynamic . . . emerged plays that fascinate still, plays like Shakespeare's *The Comedy of Errors* and *Titus Andronicus*."[62]

In the course of an essay entitled "Thrusting Elysium into Hell: The Originality of *The Spanish Tragedy,*" Edwards makes a number of relatively brief but illuminating comments on *Titus*. His aim is, in part, to examine the relationships between plays of "dramatists who used Seneca widely," specifically to "look at the tragedies of Marlowe and Shakespeare, which are companions of *The Spanish Tragedy—Tamburlaine, The Jew of Malta,* and *Titus Andronicus* . . . [in doing so]

> we may observe two things: one, that they share with *The Spanish Tragedy* a view of human life not remotely identifiable or compatible with a Christian view of providence, and secondly that unlike *The Spanish Tragedy* they make no attempt to substitute an alternative view of the government of the cosmos. *Titus Andronicus* has no metaphysical frame of reference at all. Divine and Satanic intervention is tangential, and treated with pervasive irony. Not until the rape and mutilation of Lavinia and the severing of Titus's hand is the issue of divine presence or absence raised at all. Then, "lifting this one hand to heaven," Titus makes a typical Senecan appeal to the unappearing gods of compassion.
>
> > If any power pities wretched tears,
> > To that I call.
> >
> > > (3.1,207–8)
>
> This is followed by the Senecan rhetoric of Cosmic challenge, reminiscent of Hieronimo.

Titus reproaches the gods for their indifference, quoting "directly from *Hippolytus* . . . Like Hieronimo, Titus proclaims that Justice has fled from the earth . . . The gods he has expected, those he has been educated to believe in, have failed to make an appearance. In his craziness, in lines that directly imitate *The Spanish Tragedy,* he turns to try a different set of gods, the darker gods who live in the underworld . . . there is no sense in *Titus Andronicus* that the hero's insane imaginings have touched on the secret truth of the universe . . . if you want . . . [revenge] you must initiate it yourself . . . Such a revenge is said to be in *Spanish Tragedy* terms, a revenge inspired by Pluto's court . . . There follows the *reductio ad absurdum* of the revenge hero's appeal for divine intervention: the shooting of arrows" to solicit heaven. Tamora decides to mock Titus by disguising herself as Revenge. "It seems likely that the 'strange and sad habiliment' which she wears was a direct allusion to the costume Revenge wore in *The Spanish Tragedy.*" Like Hieronino, Titus is subject to frenetical imaginings "but his vengeance is terrifyingly sane. He may be deceived by the gods but he knows Tamora . . . In writing of a Rome from which the gods have departed, Shakespeare has written a play from which the gods have departed."[63]

Miola studies the influence of Seneca's tragedies on English drama in the age of Shakespeare. He analyzes the relationships between the individual plays of Seneca and six Shakespearean tragedies including *Titus Andronicus.* He identifies significant elements in Shakespeare's first tragedy with passages in Seneca's *Phaedra,* including two "slightly altered [Latin] lines" (2.1.136 and 4.1.80–81). As to Seneca's *Troades,* whether Shakespeare knew the play "directly or indirectly [through translation or from Kyd's tragedy], it became an important influence on him in the early 1590s . . . *Troades* informs the symbolic design of *Titus Andronicus* as well as its dramatic configuration . . . Like *Phaedra,* it contributes importantly to Shakespeare's topography." The tomb in *Troades* "appears as a potent ironical symbol." Shakespeare, "Like Seneca, employs the tomb as a setting for dramatic action and ironic commentary . . . a place of repose from earthly strife: the noble dead rest there 'In peace and honor.'" Yet Miola believes that the play raises serious questions about the warrior ethos. "Alarbus merely dies a helpless victim [but] He is a spiritual brother to Mutius, whom Titus makes another offering to the insatiable and gaping mouth of the tomb."

A "haunting presence" in *Titus* is Seneca's *Theyestes,* "a deep source of the energy and the aesthetic of violence" in Shakespeare's play. Despite this, he works major changes on his archetype. He divides Atreus's revenge action among Tamora, Aaron, and Titus, which "multiplies rather than diffuses the shock value and allows for a greater complexity of perspective." Erotic and deadly Tamor recalls "the Fury who appears in the opening scene of *Theyestes,* hot from the underworld, exulting in blood . . . [and she] impersonates Revenge." Shakespeare here departs from traditional stage practice, "us[ing] the convention to show that Revenge, along with Rapine and Murder, has a familiar face and familiar hands. Tamora's art reveals herself, the artist. Chthonic power and supernatural evil . . . lie not outside but inside the hungry gorge of the human heart." While Titus "becomes alternatively pathetic and heroic in his quest for revenge, Aaron . . . plays Atreus with increasing flair." He reveals "a thirst for bloody vengeance . . . show[s] contempt for the gods, and derid[es] respect for conscience and for oaths." Like Atreus, Aaron employs a "rhetoric of defiant insatiability; proudly revealing the whole story of his villainy, he shows himself similarly unrepentant, regretting only missed opportunities for evil."

Titus as revenger is modeled on "Medea, Clytemestra, and Atreus . . . [he] imperiously dismisses the counsel of reason and moderation, sanctifying his passion, insisting on its full and terrible expression. Titus' rhetoric here, particularly the fusion of self and natural elements, is distinctly Senecan, with traceable origins in Stoic cosmology.

To portray the revenge such passion motivates, Shakespeare again makes use of the Atrean model. Titus's banquet draws upon *Theyestes* as well as on one of Seneca's own sources, Ovid's tale of Philomela . . . there are, however, important differences between Atreus' weird ritual and Titus' mad cookery, between the parallel scenes of feasting and revelation. Seneca dwells upon the victim's gross eating and on his premonitions of evil. The revelation is long and drawn out . . . The entire banquet sequence takes . . . almost one-fifth of the play. Relying on lurid rhetoric, exploiting the Stoic nexus relating appetite and disaster, Seneca plays the scene for maximum pathos. Shakespeare, in contrast, moves rapidly through the banquet and revelation . . . Titus' resolution to act 'worse than Progne' . . . suggests that Shakespeare, despite the Senecan elements and details, conceives the scene in Ovidian terms. For Ovid, likewise, combined the revelations of the murder and the banquet into one painful anagnorisis . . . Seneca's depictions of forbidden passion and unspeakable crime *(scelus),* his revelation of the hell deep within the human soul, clearly excited the author of *Titus Andronicus.* Titus here self-consciously strives to surpass his classical models, to outdo Senecan figures of revenge . . . To accomplish such overreaching, Shakespeare focuses on a classical motif variously repeated—the slaying of children. The shades of Priam's sons, Astyanax, Hippolytus, Theyestes' sons, Itys, and Virginius' daughter all hover behind Alarbus, Mutius, Martius, Quintus, Chiron, Demetrius, and Lavinia . . . [T]he adoption of Senecan localities, conventions, and rhetoric in *Titus Andronicus* marks the beginning of a long and fruitful engagement . . . important as well is the use of Senecan character. Seneca bequeathed to later ages the prototype of an unspeakably evil revenger whose sheer force could dominate a play . . . Shakespeare, like others, reformulates the revenger . . . [his] transformation of his Senecan legacy here reveals much about his notions of tragedy and theatre.[64]

Shakespeare was, of course, influenced by literary predecessors. The persuasive arguments of the critics cited above certainly establish Seneca as one of those whether the influence was direct, as seems likely, or through intermediaries. Some of the motifs regarded as Senecan may have commended themselves to Shakespeare indirectly, but that does little to dilute the palpable contribution of the Roman playwright to *Titus Andronicus.*

Appendix

If the surviving chapbook, *History of Titus Andronicus,* which was printed, according to Adams,[65] at some date between 1736 and 1764, represents an earlier print of some date in the 1580s, it could have provided to Shakespeare the general outline from which he developed the structure that informs his play, as well as many of the specific incidents he presents. Evidence that this is what could have happened is set forth below by means of a comparison of passages in parallel columns from the chapbook and the play concerning similar incidents in the two versions.[66] The *History* is divided into six chapters. Of these, Chapter 1 describes the lifting of the Gothic siege of Rome by means of a night attack led by Titus and his twenty-five sons. The play does not specifically mention this feat. In Chapter 2, after "he rode in a triumphant Chariot through the City, crowned with an Oaken Garland,"[67] Titus gathered additional forces and pursued the remainder of the Gothic army. He gave battle, personally killed the king of the Goths, Tottilius, dispersed the enemy host, and captured the Gothic Queen.[68] Only this last event of Chapter 2 is in Shakespeare's play. Of the elements in Chapter 3 a few were adapted to the play. The most important of these are the marriage of the Emperior to the Queen of the Goths, the description of the character of the Empress, her relationship to her Moorish lover, the birth of their illegitimate son, and the formation of the empress's plot to murder the Emperor's son by his former wife. The playwright, in addition to omitting much of Chapter 3, also changed, in some cases, the order of what he retained. For example, the birth of Tamora's and Aaron's black son is reset in the play to occur after the murder of Bassianus. Furthermore, Shakespeare's handling of the incidents following the baby's birth is more realistic than that in the *History,* where Attava explains to the Emperor that the child was "conceived by the Force of Imagination," an account that Waith rightly considers "fantastic."[69] Two significant happenings in Chapter 3 not in the play are the Emperor's banishing of Aaron over the birth of the black baby and Attava's successful stratagem to have him recalled.

Almost all of the events in the last half of the chapbook are found in the play. From Chapter 4 only two elements are dropped: the false swearing by Aaron and Attava's two sons against Titus's sons to implicate them in the murder of the son of the Emperor, and Titus's fainting away on his two sons' dead bodies.[70] Of the incidents of Chapter 5 the only significant omission is Lavinia's "retiring to Woods and Groves, to utter her piteous Complaints and Cries to the senseless Trees,"[71] which led to her undoing. All of the events of Chapter 6—some modified and elaborated to meet dramatic requirements—are found in *Titus*. The shooting of arrows in petition to the heavens, the ambush of Attava's sons, Titus's execution of them by cutting their throats while Lavinia held a bowl to receive their blood, the baking of the pasties, the Thyestean dinner, the slaying of the Emperor and Empress, the confession of the Moor and his sentence to death by starvation, Titus's killing of Lavinia, and his own death—all find their place in the play. Shakespeare of course did not limit himself to the plot materials of the chapbook. His conclusion, including most notably the promise of a better future for Rome under Lucius, has no counterpart in the *History;* and the sequence of the deaths of the terminal hecatomb in the play are different from that in the tale. Nevertheless, Shakespeare made theatrical use of all of the events of Chapter 6.

Comparison of Incidents in *The History of Titus Andronicus* and in Shakespeare's *The Most Lamentable Tragedie of Titus Andronicus*

The History of Titus Andronicus	Shakespeare's *Titus Andronicus*
Chapter 2	
	Enter a Captaine.
	Romaines make way, the good *Andronicus*,
	Patron of vertue, Romes best Champion:
	Successfull in the battailes that he fights.
	VVith honour and with fortune is returnd,
	From where he circumscribed with his sword,
	And brought to yoake the enemies of Rome.
In the Pursuit he took the Queen of the Goths Captive and brought her to Rome; for which signal Victory he had a second Triumph, and was stiled the Deliverer of his Country.	
(p. 198)	
	Sound Drums and Trumpets, and then enter two of Titus sonnes, and then two men bearing a Coffin couered with black, then two other sonnes, then Titus Andronicus, and then Tamora the Queene of the Gothes and her two sonnes Chiron and Demetrius, with Aron The More, and others as many as can be, then set downe the Coffin, and Titus speakes.
	(1.1.63.1–69.8)
Chapter 3	
Tottilius's two Sons Alaricus and Abonus . . . made a Desolation in the Roman Provinces, continuing a ten Years War.	*Marcus.* Tenne yeares are spent since first he vndertooke This cause of Rome.
(p. 199)	(1.1.31–32)

Satur. Behold I choose thee *Tamora* for my Bride,
And will create thee Emperesse of Rome.

(1.1.319–20)

N[urse]. A Ioyles, dismall, blacke, and sorrowfull issue,
Here is the babe as loathsome as a toade,
Amongst the fairefast breeders of our clime,
The Empresse sends it thee, thy stampe, thy seale,
And bids thee christen it with thy daggers point.

(4.2.66–70)

Bassianus. And so I loue and honour thee and thine,
Thy Noble brother *Titus* and his sonnes,
And her to whom my thoughts are humbled all,
Gratious *Lauinia*, Romes rich ornament.

Saturnine. Surprizde, by whom?
Bascianus.   By him that iustly may,
Beare his betrothde from all the world away.

(1.1.49–52; 285–86)

Vengeance is in my hart, death in my hand,
Blood and reuenge are hammering in my head.
Harke *Tamora* the Empresse of my soule,
Which neuer hopes more heauen than rests in thee,
This is the daie of domme for *Bassianus*,
His *Philomel* must loose her tongue to daie,
Thy sonnes make pillage of her chastitie,
And wash their hands in *Bascianus* blood.

(2.3.38–45)

The Emperor, desiring Peace, it was agreed
to, in Consideration he should marry Attava,
Queen of the Goths.

(p. 199)

[Attava] had a Moor as revengeful as herself,
whom she trusted in many great Affairs and was
usually privy to her Secrets, so far that from
private Dalliances she grew pregnant, and
brought forth a Blackmoor Child.

(p. 199)

Andronicus . . . had a very fair and beautiful
Daughter, named Lavinia, brought up in all
singular Virtues, humble, courteous and modest,
insomuch that the Emperor's only Son, by a
former Wife fell extreamly in Love with her,
seeking her Favour by all vertuous and
honourable Ways, insomuch, that after a long
Courtship with her Father and the Emperor's
Consent she was betrothed to him.

(p. 200)

The Queen of the Goths hearing this, was much
enraged, because from such a Marriage might spring
Princes that might frustrate her ambitious Designs,
which was to make her Sons Emperors jointly;
wherefore she laboured all she could to frustrate
it, by declaring what a Disgrace it would be to the
Emperor to marry his Son to the Daughter of a
Subject, who might have a Queen with a Kingdom to
her Dowry: But finding the Prince constant, she
resolved to take him out of the Way; so it was
plotted between her, the Moor, and her two Sons,
that they should invite him to hunt in the great
Forest, on the Banks of the River Tyber, and there
murder him.

(p. 200)

This was effected, by shooting him thro' the Back
with a poysoned Arrow, which came out at his
Breast, of which Wound he fell from his Horse and
immediately died. Then they digged a very deep Pit
in a Path-way, and threw him in, covering it
lightly with Boughs, and sprinkling Earth on it.

(p. 200)

Chapter 4

Lavinia . . . entreated her Brothers to go in search of
him, which they did with all speed; but being dogged
by the Moor and the Queen of Goths two Sons, they
unluckily coming in the Way where the Pit was digged,
they fell both in upon the dead Body, and could not
by reason of the great Depth, get out.

(p. 200–1)

Their cruel Enemies no sooner saw this, but they
hasted to the Court, and sent the Guards in search
of the murdered Prince, who found Andronicus's two
Sons with the dead Body.

(p. 201)

Demetrius. This is a witness that I am thy son. *stab him.*
Chi And this for me struck home, to shew my strength.

　　　　bring thou her husband,
This is the hole where *Aron* bid us hide him.

(2.3.116–17; 185–86)

Aron. Come on my Lords the better foot before,
Straight will I bring you to the lothsome pit,
VVhere I espied the Panther fast asleepe.
Quintus. My sight is verie dull what ere it bodes.
Mart. And mine I promise you, were it not for shame,
VVell could I leaue our sport to sleepe a while.
Quintus. VVhat are thou fallen what subtill hole is this,
VVhose mouth is couered with rude growing briers,
Vpon whose leaues are drops of new shed blood,
As fresh as morning dew distild on flowers,
Averie fatall place it seemes to mee,
Speake brother hast thou hurt thee with the fall?
Quint. Thy hand once more, I will not loose againe,
Till thou art here a loft or I belowe:
Thou canst not come to me, I come to thee.

(2.3.192–203; 243–45)

Aron. Now will I fetch the King to finde them here,
That he thereby may haue a likely gesse,
How these were they, that made away his brother.

Saturnius. Along with me, Ile see what hole is here,
And what he is that now is leapt into it.
Say who art thou that lately didst descend,
Into this gaping hollow of the earth.
Martius. The vnhappie sonnes of old *Andronicus,*
Brought hither in a most vnluckie houre,
To finde thy brother *Bassianus* dead.

(2.3.206–8; 246–52)

King. Sirs drag them from the pit vnto the prison,
There let them bide vntill we have deuised,
Some neuer hard of tortering paine for them.

Moore. Titus Andronicus, My Lord the Emperour,
Sends thee this word, that if thou loue thy sonnes,
Let *Marcus, Lucius,* or thy selfe olde *Titus,*
Or any one of you, chop off your hand
And send it to the King, he for the same,
will send thee hither both thy sonnes aliue,
And that shall be the ransome for their fault.

Titus. Come hither Aron, Ile deceiue them both
Lend me thy hand, and I will giue thee mine.

Moore. If that be calde deceit, I will be honest,
And neuer whilst I liue deceiue men so:
But Ile deceiue you in another sort,
And that youle say ere halfe an houre passe.
He cuts off Titus hand.

(3.1.150–56; 184–190.1)

They drew [them] up, and carried [them]
Prisoners to the Court, where the Moor and the
other two falsely swore against them, that they
had often heard them threaten Revenge on the
Prince, because he had put them to the Foil,
in a Turnament at Justing.

(p. 201)

The Queen designing to work her Revenge on
Andronicus, sent the Moor in the Emperor's
Name, to tell him, if he designed to save his
Sons from the Misery and Death that would
ensue, he should cut off his right Hand and
send it to Court. This the good-natur'd
Father scrupled not to do, no, nor had it
been his Life to ransom them, he would have
freely parted with it; whereupon laying his
Hand on a Block, he gave the wicked Moor his
Sword, who immediately struck it off.

(p. 201)

[The Moor] inwardly laugh'd at the Villainy; then departing with it [Titus's hand] he told him his Sons should be sent to him in a few Hours.

(p. 201)

But whilst he was rejoicing with the Hopes of their Delivery, a Hearse came to his Door with Guards, which made his aged Heart to tremble. The first Thing they presented him was his Hand, which they said would not be accepted; and the next was his three Sons beheaded.

(p. 201)

At this woful Sight, overcome with Grief, he fainted away on the dead Bodies; and when he

recover'd again, he tore his hoary Hair, which

Age and his lying in Winter-Camps for the defense of his Country, had made as white as Snow, pouring out Floods of Tears.

(p. 201)

Aron. I goe *Andronicus*, and for thy hand,
Looke by and by to haue thy sonnes with thee.
Their heads I meane: Oh how this villanie,
Doth fat me with the verie thoughts of it.
Let fooles doe good, and faire men call for grace,
Aron will haue his soule black like his face.

I plaid the cheater for thy fathers hand,
And when I had it drew my selfe a part,
And almost broke my hart with extreame laughter,
I pried me through a creuice of awall,
when for his hand he had his two sonnes heads,
Behelde his teares and laught so hartilie,
That both my eyes were raynie like to his.

(3.1.199–204; 5.1.111–17)

Enter a messenger with two heads and a hand.
Messenger. VVorthy *Andronicus*, ill art thou repaid,
For that good hand thou sentst the Emperour:
Here are the heads of thy two Noble sonnes,
And heres they hand in scorne to thee sent backe:
Thy griefe, their sports: Thy resolution mockt:
That woe is me to thinke vpon thy woes,

More than remembrance of my fathers death.

(3.1.232.1–39)

Titus. VVhen will this fearefull slumber haue an end?

Mar. Ah now no more will I controwle thy greefes,

Rent off thy siluer haire, thy other hand,
Gnawing with thy teeth, and be this dismal sight
The closing vp of our most wretched eies:
Now is a time to storme, why art thou still?
Titus. Ha, ha, ha.

Chapter 5

M. VVhy dost thou laugh? It fits not this houre.
Titus. VVhy I haue not another teare to shed;
Besides this sorrow is an enemie,
And would vsurp vpon my watrie eies,
And make them blinde with tributarie teares.

(3.1.251; 258–68)

Tamora. Giue me the poynard, you shall know my boies,
Your Mothers hand shall right your Mothers wrong.
Demetrius. Stay madame here is more belongs to her,
First thrash the corne, then after burne the straw:
This minion stood vpon her chastitie,
Vpon her Nuptiall vow, her loyaltie
And with that painted hope, braues your mightienes,
And shall she carrie this vnto her graue.
Chiron. And if she doe, I would I were an Euenuke,
Drag hence her husband to some secret hole,
And make his dead trunke pillow to our lust.
Tamora. But when yee haue the honie we desire,
Let not this waspe outliue vs both to sting.
Chiron. I warrant you maddame we will make that sure:
Come Mistris now perforce we will enioy,
That nice preserued honestie of yours.

(2.3.120–35)

Lauinia. Oh *Tamora* be calld a Gentle Queene,
And with thine owne hands kill me in this place,
For tis not life that I haue begd so long
Poore I was slaine when *Bascianus* dide.

The fair and beautiful Lavinia . . . retir[ed] to
Woods and Groves to utter her piteous
Complaints . . . when one Day, being watched
thither by the Moor, he gave notice of it to the
Queen's two Sons, who, like the wicked Elders
and chaste Susanna, had a long time burned in
Lust, yet knew her Virtues were proof against
all Temptations, and therefore it could not be
obtain'd but by Violence; so thinking this an
Opportunity to serve their Turns, immediately
repaired to the Grove, and setting the Moor to watch
on the Outborders, soon found her pensive and
sorrowful, yet comely and beautiful in Tears,
when unawares, before she saw them, like two
ravenous Tygers, they seized the trembling Lady,
who struggled all she could, and cried out
piteously for help;

(p. 202)

seeing what their wicked Intentions bent at,
she offered them her Throat, desiring they would
bereave her of her Life, but not of her Honour.

(p. 202)

Tamora. Farewell my sons, see that you make her sure,
Nere let my hart know merry cheare indeede,
Till all the *Andronicie* be made away:
Now will I hence to seeke my louely *Moore*,
And let my spleenfull sonnes this Trull defloure,

(2.3.187–91)

In a villainous Manner, staking her down by
the Hair of her Head, and binding her Hands
behind her, they turned up her Nakedness and
forced their Way into her Closet of Chastity,
taking it by Turns.

(p. 202)

Enter the Empresse sonnes with Lauinia, her handes
  cut off, and her tongue cut out, & rauisht.
Deme. So now go tell and if they tongue can speake,
VVho twas that cut they tongue and ravisht thee.
Chi. VVrite downe thy minde bewary thy meaning so,
And if thy stumps will let thee play the scribe.
Deme. See how with signes and tokens she can scrowle.
Chi. Goe home, call for sweet water wash thy hands.
Demet. She hath no tongue to call, nor hands to wash,
And so lets leaue her to her silent walks.

(2.4.01–04; 1–8)

They [the Empress's sons] began to consider how
they should come off when such a Villainy was
discovered; whereupon, calling the Moor to them,
they asked his Advice, who wickedly counselled
them to make all sure, seeing they had gone thus
far, by cutting out her Tongue to hinder her
telling Tales, and her Hands off to prevent her
writing a Discovery. This the cruel Wretches
did . . . in this woful Condition they left the Lady.

(p. 202)

—

    Enter Marcus from hunting.
VVho is this, my Neece that flies away so fast,
Cosen a word, where is your husband:
If I doe dreame would all my wealth would wake me.
If I doe wake some Planet strike me downe,
That I may slumber an eternall sleepe.
Speake gentle Neece, what sterne vngentle hands,
Hath lopt, and hewde, and made they body bare,
Of her two branches those sweet Ornaments,
VVhose cycrling shadowes, Kings have sought to sleepe in,
And might not gaine so great a happines
As halfe thy loue: VVhy dost not speake to me?
Alas, a crimson Riuer of warme blood,
Like to a bubling Fountaine stirde with winde,

Her Uncle Marcus happened accidentally, soon
after, to come in search of her, who at the
woful Sight, overcome with Sorrow, could hardly
keep Life in himself.

(p. 202)

Doth rise and fall betweene thy Rosed lips,
Comming and going with thy honie breath.
But sure some *Tereus* hath deflowred thee,
And lest thou shouldst detect them cut thy tongue.

(2.4.10.3–27)

Titus. Speake *Lauinea*, what accursed hand,
Hath made thee handles in thy fathers sight?
what foole hath added water to the sea?
Or brought a faggot to bright burning *Troy*?
My griefe was at the height before thou camst,
And now like *Nylus* it disdaineth bounds.
Giue me a sword Ile chop off my hands too,

For they haue fought for Rome, and all in vaine:

(3.1.65–73)

Titus. Giue signes sweet gyrle, for here are none but friends,
VVhat Romaine Lord it was durst doe the deede?
Or slonke not *Saturnine* as *Tarquin* erst,
That left the Campe to sinne in *Lucrece* bed.

(4.1.60–63)

Marc. This sandie plot is plaine, guide if thou canst
This after me, I haue writ my name,
Without the help of any hand at all,
Curst be that hart that forc'd vs to this shift:
VVrite thou good Neece, and here display at last,
VVhat God will haue discouered for reuenge,
Heauen guide thy pen to print thy sorrowes plaine,
That we may know the traytors and the truth,
*Shee takes the staffe in her mouth, and guides it with her
stumps and writes.*

(4.1.68–75.2)

Poor Andronicus's Grief for this sad Disaster
was so great, that no Pen can write or Words
express; much ado they had to restrain him
from doing Violence upon himself; he cursed
the Day he was born to see such Miseries fall
on himself and Family.

(p. 202)

[Titus] intreat[ed] her [Lavinia] to tell him,
if she could any ways do it by signs, who had so
villainously abused her.

(p. 202)

At last the poor Lady, with a Flood of Tears
gushing from her Eyes, taking a Wand between her
Stumps, wrote these Lines.

(p. 202)

The Lustful Sons of the proud Emperess
Are Doers of this hateful Wickedness.

(p. 202)

[Marcus.] Oh doe yee read my Lord what she hath writ,
[Titus.] *Stuprum, Chiron, Dmetrius.*
Marcus. What, what, the lustfull sonnes of *Tamora,*
Performers of this haynous bloody deede.

(4.1.76–79)

Hereupon he [Titus] vowed Revenge, at the Hazard
of his own and all their Lives.

(p. 203)

Marcus. My Lord kneele downe with me, *Lauinia* kneele,
And kneele sweet boy, the Romaine Hectors hop[e]

And sweare with me as with the wofull feere,
And father of that chast dishonoured Dame,
Lord *Iunius Brutus* sweare for *Lucrece* rape,
That we will prosecute by good aduice
Mortall reuenge vpon these Traiterous *Gothes,*
And see their blood or die with this reproch.

(4.1.86–93)

Chapter 6

Adronicus, upon these Calamities, feigned
himself distracted, and went raving about the
City, shooting his Arrows towards Heaven, as in
Defiance, calling to Hell for Vengeance, which
mainly pleased the Empress and her Sons, who
thought themselves now secure.

(p. 203)

He [Titus] giues them the Arrows.
Ad Iouem, thats for you, here *ad Apollonem,*
Ad Martem, thats for my selfe,
Here boy to *Pallas,* here to *Mercurie,*
To *Saturnine,* to *Caius,* not to *Saturnine,*
You were as good to shoote against the winde,
Too it boy, *Marcus* loose when I bid,
Of my word I have written to effect,
Ther's not a God left vnsollicited.
Marcus. Kinsemen, shoot all your shafts into the Court,
VVee will afflict the Emperour in his pride.

Titus. Now Masters draw, Oh well said *Lucius,*
Good boy in *Virgoes* lappe, giue it *Pallas,*
Marcus. My Lord, I aime a mile beyond the Moone,
Your letter is with *Iubiter* by this.
(4.3.53.1–67)

[Titus's] Friends required Justice of the
Emperor against the Ravishers, yet they could
have no Redress, he rather threatening them, if
they insisted on it.
(p. 203)

Saturnine. Whats this but libelling against the Senate,
And blazoning our vniustice euerie where,
A goodly humor is it not my Lords?
As who would say in Rome no iustice were.
But if I liue his fained extasies
Shall be no shelter to these outrages
But he and his shall know that iustice liues
In *Saturninus* health.
(4.4.17–24)

Titus. Know you these two.
Pub. The Empresse sonnes I take them, *Chiron. Demetrius.*
Titus. Fie, *Publius* fie, thou art too much deceaude,
The one is Murder and Rape is the others name,
And therefore binde them gentle *Publius,*
Caius and *Valentine,* lay hands on them,
Oft haue you heard me wish for such an houre,
(5.2.152–60)

They [the Andronici and their friends] conspired
together to . . . revenge themselves; lying in ambush
in the Forest when the two Sons went a hunting,
they surprized them, and binding them to a Tree
pitifully crying out for Mercy, though they would
give none to others.
(p. 203)

And now I finde it therefore binde them sure,
And stop their mouthes if they begin to crie.

Titus. Harke wretches how I meane to marter you,
This one hand yet is left to cut your throats,
VVhiles that *Lauinia* tweene her stumps doth hold,
The bason that receaues your guiltie blood.
(5.2.180–83)

Andronicus cut their Throats whilst Lavinia, by
his Command, held a Bowl between her Stumps to
receive the Blood.
(p. 203)

Then conveying the Bodies home to his own House privately, he cut the Flesh into fit Pieces, and ground the Bonds to Powder, and made of them two mighty Pasties.

(p. 203)

[Andronicus] invited the Emperor and Empress to Dinner, who thinking to make sport with his frantlike Humour came.

(p. 203)

When they had eat of the Pasties, he told them what it was.

(p. 203)

[Andronicus] thereupon giving the Watch Word to his friends, they immediately issued out, slew the Emperor's Guards, and, lastly, the Emperor and his cruel Wife.

(p. 203)

Then seizing on the wicked Moor, the fearful

Titus. You know your Mother meanes to feast with me,
And calles herselfe Reuenge and thinks me mad.
Harke villaines I will grinde your bones to dust,
And with your blood and it Ile make a paste,
And of the paste a coffen I will reare,

And make two pasties of your shamefull heades.

(5.2.184–89)

Titus. This is the feast that I haue bid her too,
And this the banket she shall surfet on.

(5.2.192–93)

King, Goe fetch them [Chiron and Demetrius] hither to
(vs presently.

Titus. VVhy there they are both baked in this Pie,
VVhereof their Mother daintilie hath fed,

Eating the flesh that shee her selfe hath bred.

(5.3.58–61)

Titus. Tis true, tis true, witnes my kniues sharpe point.
He stabs the Empresse.

Emperour. Die franticke wretch for this accursed deede.
Lucius. Can the sonnes eie behold his father bleede?
Ther's meede for meede, death for a deadly deede.

(5.3.62–65)

Aron. Lucius saue the child;

And beare it from me to the Empresse:
If thou do this, ile show thee wondrous things,
That highly may aduantage thee to heare,
If thou wilt not, befall what may befall,
Ile speake no more, but vengeance rotte you all.
Lucius. Say on, and if it please me which thou speakst
Thy child shall liue, and I will see it nourisht.

(5.1.53–60)

Villain fell on his Knees, promising to
discover all.

(p. 203)

Aron. Twas her two sonnes that murdered *Bassianus*,
They cut thy Sisters tongue, and rauisht her,
And cut her hands, and trimd her as thou sawest.
I traind thy brethren to that guilefull hole,
where the dead corpse of *Bassianus* laie:

(5.1.91–93; 104–5)

[The Moore] told how he had killed the Prince,
betrayed the three Sons of Andronicus by false
Accusation, and counselled the Abuse to the fair
Lavinia.

(p. 203)

Romane. You said *Andronicie* haue done with woes,
Giue sentence on this execrable wretch,
That hath been breeder of these dyre euents.
Lucius. Set him brest deepe in earth and famish him,
There let him stand and raue and crie for foode.
If any one releeues or pitties him,
For the offence he dies, this is our doome,

(5.3.175–82)

Some stay to see him fastned in the earth.

They scarce knew what Torments sufficient to devise
for him [the Moor]; but at last, digging a Hole,
they set him in the Ground to the middle alive,
smeered him over with Honey, and so, between
the stinging of Bees and Wasps and starving,
he miserably ended his wretched Days.

(p. 203)

Titus. My Lord the Emperour resolue me this,
VVas it well done of rash *Virginius*
To slay his daughter with his owne right hand
Because she was enforst, stainde, and deflowrde?
King. It was *Andronicus.*
Titus. Your reason mighty Lord.
King. Because the girle should not suruiue her shame,

[Andronicus], to prevent the Torments he
expected, when these Things came to be known,
at his Daughter's Request, he killed her; and
so, rejoicing he had revenged himself on his
Enemies to the full, fell on his own Sword and
died.

(p. 203)

And by her presence still renewe his sorrowes.
Titus. A reason mighty, strong, and effectuall,
A patterne president, and liuelie warrant,
For me most wretched to performe the like,
Die, die *Lauinia* and thy shame with thee,
And with thy shame thy Fathers sorrow die.
(5.3.35–46)

6

Date of Composition

Limits on the date of composition of *Titus Andronicus* are set by two items of evidence. A late date of 1593 is set by the first notation of a performance of the play in Henslowe's *Diary* for 23 January 1594. For the early limit, we have Jonson's comment in the induction to his *Bartholomew Fair* (in what purports to be a legal agreement between the playwright and the audience and is therefore precisely dated 31 October 1614) to the effect that some playgoers have old-fashioned tastes:

> He that will swear *Jeronimo,* or *Andronicus* are the best plays yet, shall pass unexcepted at here, as a man whose judgment shows it is constant, and hath stood still these five and twenty, or thirty years.[1]

If the reference were to be taken literally, it would set the time of composition for the two plays ranging from 1584 to 1589. Jonson's gibe need not be taken literally, as many commentators have pointed out, but it must have been generally accurate because his little joke certainly assumes that his audience knew that these two enduringly popular plays were comparatively old. The earlier date may be thought to refer only to *The Spanish Tragedy (Jeronimo)* and the later to *Titus* without overextending Jonson's meaning. If this be granted, the range of possible dates of *Titus* is thus from *circa* 1589 to *circa* 1593.

There is some other evidence that serves to narrow the range of dates. The title page of the first quarto (1594) says that *Titus* was "Plaide by the Right Honourable Earle of Darbie, Earle of Pembrooke and Earle of Sussex their Seruants." Sussex's men is listed by Henslowe as the troupe that acted the play on 23 January 1594, the earliest of three performances that season. There is no record of a presentation by Pembroke's, but it would have to have taken place before August 1593 when, according to a letter of Henslowe's addressed to his son-in-law Edward Alleyn, the company was back in London and in a process of dissolution—they were pawning their costumes—because they had been unable to earn enough to defray their expenses while on a provincial tour.[2] If we accept the order of acting companies on the title page of the first quarto, then the

190

Earl of Derby's men—or Lord Strange's as they were known before their patron succeeded to the earldom on 25 September 1593—would have acted *Titus* before Pembroke's, certainly in 1592 and perhaps earlier.

Another item of evidence on the date is a passage in *A Knack to Know a Knave,* an anonymous play presented as "ne[w]," according to Henslowe, by Strange's Men on 10 June 1592.[3] Earl Osric greets King Edgar, who has come to visit the Earl without having been invited, saying

> My gratious Lord, as welcome shall you be
> To me, my Daughter, and my Sonne in Law,
> As Titus was unto the Roman Senators,
> When he had made a conquest on the Goths;
> That in requitall of his service don,
> Did offer him the imperiall Diademe:
> As they in Titus, we in your Grace still fynd
> The perfect figure of a Princelie mind.[4]

These lines convey four elements of information. They tell of Titus's welcome by the Senators, his conquest of the Goths, the offer of the imperial crown and the description of Titus as "the perfect figure of a princely mind." There are three versions of the story of Titus Andronicus: the prose *History of Titus Andronicus,* the ballad entitled *The Lamentable and Tragical History of Titus Andronicus,*[5] and the play. Only in the latter is Titus welcomed by Tribunes and Senators after a conquest of the Goths and offered the imperial throne. In neither of the other extant versions of the story—the prose *History* and the ballad—is Titus welcomed, except by the Emperor; is a contender for the throne; or is offered the crown. The fourth element of the allusion further supports the hypothesis that it is the play to which the author of *A Knack* was referring. Depicting Titus as the "perfect figure of a princely mind" is consistent with the Elizabethan view of the stern virtues of Rome, precisely the way a sixteenth-century Englishman would have described Shakespeare's hero.[6]

Certain critics have questioned the identification. Some have been inhibited by the corrupt quality of the text of *A Knack,* but there is certainly nothing about this passage to cause doubts concerning its authenticity. It is unequivocal, shows no signs of corruption, and can be accepted at face value even though elements of the rest of the play may be suspect. Another question about the allusion has arisen because a play entitled *Titus and Vespasian* was in Strange's repertory in 1592 and was acted only four days before the first performance of *A Knack to Know a Knave. Titus and Vespasian* is lost, and we know only the title and the fact that it was performed ten times between 11 April 1592, when Henslowe marked it "ne," and 25 January 1593. Some scholars have speculated that the anonymous author of *A Knack* may have referred to *Titus and*

Vespasian, and that it may have been an earlier version of *Titus Androni-cus* written either by Shakespeare or by another dramatist or collabora-tion and later revised by Shakespeare to produce the text we have. In support of this hypothesis, they adduce such data as traces of revision in *Titus,* Henslowe's designation of the performance of *Titus Andronicus* of 23 January 1594 as "ne," similarities mostly in the first act of *Titus* to the style of George Peele, the numerous parallels between *Lucrece* and *Titus,* and the renaming of Lucius as Vespasian in the German *Tragoedia von Tito Andronico.* But each of these items of evidence is susceptible of interpretation that does not require us to assume *Titus and Vespasian* to be predecessor of *Titus Andronicus.*

That there is evidence of revision in the play is apparent and is dis-cussed in the essay on revision in this collection, but the alternations in the text can scarcely be cited in support of an assertion that *Titus and Vespasian* is a predecessor text to *Titus Andronicus* since no text of that play is extant. Henslowe's "ne" has been shown by Foakes and Rickert to be applied by him when plays were not newly composed. The admittedly Peelean diction of Act 1 may be explained as an imitation by a younger playwright of the style of an established dramatist. The links to the poems, especially *Lucrece,* could be traceable to similarity in subject and to a common "classical" setting. The use of Vespasian in the German text is probably a result of natural association in a play whose hero is named Titus, both having been Flavian emperors.[7] The manifest conclusion is that the allusion in *A Knack to Know a Knave* is a reference to Shake-speare's play substantially in its extant form and that *Titus Andronicus* must have been on the boards before the first performance of *A Knack* on 10 June 1592. To conclude differently, Alexander tells us, "seems to attribute powers of divination to the audience at the Rose of an excep-tional kind, for if they weren't thought-readers what could they make of a reference to a story which, if it existed then, could only have been an obscure pseudo-historical romance."[8] And Chambers sums up: "the allusion in *Knack to Know a Knave* . . . points to a knowledge of Titus and the Goths . . . in 1592, and no such combination is known outside *Titus Andronicus.*"[9]

Maxwell draws attention to two passages in the anonymous *Trouble-some Reign of John King of England* (published in 1591) that share words and images with *Titus Andronicus:*

How, what, when, and where, have I bestowed a day
That tended not to some notorious ill?[10]

Maxwell believes that this "can hardly be independent of Aaron's"

Even now I curse the day—and yet I think
Few come within the compass of my curse—
Wherein I did not some notorious ill.

(5.1.125–27)

And from *The Troublesome Reign* Maxwell found

> lo Lords the withered flowre
> who in his life shind like the Mornings blush,
> Cast out a doore, denide his buriall right,
> A pray for birds and beasts to gorge upon.

to have a "connection" to this passage from *Titus:*

> No funeral rite nor man in mourning weed
> No mournfull bell shall ring her burial;
> But throw her forth to beasts and birds to prey;

(5.3.195–97)

A further comparison of the two plays reveals additional locutions that may have a similar "connection:"

Tit.:	Confusion fall—

(2.3.184)

Reign:	Confusion light upon their damned soules
Tit.:	Patient yourself, madam and pardon me. These are their brethren whom your Goths beheld Alive and dead, and for their brethren slain Religiously they ask a sacrifice.

(1.1.121–24)

Reign:	Have patience, Madame, this is the chance of war: He may be ransomde, we revenge his wrong.
Tit.:	Saucy controller of my private steps . . .

(2.3.60)

Reign:	Saucie, uncivill, checkers of my will . . .
Tit.:	I will not hear her speak; away with her!

(2.3.137)

Reign:	I am deafe, be gone, let him not speake a word.

Of these additional parallels the passages counseling patience are the most significant. In both cases, a distracted mother is urged to suppress protest over the fate of a doomed son by a powerful political and military leader who could—either certainly or probably—save the young man, but does not do so.

There is a question as to which author was the borrower. Alexander finds the "writing [of *the Troublesome Reign*] like a tissue of borrowed and only half-assimilated phrases from *Henry VI, Richard III* [and] *King John.*[11] Maxwell calls the anonymous author "a shameless borrower,"[12] and Sykes notes numerous parallels to several of Peele's plays.[13] If then *The Troublesome Reign,* printed in 1591, contains borrowings from *Titus Andronicus,* Shakespeare's play must have been extant in that year.

Baldwin,[14] accepting an idea first proposed by Robertson, finds another parallel of about the same date between *Titus* and Peele's *Edward I* (published 1593 but, according to Chambers,[15] probably written in 1590–91). Robertson links two separate lines from Peele's play and draws a comparison with two consecutive lines of *Titus:*

> *Edw. I*   To tie Prometheus' limbs to Caucasus (sc. iv. 21)
>   Fast by those looks are all my fancies tied (sc. x. 201)
>
> *Tit.*   And faster bound to Aaron's charming eyes
>   Than is Prometheus tied to Caucasus.

(2.1.16–17)

Baldwin, arguing for Peele's authorship of *Titus,* concludes that, since Peele had used the two figures separate, if he had combined them "he would have got very much the result of phraseology which we find in *Titus.*" Considering only the question of influence and setting aside that of authorship, there can be no doubt that Baldwin finds a common element shared by *Titus* and a play written no later than 1591.

Many scholars accept the twofold proposition that *Titus* exhibits, in its fundamental conception, the influence of *The Spanish Tragedy* usually attributed to Kyd; and that the character of Aaron is modeled after both Barabas and Ithamore in *The Famous Tragedy of the Rich Jew of Malta,* said on the title page of a 1633 quarto to have been "Written by Christopher Marlo." Chambers dated Kyd's play "c. 1589" based on Jonson's allusion in *Bartholomew Fair,* and some critics, on the same evidence, think it is as early as 1587; and he dates Marlowe's play also "c. 1589," citing a reference in the prologue to the death of the Duc de Guise, which occurred on 23 December 1588. It was in Stranges' repertory somewhat later (June 1591) and might have been acted by them earlier. In his own chronology, Chambers dates *Titus* during the 1593–94 theatrical season taking into account only the evidence of Henslowe's *Diary* and of the *Stationers' Register* and the title page.[16]

Dover Wilson notes that in regard to date he is "widely departing from previous critical opinion which has generally inclined to a much earlier period." The original play which he believes was written by Peele, he dates from May–June of 1593, about the same time that Peele was writing his poem, *The Honour of the Garter.* This determination is based in part on the fact that the play and the poem share the rare word *palliament.* Similarly Wilson hypothesizes that Shakespeare was revising Peele's play while completing *Lucrece*, "as close parallels with it [*Lucrece*] strongly suggest . . . Is it a wild guess" Wilson asks rhetorically, "that Shakespeare spent the first fortnight or so of this period in remoulding the last four acts of *Titus* so that it would be ready in time for the performance on 23 January [1594]?" Maxwell has reservations about the evidentiary value of the reference in *A Knack*—"it might be an allusion to Shakespeare's source"—but he observes that "A date about 1590 or a little earlier would be consistent with the immaturity of the play as a specimen of Shakespeare's art and would also be easier to reconcile with the famous allusion by Ben Jonson." He reviews other evidence—finding, for example that the "notorious ill" line is "more at home in Aaron's speech than in John's . . . [it] is happier as a boast than in a penitential context"—and concludes that "it forms a tangled web [that is] fragmentary and conflicting . . . But there does not seem to be anything that flatly contradicts a date of about 1589–90." Schlösser believes that 1593–94 is too late, that *Titus* must be measurably earlier than *Richard II;* that a comparison of elements of style make it probable that it preceded the *Henry VI* trilogy; and therefore it is "Shakespeares frühestes Drama," which he dates 1589.[17]

Barnet concludes a discussion of the date of composition by noting that "a date widely favored is 1592–94 but there is no compelling reason to believe that *Titus* could not have been written in the late eighties." Cross surveys the evidence of the 1594 title page and decides that "An original date of 1590 or even earlier is not precluded." Kermode points out that the "possible allusion to *Titus* in *A Knack* . . . creates some presumption that *Titus* existed by 1592" and the "two echoes of *Titus*" in *A Troublesome Reign* (published 1591) implies its existence in that year, but that links to *Venus* and Lucrece "support an hypothesis that Shakespeare also wrote *Titus* . . . during the long closure of the theatres due to the plague in 1592–93." Bevington tells us that "*Titus Andronicus* is the kind of revenge play one might expect of a gifted young playwright in the early 1590's." Tobin cites the occurrence of the names Titus and Saturninus and the theme of maternal cannibalism in Nashe's *Christ's Tears over Jerusalem* as evidence that *Titus Andronicus* derives in part from Nashe's pamphlet, registered 8 September 1593. He dates the play "in the latter part of 1593."[18]

Waith accepts a date earlier than 1594 in consideration of the title-page list of playing companies, and also accepts that the passage in *A Knack* alludes to *Titus* "even though it is not the Senators but the Roman people who offer Titus the crown." He is less certain regarding the passages in *Troublesome Reign* because "in such cases . . . it is impossible to prove who was the borrower," and notes the possibility of similar sharing with Peele's *Honour of the Garter* and Nashe's *Unfortunate Traveller* (see the essay in this collection) with the same reservation. He adopts Foakes and

Rickerts's suggestion that Henslowe's "ne" probably indicates revision of *Titus* requiring a new license from the Master of the Revels, discusses metrical and vocabulary evidence that he finds contradictory, and settles on "a date preceding 1592 for the original composition of the play with a revision in late 1593."[19]

Honigmann, in two of his books, mounts a determined assault on what he terms the "late start" chronology of Shakespeare's plays, notably as exhibited in the efforts of Malone and the even-more-influential dating set forth by Chambers. Both of these scholars, among others, assumed Shakespeare had written only a few plays before the well-known attack on him by Greene in his *Groat's Worth of Wit* (entered on the *Stationers' Register* 20 September 1592 and published in the same year). Honigmann postulates an "early start" chronology beginning during the decade of the 80s, based in part on the note by Aubrey that Shakespeare "had been in his younger years a Schoolmaster in the Countrey,"[20] and other persuasive evidence that he presents, arguing that by 1592 Shakespeare had written a dozen plays.[21] As part of his new chronology, and citing the allusion in *Bartholomew Fair* indicating an early date for *Titus Andronicus*, which he insists should be treated more seriously than it had previously been, and the echoes in *The Troublesome Reign* (1591), Honigmann designates *Titus* as Shakespeare's first play and assigns a date of composition of 1586.[22]

In a balanced and thoughtful assessment of the date of *Titus*, Taylor sets forth comprehensively the considerations that have to be taken into account. He notes the performances by Sussex's Men beginning on 24 January 1594 and says that they cannot have been the first, since the title page of Q1 says that Derby's (Strange's) and Pembroke's also had "Plaide" the tragedy, he believes, "in sequence." He accepts the allusion in *A Knack* as relating to *Titus* but questions its value as evidence, since the text is a memorial reconstruction dated, on its title page, 1594, and "might result from a . . . memory" of that year. *Titus* does not appear in Strange's four months' season of playing at the Rose in 1592 and therefore it "must have belonged to Strange's Men either long before 1592 or not until after January 1593." The earlier possibility could "indicate that the story of *Titus Andronicus* was well known to London audiences by mid-1592." Jonson's rueful mock he judges to be "of uncertain value in arbitrating between the late 1580s or early 1590s as its most probable period of composition." Important to a determination of date are its links to Strange's Men and "the large size of its cast which associates it with the pre-plague plays . . . the only feasible alternative [to a completion in summer 1592] would be to assume that *Titus* belongs to the very beginning of Shakespeare's career, and hence that it was written in 1590 or before." He settles on a date of 1592.[23] No date is specifically assigned by Stanley

Wells in his introduction to *Titus* in the Oxford Complete *Works,* but the arrangement of the plays is chronological, and *Titus* is fifth following *Two Gentlemen of Verona, Taming of the Shrew,* and *2* and *3 Henry VI.* Wells also observes that the play "combines sensational incident with high flown rhetoric of a kind that was fashionable around 1590."[24]

The evidence regarding the date of composition, while not plentiful, is at least reasonably ample, more so than that for most of the plays of other early dramatists. Much of it has been the subject of discussion since the days of Malone, who first attempted to arrange the plays in order more than two centuries ago. Even at that early date, he noted the presence of *Titus* in the First Folio and in Meres's list, and cited Jonson's 25 or 30 years before 1614. All the evidence that has been adduced since then has been familiar to the quite considerable body of scholars whose determinations have been discussed above, but no clear consensus has emerged. It appears manifest that the specific dates endorsed have been arrived at by the degree of cogency that the individual commentator finds in various items of evidence. Thus we find a range from 1586 to 1593–94 although there are two clusters of opinions favoring 1589–90 and 1593–94.

It seems to me that Jonson's "25 or 30 years" is not as vague as it has been generally thought to be. It is in fact reasonably definite, especially as to the later part of his range, and in consideration of his implicit inclination to deny that the two plays continued to be uninterruptedly popular as late as 1614. With Honigmann, I believe that "'five and twenty or thirty' is more carefully precise than a single round number would be," and is supported, as he points out, by another Jonsonian comment on *The Spanish Tragedy* in *Cynthia's Revels.*[25] The echoes of *Titus* in *The Troublesome Reign* and the reference in *A Knack,* dated on their title pages 1591 and 1592 respectively show that Shakespeare's play was on the boards in 1590. Without pressing Jonson's comment too urgently, I conclude that the date of composition that fits with the facts we have is 1589. I do not believe it was his first play, although it may have been his first noncollaborative effort at drama.

73. A STAGE FOR *TITUS ANDRONICUS*

Drawing by C. Walter Hodges entitled "A Stage for *Titus Andronicus,*" *The Globe Restored*, plate 73, 1968. Reproduced by permission of C. Walter Hodges, the Folger Shakespeare Library and Oxford University Press.

7

Stage History: 1970–1994

THE performance record of *Titus Andronicus* in the twentieth century[1] began with the Old Vic production of 1923 and intensified notably during the years since 1951. The high level of interest on the part of producers, directors, actors, and, presumably, audiences has continued unabated, and the play has extended itself histrionically and geographically in the most recent decades. The number of international productions has risen significantly since 1970. In consideration of its relative neglect from the eighteenth century to our own, this is a good showing, rivaling that of the immediately preceding quarter of a century. In quality the standard has been high, and two superior productions have been mounted.

Friedrich Dürrenmatt, the noted Swiss playwright, who earlier had been inspired by attending a performance of the Olivier-Brook production of *Titus* at Paris to write his *Frank der Fünfte,* composed in 1970 his own *Titus Andronicus* based more directly on Shakespeare's text. Under the title *Titus Andronicus: Eine Komödie Nach Shakespeare,* his play was staged at Düsseldorf in December of that year. Dürrenmatt's adaptation included, among other departures from Shakespeare's play, the introduction of Alaric as a principal character and the transmutation of Aaron into a male prostitute. Some of his more heinous Shakespearean deeds are transferred to other characters. In his text, Dürrenmatt emphasizes piety and justice and the absurdity of human life. The Düsseldorf production was a sensation, but audience reaction was less than favorable. Since they were unfamiliar with Shakespeare's play, the horrors, which, it is reported, they found hard to bear, were attributed to Dürrenmatt. He was characterized as a sadist. Hans Schwab-Felisch, the *Theater Heute* reviewer, reported the negative outcry of the unruly audience over the horrors that was directed against Dürrenmatt rather than Shakespeare. He points out, however, that the adaptation, of which he expresses a low opinion, did not materially alter the shocks in the original text. Nevertheless Dürrenmatt's changes tend to degrade Shakespeare's dramaturgy to a level comparable, Schwab-Felisch says, to *Porgy and Bess* or *The Threepenny Opera.* The introduction of modern political themes and of the character Alaric did not succeed. Karl Heinz Stroux's production and the musical accompaniment emphasized the bloody stage pictures in Grand Guignol style, while Günter Walbeck's costumes were a medley, Titus appearing in nineteenth-century battle dress with military decorations, the Goths in Wehrmacht uniforms, and Tamora bare-breasted. The acting was mediocre except for Libgart Schwarz's intense struggle as Lavinia to write her tormentors' names in the sand, an effort that lit up the performance.[2]

V. Cankov produced a *Titus* at the Pozardzik Theatre, Bulgaria in 1975; in the same year, Peter Miller, a fifteen-year-old freshman at Lamoille Union High School, Hyde Park, Vermont, presented as his third Shakespearean production (*The Taming of the Shrew* and *Richard III* were the first two) "Shakespeare's Old Men:" Polonius, Lear, Prospero, Macbeth, and Titus Andronicus. For the last "cameo" he chose Titus cutting off his hand—impressively, according to one reviewer.[3]

1977 saw two presentations on the opposite coasts of the United States going on in an almost uninterrupted sequence. R. Thad Taylor, the founder and artistic director of the Shakespeare Society of America's Globe Playhouse in Los Angeles presented thirty performances from 3 June to 2 July. Paul Barry, artistic director of the New Jersey Shakespeare Festival at Drew University, Madison, directed twenty-two performances from 5 July to 21 August. A. R. Braunmuller and William L. Stull found Frank Geraci's direction and the acting of the cast at the Los Angeles Globe "excellent." The tragedy was "played straight as a lamentable tragedy, with a strong local Shakespearean actor, William Frankfather, in the title role. Religiously abiding by the Elizabethan conventions as we know them, Geraci nonetheless made the play a timeless study of violence . . . Frankfather, a large man, developed Titus subtly as a sympathetic moral blunderer. The mutilation of a pathetic Lavinia (Colleen McMullen) was horrific but not grotesque . . . Geraci made the characters in this inhumane play all too human, and the production rang true."[4] Joseph Stodder was "delightfully surprised" at the evenness and depth of the casting, design, and direction. He especially cited Frankfather's "strong and versatile" Titus, McMullen's "skill in handling the silences as well as the dialogue" in the role of Lavinia, and J. D. Hall's Aaron.[5]

The late Bernard Beckerman noted that the emphasis of the New Jersey Shakespeare Festival production was "on the play as ensemble. The entire cast remained on stage for much of the time, individuals stepping forth as needed to join the action. A few properties—seats, benches, braziers—provided a constant decor, fixed in the sight of the audience throughout the performance. Indeed, we were purportedly witnessing an ancient rite," which was presented without intermission in one hour and fifty-five minutes. The physical horrors were handled effectively. "Without shrinking from presenting the bloody business of hacked limbs, the director succeeded in throwing attention on human reaction to horror rather than on the horror itself." The presentation "showed ingenuity and boldness of imagination."[6] Press reviewers generally expressed opinions similar to those of Professor Beckerman. The Philadelphia *Inquirer* critic noted that the producer "mounted the play as a ritual . . . Barry calls it 'a Roman black mass' . . . The violence is committed in a ceremonial style [but] . . . the elevated demands of ritual behavior are not allowed to interfere with the open throttle acting that is characteristic of Barry's troupe . . . the effect is roughly Elizabethan, a show for the groundlings." The faint lines of the later King Lear could be seen in Titus. The New York *Daily News* reviewer appraised the production, in spite of the horrors, "a good show. The direction is sharp and fast and the acting is flawless." *Titus Andronicus* is "rather bloody, rather gruesome . . . a play about incredible revenge and agony."[7]

Fabia Puigserver and his Teatre Lliure produced an abbreviated *Titus* in a Catalonian translation by Josep de Sagarra at Barcelona in 1977, revived at Madrid in 1978 and again in Barcelona in 1980. The cast was limited to fourteen, which, with even more severe cuts in the text, reduced the playing time to two hours and a-half. The conflict between Titus and Tamora was the center of the action in a Rome whose decadence was emphasized, and in which Titus was made to seem an anachronism.[8]

The respected Stratford, Ontario, Shakespearean Festival had not essayed a *Titus Andronicus* until 1978. The production was repeated in 1980 with the same director, Brian Bedford, the same production staff, and, with some exceptions, virtually the same cast. Ralph Berry found much to commend in the 1978 version and much to criticize. Bedford, in his debut as director, required of the cast a taut and disciplined exposition that imparted clarity and lucidity, but to Berry it was not uniformly successful. There were strategic gains, but there were also "losses in passages that called for greater voltage than Bedford was ready to permit. I cannot imagine a more restrained *Titus* than this one." Jennifer Phipps's Tamora's encounter with Aaron "was staged with an unbelievable lack of passion . . . Alan Scarfe's Aaron . . . had little time for Tamora . . . his sexual charisma was reduced." These were the losses; the gains included "Domini Blythe's Lavinia, superior in acting quality to Vivien Leigh's . . . her slow, cross-stage movement in the aftermath of the rape was especially moving." While William Hutt as Titus demonstrated an eerily quiet, matter-of-fact puzzlement rather than a Titan's rage, "Max Helpmann's sturdy, oaken Marcus stood out. He missed no chances." Bedford's directorial restraint was rewarded in the final scene when Titus kissed Lavinia as she was ceremoniously sacrificed, lost his control as he stabbed Tamora repeatedly, and, upon receiving his death wound from

Saturninus, still has the strength to strike him in return. The concluding 120 lines or so following the death of Saturninus were cut, and for them was substituted the Sybilline Oracle's prophecy of the fall of Rome, which, Berry says, "was an abrupt and ominous ending, shorn of the restorative elements in Shakespeare's design." He concludes that, "with reservations, one recognizes here a cerebral and finely wrought exposition of a difficult text."[9] Berry also reviewed the 1980 production, finding "Pat Galloway's ferociously sensual Tamora . . . the most important of the casting changes." The ending was cut again and with it Shakespeare's statement of the forces of healing and renewal, but this time Berry thought that "the ominous truncated ending . . . is perhaps truer to the organic logic of the text . . . In all, an improved version of a most striking production, one that deserves to be mentioned in the same breath as Brook's." Roger Warren praised Bedford's conception, the staging, "Errol Slue's superb Aaron . . . and Stephen Russell's lithe Demetrius," but found William Hutt's Titus less than satisfactory. "The final ritual slaughter was superbly controlled by Mr. Bedford's unerring sense of rhythm," but the truncated ending was a "falsification . . . The final impression was of an uncomplicated but very powerful revenge play."[10] In 1978 there were thirteen performances; and, in 1980, nineteen.

The first production of *Titus Andronicus* in Hungary was mounted by Ferenc Sik at the Pecs National Theatre in 1978. All the horror and violence in the play were faithfully reproduced. There was even more violence than the text provides: the rape of Lavinia was enacted on stage in the form of a highly stylized yet appallingly grotesque pantomime. I. Palffy noted that "Sik was right in surmising that a naturalistic representation of concentrated violence must arouse a defensive reaction . . . but in the midst of all this horror and violence the very idea that Sik had professed was inevitably and irretrievably lost. Spectators were left with nothing but a smart stage version of a melodrama."[11] The Triple Action Theatre, a touring troupe headquartered in Mansfield, Nottinghamshire, produced in 1979 a version of the play, heavily cut by its artistic director, under the title "Stephen Rumbelow's *Titus Andronicus*." The cast consisted of five parts: Titus, Tamora, Saturninus, Lavinia, and Aaron. The technique employed in this truncated production is called by Rumbelow episodic or interrupted symbolism, which seemed to the press critics to be the substitution of shock effects for Shakespearean poetry. To one reviewer it amounted to an effort to outhorror the original, employing screams, farmyard noises, flagellations, mutilations, atrocities, and buckets of blood. The reviews were not favorable.[12]

Cleveland's Great Lakes Shakespeare Festival presented a *Titus* in 1980 under the direction of Vincent Dowling, who strove "to hold a powerful mirror up to the darker side of our life." The performance was so realistic that Patricia Olsen noted that "there was little applause, and the audience seemed, at times, to be in mute shock." She commended the range of Emery Battis as Titus, who "ran the gamut from wicked to caring, triumphant to sorrowful"; and she found the Lavinia of Madylon Branstetter, who won for her performance the Cleveland Critics Circle nomination for Best Actress, "delicate, fragile, and beautiful." Other observers singled out for praise the acting of Robert Ellenstein as Marcus, who lovingly ministered to the mutilated Lavinia. The play was performed seven times.[13]

The American Players Theatre of Spring Green, Wisconsin, not far from Frank Lloyd Wright's Taliesin, launched its premier season (1980) in an outdoor theatre with productions of *A Midsummer Night's Dream* and *Titus Andronicus*. The artistic director, Randall Duk Kim, directed by Edward Berkeley, played the title role in *Titus* to the universal applause of all the commentators. Rhoda-Gale Pollack said his performance was "a joy to watch . . . [he] plummeted to the depths of Titus, revealed the aged warrior's righteous passions, and allowed the many turns of emotion to emanate naturally from his core. Never did he rant, rave, or bluster." Memorable also were Henry Strozier as Marcus and Julia Kiley as Lavinia, "who convincingly and sensitively played the discovery scene . . . The action was violent and bloody but never merely sensational." There were some grisly moments, but Berkeley "masterfully staged this production so that it flowed effortlessly from one strong moment . . . to the next." One reviewer pronounced this *Titus* "the find of the season."[14] The fly scene was cut from the production (of which there were forty-eight performances) to the regret of Charles J. Bright, the Managing Director; it was restored as part of five additional performances in 1981.

John Barton produced a double-bill by the Royal Shakespeare Company at Stratford in 1981 consisting of *Two Gentlemen of Verona* and *Titus Andronicus*. The playing area was restricted by onstage arrangements of coatracks, costumes, mirrors, properties and property baskets, weapons, and wicker hobby horses that were used in both plays. It was apparently intended to convey the impression of a touring company, but, unlike a similar Old Vic production of 1957 linking *The Comedy of Errors* with *Titus*, which was well received by the critics, it was not successful. Gareth Lloyd Evans described Shakespeare's first tragedy as "the victim of production and acting that mocked it beyond reason. Even Shakespeare's sow's ears give some glimpses of being capable of transformation into silk purses, but this Senecan hangover was studiedly subjected to denigration. The players indulged in in-jokes—an unforgivable practice in any production . . . words were knowingly mispronounced with the suggestion that 'we don't know what they mean, let's have a giggle.' It is tedious and unpleasing to recall all the aberrations, but they all emanated from a failure to recognize and express the play's Elizabethan reality—a serious if exaggerated exercise in moral turpitude, mindlessness, and cruelty." He designated the production as "disastrous." Stanley Wells agreed that *Titus* suffered more than *Two Gentlemen*. Having the actors not directly part of the action "resting" on the stage, while generally acceptable, did not convey the austerity required for tragedy; and the substantial cuts—850 lines—were "damaging . . . Amplification is an essential rhetorical device in *Titus Andronicus;* to reduce it overemphasizes the action, detracts from its steady-paced grandeur, its sombre meditativeness." Wells was complimentary about the acting of Patrick Stewart as Titus, Hugh Quarshie as Aaron, Leonie Mellinger as Lavinia, and Ray Jewers as Marcus. Roger Warren was favorably impressed by the staging, especially of the forest sequence, which varied with the mood, lyrical at first, changing to erotic in the meeting of Aaron and Tamora, then to the gloom of the "barren detested vale" of the rape. He thought Mellinger's performance upon her return to the stage "amazing" and Stewart's Titus "superb." Sheila Hancock's Tamora "began uneasily . . . but later she had some nice moments of variety and welcome humour." He noted that Barton's *Two Gentlemen* had to be considered in relation to his treatment of *Titus*. References in the second play to *Titus* made it clear that, at least in part, the tragedy was conceived to be a foil for the comedy.[15]

In the same year, beginning 13 June, Jozef Bednarik produced *Titus Andronicus* in a Slovak translation by Josef Kot at the Andrej Bagar Theatre, Nitra, Slovakia.[16] In the following year, beginning 10 December 1982, Christof Nel directed a German version in a translation by Erich Fried at the Deutschen Schauspielhaus Hamburg. The *Theater Heute* reviewer found much to commend in Erich Wonder's production: the setting, the staging—particularly the choreographed confrontations between the Andronici and the imperial party—the costuming, and the acting, specifically Gerd Kunath as Titus and Rotraut de Neve as Lavinia; but he had reservations as to why such a senseless bloodbath should be produced at all. He expressed skepticism about the value of portraying inhuman situations, emotions, and deeds.[17] The Australian W.A.I.T. acted *Titus* at Perth from 14 to 25 June 1983, employing techniques of Artaud's "Theatre of Cruelty" to present bizarre and horrific images.[18]

Kestutis Nakas mounted a serialized "punk" production at the Pyramid Cocktail Lounge in Brooklyn, New York, in August and September 1981, repeated at Greenwich Village's Pyramid Club in August 1983. One act was presented on each of five successive Monday evenings, "in a variety of acting styles [including burlesque, which] made the performances unusual."[19] Pierre Peyrou's Parisian production in French in December 1983 was but one of three Shakespearean presentations in the French capital that year (the other two were *Hamlet* and *King Lear*). The Theatre Present mounted *Titus* in a former slaughterhouse, whose auditorium is adapted so that the actors had "the whole of the ground floor . . . while the audience are seated on tiers elevated all round." The reviewers noted that the use of "a modified abbatoir adds an ironic though harmonious touch." A full text was employed, adapted from Francois-Victor Hugo's translation, which conveyed a "rough tragic tone." The performance lasted three and a-half hours. It was Peyrou's "first encounter with Shakespearian drama and definitely comes down as a great success." The acting was generally accomplished, notably "Brigitte Lechanteur's pretty and moving Lavinia, Tonia Galievsky's deep-voiced Tamora, Pierre Payrou's dark-spectacled Aaron, [and] Roger Mollien's Titus." Mollien's reaching out for the missing hands of the mutilated Lavinia, the fly-killing episode, the cropping of Titus's hand by Aaron using a rusty scythe, and the disguising in Act 5 were highlights.[20]

Titus was the last play in the BBC series of televised productions that was presented under the title "The Shakespeare Plays." Rehearsals began early in 1984 and video recording was completed in February 1985. Jane Howell, the producer, featured young Lucius from the opening scene, even though in the Folio text he does not appear until 3.2 (and not until 4.1 in the quartos) and consequently has no lines to speak until the play is half over. Stanley Wells in his review found this a "brilliant stroke," providing an unspoken reaction to the early bloody deeds in contrast to the verbalized responses of the other characters. Wells notes that the horrors are not flinched, but

> "the tableaux of grief are comparatively unaffecting, partly because the camera dwells too much on the object of suffering, too little on the sufferer—as when Marcus describes his mutilated niece—partly because the performers do too little to move us. The play's rhetoric may need to be scaled down for television, but it must not be evaded. Edward Hardwicke, as Marcus, tries, and fails, to take command of the verse . . . Trevor Peacock begins splendidly as Titus, a grizzled, sombre warrior with the authority of experience, sternly stoical in the face of grief. But as his sufferings take the centre of the stage his gravelly voice does not realize the emotion latent in his anguished arias, there is no sense of consolation deriving from the power to verbalize sorrow; nor does he create any impression of madness, real or feigned.

Wells found the less articulate roles (Anna Calder-Marshall's Lavinia and Paul Davies-Prowles's boy Lucius) the production's most touching figures, and sums up: "the play's emotional impact is not fully realized."[21]

In Germany in 1984–85 there were three productions of widely varying character. At the Schauspielhaus, Bochum, the well-known, innovative East German playwright Heiner Müller presented *Anatomie Titus Fall of Rome: Ein Shakespearekommemtar,* which, Marga Munkelt tells us aim[ed] at presenting three levels: a personal, a political, and an intellectual. Müller's version consists of a German translation of Shakespeare's text in verse, intermingled almost furtively with smaller additions every now and then, and expanded by set-off commentaries spoken by a Narrator, whom Müller adds to the cast. Some of his comments are summaries of parts of the action, others are discussions of topics which Müller thinks are inherent in the play.

She notes that Müller's text incorporates, among other things, his "biased outlook on class and race . . . a filthily distorted view of the Resurrection . . [and an] obsession with recurring characteristics—Tamora's trademark, for instance, is her breasts, and Saturnine perspires permanently . . Müller's stylistic incongruities come close to being stylistic lapses— whether inadvertently so or consciously is hard to say."

Other critics denigrated Müller's pervasive tinkering with and mistranslation of Shakespeare's text, as well as what was judged to be an excessive emphasis on the horrors. Wilhelm Hortmann observed that "To Müller the world is a slaughterhouse . . . kings dung their fields with the bones and blood of their subjects; whoever dabbles in power or sex is invariably butchered, and every victim drags others to the block. Directors Manfred Karge and Matthias Langhoff took the audience through a macabre dance of death—15 corpses in varying stages of decomposition waking up to begin the play—in which the emotional shocks of a theatre of cruelty alternated with slapstick horrors of the video age."[22]

The second presentation was in part a reaction to Müller's: a humorous version entitled *Titus Androgynous* intended by Munkelt and her partner and "co-producer," Krishnan Venkatesh, as a satirical comment on "directorial experiments" with Shakespeare's play, "merging the styles and approaches of various producers and even going beyond their distortions." It was recorded on audio tape with Munkelt and Venkatesh taking all the parts in a shortened text and in numerous variant voices. The role of Titus is played by Munkelt, the first on record by a woman. There was one "semi-public presentation" in the English Seminar of the University of Münster on 6 December 1984.[23]

Johann Weissenbacher and the students of the Alexander von Humboldt Gymnasium at Schweinfurt presented the third *Titus* of 1984–85 three times. It was selected for production because of the theme of justice and because it could, with appropriate alterations, be made suitable for student actors. Weissenbacher employed Dürrenmatt's text cut by approximately 30 percent and with a few other adjustments. The audience response was mixed: fellow students of the actors received the play well; their elders had reservations.[24]

The Oregon Shakespeare Festival at Ashland rendered its third *Titus* in 1986 as part of the season that included *As You Like It, Measure for Measure,* and *The Tempest,* and seven non-Shakespearean plays. The earlier versions of the woes of Titus were mounted in 1956 and 1974. Pat Patton, associate festival director and director of the 1986 production, viewed his task as not to make the play palatable but to have it be comprehensible. "I tried to make it hard, strong, and fast," and in this he was successful. Reviewers noted that the staging was lean and that the pace carried the audience along while neither stinting nor overstating the horrors. Stage blood was eschewed, blood-red streamers being substituted, and a range of sound effects—notably "eerie echoic gongs"—reinforced the action. The general effect was "pulsating," especially in the attack on Lavinia, which one reviewer said was "stunning." Nancy Carlin as Lavinia, Peter Temple as Aaron, and Joan Stuart-Morris as Tamora were applauded. Henry Woronicz was commended but some thought he was a bit too restrained as Titus. Thirty performances were given on the Ashland outdoors Elizabethan stage.[25]

In sharp contrast to most *Tituses,* which intend to take the play seriously, was the 1986 presentation by the Source Theatre, Washington. The director, William Freimuth, jettisoning any attempt at earnestness, mounted a thoroughgoing parody instead. In a critique marked by genial good humor in the face of such a production, Margaret Tocci characterized the Source Theatre's effort as a compound of "knockabout farce and cheerful mayhem sprinkled with gallons of stage gore . . . [which] reaches an apogee of absurdity." Feimuth was successful "in evoking constant laughter." Inspired by Dover Wilson, who characterizes the play as a "broken-down cart, laden with bleeding corpses . . . driven by an executioner from Bedlam dressed in cap and bells . . . [a] burlesque and melodramatic travesty . . . a huge joke" and who perceives Shakespeare "laughing behind his hand through most of the scenes," Freimuth included and exploited such devices as a large trash can at the play's opening filled with the mutilated limbs of Titus's dead sons killed in battle; the heads of Quintus and Martius delivered to Titus in a newspaper bag by a messenger on a bicycle—Titus carried one around by the nose; handless Lavinia's frustrated efforts to eat chips and dip; the Thyestean banquet as a food fight; a Lucius who faints whenever events turn gory; a Marcus who wears red passion flowers behind his ears; a Tamora who is "a sort of deep-South iron butterfly cum evangelist;" and a chef's apron worn by Titus "bearing the banner, 'This is no dress rehearsal. This is it.'" Tocci found the costumes "cheerful and looney:" Bassianus "sports a bow tie with his tunic . . . Titus favors epaulets . . . [Tamora wears] silver dance shoes, a navy velvet gown, and fox neckpiece, [and Lavinia] a moth-eaten dance recital costume." Tocci summed up the performance as "fast paced, utterly camp . . . freely interpreted," the text heavily cut—"this production of *Titus Andronicus* will amaze many and irritate not a few . . . Freimuth and his cast go for the gusto and leave any serious intent in the dust." Press reviewers found it "hilarious," "a real scream," and "unruly, undisciplined, often unfunny," but still worth seeing. There were thirty-two performances.[26]

The Royal Shakespeare Company mounted its fourth *Titus* in thirty-six years after having totally neglected the play during the first seventy years of the company's existence. This production, which opened in April 1987 at the relatively new Swan in Stratford-upon-Avon, was directed by Deborah Warner, who presented the uncut text—a rare theatrical event—and allowed herself only one minor but effective nonverbal intrusion (whistling). Stanley Wells noted the absence of "theatrical glamour" from Warner's conception. There was "none of the allurements of pageantry or of sumptuous costumes" frequently employed by other directors. "Her staging . . . seemed based on the most austere of Elizabethan methods" and made no effort to point out modern parallels nor to probe "a subtext for psychological resonances." There was no shirking of the violence.

> The director worked on the premise that everything in the text was there for a purpose, that the dramatist knew what he was about . . [she was] determin[ed] to test the text at every point with relentless rigour . . . the result was overwhelmingly impressive . . . Warner's approach . . . revealed the hand of an immensely skilful, even cunning, director. The rhetoric was plumbed for its deep sources, which were then brought to the surface so that even the most artificial verbal structures became expressive of emotion. Marcus' description of Lavinia immediately after her rape may read like a heartless verbal exercise by a bright boy from the local grammar school; spoken in Donald Sumpter's hushed tones it became a deeply moving attempt to master the facts, and thus to overcome the emotional shock, of a previously unimagined horror. We had the sense of a suspension of time, as if the speech represented an articulation, necessarily extended in expression, of a sequence of thoughts and emotions that might have taken no more than a second or two to flash through the character's mind, like a bad dream.

Warner managed to obviate audience laughter at inappropriate moments by taking full advantage of the comedy "latent in the text." She had Brian Cox as Titus stuff

> his fingers into his ears, pretending not to hear his brother and sons pleading for Mutius' burial. Estelle Kohler, as Tamora, and her two sons, played her bombastic accusation of Bassianus as if it were a burlesque playlet put on for their victims' entertainment; Demetrius' sudden stabbing of Bassianus seemed all the more horrific as a result. Acknowledgement of the comedy in the situation when Titus, Lucius, and Marcus squabble over who shall have the honour of losing a hand in the hope of saving Titus' sons intensified the pain of the moment when Titus outwits the others by getting Aaron to mutilate him while they have gone to fetch an axe.

The high point attained by Warner's exploitation of comedy came in the fly scene, in which Titus repeatedly stabbed at the "black ill-favoured fly" (3.2.66), "his enemy's surrogate," while sprawling across the dinner table. "Cox made a marvelous moment of the transition . . . from the tragicomic absurdity of his initial reaction, through dawning acceptance of the validity of Marcus' excuse [in first stabbing the fly], to the ferocity of frustrated despair with which he cast himself on the table. This was masterly acting." In the final scene, Warner "permitted herself a wordless interpolation: servants whistled a merry tune as they carried on the furniture for the Theyestean banquet." Wells was also favorably impressed by the representation of the comedic elements of the brief clown sequence (4.3.76–110).

Like any strong production this one impelled its audience to revalue the play. *Titus Andronicus* stood in greater need of revaluation than most of its author's works, and this production gave it what it needed at this point in its history. It emerged as a far more deeply serious play than its popular reputation would suggest, a play that is profoundly concerned with both the personal and social consequences of violence rather than one that cheaply exploits their theatrical effectiveness. I was impressed as never before by the art of its structuring: its twin climaxes of violence, one directed at Titus, the other directed by him; by the force of the counteraction, led by Lucius; and by the part played within the whole by details of language, such as by the recurrent, increasingly horrific emphasis on 'hand' and 'hands' . . . [the play] did not emerge as an unflawed masterpiece in this revelatory production, but subsequent directors will have far less excuse than before for evading its problems by textual adaptation or by evasive theatricalism.

In addition to the performance by Cox, Wells noted Richard McCabe's giggling, psychotic Chiron; Sonia Ritter's quiveringly traumatized Lavinia; and Kohler's stingingly waspish Tamora; but found it "perverse to give the role of Aaron to an actor [Peter Polycarpou] who looks Greek instead of the raven-black Moor of the text."[27]

Alan Dessen judged Warner's production to be "extremely powerful, for some even overwhelming. If one ranks productions by what percentage of the potential in the script is realized, Warner's *Titus* was one of the best Shakespeare shows I have seen in recent years . . . this director's methods were revolutionary and extraordinarily fruitful . . . scenes that editors, scholars, and directors have assured us were unplayable emerged as powerful and highly meaningful." One of these was the meeting between the unforewarned Marcus and his savaged niece, Lavinia. In spite of the impression conveyed by the text, in this production it "is a two-actor scene, wherein we observe Marcus, step-by-step, use his logic and Lavinia's reactions to work out what has happened and, in the process, filter the horror through a human consciousness." Other so-called "'unplayable' moments also came across with great force . . . Thanks to some fine acting and inventive staging," notably in Tamora's description of "the woods as a 'barren detested vale' in II.iii, [where it] was played by Estelle Kohler as a joke or deliberate exaggeration, so that Bassianus, Lavinia, and the audience laughed as Chiron and Demetrius pantomimed the hissing snakes and swelling toads. The payoff was an even greater shock when an apparently funny moment erupted into violence. Dessen points out that "the ultimate test for any Titus" is the scene (3.1) in which the old warrior undergoes a series of horrors—the arrest of two of his sons on trumped-up charges of murder, the banishment of Lucius, his third remaining son, the presentation to him by Marcus of the martyred Lavinia, the sacrifice of his hand in an effort to redeem his accused sons, and the brutal return of his severed hand with his sons' heads—climaxed in this production by a "long chilling laugh that signaled his [Titus's] total break with Rome and with ordinary humanity . . . The effect was stunning." But most revealing for Dessen "were two lessons: that in Titus, laughter (when under control) can mix with tragic effect; and that, given the right conditions, the 'unplayable' can become the theatrically potent."

In a later essay, described by Dessen as "highly selective (and admittedly idiosyncratic)," he chooses certain "exciting and revealing moments" from a few Shakespearean presentations, avoiding those "that did not work for me." From Warner's mounting of Titus he calls attention to, among other times the emphasis by Aemilius on the word your in the line "Your bidding shall I do effectually" addressed to Saturninus (4.4.107) which makes a "useful distinction by signaling a possible ground swell among non-aligned Romans against the power and influence of Tamora; [the] uncut and very powerful rendition of Marcus's supposedly unplayable forty-seven-line speech to the maimed Lavinia" (2.4.11–57); and the acting of Ritter as the "near-catatonic Lavinia" during the execution of Demetrius and Chiron and at the moment of her own death. In sum, he cites the work of Warner in Titus and King John as the most telling combination of theatrically and thoughtfulness and hence . . . the best example in 1988 of exciting Shakespeare."[28]

H. R. Woudhuysen commended Warner, who, he says, "succeeds powerfully in presenting a spectacle in which Titus has to be taken on its own terms . . . On a starkly bare stage, with a minimum of props, with costumes which discreetly manage not to draw attention to themselves and only a few highly effective lighting changes the play moves unerringly between high tragedy and the most painful comedy. The audience is allowed to laugh, but at the right moments, and is made to feel that here laughter need neither be innocent nor happy." The pace "is disciplined and well-controlled" with no slackening in the second half. Indeed, the production becomes "more moving" as Titus sinks into the wilderness of tigers. The gruesome parts were appalling but credible: "blood is used sparingly and almost always on spotlessly white linen." Woudhuysen noted that "the production places a great burden on the actors" especially Cox, Kohler, and Ritter, who rose to the occasion and performed with conviction. However, Polycarpou he found to be "too pale . . . and too decent to enjoy the wickedness he should revel in."[29]

The production was moved to The Pit theater at Barbican, London, and performances resumed in August 1988, continuing intermittently to January of the following year. Press reviewers pointed out that the staging seemed to have intensified somewhat as compared to that at The Swan, perhaps traceable to the "studio" atmosphere of the smaller Pit, which, in Irving Wardle's assessment, cleared the way "for an unobstructed rhythm of calamity and lamentation . . . achiev[ing] some breathtaking imagery." "Under the low ceiling of the Pit," Michael Ratcliffe noted, "nothing comes between us and the core of the play, which is not violence and cruelty but grief . . . Heroic theatre and a comedy of terrors march side by side." Michael Billington had admired the play at the Swan but found it "even greater in the intimate confines of the Pit . . . it translates what can easily seem a grotesque catalogue of horrors into an unforgettable symphony of grief . . . The production also gains in claustrophobic power . . . The central performances are . . . even richer than at Stratford." Other observers also expressed high opinions of the Pit presentation, employing terms such as "galvanic ensemble work"; "admirably spare cogent production"; "tragic grandeur" "extraordinarily powerful theatre"' "powerful . . . cumulative effect." Most comments regarding the acting singled out Cox, Kohler, Ritter, and Donald Sumpter, a Marcus, for favorable mention.[30]

Warner's *Titus* was performed 76 times at Stratford, 10 times at Newcastle, 47 times at Barbican, 2 at the Riverside Studios, London, and 28 on a continental tour including Madrid, Paris, Copenhagen, and Aarhus, Denmark, for a total of 163 performances over the period from 28 April 1987 to 14 April 1989, a record for any production, exceeding even the Brook-Olivier total of 90 at Stratford, on the Continent, and in London. More important is the fact that, in the judgments of reviewers, both scholarly and journalistic, it compared favorably to the Brook-Olivier production of 1955–57, the Papp-Friedman presentation of 1967, and that by Brian Bedford in 1978–80.

Three American Shakespeare Festivals mounted the play in 1988. The Colorado Festival's was its second, the earlier one having occurred in 1967. In the same summer, Shakespeare Santa Cruz and the Idaho Shakespeare Festival each presented *Titus*. Michael Mullin observed that the Colorado version "was a revelation. By using ceremony and *tableaux vivants* to distance the sensational gore, director Joel G. Fink unleashed the play's raw power. Borrowing from Japanese theatre, he treated Lavinia's maiming as a coup de theatre, the robed girl standing stage center as black-robed stagehands . . . drew long streamers of red silk from each sleeve. At once horrifying and beautiful, this and the other powerful tableaux formed a series of stark, haunting stage pictures that stunned the audience . . . For all its horror the production did not degenerate into thriller-diller Grand Guignol . . . the grisly banquet could be greeted with laughter and derision . . . Instead . . . The banquet scene played to stunned silence . . . the play swept along, riveting everyone's attention and creating a deeply moving sense of how close to our own experience are the emotions that wreak such horrors." He sums up: Director, designers, and actors remained true to the play, "even as they discovered unusual and unfamiliar ways to express it. *Titus* was theatre at its best." Press reviewers found the play "consistently compelling," "spirited, crude, bloody, vivid, and violent," "staging and decor . . . bewitching and handsome." While reaction to the acting was mixed, the Denver Drama Critics cited the production for the quality of the direction. There were twelve performances.[31]

As in the case of the RSC's *Titus Andronicus,* Dessen selects elements of Mark Rucker's Shakespeare Santa Cruz's presentation for comment. He found Bruce Young's Aaron "particularly interesting." He was

> wily, witty, and intelligent, he was not so much the proto-Iago or Richard III (although such elements were present) but was rather a warrior figure. Here one key was Young's size, for among his many assets as an actor (e.g., his fine diction, his control of verse, his resonant voice) is his physical stature—he is 6'4" and weighs about 240 pounds. Such size and stage presence gave him some grand opportunities, starting in 2.1 where he towered over Chiron and Demetrius whom (here and in 4.2) he tossed around with ease . . . Like those who have played Aaron in other productions, Young got some of his strongest effects . . . when defending his son. Standing with his scimitar and his baby on the hill . . . Aaron towered over the smaller figures below who seemed puny in comparison . . . the key to this interpretation lay in the soliloquy that ends the scene, for Young . . placed special emphasis on this moment . . The politician-manipulator at Saturninus's court clearly has been superseded here by the warrior.

A second powerful feature of Rucker's production was, to Dessen, directly involving Elizabeth Atkeson's Lavinia in the seizing of Chiron and Demetrius by stamping her foot to spring a trap that caught their feet. Her tormentors were overpowered, suspended upside down, and their throats cut. Lavinia received their blood in her basin. By this stamping of her foot

> Lavinia signaled to the audience that she was . . . a knowing agent in the revenge process. This choice then set up a moving death scene . . . for at the

outset of Titus's last speech to her, Atkeson rose and, with her arms raised and outstretched, slowly walked towards her father and his visible knife as if walking towards an embrace. Now that Chiron and Demetrius are dead and Tamora has eaten the meat-pie, this Lavinia was clearly *choosing* to walk to her death as a release from shame and pain . . . this moment emerged . . . as a visibly willed action that conveyed a poignancy, even a strange kind of beauty.

Press critics took notice of the Festival setting—all the performances took place at night in a grove of substantial redwood trees on the campus of the University of California, Santa Cruz—and they were favorably impressed by the acting of Young, of J. Kenneth Campbell as Titus, and Molly Mayock as a "vulpine Tamora," as well as Atkeson. The play was acted twelve times.[32]

Rod Ceballos, the director of the Idaho Shakespeare Festival's *Titus*, viewed the play as a portrayal of the conflict between the family and society, a problem of the "delicate balance that exists between personal integrity and the demands of the state." This "clear, solid production . . . [a reviewer said] is a brilliantly constructed contribution to the genre . . . of pride, honor, intrigue, and revenge." The director and his cast convey "the feeling of Roman pageantry, the fickleness of its citizens and the angry onslaught of the invading Goths . . . The story is a mixture of barbaric revenge and pure evil." Critics commended Will Casey as Titus, A. Bernard Cummings as Aaron, and Sandra Lindberg as Tamora. The play "leaves the audience's emotions drained and almost numbed with horror, although satisfied that justice finally prevails." There were ten performances.[33]

New York City's Riverside Shakespeare Company also mounted the play in 1988 in what Seymour Rudin designated as "the minimally furnished choir loft of the West Park Presbyterian Church . . . seating about sixty" (actually ninety-nine). In spite of the cramped quarters, the company offered "a thoughtful, responsible, mostly engrossing version of the first . . of the tragedies." Artistic director Timothy W. Oman chose "to play it as a series of escalating episodes of bloody aggression and revenge . . . [featuring a] monstrously willful, monstrously suffering, monstrously vengeful Titus . . . a kind of proto-Lear." Rudin found that while "not all the actors were . . . up to their tasks," Herman Petras in the title role "conveyed a good measure of the basic indignation and passion" required by the part. William Beckwith "was a quietly supportive, effective Marcus [and] Lisa Nicholas was a powerfully affecting Lavinia." There were sixteen performances.[34]

The year 1989 saw four productions in the western hemisphere. The Stratford [Ontario] Festival led off the year with a double bill of *The Comedy of Errors* and *Titus*, with each play adapted by its director to about eighty minutes playing time. Jeannette Lambermont viewed her adaptation as an opportunity to explore themes of *King Lear* in an early Shakespearean play, employing a kabuki design. The effect of this, according to C. E. McGee, was "to make the play a domestic tragedy of the Andronici, at the heart of which tragedy was the relationship between Titus and his daughter." Lucy Peacock "captured Lavinia's suffering powerfully . . . Her discovery [by Marcus] intensified her suffering because Marcus's gentleness and concern could not alleviate her sense of shame." Lambermont elected to shrink all the roles that made "caricatures of characters . . . Saturninus was a luxuriate booby . . . Tamora . . . too simply villainous . . . [and the] race to finish on time cost the production Aaron's moving appeal on behalf of his baby boy. In this shrunken *Titus* only Romans had genuine emotions." Nevertheless, Lambermont's production "had more of Shakespeare . . . in a sense" than the abbreviated *Errors*.

Wallace Sterling points out that the production lacked

> "a focus or clearly defined concept. The magnitude of the play and the scope of the title character as he seeks full retribution are sadly lacking. Instead we get pedantic line readings and stagy posturings . . . The Oriental puppet show . . . might have worked in a fuller, broader version . . . [but in this] it seemed more like an unnecessary appendage. In other words, the parts of this production did not cohere. Nicholas Pennell as Titus . . . does not generate the emotion of a man . . . seeking meaning in the maelstrom . . . Goldie Semple as Tamora, though rising significantly above the production approach, is also hampered in her attempt to present a full portrait of the powerful Queen of the Goths . . . I got the impression from the hasty and unimaginative curtain call that the actors were ready to have this production over with."

Media critics reported mixed reactions in two senses: that *Titus* in itself was uneven—"what is missing is the color, the resonances and the connections"; and that, by contrast, *Errors* was the better production. They praised the performances of Pennell, Semple, and Peacock. This second presentation of *Titus Andronicus* in a decade by the Stratford Festival was acted an even half a hundred times.[35]

The New Jersey Shakespeare Festival presented its second mounting of *Titus* beginning in June 1989, followed in August by the New York and the Alabama festivals. Paul Barry, the New Jersey's Artistic Director, who produced the play and took the part of Titus, started off with a mood-setting funeral for the previous Emperor, the father of Saturninus and Bassianus, an event that is not in Shakespeare's play. Naomi Conn Liebler noted that "As with Shakespeare's own creative endeavors authenticity and historical accuracy may on occasion be set aside for the sake of creating an overarching mood. That is what the director has done in this production, and it works through a consistency and integrity that are sustained for the length of the play." By emphasizing ritual, and involving Titus in it, Barry enlivened and unified his presentation and "humanized Titus more than the text denotes," especially in the Mutius incident. Thus the horrors are

> less surprising, less disjunctive, more intelligent and interesting than they appear to readers and audiences. This Titus is a complicated and torn character from the beginning, and, from the beginning, then, he is marked as a tragic protagonist rather than a monomaniac . . . In presenting a play that is often taken as an excuse for excess, director and actors cooperate in the exercise of restraint . . . [for which] Barry is to congratulated.

Liebler commended the playing of Diana LaMar as Lavinia, Leland Gantt as Aaron, Geddeth Smith as Marcus, and Barry in the title role. Press commentators generally registered mixed responses, though many thought some aspects of the production praiseworthy, and almost all found the acting impressive. The play was presented twenty-six times.[36]

The New York Shakespeare Festival's third production of *Titus* was offered as part of festival director Joseph Papp's announced plan to produce all of Shakespeare's plays over a six-year span. He had first mounted the play in 1956; his second production was the widely acclaimed version directed by Gerald Freedman in 1967. The latest (1989) presentation in the open-air Delacorte Theatre in Central Park offered a text substantially cut—some six hundred lines were omitted—by the director, Michael Maggio. Reviewers, both scholarly and journalistic, found little to commend either in the conception or in the acting. Dorothy and Wayne Cook judged Maggio's *Titus* "an oversimple reading [of a complex play:] to make Titus merely a vengeful victim is to distort the play as badly as do those glib commentators who dismiss the work as an example of youthful preoccupation with sensational event." They designated the acting "competent," the supporting roles almost without exception being uninspired or misconceived. Donald Moffat as Titus "emerged largely a figure of pity, without the responsibility either of his self-immolation or of his becoming a scourge of the gods." The only parts well-played were Aaron and Tamora, in which Keith David and Kate Mulgrew "were superb . . . David's Aaron was a malevolent genius . . . [and] Mulgrew as Tamora was Faulknerian." Between them they "raised the performance from second-rate thriller to a Shakespearean level of tragedy. Ironically . . . it was their vengeance that, despite its terrible and unwarranted gratifications, was the more dramatically justified."[37] Press reviews adopted the same tone. The Festival's presentation was described by Frank Rich as "a genteel *Titus Andronicus* . . . a routine sandal-and-toga recital of an early, infelicitously written work that . . . demands extravagant imagination and passion to rouse audiences . . . the performance like the production is too muted and patrician in adversity" especially that of Moffat as Titus. And even David as the Moor is not given "the histrionic room to unleash the irrational evil of a motiveless mass murderer." Clive Barnes contrasted the production with those mounted by Peter Brook and Deborah Warner and pointed out that "Those two productions are examples of what *can* be done with *Titus*" but was not in this instance. As to the acting, he found Moffat's Titus "a man of bumbling folly and gruff dignity . . . Mulgrew neither vicious nor seductive enough for the sensuously homicidal Tamora . . . [and] Alan McManus . . . more wimp than villain as the uxorious Emperor. By far the best performance comes from . . . David . . . madly exultant in his wickedness, glorying in his crimes, and celebrating his blackness."[38] There were eighteen performances.

The Alabama Shakespeare Festival at Montgomery presented its first *Titus* in 1989. Director Will York's conception comprehended an "abstract style influenced by an oriental discipline." The ethos of Chicago mob wars and of Los Angeles street gangs was mixed with the cultures of the play as part of York's "contemporary treatment."[39] The responses of reviewers were mixed. Press comment ranged from outright condemnation: "The production concept is confused and confusing. The direction is unfocused and erratic. The acting is slipshod" to grudging approval: "the violence was grotesque, literal, and horrifying . . . There were highquality performances . . . Edward Furs as Aaron . . . was especially fine" to general endorsement: "images . . . [were] built upon a foundation of brilliantly realized characters . . . the production . . . is as effective as it is unconventional." There were two casting oddities: Marcus was played by actress Ingrid MacCartney; and Furs, a white actor, portrayed Aaron without blackface. The play was presented ten times.[40]

The first Utah Shakespearean Festival presentation of *Titus* took place in 1990, in the Festival's twenty-ninth season. The director, Richard Risso—Chairman, Theater Department of California, Riverside—aimed at a balance between stylization and realism to make the staging "tough" without stressing "its savage violence."[41] In this he was successful, as reflected in the response of press reviewers who found the production "marvelous," the play "treated with intelligence, grandeur, and dignity," and presented "with striking effect." Ken Ruta as Titus exhibited "power and credibility," Megan Cole was a "subtle and vicious" Tamora, LeWan Alexander was "as nasty a villain as Shakespeare ever created," and Melanie van Betten "portrayed [an] "emotionally . . . wrenching" Lavinia. Risso "looked deep into the tragedy and discovered more than . . . a series of atrocities."[42] There were eighteen performances.

Paul Hunter, in the 1990 Edinburgh Festival Fringe, presented *Shakespeare's Fools,* the "wonderful clown parts" in the plays portrayed "most probably by Dick Tarleton but possibly by Will Kemp," including the Clown in *Titus*."[43]

The Theatre for a New Audience mounted *Titus* off-Broadway at New York's St. Clement's Church in 1994. Julie Traymore's production was straightforward and no effort was made to soften the impact of the play. Clive Barnes thought it "a classical Senecan revenge play," exhibiting "a fine ritualistic momentum." Another press reviewer noted that it was "a veritable slaughterhouse . . . gore is all." Vincent Canby summed up the production as "inventive, funny, fascinating, consistently engaging." New York *Times,* 4 March 1994; New York *Post,* 14 March, 1994. There were thirty-one performances.

In the course of the descriptions above of modern productions there are frequent discussions of staging. As to the early staging, though there is a little information in Jacques Petit's brief letter and in the Longleat drawing,[44] no comprehensive contemporary account of staging has come down to us. As a consequence of this deficiency, if we are to understand how the play was staged in Shakespeare's day, we must rely on the interpretation of evidence such as hints in the dialog and, undoubtedly much more fruitfully, though still scant, in the stage directions. This situation has, sometimes unfortunately—or perhaps only as might have been expected—resulted in contradictory scholarly speculations. Thus, we confront the spectacle of respected students of Elizabethan staging at odds as to whether *Titus Andronicus* supports the contention that Elizabethan playhouses had two or three stage doors,[45] or alternatively had two stage doors, one each at the left and the right, with an "inner stage" or "discovery space" situated in the center of the tiring-house wall.[46] This debate is, of course, much broader than any single play, but advocates, for example, of the two-door only hypothesis give little credence to the possibility, subscribed to by equally eminent scholars, that there is a hint in the text of Act 1 of *Titus* of three stage doors. Similarly, some close readers of the play believe that, in the final scene, there is an indication in the dialogue that Lucius and Marcus mount to the gallery from which to address the Romans; others deny the inference, since there is no stage direction explicitly calling for the two to exit from the platform nor to reenter above. In the general view and evaluation of the evidence of such aspects of the early staging of plays, *Titus* does not carry much weight, not only because it is a single play among many, but also because it is early, and because there continues to exist in the opinion of some commentators a lingering doubt concerning its authorship. In spite of these difficulties, the conjectures of certain critics have proved illuminating. In our exploration of the early staging and of the opinions and conclusions of others concerning it, we will direct our attention almost exclusively to *Titus;* secondarily to the other plays of Shakespeare; and will only occasionally take into account parallel situations in non-Shakespearean works.

In his essay on the use of a gallery over the platform of Elizabethan public-theater stages, Hosely adopts as "a working hypothesis the assumption that each of Shakespeare's plays was designed for production in a theatre having a gallery . . . similar to the Lords' room shown in the Swan drawing."[47] He points out that Shakespeare in his use of the gallery "generally introduces a secondary action aloft in support of an original action on the stage below," and this is true of *Titus Andronicus,* possibly with one exception. He lists three uses of the gallery in Act 1 but rejects "ten variously supposed uses of the gallery in five plays," including the two in Act 5 of *Titus,* which are accepted by many other scholars. In doing so, he says he has "the support of at least one modern editor [who is not named] in all but one case (*Titus* V.ii)."[48] This scene is the one in which Tamora, disguised as Revenge and accompanied by her sons as Rape and Murder, visits Titus to entreat him to restrain Lucius from marching on Rome. They knock, and Titus "opens his study door." There is no indication in the form of a stage direction in either Qq or F where the study is. Most such studies in plays of the era are located in the discovery space. However, in the dialogue, after identifying herself, Tamora says to Titus

> Come down and welcome me to this world's light;
>
> > (5.2.33)

Titus asks:

> Art thou Revenge? And art thou sent to me
> To be a torment to mine enemies?
>
> > (5.2.41–42)

to which she responds

> I am; therefore come down and welcome me.
>
> > (5.2.43)

Some lines later, Titus exclaims

> O sweet Revenge, now do I come to thee
> And if one arm's embracement will content thee,
> I will embrace thee in it by and by.
>
> > (5.2.67–69)

Tamora then speaks eleven lines addressed to her sons, the last of which is

See, here he comes, and I must ply my theme.

(5.2.80)

According to Hosley, the "amount of dialog provided to 'cover' a stairway descent ranges [in ten plays] from none to sixteen lines, the average being four; and the time required for such a descent, as determined by experimental productions on [two] replica Elizabethan stages must have been around eight to ten seconds."[49] The ten lines Tamora speaks before she sees Titus is two and a-half times Hosley's average, ample even for a character presumed to be of advanced middle age and having only one hand. This evidence is not as compelling in establishing that Titus's study was on the gallery as would be a stage direction noting that he is "aloft;" but, on balance, the dialogue makes it reasonably clear that he is.[50]

The other use of the gallery rejected by Hosley occurs in the concluding scene of the play. Again there is no stage direction indicating that any part of the scene is acted "aloft." After the sudden hecatomb that leaves the bodies of Lavinia, Tamora, Titus, and Saturninus scattered about the stage, Marcus addresses the "people and sons of Rome" to teach them "how to knit again" the commonweal (5.3.66–71). In Qq, a significant part of the speech is assigned to a "Romane Lord," and in F to a "Goth." Many modern editors, though not all, continue Marcus as the speaker, and at the conclusion of his address he calls on Lucius to speak, who recites the atrocities of Tamora and her sons. Marcus then speaks to the Romans again, denouncing Aaron and justifying Titus's revenge, then asking

> what say you, Romans?
> Have we done aught amiss? Show us wherein,
> And from the place where you behold us pleading
> The poor remainder of Andronici
> Will hand in hand all headlong hurl ourselves,
> And on the ragged stones beat forth our souls,
> And make a mutual closure of our house.
> Speak, Romans, speak, and if you say we shall,
> Lo, hand in hand, Lucius and I will fall.

(5.3.127–35)

In the course of these nine lines, Marcus twice makes clear that he and Lucius are located at a significant height (11. 5.3.131 and .135), sufficiently so that to fall would result in the death of both of them and bring about the "closure of . . . [the] house" of the Andronici. If that be so, they must have been on the gallery.[51]

Adams[52] finds that the opening scene of *Titus* is "longer, more varied, and theatrically bolder than anything Shakespeare had written previously," and that "it is probably the first action in English dramatic history to employ three stages simultaneously." the three are the platform, the gallery, and a "curtained rear stage," the inner stage that he locates between the two main stage doors, and that "came into general use in London playhouses after 1587." It was employed in *Titus* to represent the family monument of the Andronici. Adams also thinks that the presence of the three and a-half lines (following 1.1.35) in Q1, but absent from the three succeeding texts, alluding to the sacrifice of the noblest Gothic prisoner, "indicates that in the original [possibly non-Shakespearean] play no attempt was made to represent the Tomb on stage." The gallery was directly above "the Study used as a Tomb," and those aloft could not see into it, which created "a minor problem of versimilitude that Shakespeare overcame by developing considerable activity *in front* of the Tomb." The episode of placing the coffin inside the monument—the inner stage—"was concluded . . . by closing the curtains." The recessed stage, Adams tells us, is equipped with "a distinctive inner-stage trap," which is the site of the "unhallowed and bloodstained hole" (2.3.210) that contains the body of the murdered Bassianus and into which Martius and Quintus fall. When the scene is concluded

> the Emperor with Tamora departs through one of the two platform doors, and Titus with Lucius departs through the other, the inner-stage curtains close, shutting off the audience's view of the pit with Martius, Quintus, and the body of Bassianus yet inside and with Attendants grouped about the pit as if about to carry out the Emperor's order.

Adams says that the scene "from beginning to end . . . is contrived with technical skill of a high order." The rear trap is "apt for the business in hand [and], distinguishing . . . it from the Platform trap, it could be kept open indefinitely." He also thinks that two scenes (3.2 and 4.1) "were never performed as printed, for too many details are at loose ends . . . one [scene] fails to advance the plot . . . [the other] exposes the criminals . . . in the one Titus is exhausted and senile, in the other, [the later, he is] vigorous and alert." This scene (4.1) begins on the platform, but the writing in sand takes place on the inner stage "for the making ready of the bed of sand as well as its subsequent removal are details best performed out of sight of the audience." The arrow shooting in 4.3 recalls to Adams an episode in 2 *Tamberlaine*. In both, the arrows are "launched . . . into the stage Gallery—the only reasonably safe target afforded by playhouse design." Scene 4.4 takes place in the imperial palace "where seats for the Emperor (and his Queen?) are provided . . . These indications of an audience chamber . . . suggest that the rear stage, pre-set with suitable furniture, has been brought into use." In scene 5.2, Tamora's reiterating to Titus to "come down," and the lines she subsequently speaks to cover the interval from the time he exits until he reenters "makes it evident that Titus, on emerging from his 'study,' first appeared aloft in the Gallery . . . It makes a better stage tableau, of course, to involve the Gallery in this byplay."

In the concluding scene, Marcus's invitation to Saturninus and Lucius to "take your places" at table (5.3.24) could, to Adams, "be taken to mean an opening of the stage curtains and a discovery of the table being made ready in the rear stage. An inner-stage setting would accelerate matters here and would serve later in the scene as a suitable exit for those carrying off the dead bodies of Titus and Lavinia." Following the concluding slaughter, Marcus and Lucius detail to the assembled Romans the crimes perpetrated against their family and offer to hurl themselves downward to their deaths. Adams point out that these lines "constitute the only evidence the text affords . . . that Marcus, Lucius, and young Lucius escaped during the melee to the safety of the upper gallery . . . their elevated position considerably enhances the stage grouping of the finale . . . and creates a tableau reminiscent of the first scene of the play." Then the bodies of Titus and Lavinia were conveyed into the inner stage and "the curtains . . . closed . . . the body of the Emperor was carried . . . out through one stage door, and . . . Aaron, together with the body of Tamora, were dragged off through the other."

Adams concludes that the surviving text of *Titus* constitutes a "full-scale revision of an older play . . . [that] introduced the Tomb as a 'discovery' in the rear stage . . . the unambiguous reference to an off-stage pit;" and the "Folio's preservation of the cancelled Fly Scene . . . the original Titus appears to have been written for a stage of two units (the Platform and Gallery), whereas the revised *Titus* was written for three (Platform, Gallery, and Inner Stage) . . . The revised *Titus* made theatrical history. It was the first Elizabethan play to begin and end with episodes involving three stages at once."

Stamm analyzes the staging of the scenes following the rape and mutilation of Lavinia, and in which she plays a significant part, "to show how the young playwright . . . experimented in this play with various methods of coordinating speech and gesture, elaborate poetical patterns and effective stage situations, in order to create a poetic tragedy."[53] Because she has been deprived of speech in scene 2.3, Lavinia "is in danger of being no more than a passive image of horror," but Shakespeare is "at pains . . . to give her sparks of an active life and touches of individuality." When her Uncle Marcus finds her, he delivers a patterned rhetorical speech that constitutes a double process of comparison, in the course of which Lavinia's present condition is, on the one hand, expressed by poetic imagery and, on the other, confronted with her former state of perfection . . . the passage is open to criticism as an attempt to amalgamate dramatic speech and epical description . . . it oversteps the limits within which the relation of imagery to fact can be dramatically effective.

But the playwright did not abandon "his ambition to integrate this [rhetorical] pattern in a thoroughly dramatic event, and he was at least partially successful in realizing it." From the first line of his speech, Marcus weaves in a series of questions and comments, so propounded that the boy playing Lavinia can respond with appropriate body movements, and thus we find "Marcus, seeking his way, step by step, from his happy ignorance to the knowledge of the full extent of Lavinia's violation." Stamm tells us that in "this fascinating speech . . . its author tried hard to integrate a pattern derived from epical poetry in a dramatic event and that, although he did not fully succeed, he was able to create a scene with a greater theatrical potential than is usually conceded." In the subsequent scenes (3.1 and 3.2), Lavinia "plays a secondary role . . . [y]et the playwright tries to make more of Lavinia than a passive emblem of suffering by giving her opportunities of reaction and, on rare occasions, even of spontaneous action." One of these is her effort to "express her sympathy with her father" in his woes by kneeling with him when he tries to pray; and another, in 3.2, is when, as Stamm posits, she makes "an imploring gesture . . . in order to assuage the agitation of her father." In the next scene (4.1), "Lavinia is more active and shows more initiative than anywhere else in the play. This scene, especially its first part leading up to the disclosure of Lavinia's secret, aims at the same kind of interaction of speech and gesture as the fly-episode, but it lacks its finish. The theatrical notation in it is so defective as to suggest that it was printed without having gone through the author's final revision." She pursues young Lucius to obtain one of his books, which, at first, neither Titus nor Marcus comprehends, but which, when she does pick it out, they recognize as Ovid's *Metamorphoses*. She seeks out specifically the "tragic tale of Philomel," and Titus exclaims "rape, I fear, was the root of thy annoy" (4.1.49). Marcus suggests the writing in sand to identify the "traitors," which Lavinia succeeds in accomplishing. After that

Lavinia kneels down in the new ceremony in which the family swear again to revenge their wrongs, and then disappears from the stage until she is called upon to play her part in Titus' cruel rites of revenge and, finally, to become a willing sacrifice to her father's and her own sense of honour . . . our author's experiments with his mute heroine come to an end at the beginning of Act IV. We hope to have shown that they were important experiments because they permitted him to train himself in one of the playwright's most essential skills, in the art of expressing emotion and meaning not through language alone, but through gesture and the other visual elements of the theatre as well.

In the course of an essay on "the Elizabethan language of visual effects" on the stage, Hunter examines the staging of Act 1 of *Titus*.[54] He notes that the bareness of the Elizabethan stage "was a neutral precondition which allowed other visual effects to make their full impact. The number of these effects was limited; but his means less that the visual language was starved than that each item in it had to carry a disproportionately wide range of significances." The play's opening action establishes on the main stage a "three-pointed diagram" composed of the contending Saturninus and Bassianus, each with his supporters, as candidates for the imperial crown, and the as-yet-uncommitted Tribunes and Senators aloft. Marcus joins them[55] with the crown, tells the two brothers that Titus has been "chosen" by the people (plebs) of Rome and persuades them to dismiss their followers, which they do. Then, Hunter says, "*They go up into the Senate-house* (by separate doors, one must assume)."[56] The platform stage is cleared and a captain enters to herald "a formal processional entry (in reminiscence of a Roman Triumph) by Titus, his sons, and his prisoners . . . The next phase of stage movement appears when *A Tomb* is opened (over the stage trap, presumably) . . . and into this there are two processional exits, one with the 'proudest prisoner of the Goths' and one with the coffins of the dead Andronici.[57] Next, the Tribunes, with Saturninus, Bassianus, *and others* . . . re-appear (above), marking the climax of the stage use, with a group of at least sixteen persons occupying two levels of the stage (and a number of named corpses in the space below)." The parties deliberate on the question of the succession, which is "soon settled." After "several scuffles" associated with the abduction of Lavinia, Saturninus, Tamora, and her faction *Enter aloft.* "A new upper/lower polarization is thus created . . . This pattern of the preceding diagram is now repeated . . . The [subsequent] confrontation of the two brothers [Saturninus and Bassianus] (now reinforced by their wives) takes one back to the opening of the play; but there is now no *above* to represent the overarching stability of Roman institutions. Personal reconciliations at this level now mark only the space for treachery."

The use of the stage spaces in the first scene of *Titus Andronicus* indicates the basic polarizations of the play. The upper stage denotes (on this occasion) the seat of Roman political power, whether Imperial or Republican. The space beneath the stage locates the metaphysical commitment of the traditional Roman to stern self-sacrifice in the interests of the state, to warrior citizenship based on family piety. The space between these two (the main stage) gives to the principal characters, Titus and Lavinia, who are responsive to both these pressures, a field appropriate to their endeavour throughout the play to bridge the gap between the world of Power and the world of Right.

In what is "both an answer [to Titus's demand for redress] and a mockery of his need for an answer . . . "

Tamora appears as Revenge, 'sent from below/To join with him and right his heinous wrongs' . . . But what begins as cruel mockery ends as cruel justice. After the slaughter of Act V editors usually state that *Lucius, Marcus, and their friends go up into the balcony,* so that it is from this significant vantage-point that they deliver their pacificatory speeches to the populace and see Lucius elected Emperor. They only descend, it would seem, when the transfer of power is complete and then the family tomb can be re-opened and the dead Titus and Lavinia interred there . . . the visual diagram of meaning has been re-stabilized, and the movement of persons to their proper and appointed places assures us that the action is at an end.[58]

Hunter's assumption that Saturninus and Bassianus ascended to the gallery in Act 1 "by separate doors" is reasonable but not strictly necessary, as Wells pointed out (see n. 56). His presumption that the tomb is positioned over the "stage trap" is less persuasive, especially if he means the trap in the main platform. Titus tells us

This monument five hundred years hath stood,
Which I have sumptuously re-edified.

(1.1.350–51)

It would seem therefore that the tomb was a substantial stage property that, if placed over the trap located approximately in the middle of the platform, as the external evidence would seem to indicate, would have impeded the actions of the players.[59] It appears more likely that such a large property would be more conveniently located immediately in front of the tiring-house wall and spanning the third stage door at the center rear, if there was a third door.[60]

As part of a thoroughgoing analysis of Elizabethan plays in performance, Hattaway presents an evocative review of *Titus,* including a reconstruction of the early staging.[61] He points out that the play's "structure . . . is visual rather than literary . . . it is not just a bloodbath of classical horrors but does make a political statement—as a pageant, however, and not in conventional literary-dramatic terms." In *Titus,* Shakespeare concentrated his attention on "the creation of dramatic images, explored kinds of spectacle that produce a compulsive response from the audience, and . . . tried to work towards a dramatic rhythm based on word, gesture, and music in which concord is invaded by discord." The overall pattern, he tells us, "is simple: the play begins and ends with the election of a

Roman Emperor; the middle is occupied by a grim vision of the wild justice of revenge." The playwright may have thought that earlier tragedy had "excluded direct experience of horror and suffering, [and] he was as concerned to demonstrate how we perceive violence as well as the violence itself. Marcus, confronted with the mutilated figure of his niece, anaesthetizes himself by attempting to see her as an emblem" in his well-known reaction to coming upon her in the forest (2.4.11–57).

The opening sequence presents a series of tableaux intended to convey the significance of the "constituted power of Rome," arrayed in the gallery. From there the Tribunes, Senators, Saturninus, and Bassianus witness the procession of power accompanying the triumphal entrance of Titus. "Lucius's demand that the son of Tamora be sacrificed 'Before this earthly prison of their [his brothers'] bones,'" concentrates attention on the tomb, which suggests to Hattaway "that the discovery space would have been used rather than the stage trap . . . the architecture of the tiring-house was such that these images of senate house and tomb were placed, significantly, one below the other—and the two leading ideas of the play have been economically established . . . The act ends with the return to a kind of equilibrium as the Emperor and Tamora, Bassianus, and Lavinia enter symetrically at opposite doors to stage a reconciliation and plan 'to hunt the panther and the hart.'" This use of different stage levels, the emblematic rhythm "and its consequent ironies" indicate that the scene was "firmly planned."

The second Act is also symmetrical in that it begins and ends with soliloquies. Between these is unfolded the chaos and violence wreaked upon the innocent. "The effect is of a cancer working fearful change on the body politic. Evil has moved inside the city, and innocent and active alike succumb" in one of the principal sequences of violence in the play. Bassianus is stabbed to death, Lavinia is led off to be raped, and her brothers are falsely accused of the murder of her husband. Hattaway "think[s] that Shakespeare's mind was captured by the idea of translating to the playhouse images of violence he had found" in Ovid.

Act 3 begins with the portrayal of Titus for the first time as "an object of pity." He begs in vain for the lives of Quintus and Martius and has presented to him his violated and mutilated daughter, to which he responds with "gnomic utterances." Aaron enters to announce that Titus's two sons can be ransomed if his hand or one of Marcus's or Lucius's will be chopped off and offered "to the King" (3.1.150–54). Titus's hand is severed and sent, only to be returned shortly along with the heads of his sons. This time he responds by laughing. "Shakespeare uses the device to mark the moment when Titus realizes that his compulsive energies must be harnessed to revenge . . . to the half-crazed half-witty contrivances of the revenger." Hattaway considers it possible that "Aaron might have concealed himself in the discovery space" and ironically joined Titus "in a gale of laughter," as he later confesses to Lucius. In the "fly scene," Shakespeare "confirms this impression of Titus' monomania . . . [the banquet] prefigur[es] the final Theyestean banquet [and is] an emblem of Titus' derangement . . . The scene works, concentrating the audience on the effects rather than the sensational spectacles of violence."

In Act 4, "The succession of violent spectacles abates in intensity for a while in preparation no doubt for the enormities of the play's conclusion." The means employed in the scene to reveal Lavinia's attackers is "too obviously emblematic," however it serves to remind the audience "that horror does not cease when physical violence has abated." Aaron's "sight of his child inspires him to . . . vitality and confidence," but it also causes him to stab the nurse "coldly and cruelly." He "displays a nascent self-sufficiency and a celebration of natural values that is in its way attractive." The arrow-shooting scene (4.3) "[i]n its mixture of grotesquerie . . . [its] pathos as we hear the rantings of Titus, [its] cheerful obscenity when he remarks that [young] Lucius has hit the virgin in the lap, and bathos when the Clown emerges to be the messenger . . . serves as an emblem of the confusion in Titus' mind. It is a play within a play . . . and the deliberate violation of decorum . . . occurs when a grand anagogic concept—communicating with the gods—is literally enacted on the stage." Hattaway concludes:

> With the Thyestean banquet, the final horror of the sons baked in a pie and served to their mother, and the swift successions of stabbings, Act V offers a culmination to the nightmare of violence in the play. But it also contains a rising movement that is as strong as any in Shakespearean tragedy. It is not a question of good supplanting evil—the Thyestean banquet will strip Titus of any sympathy—but of a victory by main force of those who respect the state over those whose respect is only for themselves. There is an uncomfortable pause when it looks as though Lucius [in 5.1] will hang Aaron's baby on the stage, but mercy prevails, and the scene is resolved with a long confession of dastardly deeds from the captured Aaron . . . The speech is at the centre of the first of two scenes in which Shakespeare, perhaps rather desperately, crystallizes themes out of the play's action, having, if my interpretation is correct, tried to eschew significance in some of the preceding sequences. Aaron . . . becomes the evil which Lucius must purge from the body politic . . . In the second scene [of Act 5] Shakespeare resorts to actual allegory as Tamora invests herself in the costume of Revenge . . . Titus, in his madness, recognizes her immediately and begins the grim stage game that will end only with the deaths of them both. He names her sons Rape and Murder and invites her to 'Stab them, or tear them on thy chariot-wheels' . . . Tamora . . . repeated[ly] bids Titus to come down [which he does] . . . Shakespeare may in fact have used the gallery as an ironic reminder of the action in Act I. There Tamora appeared aloft while her power was in the ascendant, here Titus has seen through to her true nature and is in a position to have her seized and brought to summary justice . . . Once the spectacle is established the action moves

very quickly as the pie is brought in, Lavinia is slain in imitation of the legend of Virginius' slaughter of his daughter, and Tamora, Titus himself, and Saturninus are despatched . . . [T]he scene has [a] combination of grotesquerie, savagery, and fundamentalist detachment from what is inhuman and inhumane . . . Shakespeare, in other words, has taken what is naive in folk culture and turned it into a sophisticated and serious kind of theatre. He marks this by turning from surrealist and fanciful nightmare to customary theatrical ceremony: the play must have ended with a double funeral procession, probably . . . without music: the noble borne out shoulder high with due honour, the base drawn out ignominiously by their feet.

Wells conducts an examination of the staging of Act 1 of *Titus* as exhibited in both Q1, "printed from Shakespeare's own, 'foul' papers;" and in F1, which "could represent a staging of the play later than, and different from, that which it originally received."[62] He chose this long "expository" scene "because it offers . . . particular difficulties in understanding and visualizing the staging," as evidenced by the different solutions to problems of stage directions developed by recent editors including Dover Wilson, Waith, Bevington, and particularly Maxwell and Blakemore Evans. He also takes into account the comments of such scholars as Greg and Hunter; and, those by McKerrow in the surviving galley proofs of his text of the play in a projected Oxford Shakespeare that was never published.

An example of such difficulties is a crux that occurs early. The first quarto reads:

Marcus Andronicus with the Crowne.

(1.1.17.1)

The line is centered, is italicized and is followed immediately by a speech manifestly spoken by Marcus as a Tribune of the people.

The Folio reads:

Enter Marcus Andronicus aloft with the Crowne.

(TLN 25)[63]

Wells points out that the reading of Q "is not necessarily an entry direction" though later in the scene there occurs a similarly centered and italicized line, which reads

Enter a Captaine.

(1.1.64.3)

He observes that the line regarding Marcus in F could "represent simply a scribe's or compositor's misguidedly helpful but unauthoritative and mistaken interpretation of the Quarto direction . . . The addition merely of '*Enter*' may be regarded as no more than officiousness, but the further addition of '*aloft*' looks suspiciously like carefulness . . . since the Quarto direction does not deny the possibility that he [Marcus] first appears 'aloft' at 1. 17, and since the text influenced by the prompt-book actually says he does, the evidence supports the Folio direction, and this should be preferred."

An equally puzzling disparity between the quarto text and that of the Folio is apparent in the stage directions regarding a coffin or coffins, the first occurring immediately preceding the entrance of the triumphant Titus. Q1 reads:

> *Sound Drums and Trumpets, and then enter two of* Titus *ſonnes, and then two men bearing a Coffin couered with black, then two other ſonnes, then* Titus Andronicus, *and then* Tamora *the Queene of Gothes and her two ſonnes* Chiron *and* Demetrius, *with* Aron *the More, and others as many as can be, then ſet downe the Coffin, and* Titus *ſpeakes.*
>
> (1.1.69.1–8)

F has:

> *Sound Drummes and Trumpets. And then enter two of Titus Sonnes; After them, two men bearing a Coffin couered with blacke, then two other Sonnes. After them, Titus Andronicus, and then Tamora the Queene of Gothes, & her two Sonnes Chiron and Demetrius, with Aaron the Moore, and others, as many as can bee: They set downe the Coffin, and Titus speakes.*
>
> (TLN 83–89)

The interment of the dead is delayed by the sequence leading to the sacrifice of Alarbus, after which they are entombed. The direction in Qq is consistent with the earlier one:

> *Sound Trumpets, and lay the Coffin in the Tombe.*
>
> (1.1.149.1–2)

but the F direction at the entombment varies from the earlier F reference:

> *Flourish.*
> *Then Sound Trumpets, and lay the Coffins in the Tombe.*
>
> (TLN 174–75)

Wells cites Maxwell's reasonable note regarding this manifest discrepancy between the two texts: "The singular is surprising . . . But this is probably how the author envisaged the staging;"[64] and Wells further comments: "The author does seem to have 'envisaged' a 'staging' with only one coffin *as he wrote the direction,* but shortly afterwards he was envisioning more than one corpse." He doubts that there were coffins large enough to hold "more than one of Titus' sons," and he cites McKerrow's observa-

tion that if so "it would surely have taken more than two men to carry
it." Despite the reservations of such sound scholars there can be little
doubt that a large coffin, adequate to appear large enough to hold two
bodies, could have been so constructed that it was light enough to be
carried by two burly extras hired specifically for that trait, especially
since they have no lines to speak. Wells concludes: "It seems strange
that Shakespeare should have repeated the singular form in the direction
at 1. 149 [of Q], since both the line before the direction and the line after
it refer to the fact that this is a multiple burial. It might be a misprint;
indeed, were it not for the repeated use of the singular in the earlier
direction, one would feel fairly sure that it was."[65] Perhaps, alternatively,
the single F plural—the other two in that text being singular—may be
a misprint.

The election of Saturninus as Emperor is accomplished while he, Bassianus, and Marcus are still "aloft" in the gallery. Qq has no stage direction
moving them to the platform below, but F reads:

A Long Flouriſh till they come downe.

(TLN 264)

Wells reasons that the "flourish is not, perhaps, absolutely indispensable,
but it seems entirely natural to emphasize the importance of the proclamation" and to provide time to cover their descent. It is "warranted by
the Folio, presumably by way of the prompt-book, so I should include it."

A difficult staging tangle is presented in the incident of Bassianus's
abduction of Lavinia, including the death of Mutius, which was probably
an interpolation. Saturninus had proposed making Lavinia his Empress,
and Titus had agreed. She is not consulted but, as a dutiful daughter, she
raises no objection. Titus in gratitude "consecrates" to Saturninus his
sword, his chariot and his prisoners, which are gracefully accepted. Saturninus comforts Tamora and observes that she is

A goodly Lady trust me of the hue
That I would chooſe were I to chooſe a new:

(1.1.261–62)

Wells observes that the lines "are traditionally marked 'aside,' following
Capell"; but he thinks "the *'aside'* direction is simplistic, and better omitted." Saturninus then says

Romans let vs goe,
Raunſomles here we ſet our priſoners free
Proclaime our Honours Lords with Trumpe and Drum.

(1.1.273–75)

Wells points out that neither Q nor F provide a stage direction but that almost all editors "Following Rowe's wording and Capell's placing," add:

Flourish. Saturninus courts Tamora in dumb show.[66]

While this is taking place, Bassianus, assisted by Marcus and Titus's sons, seizes Lavinia so as to, as he says,

Bear his betrothed from all the world away.

(1.1.286)

Titus calls to Saturninus that Lavinia is "surprised" and that he will "soon bring her back," (1.1.284 and 289) but Mutius attempts to restrain his father from following Lavinia, which so incenses Titus that he thereupon fatally stabs his own son. Wells recasts this entire sequence and posits an original Shakespearean version, rearranging though not altering the dialogue to smooth out the action so that the Emperor and his party leaves the platform during the contention over Lavinia and ascends to the gallery in time to respond to Titus's urgent cries:

No *Titus* no, the Emperour needes her not,

(1.1.299)

Wells finds it "an oddity of the stagecraft that, so far as the directions in the Quarto and all later editions are concerned, Mutius' body has had to remain, ignored, on stage throughout the upper-level episode . . . The problem is resolved, however, if we make the quite reasonable assumption that Mutius' body should not remain on stage, but should be dragged off by Lucius after the killing and carried back again by Marcus, or by one or more of the sons, on the line 'O *Titus* see: O see what thou hast done' . . . It is true that Shakespeare appears not to have written directions for these happenings, but neither did he write [other important] directions" and he lists several.

Wells sums up his intensive investigation of the staging of the first act of *Titus*. He has, he tells us

> dealt empirically with a variety of features to which the editor needs to devote his attention. Some of my comments affect no more than mechanical aspects of presentation. But others, I think, help to show that this long span of action is a more consciously wrought and sophisticated piece of dramatic artistry than is usually granted, and in particular that it employs visual effects to convey and reinforce meaning . . . Most of these editorial procedures depend on straightforward deductions based on information supplied by the text itself; only those relating to the episode of Lavinia's abduction and the subsequent killing of Mutius seem to me to be at all speculative . . . The episode is patently

unsatisfactory as it stands in both the Quarto and the Folio. In a modern edition, it might be reprinted exactly as it stands in either of these texts.

He discusses the editorial problems presented by differences between the texts of the Qq and that of the F.

> I suggest that whenever we have as authoritative texts a quarto based on foul papers and a Folio text which appears to be reprinted either from a quarto annotated from a theatrical manuscript, or directly from a theatrical manuscript, then the basic editorial procedure to be followed in a fully edited version for the general reader should be to accept the evidence offered by the Folio that supplements or substantially replaces that offered by the quarto.

and he concludes by acknowledging the usefulness of other types of editions such as one that attempts to present a "text that lies closest to Shakespeare's manuscript."[67]

In an Appendix, Wells presents "A Conjectural Reconstruction" of Shakespeare's first draft of Act 1 that "follows the text of the First Quarto (1594) but omits the passages which there is reason to believe that Shakespeare added after his initial act of composition," such as the sacrifice of Alarbus, and the killing and entombment of Mutius. "This is . . . an attempt at . . . [a] diplomatic" rendering of the first act, one that "makes only minimal corrections of errors and anomalies in the text as originally printed." The result is a successful and informative reconstruction of the text that involves only nine substantive emendations and eleven incidental emendations.[68]

Longleat drawing, ca. 1595, depicting a performance of *Titus Andronicus*. Reproduced by the kind permission of the Marquess of Bath, Longleat House, Warminster, Wiltshire, England.

8

The Longleat Manuscript

Iɴ the library of the Marquess of Bath at Longleat there is a manuscript (*Harley Papers* vol. 1, fol. 159ᵛ) consisting of a single sheet folded to form two leaves, or four pages. On the inner side of the first leaf is a drawing, apparently intended to represent action from *Titus Andronicus,* accompanied by forty-two lines of verse copied, with the exception of two improvised connective lines, from a text of the play.

The sketch presents seven human figures divided by an upright staff at the center into two groups, three on the left confronting four on the right. Five of the persons are readily recognizable from the drawing itself, confirmed by the text. They are Titus, Tamora, Chiron, Demetrius, and Aaron, who is black. The identity of the remaining two, armed men standing behind Titus, is not clear and, like several other features of the picture, is in dispute. Tamora, Chiron, and Demetrius on the right of Titus's staff (which may be a spear or the Roman *hasta,* a ceremonial staff) are kneeling, apparently in supplication to Titus, whose attitude suggests a negative response. It is not certain from the picture for whom they are pleading, but in the text Tamora speaks four times of her "sonnes" (11. 5, 6, 7, 11, Chambers's numbering),[1] and once of her "first borne sonne" (1. 19). At the far right, standing behind Chiron and Demetrius, whose hands are bound—and perhaps Tamora's are also—is Aaron brandishing a sword in his left hand. He is pointing with his right hand, but it is not apparent whether he is pointing at the sword, at Tamora's kneeling sons, or at Tamora herself. On the ground at Titus's feet there is a short rod that may or may not be a discarded scepter. The drawing, while it has no intrinsic value, is not totally lacking in design quality. The division of the drawing by the upright spear or *hasta* in Titus's hand is the focus of the picture around which the human figures are organized. The parallel thrusts from both the left and the right—from the left, the halberds in the hands of the armed men and the line of Titus's right arm, and from the right the angle of Aaron's sword and Tamora's pleading arms and hands—direct attention to the key figures on either side of the upright central staff. This is, as Thomson notes, "a formal arrangement to provide a focus on the confrontation of Titus and Tamora, but with a sensationally black Aaron as a challenge to symmetry."[2] The draftsmanship is fairly elementary and purely documentary. The value of the drawing is in its content, not in its artistic merit, which is virtually nil. This is, as Chambers designated it, "the first illustration to 'Shakespeare.'"

The manuscript was first calendered in 1907 by a royal commission (*Longleat Papers*, 2.43), and called to the attention of Shakespearean scholars by Chambers in his 1925 note. His paper, while reproducing the drawing and the text, is devoted largely to the latter, but it briefly touches on other matters. At the lower left of the manuscript sheet opposite 11. 35–37 (Chambers's numbering) there is a legend, in italics in either the same hand as the text or in a hand contemporary with the text, that Sir Edmund reads as "Henricus Peacham Anno m°q°qq°." He interprets the final $q°$ as either *quinto* or *quarto*, i.e., *millesimo quingentesimo quinto* (1595) or *quarto* (1594). The second q is a little doubtful, and Chambers considers momentarily but discards the notion that it might be a slip for an arabic 9. Later, without discussion, he prints it as 9.[3] He interprets the manuscript briefly. He thinks that the deaths of two sons are "contemplated" in the manuscript. He also puzzles over the significance of Aaron's posture and asks: "Are we then to infer that Peacham had before him an early version of the play and that this was afterwards rearranged? It would be a hazardous conclusion, and it would of course be more hazardous still to suggest that Peacham was the 'private author' whose work, according to the tradition reported by Edward Ravenscroft in 1687, was touched up by Shakespeare." It is even hazardous to assume on the basis of the Latin legend, as Chambers does but some other critics do not, that the sketch was drawn by Henry Peacham, author of *The Compleat Gentleman*, even though there is another notation in the manuscript (fol.2[a]), evidently of a later date, reading "Henrye Peachams Hande 1595." This may, however, be nothing more than an English rendering of the Latin. A friend suggested to Chambers that the sheet may have been done by Peacham for a competition in penmanship, but he rejects the suggestion.

Adams thinks of the drawing as intended to illustrate the text, saying that it is "difficult to understand why the carefully executed drawing fails to agree with the text it is supposed to illustrate." He assumes that Tamora is pleading for the lives of the two sons kneeling behind her, and that the figure of the black man at the far right is pointing at Tamora's doomed sons as though he were an executioner. "It may be that this figure was indeed originally intended to represent the executioner, and later was blackened to represent Aaron, after the transcriber had decided to add to his text the Moor's boast of villainy." Titus's two armed attendants are "possibly Lucius and Marcus." Adams reads the notation on the date as

"Anno m°q°gq^{to}." As to the last two letters he is certainly correct and Chambers, who reads $q°$, is in error, but the immediately preceding symbol is not clearly g and Adams admits that what it represents, assuming it to be g, "is not apparent:" the date may be interpreted as either 1594 or 1595. The legend "Henrye Peachams Hande 1595" he thinks is merely a translation of the Latin. By a comparison with John Payne Collier correspondence and known forgeries in the Folger Library, he concludes it was written by Collier, as were some other notes in pencil at the top of the drawing and to the right of the verses. These read, at the top, "Tamora pleading" and "Written by Henry Peacham—author of the complete Gentleman," and, at the side, "so far from Shakspear Titus Andronicus Sc. 2." Concerning them, Adams says: "That these annotations were made by John Payne Collier seems highly likely." His evidence is the handwriting and the fact that "in certain editions of the play, including Collier's, these lines appear in Scene 2." He may be right about the date on fol. 2^a, but the pencil notations on the drawing were not made by Collier, but by Canon John Edward Jackson (1805–91), who was librarian to the marquess of Bath and, according to *DNB*, "arranged and indexed the bulk of the manuscripts at Longleat." Numerous examples of his handwriting are preserved in the library there. Another note in the left-hand margin reads "temp. Jn. Thynn J°." or possibly "J^r." The hand is uncertain. Adams thinks this refers to the son of the builder of Longleat House (d. 1623). He then compares the writing in the Longleat manuscript with that in a holograph manuscript of Peacham's *Emblemata Varia* in the Folger Library and finds some resemblance between the two but also some very distinct differences. He lists five of the most significant of these and offers the judgment that the writing in *Emblemata Varia* is "distinctly inferior" to that in the *Titus Andronicus* document. A comparison of the Longleat picture with twenty pen drawings in the *Emblemata Varia* leads to the determination that the latter are "quite obviously different in style and inferior in craftsmanship to the *Titus* drawing," thus rejecting Peacham as the author of the Longleat sketch. At Adams's request, Greg examined drawings and the writing in a Peacham manuscript of emblems in the British Library (*Basilicon Doron*, MS Royal 12A 1xvi). Greg concluded: "The *Titus* drawing seems to me better done, and the writing, which bears no likeness to that of the emblems, is distinctly superior," supporting Adams's opinion.[4]

Wilson finds that the drawing presents several puzzling features that can be resolved only in relation to the text. He notes that Chambers and Adams have decided neither the exact incident the drawing attempts to depict nor its date. He accepts Adams's determination that Collier made the notations in the manuscript and the English rendering of the Latin date. On the basis of what he calls the "dated signature or attribution," he thinks that "there can be little doubt, that the document was, to some extent at any rate, the work of one Henry Peacham," but he stops short of identifying him with the author of *The Compleat Gentleman* and concludes by saying that "it is safest to regard [the identification] with suspicion." He poses five questions on the "puzzles" presented by the manuscript, all relating aspects of the picture either to the accompanying text or to one or more of the *Titus* prints. "I find it impossible," he says, "to escape the conclusion that the text was at any rate added to the drawing by another man," at a date much later than that of the sketch. This is based on Adams's argument that the manuscript text was transcribed from either Q3 (1611) or F1. The stage situation shown in the drawing is the "tableau" immediately after Titus refuses Tamora's prayer, and his sons have led away the doomed Alarbus. This Wilson supports in part by noting the presence in the picture of only two of Tamora's sons and none of Titus's. The attendants behind him are men-at-arms, the one in helmet and armor being perhaps an officer, because all the Andronici would be dressed like Roman gentlemen, as are Titus, the Gothic princes, and Aaron. The latter's gestures exhibit the bitter indignation of the Gothic party at the sacrifice of Alarbus. The drawing is "the work of a cunning pen-and-ink artist who depicts . . . what he actually saw at a performance of the play . . . The actors shown in the drawing were probably members of Shakespeare's company—does that black profile belong to Burbage?—or at any rate of some London troupe like the Earl of Sussex's men." The costumes show that the lower classes were played in "modern [i.e., Elizabethan] dress," while efforts were made "to attain accuracy in the attire worn by patricians" in Roman times.[5] Wilson presents a summary of these arguments in "A Note on the Frontispiece" (the Longleat drawing) in his edition of *Titus Andronicus*, with little deviation except to place more emphasis on Adams's assertion that Henry Peacham is not the artist and to add to his earlier hypothesis that the drawing depicts "the actual action and grouping of Shakespeare's fellows in Shakespeare's theatre at a particular moment" the further speculation that possibly "the beard of Titus conceals the features of Shakespeare himself."[6] In a kind of postscript to his essay, Wilson expresses the hope that his paper will induce others to join a symposium to elucidate the complex problems of the manuscript. In this he was, to a limited degree, successful.

Munro, who was the first to respond to Wilson's invitation,[7] is also the first commentator to treat the drawing and the text as of equal significance. He rejects the "supposed discrepancy between the picture and the extracts from the play" and Wilson's notion that the two parts of the manuscript were executed at different times. To Munro "the word and the picture match satisfactorily," and are of the same date. The source of the text was "perhaps Q1." He came to consideration of the picture and the text after a reading of the play, and suggests that his procedure obviates some scholarly difficulties. Wilson is led astray in placing the sketch slightly later in the play than the text indicates by the absence of Alarbus from the picture, but, Munro asserts, "there never had been an Alarbus in the Shakespearian play." Whatever we may think of the soundness of this opinion, it certainly is a conclusive explanation for Alarbus's absence from the drawing. He arrives at his view because of the lack of an entry for Alarbus in the Q1 stage direction following 1.1.69; the fact that he has no lines to speak in the face of his imminent sacrifice—"a mute Alarbus . . . is incredible"—and his absence from other versions of the Titus story. He explains away the stage direction following 1.1.129 *(Exit Titus sonnes with Alarbus.)* by hypothesizing that "somebody" added the final two words to the authorial Q1 direction "in contradiction to the main stage direction" at 1.1.69.[8] As to Titus's men-at-arms, he notes that "Adams suggested that they might be sons of Titus, and this, I think is what they are." Aaron presents a potential different problem but not if he is accepted as the person he describes himself to be in the text, "inscribed by way of explanation below the picture," for the drawing is "a very simple example [of the] comprehensive method of illustration" in which incidents and persons are portrayed in one compass though actually separated by periods of time and considerable distances. He cites some authorities and several examples of this technique usually termed "simultaneous representation," and that is in fact both common in the art of the Middle Ages and the Renaissance and well-recognized. An example of simultaneous representation that is of some interest in this connection is Shakespeare's description in *Lucrece* of a pictorial rendering of the Siege of Troy, probably based, Munro says, on a "contemporary tapestry."

In his reply to Munro, Wilson reiterates his position, at the same time clarifying and sharpening some of the issues. He tells us that he had considered the type of solution Munro put forth but rejected it because it did not solve the central puzzles, and adds, erroneously, that Munro regards the document as one "of that continuous [*sic*] type of pictorial art familiar to all who know anything of medieval or renaissance tapestry or drawing." Munro actually describes five methods of illustrating a story or play, including the "continuous," but he does not advocate that as the type that the Longleat drawing is, because it manifestly does not conform to the continuous convention. Munro really suggests that the picture is of the "comprehensive" type, that is, simultaneous representation. Wilson also says that Munro "maintains that the picture was drawn to illustrate the extracts," whereas Munro considers the two elements of independent significance, leaning a little to the view that the text may have been added to elucidate the drawing. In a rebuttal, Munro points out Wilson's confusion over the two different techniques of illustration—the continuous and the comprehensive—and his failure to understand Munro's argument for the latter method. He again explains that Aaron is depicted not as the action of the play requires but as "the man in his speech describes himself to be, a truculent and unrepentent villain," and repeats his reasons for thinking that Alarbus was not in Shakespeare's original play "until the editors put him there." Later in his edition of the plays, he summarizes his position on the Longleat manuscript but adds nothing new.[9]

Perrett challenges Munro's argument that Alarbus was not in Shakespeare's original, noting that "the positive evidence of the exit is weightier" than the absence of Alarbus from a crowded entrance. As a parallel, he points out the absence of an entrance for the Clown in *Love's Labour's Lost* (Q1, 5:1) "yet he has lines to utter," and notes that Heminges and Condell would be unlikely to foist an exit for Alarbus into the Folio "if he made no appearance in a play in which they themselves would have taken part." He calls attention, as another item of evidence for the simultaneous type of illustration, to the sceptre lying at Titus's feet in the drawing. "Thus in one and the same picture we have . . . Tamora . . . in the act of pleading and . . . when the pleading is quite finished . . . the sceptre [that] has been cast aside by Andronicus."[10]

Parrott reviews the contentions presented in the foregoing discussions and adds one bit of argument: a doubt that the object at Titus's feet really is a sceptre. An artist (not identified) who examined three reproductions of the drawing assures Parrott "that the object is not lying on the ground, represented by a line clearly drawn across the sketch, but apparently fixed to, or penetrated by, the staff," in which case it is probably a base for the staff. Parrott concludes by agreeing with Wilson that the picture shows Shakespeare's characters in action on the stage and is not an example of simultaneous representation for if "the sketch does not represent a definite scene on Shakespeare's stage . . . its value diminishes almost to a vanishing point." Having accepted Wilson's general position, he also accepts the hypothesis that the text was written after the picture was drawn.[11]

Maxwell notes the "Henricus Peacham" of the manuscript and Adams's reading of the date in Latin. "A later hand has interpreted [it] as '1595.' Who this Peacham was, and whether the date has any authority, we do not know." He rejects Wilson's idea that the writer of the text did not understand the illustration. "I cannot help thinking that drawing and text belong together. Perhaps the compiler's purpose was to string together (for private theatricals?) two striking and popular speeches from the play, and perhaps it is a private performance that the drawing represents." A remaining problem is "the incongruity between the representation of Aaron and his situation in either Act I or Act V."[12] Merchant briefly alludes to the Longleat drawing and quotes Wilson regarding costuming, but does not discuss its significance nor the method of simultaneous representation; and although he reprints an engraving from the *Universal Magazine* (1749) showing "a curious 'simultaneous setting' [of] both the meeting of Coriolanus and his mother and his later murder," he does not call attention to the similarity in technique between the *Coriolanus* illustration and that of the Longleat sketch. Oppel reviews and accepts Munro's explanation and concludes that three principal incidents were brought together in simultaneous representation.[13]

Holmes discusses the costumes and particularly the armor depicted in the Longleat drawing. He points out that six of the seven figures are wearing armor of sorts. Titus has a classical-looking cuirass and buskins, a military cloak knotted on the left shoulder, and carries a tasselled spear. The armed men behind Titus, whom Holmes accepts without discussion as sons of Titus, wear half-armor of different types. The man on the extreme left is costumed very much like an Elizabethan infantry officer. He wears a tall, plumed bonnet in Spanish style and his breeches are cut after the fashion of the Swiss mercenary infantry of the sixteenth century. His companion wears armor of the late-fifteenth-century German type known as "Gothic," which was completely out of use by 1595 and which therefore must have been old armor of about 1480 that had found its way eventually into a theatrical wardrobe. If so, the sketch may represent what the draftsman saw on the stage. The headpiece, less fashionable than that of his companion, is a kind of helmet known as a combed morion. He also has on leg armor. Tamora's sons and Aaron are wearing Roman-type cuirasses and buskins like Titus's. Holmes conjectures that old armor was apparently familiar to Shakespeare, and he cites a line from *Richard III* about "bruised arms hung up for monuments" (1.1.6)[14] To Cerumen "The 'Longleat Manuscript' . . . consists of a drawing . . . showing Tamora begging Titus to spare her sons over whose heads Aaron holds a sword . . . the textual extracts which accompany it . . . seem to have been added later. They do not fit the picture which in any case does not represent a scene in the play; and the manuscript has no importance." The caption, which is anonymous, to a reproduction of the drawing reads: "The artist (possibly, though probably not, Henry Peacham) has confused the action of the moment in *Titus Andronicus* Act I: Tamora is apparently pleading with Titus to spare two of her sons, not one, and Aaron the Moor, with drawn sword in hand, it taking a more active part than his mute role in Act I allows him." The mixture of Elizabethan and Roman costumes is noted. Unaccountably, this edition, The Riverside, which, in Kermode's introduction to *Titus* and in the caption to the reproduction of the Longleat drawing, fails to recognize the type of illustration it is, also includes, and does properly appreciate two other examples of simultaneous representation. One is a reproduction (on p. 1022) of a woodcut from a broadside ballad in the Folger Library depicting in a single illustration five events that occur in the story of Titus, plus a picture of a palace. The accompanying legend says that "the woodcut is a composite representation of several of the principal scenes in both the play and the prose story." The second plate is a reproduction of a print from *Scarron's Comical Romance of a Company of Stage Players* (1676), also in the convention of simultaneous representation, which depicts a group of strolling players arriving at an inn and their later performance in a village square.[15]

Miola, who sees *Titus Andronicus* as an evocation of the classical iron age, finds support for his thesis in the display of weaponry in the illustration. He cites the debate between Wilson and Munro but concludes that "there has been advanced no satisfactory solution to the various problems which this drawing raises."[16]

Waith in his Oxford edition of *Titus Andronicus* comments that to "the most important questions" about the Longleat picture "there are no universally accepted answers," and that it is "a puzzling document." He is inclined to accept Munro's explanation that the technique is simultaneous representation and notes that wood cut illustrations to other plays— notably *The Spanish Tragedy*—employ the same technique, but he emphasizes that the *Titus* drawing "combines episodes from two widely separated points in the play" and the speech prefix "Alarbus" remains a mystery, to which "no one has offered a satisfactory solution." Concerning the attribution of the drawing to Henry Peacham, Waith examined manuscript collections of Peacham's emblems in the Bodleian and British Libraries and found no reason to be skeptical, unlike Adams, Greg, and Dover Wilson. He reports that Peter Croft, a King's College, Cambridge librarian and paleographer, thought that Peacham wrote the cento, which is an example of fair writing in the secretary hand comparable to the fair writing in italic style in Peacham's emblem books. Furthermore, Croft believed that "the probabilities are in favour of the signature on the Longleat MS being in the same hand as those in the two emblem books," therefore it is Peacham's own signature. In addition, he noted that the "Anno" in the date immediately below the signature "looks as though it is in the same hand as the text and . . . the signature," which means that Peacham also wrote the cryptic date, "the form of which," says Waith, referring to the anomalous *g,* "has so far defied explanation." Concerning the date, he determines that it is 1595 since, if it were intended to be 1594, the concluding letters would include "one of various possible symbols for 'r.'"[17]

Foakes finds that there are in the manuscript four separate elements to consider: the drawing; the passage of text drawn from the play; the signature and date, which may be in the same hand as the text; and the endorsement (the date on p. 3), which is "in a different hand altogether, and is probably to be discounted as a forgery by John Payne Collier." In trying "to discover what part of the action of the play the drawing illustrates [the scribe] in fact . . . got it wrong." He may also have been "puzzled by the stance of Aaron . . . it looks as though the text has no direct relation to the drawing, and could have been added later, and by another hand . . . In any case there is no necessary connection between the text with the signature and date, on the one hand, and the drawing on the other." Foakes thinks that the Henry Peacham of *The Compleat Gentleman* "could well . . . be the artist who made the drawing but various puzzling questions about it . . . remain insoluble." He notes Wilson's comment that the picture represents an actual performance, but adds that "this is to overlook certain puzzling features of the drawing," notably the absence of characters and properties present in Act 1. In fact, there is "no reason to suppose this drawing was made at a staging of the play; it is more likely that it was drawn from recollection." Aaron is a prisoner in Act 1 "and has no speaking part, so it is inconceivable that he could have appeared as he does in the drawing . . . [which] does not fit any point in the action and probably was not drawn from the life." Nevertheless, the sketch may relate to a performance and if so it should be viewed as Munro suggests as an example of "multiple representation . . . conform[ing] to the same convention as the woodcuts illustrating the title-pages of such plays as *The Spanish Tragedy . . . A Maidenhead Well Lost . . .* and *The Witch of Edmonton.*" Foakes thinks "the most striking aspect of the group shown is the variety of costume." It is a medley that "suggests a casual attitude towards both historical accuracy and consistency." He rejects Wilson's interpretation that costuming for common characters was contemporary while that for patricians made some attempt at historical accuracy and concludes that "the two soldiers on the left may be Titus's sons and 'patricians.'"[18]

Students of the Longleat manuscript from Chambers to Foakes have experienced difficulties to a greater or lesser degree in understanding the picture, especially the seeming failure of the drawing to conform to either the accompanying cento or to the play. Parrott says: "The truth is that Chambers was puzzled by the picture. He accepted sketch and text as the work of Peacham, but made no attempt to explain the discrepancy between them." Adams finds it hard to understand why the transcriber altered the text and why the carefully executed drawing fails to agree with the text it is supposed to illustrate. Wilson can only extricate himself from his problems in comprehending the manuscript by positing two hands in it, one—who is not the illustrator—providing a text at some time from sixteen to twenty-eight years after the drawing was made, which in any case the copyist misunderstood. Munro, though he perceives much of the significance of the drawing and of the technique of simultaneous representation employed in it, is unfortunately diverted by his preoccupation with the conception that Alarbus is a ghost character who "should be withdrawn from the *dramatis personae*." Maxwell sums up: "I do not see how a scribe at a loss to interpret the drawing would have been made any happier by constructing his cento, which he himself must have realized did not represent any single situation in the play."[19] Waith and Foakes, while elucidating much, acknowledge that they find the whole matter challenging.

In an effort to understand and interpret the Longleat drawing, modern critics must first clear away some preconceptions and misconceptions. Commentators assume the primacy of the cento with or without acknowledgement, even though it is a mere pastiche exhibiting over two dozen departures from the authentic texts. Wilson, after a discussion of the cento, says that it "is of small interest to an editor or to anyone else," yet he continues to view it as primary and the drawing as secondary. While a case could be made for regarding the drawing as primary and the text as explanatory—an aid to the understanding of the picture—it is not necessary to do so for a proper grasp of the significance of the manuscript. To appreciate the drawing it is necessary only to assume that it is equally as important as the text. It should be studied directly, not through or under the guidance of or influence of the appended verses. A second preconception that must be dispensed with is the notion that the sketch is the Elizabethan equivalent of a modern photograph that has the capability of preserving an intensely active moment without loss of vitality or dynamics. The Longleat drawing is both more and less than a photograph. It is more in that certain characteristics and qualities of the action selected by the draftsman to be presented can be emphasized without the distraction of unwanted features, and by this means highlighting those elements that he considers most significant. It is less than a photograph in that many things, albeit some subsidiary, that we would like to know about an Elizabethan production of a Shakespearean play have been excluded. Of first importance to be understood is that the drawing, unlike a photograph, need not be limited by time to a specific instant. There are also other scholarly preoccupations in connection with the Longleat document that have to be set aside as peripheral or secondary in understanding the picture. We need not conclusively determine the date of the manuscript, although the interpretation of the cryptic Latin inscription as meaning 1595 is probably correct.[20] Nor is it necessary to settle the question of the identity of the artist. It may or may not have been Henry Peacham, but an appreciation of the sketch can be attained independently of knowing who the draftsman was. And while it is interesting to speculate with Wilson on whether Burbage played Aaron, or Shakespeare played

Titus (if Alleyn was in the company at the time what part did he play?), such guesses do not contribute to an understanding of the picture. Finally, it is essential to recognize that the Longleat drawing was executed for the single purpose of presenting information on a dramatic performance that the artist witnessed. He conveyed the amount of information he thought desirable and necessary within the compass he allotted, omitting, unfortunately, much more that we would like to know. The technique employed is in the tradition of simultaneous representation, frequently employed in Renaissance times, in which events that actually took place at different times or in different places are presented as though they are contemporaneous. This is the style to which Munro alludes when he speaks of the comprehensive method. An understanding of the simultaneous representation convention would obviate the scholarly complaints that the drawing does not represent any given moment in the play—as indeed it appears quite clear that it does not, and was never intended to do so.[21] Having cleared away the impedimenta, we are in a position to appreciate the picture.

The Longleat drawing is a representation of a performance of Shakespeare's *Titus Andronicus,* possibly at Newington or at the Rose in 1594 or shortly before, by the combined Strange's and Admiral's company; or alternately by the newly constituted Chamberlain's Men in 1594 or 1595; or at Burley-on-the-Hill in January 1596. The artist has not with certitude been identified, but on the basis of Croft's finding we may conclude that he was probably Henry Peacham the younger. We can be sure it is Shakespeare's play because five of the characters depicted are readily recognizable: Titus Andronicus, the Roman conqueror, with his crown of laurel (*pace* Speight, who thinks the figure represents Saturninus);[22] Tamora, the Gothic queen, with her regal crown; Tamora's sons Chiron and Demetrius, kneeling, as she is, in supplication to Titus; and Aaron, defiant, Tamora's Moorish paramour. The appended verses, whatever limits they may have and whatever puzzles they present to textual scholars (see below), affirm at the minimum the fact that the drawing records scenes from Shakespeare's play. Scholarly complaints that the sketch and the text do not go together overlook the essential fact that whoever copied the verses, whether it was Peacham or another, knew that the play was *Titus.* The technique is in the convention of simultaneous representation—Munro's comprehensive method—and he is undoubtedly right in his identification of it.

Four events from the play are presented. The first is Tamora's plea addressed to Titus (1.1.104–20) to spare the life of her eldest son, Alarbus, who is about to be sacrificed to appease the *manes* of Titus's dead sons killed in battle. Chiron and Demetrius also kneel in petition to Titus. The second is Wilson's "tableau" (1.1.130–42) of Gothic disappointment and resentment, which follows immediately on Titus's decision to grant to his sons the sacrifice of Alarbus. Lucius, Quintus, Martius, and Mutius have taken Alarbus offstage to the place of sacrifice. Marcus does not participate. Aaron personifies the indignation of the Gothic queen and princes. His sword is extraneous to the tableau. He is pointing to Tamora and her two remaining sons to emphasize the urgency of their prayer for mercy. The men-at-arms behind Titus are members of his guard. Clearly they are not his sons Quintus and Martius, as Foakes thinks possible, nor Lucius and Marcus, as Adams suggested. Lucius is offstage with his brothers at the sacrifice, which he subsequently reports to Titus at 1.1.142–47 when it has been accomplished. Marcus had entered aloft at the beginning of the scene, before Titus's entry. He remains aloft until much later when, according to the Folio stage direction (after 1.1.233) he descends to the main stage following the election of Saturninus as Emperor. Munro's argument that Alarbus was never a character in Shakespeare's play because no entry is provided for him cannot stand up against the circumstantial account of the sacrifice and the specific mention of Alarbus by name once, most importantly, in a stage direction (after 1.1.129) and twice in the dialog (1.1.133 and 143). Adams's speculation that the figure of Aaron was originally that of an executioner and that his skin was later inked in to represent Aaron arises as a consequence of his assumed priority of the text over the drawing, a lack of understanding of the convention of simultaneous representation and an inability to explain the weapon in Aaron's hand. If Aaron had the sword early in Act 1, it would certainly be anomalous because the other members of the Gothic party are, as prisoners should be, unarmed; but Aaron's sword is, in fact, not anomalous because it is part of a later incident.

The third event represented in the drawing is Titus's refusal of the imperial crown. Invited by Marcus on behalf of the common people (plebs) of Rome to be a candidate "for the Empire," Titus responds:

Giue me a staffe of Honour for mine age,
But not a scepter to controwle the world.

(1.1.198–99)

In the picture Titus holds the staff of a tasselled, probably ceremonial, spear, and at his feet is the rejected sceptre. There is nothing to support the idea put forward by Parrott that the object at Titus's feet is a base for his staff nor the opinion of his artist that the object is not lying on the stage. The line drawn across the sketch that the artist took to be a surface is the front edge of the platform. The "ground" below the actors' feet is clearly marked by additional horizontal lines on which the sceptre rests downstage from Titus's staff.

The fourth incident represented in the picture was correctly identified by Munro. It is Aaron's defiant recital of his crimes to Lucius after his capture by a Goth with his infant son. The sword is a property intended to characterize and enhance his truculent attitude. He is, in this incident, pointing at it to emphasize the advice he gave to Chiron and Demetrius on the "trimming" of Lavinia (5.1.92–96). The latter portion of the cento (111. 23–42) supports this view, but it must be understood that, as Munro pointed out, the picture does not portray the incident in 5.1 involving Aaron when he is in imminent danger of execution, but Aaron as he describes himself in exulting in his evil doings.

The Longleat drawing is a unique and exceptionally valuable record of Shakespearean staging that provides theatrical knowledge not available from any other source nor for any other play. It visually portrays four incidents from a performance probably witnessed by the artist and preserves information on early acting and costuming in Shakespeare's plays.

Written out beneath the Longleat drawing in a fair hand of mixed italic and secretary forms are forty verse lines introduced by two scene setting lines and followed by a solitary speech prefix. The first two lines are in the form of a stage direction, which reads: "Enter Tamora pleading for her ſonnes/going to execution." It is not found in any of the printed versions of the play. The first seventeen lines of verse (Tamora's plea) are copied from the play, 1.1.104–20. It is assumed by scholars with little discussion[23] that the scribe worked from one of the four printed texts, not from a manuscript. The next line of the cento is a composite of two authentic half-lines from Titus's response to Tamora. They are the first half of 1.1.121 and the second half of 1.1.125, with "for" substituted for "and." The next two lines, addressed to Aaron by Titus, are not Shakespearean. It has been generally accepted that they are the work of the scribe. Their purpose is to provide a transition and an introduction to the succeeding speech by Aaron, which consists of twenty lines from his defiant recital to Lucius (5.1.87–144). The last line is concluded by "& cetera." Four speech prefixes are supplied, one each for Tamora, Titus, and Aaron, and one for Alarbus, who has no lines to speak in either these verses nor in any of the *Titus* texts. Aside from changes in spelling, which are fairly frequent, there are some alterations in wording and word forms. Lines 5 and 7 of the Longleat text read "ſonnes" the quartos in these lines have the singular, but the Folio in the line corresponding to 1. 7 (1.1.108) of the cento has the plural. All of the prints and the manuscript read "ſonnes" in the intervening line. The prints also have "for her ſonne? (1.1.106) where the cento reads "of her ſonnes." Aaron's speech begins with "Ah now I curſe" (1. 23) in place of the prints' "Euen now I curſe;" and in his second line (1. 24) the scribe writes "comes" for "come." Also in that line the cento agrees with the quartos in reading "within the compaſſe" after striking out an erroneous "your;" F has "within few compaſſe" Line 31 of the cento reads "barnes and hay ſtackes," which agrees with Q3 and F1 (except for the latter's capitals B and H), but Q1 has "hayſtalks" and Q2 "hayſtakes." The prints in the line corresponding to 1. 35 of the manuscript read "ſorrowes almoſt was forgot" while the Longleat scribe transposes the word "almoſt" to an earlier position so that it reads "Even almoſt when their ſorrowes was forgot." The following line (36) begins in the manuscript "And on their breſtes," in place of the print's "And on their skinnes." The first word of 1. 39 is "Tut" as it is in Q2, Q3, and F1. Q1 reads "But." The speech prefix for Tamora is "Tam:" as in F1 where, however, it is printed upside down, while Q1 spells the name out. In Q2 and Q3 it is "Tamo." The cento agrees with Qq in the speech tag "Titus;" F1 has "Tit." There is no deviation in the prefix "Aron" and of course no prefix for Alarbus in the prints. The cento has no punctuation whatsoever in the verse lines.

Some students of the play have attempted to identify which of the printed texts the Longleat scribe had before him. Manifestly, some of the alterations described above are slight as evidence. Taken as a whole they are not unequivocal and are subject to interpretation in order to be brought into harmony. Chambers classifies the substitution of "brestes" for "skinnes" with "slight verbal variants . . . not . . . beyond the compass of a transcriber more intent on his penmanship than his textual accuracy." He notes the agreement between the manuscript and F1 in "haystacks," but he also says "Obviously, if Peacham used any extant print, it would be Q1 (1594)" without explaining why he thinks so. He apparently relies on the Latin notation for the date. Adams prints a chart showing his collation of thirty-six variants, most of which are alterations in spelling, but he excludes some that appear to be of more substance. "The mere variations in orthography . . . might safely be ignored," he says, "but hardly the variants *haystalks-haystacks* and *But-Tut*. On the evidence thus revealed, we seem justified in concluding that the writer did not transcribe from the 1594 quarto, and that probably he transcribed from either the 1611 quarto or the 1623 Folio, with a slight presumption in favor of the Folio."[24] While some of his evidence points toward the Folio, other evidence does not; and some of the evidence Adams overlooks indicates that the source is Qq, for example the speech prefix "Titus." The "haystackes" variant could indicate Q3 as well as F1, as he notes, and "Tut" might have been derived from Q2 or Q3 as well as F1, which he does not point out. Adams also places some weight on the agreement of the manuscript in 1. 7 ("sonnes") with F1, but the whole sequence of "sonnes" is a tangle and moreover is undoubtedly influenced by the drawing. It is clear from some of the other alterations, which are different from all the prints, that the scribe was at least moderately free in his relationship with his text.

Wilson believes that the verses were "almost certainly taken from one of the printed texts," but he does not address himself to the question of which one, saying merely "I think Adams is probably right in believing the Folio to be the source of the text." Later in his edition of the play, he says that the text "is a curious cento, copied from what seems to have been either a late quarto or the folio." Munro finds the text "on the whole good. In one reading it seems to agree with Q against the Folio, in another with the Folio against Q, in a few cases it makes minor departures from both, and in one line (V.i.137) ['almost'] it alters the order of the words: evidently an early text was followed, perhaps Q1 (1594)." Maxwell offers the opinion that the "source seems to have been the First Folio rather than any Quarto," but he mentions as a caveat the Latin date "which a later hand has interpreted as '1595.'"[25]

In his discussion of the cento, Waith questions the significance of the different "Haystacks" spellings, pointing out that the Q1 reading may be "a dialectal variant or a printer's error which any transcriber might well alter to the standard form." In regard to the "Tut" (1. 39), he says "it is conceivable that some copies of Q1 had the reading as a result of a press correction, or alternatively that both Peacham and the Q2 compositor misread the "B," which is somewhat smudged in the one surviving copy of Q1." He notes other disparities and confusion in copying the verses that "suggest that the drawing was made some little time after the performance . . . The evidence of these mistakes does not, however, require us to conclude with Adams . . . and Dover Wilson . . . that the lines were copied years later from the Folio. No edition of the play is consistently followed."[26]

Waith is convincing in turning away from F1, and the source of the verses and the evidence of the alterations as described above tends to support his view that no print is consistently followed. However, if none of the Qq is eliminated and if the reading of the date in the Longleat manuscript as 1595—in accord with Croft's paleographic determination of the origin of the Latin date and Professor Clarence Miller's suggestion to Waith about the final digit—is valid, then it appears most likely that the text Peacham worked from in compiling the cento was Q1, 1594.[27]

9

Nashe's *Unfortunate Traveller* and *Titus Andronicus*

In *Titus Andronicus* and in Nashe's *The Unfortunate Traveller, or the Life of Jack Wilton,* there occur passages that are so closely similar that a conclusion that one writer influenced the other seems inescapable. As Chiron and Demetrius are about to lead off the chaste Lavinia to be raped, Chiron says of the murdered Bassianus:

> Drag hence her husband to some secret hole,
> And make his dead trunk pillow to our lust.
>
> (2.3.129–30)[1]

In Nashe's novel, Esdras of Granado, a notorious "bandetto," ravishes Heraclide, and Jack Wilton, watching through a chink in the floor above, says, "Her husband's dead bodie he made a pillow to his abhomination."[2] Attention was first called to these passages by Ebbs in 1951. In assessing the direction of the possible borrowing Ebbs adopts an indeterminate stance: "Unless there was a common source available to both writers, the resemblance of the lines makes an indebtedness of one to the other seem almost certain." He says that Nashe was a frequenter of the playhouses and might have seen Shakespeare's play, but that it is also possible that Shakespeare read Nashe's sensational narrative in manuscript while he was writing *Titus Andronicus.* Ebbs does not attempt to resolve the question of influence.[3]

York, apparently working independently of Ebbs, noted the same parallel two years later in 1953. He thinks that since both authors sought Southampton's patronage at about the same time (1593–94) Shakespeare may have seen Nashe's novel in manuscript and that Shakespeare certainly read it after it was published. He canvasses other versions of the Titus story, such as Ravencroft's *Titus Andronicus, or the Rape of Lavinia* and the German *Tragödie von Tito Andronico* (but neither the Dutch *Aran en Titus* nor, surprisingly, the chapbook *History of Titus Andronicus*) for

248

possible illumination on the borrowing, but finds none. York concludes that while it is possible that Shakespeare invented the detail, "it is hardly likely. More probably he remembered it from his reading of the *Unfortunate Traveller.*"[4]

Schrickx reviews the findings of Ebbs and York, and in addition cites a somewhat similar image in Nashe's *Pierce Penniless* (1592): If we had "men swine . . . then we should haue . . . a side of [human] bacon that you might lay vnder your head in stead of a bolster."[5] Schrickx considers this to be evidence that Nashe originated the idea of a dead human body being used as a pillow and that Shakespeare may therefore be the borrower. He adds neutrally: "On the one hand the gruesome incident is certainly not beyond Nashe's invention; on the other hand, in the catalog of provocative cruelties with which the sensibilities of the spectators and readers of *Titus Andronicus* are assaulted, Chiron's lurid suggestion is not out of place."[6]

Burnet notes two additional parallel phrases in *Titus Andronicus* and *The Unfortunate Traveller,* one "an exact verbal correspondence." He cites from *Titus Andronicus* "Let not your sorrow die," which occurs also in Nashe's novel; and "big-swol'n face," which is paralleled by "big swolne large face" in the story. The first of these he thinks "does strengthen the possibility that Nashe was involved in the writing of the play."[7] It should be noted that none of the other commentators on these parallels nor any of the critics or editors of the play in this century consider Nashe as a possible collaborator in the composition of *Titus,* including the archdisintegrator, Robertson, and Dover Wilson, who thinks Shakespeare revised the work of another playwright (later recanted except for Act 1).

There are other parallels in addition to those cited above. Close reading of *The Unfortunate Traveller* reveals a number of additional words and phrases shared with *Titus Andronicus,* most of which, of themselves, have only modest evidentiary value. A character in Jack Wilton's narrative, while in Rome, addresses himself to "gentlemen and noble Romans," as Bassianus does to "Romans, friends, followers," but like expressions occur fairly frequently in the literature of the time, notably Brutus's "Romans, countrymen, and lovers" and Mark Antony's "Friends, Romans, countrymen."[8] Similarly, Aaron warns the contentious Gothic princes not to "jet" on the Emperor's right; Nashe has: "a soldier & a braggart he is . . . he ietteth strouting." Aaron's catalog of atrocities is usually compared to that of Barabas in Marlowe's *Jew of Malta,* but Nashe's Zadoch recites a comparable list of intended horrors.[9] There are however no lexical echoes. Two other parallels are of somewhat more significance. Aaron counsels Chiron and Demetrius

> so must you resolve
> That what you cannot, as you would achieve,
> You must perforce accomplish as you may.

(2.1.106–8)

The Unfortunate Traveller has:

> They must shape their cotes, good men according to their cloath, and doe as
> they may, not as they wold.

(McKerrow ed., 2:238)

The expression is, of course, proverbial.

Again, Aaron tells Lucius:

> I play'd the cheater for thy father's hand,
> And when I had it, drew myself apart,
> And almost broke my heart with extreme laughter.
> . . . .
> And when I told the empress of this sport,
> She sounded almost at my pleasing tale.

(5.1.111–13 and 118–19)

Nashe notes that "*Philemon,* a Comick poet, died with extreme laughter" (McKerrow ed., 2:298), while earlier in the novel of Nashe's characters, Tabitha, under great emotional stress, "sounded and reuiued, and then sounded again" (McKerrow ed., 2:257).

Of greater consequence than these verbal correspondences is a close affinity in the action of the two rape sequences, apparently not noticed by previous commentators. In both *Titus Andronicus* and *The Unfortunate Traveller,* the victim is a virtuous matron rather than a maid, such as those whose ravishment Aaron boasts of having plotted (5.1.129). In both the play and Nashe's tale, the man (Bassianus and the zany Capestrano) who could have protected the chaste lady is first done away with, each killed before the eyes of the victim about to be attacked. There is an emotion-laden exchange beforehand in which the object of the intended crime pleads for mercy or death instead of violation, but in both the plea is brusquely denied. In neither case is the rape described. In the play it occurs offstage and in *The Unfortunate Traveller* Jack Wilton bids the reader to "conjecture the rest," but we know it happened from Heraclide's lament and because Jack says that Esdras's "whorish lust was glutted, his beastly desire satisfied."[10] In both instances, the perpetrators temporarily escape the consequences of the crime they have committed but are eventually brought to the rough justice of vengeance, although Esdras is killed in retaliation for having slain his confederate, Bartol. Neither Esdras nor

Chiron and Demetrius exhibit any remorse. In two important respects the stories diverge: Heraclide is not mutilated, nor is she "sacrificed," as Lavinia is, but commits suicide much as does Shakespeare's Lucrece.[11] The elements in this sequence are found in the chapbook *History of Titus Andronicus*, except that in the tale, Lavinia is unmarried at the time she is violated, and the rape is briefly though graphically described. That the *History* was almost certainly Shakespeare's primary source[12] is attested to by the numerous correspondences in structure, incident, and diction between the prose tale and *Titus Andronicus*. Shakespeare in his play changed Lavinia from a maid, as she is in the *History*, to a married woman and omitted the description of her rape. In these particulars, Nashe appears to have followed the play. If so, then the probability is that the verbal parallels in *The Unfortunate Traveller* are Shakespearean in origin, that Nashe heard them at one or more performances of *Titus*, and recorded them in his commonplace book for later reference.

Critics who believe that Shakespeare is the borrower place some reliance on similar possible borrowings from Nashe in other Shakespearean plays. York cites George R. Coffman, who finds parallels in passages in *1 Henry IV* and *The Unfortunate Traveller* concerned with Pegasus and "estriches." Schrickx notes Dover Wilson's twenty parallels in his New Cambridge edition of the same play; his own *Shakespeare's Early Contemporaries* for a "further echo" from Nashe in *2 Henry IV;* Davenport's discovery of parallels in *Hamlet* from Nashe's *Pierce Penniless;* and Frank Bradbrook's possible Shakespearean borrowings from *Christ's Tears over Jerusalem* in *Antony and Cleopatra* and *The Tempest*.[13] Many of these are subject to question. Some are doubtful, some commonplace, and a few are far-fetched. For example, of Dover Wilson's twenty parallels between Nashe and *1 Henry IV*, only two have any cogent evidentiary value. Wilson himself prefaces his list by saying "I have no explanation to offer" concerning the parallels. It may be of note that in his New Cambridge edition of *2 Henry VI*, published in 1952, some six years after his *1 Henry IV*, Wilson again lists such parallels but indicates he is uncertain of the direction of influence. In a section of his Introduction to *2 Henry VI* entitled "Nashe and the Jack Cade scenes," he first asserts that Nashe "was Greene's collaborator in *2 Henry VI* . . . and wrote the Jack Cade scenes in their original draft," but later he asks if Shakespeare borrowed from Nashe "or did Nashe jot down these sentences at the play for later use, as he confesses was his habit at the theatre?" In conclusion, he limits himself to the statement that the allusions he has cited "appear to be connected." In his edition of *Titus*, Wilson says that the notorious lines about the human pillow exhibit "Shakespeare's cadence," which leans toward acceptance of Shakespeare as the originator.[14] It should be remembered, however, that the playwrights of the period, as Chambers pointed out,[15] shared a common stock of diction deriving ultimately from Spencer, from the translators of the classics, and from Seneca, so a certain minimum of lexical parallels is only what should be expected.

Other scholars who have weighed the evidence of these potential links express reservations similar to Wilson's. Hibbard cites the parallel "pillow" passages, then neutrally comments: "It looks as though Shakespeare may have borrowed from Nashe." Kaula doubts that Shakespeare made any significant borrowings from Nashe, and Leggatt, though less explicit, seems to be of the same opinion. Rhodes, who seeks to define "Shakespeare's debt to Nashe" finds reflections of Nashe's writings and specifically of *The Unfortunate Traveller,* in *2 Henry VI, Love's Labor's Lost, Taming of the Shrew,* and *1* and *2 Henry IV,* but he does not record any Nashean links to *Titus.*[16]

Crewe thinks that "the study of Nashe contributes to an understanding of Shakespeare, if for no other reason than that the two authors are linked both chronologically and by a common and acknowledged linguistic virtuosity." He speaks of "Shakespeare's possible indebtedness" and says that "Nashe's innovativeness appears to have been underestimated in relation to Shakespeare's" but does not cite specific examples nor press his case beyond his evidence. Schäfer compares the vocabularies of Shakespeare and Nashe, and to a lesser extent those of Malory and Wyatt. By means of a statistical calculation, he arrives at a conclusion that Nashe's linguistic innovations exhibit a higher frequency than Shakespeare's, but he makes no show of borrowings. Nicoll cites approvingly McKerrow's stricture on Nashe's "systematic gutting" of Agrippa's *De Incertitudine,* says "This is fair enough criticism;" and notes in *1* and *2 Henry VI* "some striking parallels with phrases in Nashe's . . . pamphlets, though these could equally be Nashe echoing Shakespeare."[17]

It seems evident that while certain of the parallels cited exhibit a modicum of common ground between Nashe's writings and some of Shakespeare's plays, including *Titus Andronicus,* there is no certainty as to who was the borrower. In Renaissance times, imitation by one writer of another was, of course, common. Felicitous interweaving of the thoughts, images, and expressions of another author, particularly if an eminent one, into the fabric of one's own composition, was admired. All writers essayed this type of adornment, including both Shakespeare and Nashe. But while Shakespeare customarily at least altered, and sometimes completely transformed, the ideas of another, Nashe, a University man trained in classical *imitatio,* is more typically a verbatim borrower. By his own testimony, we know that he diligently collected and recorded the words of other authors. In *Lenten Stuff,* he complains that, "of my note-books and all books else here in the countrey I am bereaued, whereby I might enamell and hatch ouer this deuice more artificially and masterly, and attire it in his true orient varnish and tincture; wherefore heart and good wil, a workman is nothing without his tooles."[18] After quoting a proverbial expression in *Strange Newes,* he has a "*Memorandum:* I borrowed this sentence out of a play. The Theatre, Poets hall, hath many more such prouerbes."[19] McKerrow, in a section of his Commentary on "Nashe's Reading," says that "he, as indeed almost all the prose writers of his time, set himself deliberately to produce a kind of artistic composition . . . in which the effect should be heightened by all the well-known devices of ornament, [including] examples of similes . . . and there seems to be evidence that it was a usual practice to keep note-books in which striking phrases, images or examples met with in the course of reading might be treasured up for future use."[20]

Schrickx and Burnet, explicitly, and York, implicitly, also cite, in support of their hypothesis, the dates of composition of *The Unfortunate Traveller* and *Titus Andronicus.* They reason that since Nashe's novel was complete on 27 June 1593, a date noted on the final page, and was registered for publication on the following 17 September, while *Titus Andronicus,* according to Henslowe, was first performed by the Earl of Sussex's Men as "ne[w]" on 23 January 1594[21] and registered on 6 February (the printed versions of both the play and the novel are dated 1594), that therefore *The Unfortunate Traveller* must be the earlier at least by some months and consequently Shakespeare borrowed from Nashe. No account is taken of a body of evidence for a date significantly earlier than 1593–94 for Shakespeare's play. Schrickx notes in passing that the title page of the first quarto of 1594 lists the troupes of the Earls of Derby and Pembroke as having played *Titus* presumably before Sussex's men did, but he neither evaluates nor interprets the evidence. None of the commentators cites the well-known passage in *A Knack to Know a Knave* that not only names Titus but also mentions important details of the story which, of the versions of the tale still extant, occur only in Shakespeare's play. Osric tells King Edgar:

My gratious Lord, as welcome shall you be,
To me, my Daughter, and my sonne in Law,
As *Titus* was unto the Roman Senators,
When he had made a conquest on the Goths:
That in requitall of his seruice done,
Did offer him the imperiall Diademe:
As they in *Titus,* we in your Grace still fynd,
The perfect figure of a Princelie mind.[22]

Sir Edmund Chambers says that "no such combination [of Titus and the Goths] is known outside *Titus Andronicus.*"[23] None of the other versions of the story—the *History of Titus Andronicus,* the ballad, the German and Dutch versions, Ravenscroft's derivative *Titus Andronicus, or the Rape of Lavinia*—include a senatorial welcome for Titus, an offer of the imperial crown, or a description of Titus as princely. These are found only in Shakespeare's *Titus Andronicus*. It seems safe to conclude with Peter Alexander that Osric was alluding to a play that was on the boards at the time that *A Knack to Know a Knave* was first produced, or had been shortly before.[24] Henslowe notes *A Knack* as new on 10 June 1592,[25] and consequently it appears probable that both plays were written before *The Unfortunate Traveller* and *Pierce Penniless*.

Possible links between *Titus Andronicus* and *The Troublesome Reign of King John,* printed in 1591, and Peele's *Edward I* (published in 1593 but Chambers thinks it was written in 1590–91),[26] while not so conclusive as those that exist between Shakespeare's play and *A Knack to Know a Knave,* nevertheless constitute evidence not lightly to be ignored. These items of fact are further supported by Jonson's well-know comment in the induction to *Bartholomew Fair* (1614), to the effect that *The Spanish Tragedy* and *Titus Andronicus* were written twenty-five or thirty years before, which is usually interpreted to mean an approximate date of composition of 1589.[27]

The hypothesis of Shakespearean borrowings from Nashe in plays other than *Titus Andronicus* quite apparently does not apply with uniform cogency. Some passages in some plays seem to reflect Nashe, while those in other plays may be interpreted as Nashe borrowing from Shakespeare. Nashe's following Shakespeare appears particularly true in the case of *Titus.* Nothing in the parallels between this play and *The Unfortunate Traveller* identifies Shakespeare as the borrower, while the pattern of imitation shows that Nashe is far more likely to have adopted some of the incidents and language of the play. The evidence concerning the date of composition of *Titus* neutralizes the arguments put forth on the basis of the priority in time of Nashe's novel. On the whole it appears likely that Nashe saw one or more performances of *Titus Andronicus* before he began writing *The Unfortunate Traveller,* and made note of the rape incident and of some passages of verse for later use. The conclusion is that the links between the play and *The Unfortunate Traveller* represent Nashe borrowing from Shakespeare.[28]

10

Music in *Titus Andronicus*

In comparison to other Shakespearean plays, especially the comedies, there is indeed only a little music of any kind in *Titus Andronicus* but it is not altogether absent. In addition to the requirement for trumpet flourishes to be anticipated in a play including imperial entrances and exits, the play calls for music on a few other occasions. These include drums and trumpets to signal the martial displays of the first and fifth acts, the solemn funeral music upon the entombment in Act 1, and the winding of horns in the two hunting scenes (2.2 and 2.4). Such sparsity is not a characteristic peculiar to *Titus*. In a survey of Shakespeare's use of music in his plays, particularly those composed after "about 1600," Nosworthy observes that "with the notable exception of *Hamlet* [primarily in Ophelia's part], the tragedies as a whole make little use of music." He mentions, in addition, *Othello, Antony and Cleopatra*, and *Timon of Athens* and says further that "the subsequent tragic period offers little of real musical interest." Although his comments apply directly only to the later tragedies, they are manifestly pertinent to the earliest.[1]

The stage directions in *Titus* concerning music vary between the quartos and the First Folio, with those in the latter generally being fuller, more specific and, in certain cases, repetitive. Although not without exception, the Folio generally substitutes "Flourish" for the quartos' "Sound Trumpets." On two occasions it has both. In Act 5, at the entrance of Titus, dressed "like a Cooke," F1 calls for "hoboyes," where the quartos have "Trumpets sounding." The absence of the latter phrase from the later text may be traceable to the emendations to the stage direction that arose from a defect in the exemplar of Q3 from which F1 was set. The direction for "Hoboyes" is not involved in such changes, however, because it occurs on the preceding line of text, which is printed by F1 unchanged otherwise from Q3. Sternfeld, in comment on the use of hoboyes, says "That the squealing of oboes was held to be an ill omen is borne out by many stage directions in Elizabethan plays. One may assume that, essentially, all wind instruments were considered loud and piercing: trumpets, cornetts, oboes, pipes, and even flutes. When the playwright wished to express an unusually soft quality by means of a wind instrument he spoke of 'still flutes' or 'still recorders' . . . Shakespeare's earliest tragedy . . . prescribes oboes for its most gruesome scene . . . banquet, music, and bloody revenge are combined in a melodramatic manner. There is a great deal of excess in this early tragedy, as its critics customarily declare, but there is no denying that the counterpointing of cruelty and music is an effective dramatic procedure." Later he observes:

> Certain instruments or consorts of instruments might be used to signify war or peace, to suggest divine or diabolical intervention, or to announce that a scene is domestic, courtly, or military. Such contextual music depended for its effect on the significance of opposites: loud and harsh music . . . meant the opposite of soft and peaceful music . . . trumpets, cornetts, and hautboys contrasted with strings and recorders . . . Squealing hautboys (much louder and harsher than the modern oboe) foretold doom, most notably in the banqueting scenes in *Titus Andronicus* and *Macbeth* and in their ominous music under the stage in *Antony and Cleopatra*.[2]

Long, following an examination of the "musical rubrics" in *Titus* Qq and F1, points out that they differ. "While the Q texts may be closer to the author's manuscript than F, I will demonstrate that F's directions for music in no way contradict their equivalents in the Q texts. In most cases, F's directions clarify and augment those in the Q texts . . . Q's directions are more general than their parallels in F. The quarto directions never use the more specialized terms 'flourish' or 'sennet'; they state, 'Trumpets sound,' 'Sound trumpets,' or 'Sound.' Nor do directions calling for hautboys (waits, shawms) appear in these Q texts . . . For these reasons . . . I believe that F's directions for music in *Titus Andronicus* are as valid as those in the Q texts and that F supplies a more detailed account of the music as it was actually used in the play's most complete early productions."[3] Greg's opinion that "the folio alterations [in the stage directions] are for the most part due to the editor or compositor, the additions to the book-keeper" tends to support Long's judgment.[4] In this conclusion, Long differs from the determination of modern editors.[5]

As to the specific music employed, Long believes that Titus is greeted upon his return to Rome with "a military drum march punctuated by trumpet fanfares," that the slain sons are entombed as a "flourish sounds the 'larums to welcome the victorious spirits of the dead, and the trumpets sound a solemn valedictory . . . The customary flourish would do for the salutation; for the valediction I suggest the 'Retraite' shown in Appendix I [of his book] . . . The hunting scene . . . provides some variety in instrumentation via the hunting horn." He suggests "a 'hunts-up' or aubade to rouse the emperor" from Turberville's *Noble Art of Venery or Hunting,* and in order to announce the entry of Marcus to the ravished

Lavinia, another of Turberville's horn signals, "The Straking from Covert to Covert." These suggestions would provide rather more variety in the music of *Titus* than otherwise might have been anticipated.[6] The quarto stage direction for the banquet at the play's conclusion calls for trumpets, but the Folio reads "Hoboyes." "Both trumpets and hautboys," Long tells us, "were used in Elizabethan stage banquets. The normal procedure was for the trumpets to play a fanfare upon the entrance of royalty, and for the hautboys to play a processional march as the monarch and his train moved into the banqueting hall . . . It is possible that only trumpets were available for the performances reported in the Q texts; on a later occasion the trumpets may have been augmented by hautboys as directed in F. If this were the case, this scene provides the first example of Shakespeare's increasing and varying the instrumentation to emphasize a play's climax—a technique that he used frequently in the later comedies."[7]

Price finds the use of the horns in the hunting scenes admirable: "The stage direction in Qo.1 is: 'Enter Titus Andronicus, and his three sonnes, making a noise with hounds and hornes.' Titus delivers his speech, in which he says

> Uncouple here, and let us make a bay
> And rouse the Prince, and ring a hunter's peal.

Lower down there follows the stage direction: 'Here a crie of Hounds, and wind hornes in a peale.' Shakespeare is obviously working hard to obtain atmosphere. The hounds, 'match'd in mouth like bells, Each under each' combine with the music to create the mood of a jolly hunting dawn. Shakespeare uses various sorts of music. He brings in the special trumpet call when hounds were uncoupled, and another call 'for a companie in the morning.' The 'peal' was not just any tantarara, but a special musical form . . . There is only one 'parallel' to this passage, and that is *M.N.D.* iv. i. 110–30 . . . There is nothing accidental in the similarity of technique that these two passages show. So far as my observation goes, no Elizabethan dramatist, certainly none writing in 1594, was so skilful as Shakespeare in using music to create mood and atmosphere . . . Music is used with dramatic irony at ii.iv.10 . . . Fo. reads: 'Winde Hornes. Enter Marcus from hunting, to Lauinia.' Qo. 1 reads: 'Enter Marcus from hunting.' In both cases the effect intended is the same. From behind the scene the audience hears a merry hunter's peal upon the horns, and then Marcus enters in that mood of hearty cheerfulness which is always produced by a day's hunting in the forest. He enters—to find 'Lavinia ravished; her hands cut off, and her tongue cut out.' If we are looking for parallels, the closest is afforded by *Lear* i.iv.7. Horns are sounded within, presaging something jolly, and Lear enters from hunting, with an appetite born of a day in the fresh air, eager for dinner. It is the prelude to the episode in which Lear is driven to curse Goneril. If similarity of workmanship may be held to prove anything, then the same hand was at work in both these scenes."[8]

Hattaway points out that

> Like *Coriolanus* . . . *Titus Andronicus* demands more than the usual amount of music. Shakespeare's frequent calls for flourishes and trumpets are not a tacit admission that non-verbal devices are required to flesh out the text nor do they serve merely to create a martial atmosphere. Rather, as we have seen, music serves for perspective, for symbols of concord and discord, political league and political chaos, the harmony of love and the broken chords of passion.

Shakespeare also employs "musical metaphor[s]," as in Aaron's admonition to Tamora's sons

> And should the Empress know
> This discord's ground, the music would not please.
>
> (2.1.69–70)

and in Tamora's wooing of Aaron by evoking "the harmony of echoes, hounds, and horns, [which] ironically symbolizes a legitimate and decorous love." Since *Titus* can attain a resolution "only by deaths," Hattaway finds it "significant that the final lines of the play . . . explicitly forbid the sounding of ritual funeral music:"[9]

> As for that ravenous tiger, Tamora,
> No funeral rite, nor man in mourning weed,
> No mournful bell shall ring her burial;
>
> (5.3.194–96)

Ingram believes it probable that there was more music heard in Shakespeare's plays than is directly called for in the text or in the stage directions. Indications would have been inserted into the prompt-book, but he thinks not all are preserved in the printed texts. He points out that the texts we have "can ask directly for music without there being any direction for it . . . the situation may 'demand' music because of dramatic convention or social habit . . . with neither stage direction nor indication in the spoken work. Generally I believe it is reasonable to assume that social convention ruled even where its edicts are not explicitly asked for in directions, where an audience would be disconcerted if no music were heard . . . Entries and departures of rulers, returns of victorious generals, triumphant or solemn processions were always musical in real life." Ingram identifies several such occasions for additional music in Act 1 of *Titus:* following Marcus's proclamation of Saturninus as Emperor at 1.1.233 and before F1's Flourish to cover their descent; on Saturninus's call for "trump and drum" on his exit at 1.1.275; upon his announcement of his choice of Tamora as his bride instead of Lavinia, 1.1.333; and upon his exit at 1.1.337; at the entombment of Mutius, 1.1.386; and upon the reentry of Saturnius and Bassianus at separate doors at 1.1.398. Ingram also notes that "Texts change, stage business varies . . . Music might be used in one place one year but not in that place another . . . the printed texts that have come down to us do not include all of these. Even where printed texts do have prompt-book directions . . . it is arguable that not all of them have been printed," therefore more ceremonial music would have been employed "when such music would be expected."[10]

Curious marginal jottings by the "Old Corrector" in the so-called Perkins Folio rework the opening lines at the beginning of the hunt and the subsequent stage direction to rhyme Titus's opening speech, to provide for a "round," and to call for a song and an aubade in the subsequent stage direction. The Old Corrector's changes are the last word or words of six of the ten lines of the speech to produce rhymes. These and the additions to the stage direction are enclosed in brackets in the following transcription.

> *Tit.* The hunt is up, the morne is bright and [gay,]
> The fields are fragrant, and the Woods are [wide:]
> Vncouple heere, and let us make a bay,
> And wake the Emperour, and his lovely Bride,
> And rouze the Prince, and ʃing a hunters [round;]
> That all the Court may eccho with the [ʃound.]
> Sonnes let it be your charge, [and so will I]
> To attend the Emperours person carefully:
> I have been troubled in my ʃleepe this night,
> But dawning day [brought comfort and delight.]
> [*Songe then*] *Winde Hornes.* [*The Hunt is up*]
> Heere a cry of houndes, and winde hornes in a peale;[11]

The use of music in modern productions of the play has varied. Most prevalently it is limited to that required by the stage directions and sometimes additional musical accompaniment; but the most highly regarded modern production was widely praised for, among several other reasons, its music written by the producer, Peter Brook, for the Royal Shakespeare Company production of 1955. The effect was memorably described by David:

> The compulsive and incantatory nature of the production . . . was reinforced by the musical effects, all of a marvellous directness. The overture was a roll of drum and cymbal, the dirge for the slain Andronici, so strange and powerful, no more than the first two bars of *Three Blind Mice*, in the minor and endlessly repeated. A slow see-saw of two bass notes, a semitone apart, wrought the tension of the final scene to an unbearable pitch, and ceased abruptly, with breath-taking effect, as the first morsel of son-pie passed Tamora's lips. Even more harrowing were the hurrying carillon of electronic bells that led up to

the abduction of Lavinia and the slow plucking of harp-strings, like drops of blood falling into a pool, that accompanied her return to the stage.[12]

David subsequently discusses Shakespeare's use of various kinds of music with the purpose "of creating atmosphere," notably in *1 Henry IV*, *Merchant of Venice*, and *Antony and Cleopatra*. "Even such a mesmeric use of music [as in *Merchant* and *Antony*] may seem unsophisticated in comparison with those of which the director Peter Brook is the modern master, for example the extremely simple but hypnotising electronic sounds that pointed his 1955 production of *Titus Andronicus*. But Brook's procedures, considered from the point of view of their effect upon an audience, are essentially of the same kind as Shakespeare's, and twentieth-century elaborations of musical techniques should be welcomed . . . as an intensification, not a betrayal, of Shakespeare's own methods."[13]

In a discussion of Brook's staging of *Titus*, Beauman notes that he "wrote all the music . . . Brook's *musique concrete* boomed and breathed around the auditorium. All through the production strange music provided emphasis, alarum, and counterpoint; some sounds were created by using conventional instruments, distorted by recording at different speeds, or by the use of an echo chamber, others were created with an assortment of household objects—wine glasses, a toy trumpet. The music created a sense of dislocation, threat, and unease."[14]

Music presented as part of two other productions was sufficiently distinctive to draw comment. The first of these was that mounted under the direction of Gerald Freedman in the 1967 New York Shakespeare Festival. In his introduction to the Folio Society edition of *Titus*, Freedman explains his conception:

> if one wants to create a fresh emotional response . . . one must . . . shock the imagination . . . with visual images . . . with the power of poetic conventions . . . drawn from the ancient theatres . . . with instruments and sounds that nudge our ear without being clearly explicit or melodic . . . Thus the choice of music, mask, and chorus . . . The solution had to lie in a poetic abstraction of time and in vivid impressionistic images . . . and this led me to masks and music and ritual . . . The music eschewed electronics, which though non-literal are distinctly of "our" time. What I needed were those sounds that are part of our inherited primitive consciousness—drums, rattles, rubbed stones, animal horns, and stretched strings.

Critics favorably noted the contribution of the music to the production. A newspaper commentator cited the "hissing, buzzing, declaiming . . . quivering, rasping, and percussive musical sound effects;" while Kuner recalled "the music of drums . . . in the mode of a liturgy."[15]

The most recent *Titus* presentation noted for music was the Oregon

Shakespearean Festival's third mounting, which was offered during its 1986 season. Dessen observed that "Although not going to the lengths that Brook had chosen for his music in 1955, music director Todd Barton did find some distinctive and unusual background sounds—most notably what Barton termed a controlled panic scream that was heard at key moments." Journalistic reviewers were favorably impressed by the music and many noted its special quality. One cited the "sound score dominated by eerie echoic gongs;" and another the accompaniment of "ominous gongs, clangs, and booms."[16]

Notes

Chapter 1. Authorship

1. E. K. Chambers, *William Shakespeare: A Study of Facts and Problems,* 2 vols. (Oxford: Clarendon Press, 1930), 2:72.

2. Sir Aston Cokayne, *A Chain of Golden Poems.* (London: 1658), poems 7 and 35; reprinted in W. W. Greg, *A Bibliography of the English Printed Drama to the Restoration,* 4 vols. (London: Bibliographical Society, 1939–59), 3:1240–43.

3. Chambers, *William Shakespeare,* 2:194. See T. W. Baldwin, *Shakspere's Love's Labor's Won* (Carbondale: Southern Illinois University Press, 1957), passim. For a discussion of efforts to identify *LLW* with a canonical play, see Metz, "*Wonne* is lost, quite lost," *MLS* 16 (1986), 3–12.

4. Edward Ravenscroft, *Titus Andronicus, or the Rape of Lavinia* (London: 1687), sig. A2^r; facsimile reprint (London: Cornmarket Press, 1969). Chambers, in his 1924 British Academy Annual Shakespeare Lecture, notes that, although we do not know who Ravenscroft's informants were, "At least one old actor, William Beeston, whose father [Christopher Beeston] had been a 'fellow' of Shakespeare, and who may himself have known Shakespeare in his boyhood, survived to 1682. A true report is not, therefore, inconceivable"; *The Disintegration of Shakespeare* (London: Oxford University Press, 1924), 3; reprint, *Shakespearean Gleanings* (London: Oxford University Press, 1944), 1–21.

5. Gerard Langbaine, *An Account of the English Dramatick Poets* (1691; reprint, Los Angeles: UCLA, 1971), 464–65.

6. Alexander Pope, ed., *Works,* 6 vols. (London; 1723), 1:xx; Lewis Theobald, ed., *Works,* 8 vols. (London: 1857), 5:307n; Samuel Johnson, ed., *Plays,* 8 vols. (London: 1765), 6:394–65; Thomas Percy, *Reliques of Ancient English Poetry,* 3 vols. (London: 1765), 1:221.

7. Edward Capell, ed., *Comedies, Histories & Tragedies,* 10 vols. (London: 1767–68), 1:41–46.

8. Edmond Malone, "An Attempt to Ascertain the order in which the plays attributed to Shakespeare were written"; Samuel Johnson and George Steevens, eds., *Plays,* 10 vols. (London: 1778), 1:269–346, esp. 274–75, 279–80; *Plays and Poems,* 10 vols. (London: 1790), 1:lix, 293n; James Boswell, ed., *Plays and Poems,* 21 vols. (London: 1821), 21:257–61.

9. Frederick S. Boas, *Shakspere and his Predecessors,* (1896; reprint, New York: Gordian, 1968), 139.

10. J. O. Halliwell-Phillipps, ed., *Works,* 16 vols. (London: 1853–65), 13:3–6; *Outlines of the Life of Shakespeare,* 10th edition, 2 vols. (London: 1898), 1:114–15, 293–94.

11. *William Shakespeare,* 1:255–69, esp. 266–69.

12. Frederick G. Fleay, "On Metrical Tests as Applied to Dramatic Poetry, Part I. Shakspere." (*NSST, 1874*), [1874], 1–16; *Shakespeare Manual* (London: 1876, 1878), 128; Clement N. Ingleby, *Shakespeare, the Man and the Book,* 2 vols. (London: 1877–81), 2:140; *A Chronicle History of the Life and Work of William*

Shakespeare (London: 1886), 280–82; *A Biographical Chronicle of the English Drama, 1559–1641*, 2 vols. (London; 1891), 2:299–300.

13. Richard Simpson, "Table of Shakspere's Once-Used Words" (*NSST 1874*), [1874], 114–15.

14. G[regor] Sarrazin, "Wortechos bei Shakespeare," 1: *SJ* 33 (1897), 121–65; 2: *SJ* 34 (1898), 119–69.

15. F. G. Hubbard, "Repetition and Parallelism in the Earlier Elizabethan Drama," *PMLA* 20 (1905), 360–79; Alexander B. Grosart, "Was Robert Greene Substantially the Author of *Titus Andronicus?*" *Englische Studien* 22 (1896), 389–435. In regard to the authorship of *Selimus*, see *The Predecessors of Shakespeare*, ed. Terence P. Logan and Denzell S. Smith (Lincoln: University of Nebraska Press, 1973), 301–4.

16. Harold de Witt Fuller, "The Sources of *Titus Andronicus*," *PMLA* 16 (1901), 1–65; George P. Baker, "*Tittus and Vespacia* and *Titus and Ondronicus* in Henslowe's Diary," *PMLA* 16 (1901), 66–76; *The Development of Shakespeare as a Dramatist* (New York: Macmillan, 1907), 124–34.

17. Robert K. Root, *Classical Mythology in Shakespeare* (New York: Holt, 1903), 13–17; Robert A. Law, "The Roman Background of *Titus Andronicus*," *SP* 40 (1943), 145–53; Gilbert Highet, *The Classical Tradition* (1953; reprint, New York: Oxford University Press, 1957), 207–8, 214, 618n.1, 623n.84, 626n.92; J. A. K. Thomson, *Shakespeare and the Classics* (London: Allen, 1952), 51–58; Barbara A. Mowat, "Lavinia's Message: Shakespeare and Myth," *RenP 1981* (1982), 55–69; Grace Starry West, "Going by the Book: Classical Allusions in Shakespeare's *Titus Andronicus*," *SP* 79 (1982), 62–77.

18. J. M. Robertson, *Did Shakespeare Write Titus Andronicus?* (1905, revised edition, entitled *An Introduction to the Shakespeare Canon* 1924; reprint, Westport, CT: Greenwood, 1970), passim. Refs. *to Tit.* are to Eugene M. Waith, ed., *Titus Andronicus*, in *The Oxford Shakespeare* (Oxford: Clarendon Press, 1984). References to other Shakespeare plays, unless otherwise noted, are to Stanley Wells and Gary Taylor, gen. eds., *Works* (Oxford: Clarendon Press, 1986).

19. W. W. Greg, ed., *Henslowe's Diary*, 2 vols. (1904–08; reprint, Norwood, PA: Norwood Editions, 1978), 2:159–62; "*Titus Andronicus*," *MLR* 14 (1919), 322–23; *The Editorial Problem in Shakespeare* (Oxford: Clarendon Press, 1942), 3rd ed. 1954, 117, 118n1; *The Shakespeare First Folio* (Oxford: Clarendon Press, 1955) 204. He sums up a review of Robertson's book by saying: "though it seems impossible to accept Mr Robertson's argument in its entirety, his main conclusions may be recogised as sound." *MLR* 1 (1906), 337–41. The quoted passage is on p. 341.

20. T. S. Eliot, Introduction to *Seneca His Tenne Tragedies Translated into English;* reprint, London: Constable; New York; Knopf, 1927); and in Eliot, *Selected Essays* (London: Constable; New York: Harcourt, 1932) under the title "Seneca in Elizabethan Translation"; Joseph Q. Adams, *A Life of William Shakespeare* (Cambridge, MA: Riverside, 1923), 134n.1; Edgar I. Fripp, *Shakespeare, Man and Artist*, 2 vols. (London: Oxford University Press, 1938), 1:370; Mark van Doran, *Shakespeare* (1939; reprint, Garden City, NY; Doubleday, 1953), 38–43; Fredson T. Bowers, *Elizabethan Revenge Tragedy 1587–1642* (Princeton: Princeton University Press, 1940), 110. For Eliot's final opinion see "Criticism" n. 6.

21. T. N. Parrott, "Shakespeare's Revision of *Titus Andronicus*," *MLR* 14 (1919), 16–37.

22. William Allan Neilson and Ashley Horace Thorndike, *The Facts about Shakespeare* (New York: Macmillan, 1914), 70–76; Henry D. Gray, "Chronology

of Shakespeare's Plays," *MLN* 49 (1931), 147–50; Karl P. Wentersdorf, "Shakespearean Chronology and the Metrical Tests," *Shakespeare-Studien: Festschrift für Heirich Mutschmann*, Walther Fischer and Karl Wentersdorf, eds. (Marburg: Elwert, 1951) 161–93.

23. George Saintsbury, "Shakespeare: Life and Plays," *Cambridge History of English Literature*, A. W. Ward and Alfred R. Waller, eds., 15 vols. (Cambridge: Cambridge University Press, 1907–16), 5:165–222.

24. Chambers, "Disintegration," *passim*. *William Shakespeare*, 1:312–22.

25. Peter Alexander, *Shakespeare's Henry VI and Richard III* (Cambridge: Cambridge University Press, 1929), 137–43; Philip W. Timberlake, *The Feminine Ending in English Blank Verse* (Menasha, WI: Banta, 1931), 113–18.

26. Arthur M. Sampley, "Plot Structure in Peele's Plays as a Test of Authorship," *PMLA* 51 (1936), 689–701; "'Verbal Tests' for Peele's Plays," *SP* 30 (1933), 473–96. J. C. Maxwell, ed., *Titus Andronicus*, in *The New Arden Shakespeare* (London: Methuen, 1953, 3rd ed. rev., 1961), xxvi–xxvii; Hereward T. Price, *Construction in Shakespeare* (Ann Arbor: University of Michigan Press, 1951), 37–41; Ernest W. Talbert, *Elizabethan Drama and Shakespeare's Plays* (Chapel Hill: University of North Carolina Press, 1963. Corrected ed. New York: Gordian, 1973), 134.

27. George Lyman Kittredge, ed., *Works* (Boston: Ginn, 1936), 971–72.

28. Price, "The Authorship of *Titus Andronicus*," *JEGP* 42 (1943), 55–81; "The First Quarto of *Titus Andronicus*," *English Institute Essays* (New York: 1948), 137–68.

29. John Dover Wilson, ed., *Titus Andronicus*, in *The New* [Cambridge] *Shakespeare* (Cambridge: Cambridge University Press, 1948), xii, xxiv, xxxiii–xxxiv, 101, 110, 124, 133, 141, 146, 149, 152; reprint, 1968, p. lxv. The comment on Act 2 is cited by Wilson from A. K. Gray, "Shakspeare and *Titus Andronicus*," *SP* 25 (1928), 309.

30. Donald A. Stauffer, *Shakespeare's World of Images* (New York: Norton, 1949), 13; Albert Feuillerat, *The Composition of Shakespeare's Plays* (New Haven: Yale University Press, 1953), 142–84.

31. Maxwell, ed., *Tit.*, pp. xviii–xxvii; James G. McManaway, "The Year's Contributions to Shakespearian Study 3. Textual Studies," *ShS* 3 (1950), 143–46; John Munro, ed., *Works*, 6 vols. (London: Eyre and Spottiswood; New York: Simon and Schuster, 1957), 5:3; Gustav Cross, ed., *Tit.*, Pelican Shakespeare, rev., gen. ed. Alfred Harbage (Baltimore: Penguin, 1969), 823.

32. C. J. Sisson, ed., *Works* (New York: Harper, 1953; London: Odhams, 1954), 846; Nicholas Brooke, "Marlowe as Provocative Agent in Shakespeare's Early Plays," *ShS* 14 (1961), 34–44; Horst Oppel, *Titus Andronicus: Studien zur dramengeschichtlichen Stellung von Shakespeares früher Tragödie* (Heidelberg: Quelle & Meyer, 1961), 7–13, 86–110; Sylvan Barnet, ed., *Tit.*, Signet Shakespeare (New York: Harcourt, 1972), 284; S. Schoenbaum, *Internal Evidence and Elizabethan Dramatic Authorship* (Evanston, IL: Northwestern University Press, 1966), 162, 166. Anselm Schlösser, "*Titus Andronicus*," *SJW* 104 (1968), 75–84; David Bevington, ed., *Works* (Glenview, IL: Scott Foresman, 1980), 956; Stanley Wells and Gary Taylor, gen. eds., *Works* (Oxford: Clarendon Press, 1986), 141.

33. R. F. Hill, "The Composition of *Titus Andronicus*," *ShS* 10 (1957), 60–70; T. W. Baldwin, *On the Literary Genetics of Shakspere's Plays 1592–1594* Urbana: University of Illinois Press, 1959), 402–46; A. C. Hamilton, *The Early Shakespeare* (San Marino, CA: Huntington Library, 1967), 63–89. See also his "*Titus*

Andronicus: The Form of Shakespearian Tragedy," *SQ* 14 (1963), 201–13; Leonard R. N. Ashley, *Authorship and Evidence* (Geneva: Droz, 1968), 90–95.

34. W. Braekman, *Shakespeare's Titus Andronicus* (Ghent: Blandijnberg, 1969), passim.; Frank Kermode, ed., *Titus Andronicus,* in *The Riverside Shakespeare,* 1020; Waith, ed., *Titus Andronicus,* 11–20.

35. Eliot Slater, "Shakespeare: Word Links Between Poems and Plays," *N&Q* 220 (1975), 157–63; MacD. P. Jackson, *Studies in Attribution: Middleton and Shakespeare,* Salzburg Studies in Eng. Lit. 79 (Salzburg: Universität Salzburg, 1979), 148–58; Metz, "Disputed Shakespearean Texts and Stylometric Analysis," *TEXT* 2 (1985), 149–72. For an explanation of the stylometric method described in my paper, see A. Q. Morton, *Literary Detection* (London: Bowker; New York: Scribners, 1978), passim.

36. Gary Taylor, "The Canon and Chronology of Shakespeare's Plays," *William Shakespeare: A Textual Companion* (Oxford: Clarendon Press, 1987), 76–80, 113–15, 208–16. Taylor questions the validity of certain aspects of "Morton's [stylometric] techniques and conclusions," noting that the "statistical procedures have themselves been challenged." He also points out that reliable conclusions regarding Shakespeare's habits of composition cannot be based "upon the evidence of one short play *(JC)* and two of disputed authorship *(Tit.* and *Per.)*" and this is certainly so. However, the publication of the results of such studies, as far as they have progressed, was not intended to be definitive, but rather to report on the status of "a potentially valuable tool for use by literary students, [on which] much more work needs to be done." (Metz, "Disputed Shakespearean Texts," 156).

37. Marco Mincoff, *Shakespeare: The First Steps* (Sofia: Bulgarian Academy of Sciences, 1976), 112–37, 210–13.

38. William George Clark, William Aldis Wright, and John Glover, eds., *Works* Cambridge Shakespeare. 9 vols. (Cambridge: Cambridge University Press, 1863–66; reprint, Cambridge, 1867), 1891–93; New York: AMS, 1970); Sidney L. Lee, *A Life of William Shakespeare* (London: Macmillan, 1898. Rev. ed., 1915), 131; Alfred W. Pollard, *Shakespeare's Folios and Quartos* (London: Methuen, 1909; reprint, New York: Cooper Square Publishers, 1970), 14; Chambers, *William Shakespeare,* 1:321; Wilson, ed., *Titus Andronicus,* 96, 131; Price, "Mirror-Scenes in Shakespeare," *Joseph Quincy Adams Memorial Studies,* ed. James G. McManaway, Giles E. Dawson, and Edwin E. Willoughby (Washington: Folger Sh. Library, 1948), 101–13; Maxwell, ed., *Titus Andronicus,* p. 70n. Scene II; Greg, *Editorial Problem,* 119; Cross, ed., *Titus,* 125; Kermode, ed., *Titus,* 1019; Joseph E. Kramer, "*Titus Andronicus:* The 'Fly Killing' Incident," *ShakS* 5 (1969), 9–19; Waith, ed., *Titus,* 18; Taylor, "Canon and Chronology," 115.

39. Robertson, *Introduction,* 56–67; Chambers, "Disintegration," 14.

40. In "To the Reader," Ravenscroft informs us that "The Success answer'd the Labour . . . it bore up against the Faction, and is confirm'd a Stock-Play." Sigs. A2ʳ–A2ᵛ.

41. Langbaine, *Account,* 464; Charles Knight, *Studies of Shakespeare* (London: 1849; Reprint New York: AMS, 1971), 44; Halliwell-Phillipps, *Outlines,* 2:262; Parrott, "Revision," 22; Robertson, *Introduction,* 57; Kittredge, ed., *Works,* 971.

42. Hazelton Spencer, *The Art and Life of William Shakespeare* (New York: Harcourt, 1940), 208–9, 404n.2.

43. Maxwell, "Peele and Shakespeare: A Stylometric Test," *JEGP* 49 (1950), 557–61.

44. John W. Velz, "Topoi in Ravenscroft's Indictment of Shakespeare's *Titus Andronicus*," *MP* 83 (1985), 45–50; Harold Brooks, Appendix to Maxwell, ed., *Titus*, 129–31.

45. The only item of evidence that may possibly be considered as a link between *Titus and Vespasian* and *Titus* is the inclusion of the title *Titus, and Vespatian*, in Revels Office play lists preserved in BL MS. Cotton Tiberius E. X., dated by Chambers "about 1619 or 1620." He seems to doubt that the play "had an independent existence to the middle of the seventeenth century" and speculates that its appearance in the "list of the plays . . . gives some confirmation to the view that the titles are equivalent." Rev. of Frank Marcham, *The King's Office of the Revels, 1610–1622*, *RES* 1 (1925), 479–84. See also Chambers, *William Shakespeare*, 1:319; 2:346.

46. Maxwell, "Peele and Shakespeare," passim.

47. Taylor accepts Shakespeare's collaboration with Middleton in *Timon*. He alludes to the unfinished play theory but does not discuss it. See Una Ellis-Fermor, "*Timon of Athens:* An Unfinished Play," *RES* 18 (1942), 270–83; reprint in *Shakespeare the Dramatist*, ed. Kenneth Muir (London: Methuen; New York: Barnes and Noble, 1961), 158–76. He cites "compelling evidence" developed by Lake, Jackson, and Holdsworth indicating persuasively that the second hand in *Timon* is Middleton. "Canon and Chronology," 127–28. See also Kermode, ed., *Timon* in *The Riverside Shakespeare*, 1441–44.

48. In regard to Shakespeare's possible collaboration in the composition of *Ed3, Cdo.,* and *TNK,* and his contribution to *STM,* see Metz, *Sources of Four Plays Ascribed to Shakespeare* (Columbia: University Press of Missouri, 1989), 6–20; 150–62; 259–83; 378–409.

49. Taylor, "Canon and Chronology," 111–15.

Chapter 2. Twentieth-Century Criticism

1. J. Dover Wilson, ed., New [Cambridge] *Titus* (Cambridge: Cambridge University Press, 1948; Reprint, 1968), lxv. The degree of pre-twentieth-century critical neglect of *Titus* may be gauged by reference to Arthur Eastman's popular *Short History of Shakespearean Criticism* (1968). In this book, in which he admittedly "deal[s] of necessity only with the principal [critical] figures," he devotes fewer than two-score lines to the play out of four hundred pages. The longest passage is twenty-six lines, of which three are quoted from *Titus*. This does not constitute rejection by Eastman, but is rather an accurate reflection of the meagerness of interest on the part of literary critics during the first three centuries of the play's existence.

2. J. C. Maxwell, ed., New Arden *Titus* (London: Methuen, 1953, 3rd rev. ed., 1968), xxxii, n. 5.

3. For a useful series of excerpts of criticism, with helpful introductory notes, extending from Ben Jonson's 1614 comment to 1979, see Mark W. Scott, ed., *Shakespearean Criticism* (Detroit: Gale, 1987), 4:612–84.

4. H. Bellyse Baildon, ed., Arden *Titus* (London: Methuen, 1904), ix–lxxxiv, esp. xxix–xxxi, xxxiii–xxxv, xxxix–xliii, xlix–l, xvii–lxix, lxxx.

5. George Pierce Baker, *The Development of Shakespeare as a Dramatist* (New York: Macmillan, 1907; Reprint, New York: AMS, 1965), 124–34.

6. T. S. Eliot, Introduction to *Seneca His Tenne Tragedies Translated into English*. The plays were originally published at London, 1581. Eliot's introduction was included in a reprint, (London: Constable; and New York; Knopf, 1927); and

in his *Selected Essays* (London; Faber; and New York; Harcourt, 1932), under the title "Seneca in Elizabethan Translation," and frequently reprinted. In another essay entitled "Shakespeare and the Stoicism of Seneca" (1927), Eliot says he is "not so much concerned with the influence of Seneca on Shakespeare as with Shakespeare's illustration of Senecan and stoical principles . . . Seneca is the *literary* representative of Roman stoicism, and . . . Roman stoicism is an important ingredient in Elizabethan drama." London: Shakespeare Association, 1927, Reprint, New York: Haskell, 1964 in *Elizabethan Essays*), 33–54. Eliot's views on the Senecan and stoical content of Shakespeare's plays altered over the years. In the preface to his *Essays on Elizabethan Drama* (New York: Harcourt, 1956), he alluded to the "callowness" of some of his earlier opinions, which he says verged "on impudence . . . for the understanding of Shakespeare, a lifetime is not too long; and of Shakespeare, the development of one's opinions may be the measure of one's development in wisdom" (vii–viii). It seems we may deduce that Eliot's final opinion was that *Titus* exhibited a significant Senecan influence and possibly that the play is truly Shakespearean.

7. Joseph S. G. Bolton, "*Titus Andronicus:* Shakespeare at Thirty," *SP* 30 (1933), 208–24; Fredson Bowers, *Elizabethan Revenge Tragedy 1587–1642* (Princeton: Princeton University Press, 1940, Reprint, 1966, 110–18. Chambers finds that "The facts [concerning the German and Dutch versions of the play] are quite consistent with the natural hypothesis of divergence from a common source in an adaptation of *Titus Andronicus* for continental travel." *William Shakespeare,* I: 319.

8. Howard Baker, *Introduction to Tragedy* (Baton Rouge: Louisiana State University Press, 1939, Reprint, New York: Russell, 1965), passim; G. K. Hunter, "Seneca and the Elizabethans: A Case-Study in 'Influence,'" *ShS* 20 (1967), 17–26. See also Hunter, "Seneca and English Tragedy," *Seneca,* ed. C. D. N. Costa (London: Routledge, 1974), 166–204. Both of Hunter's essays are reprinted in G. K. Hunter, *Dramatic Identities and Cultural Tradition: Studies in Shakespeare and His Contemporaries* (Liverpool: Liverpool University Press, 1978), 159–73; 174–213; Barbara A. Mowat, "Lavinia's Message: Shakespeare and Myth," *RenP 1981* (1982), 55–69. For the Medieval influence, particularly of nondramatic tragedy, on Elizabethan tragic drama, see Willard Farnham, *The Medieval Heritage of Elizabethan Tragedy* (Berkeley: University of California Press, 1936), passim.

9. William T. Hastings, "The Hardboiled Shakespeare," *SAB* 17 (1942), 114–25.

10. Hereward T. Price, "The Authorship of *Titus Andronicus,*" *JEGP* 42 (1943), 55–81, esp. 70–80.

11. E. M. W. Tillyard, *Shakespeare's History Plays* (London: Chatto & Windus, 1944), 135–41.

12. Alfred Harbage, *As They Liked It* (New York: Macmillan, 1947), 13–15.

13. Frances A. Yates, "Queen Elizabeth as Astraea," *JWCI* 10 (1947), 27–82, esp. 70–72, 82.

14. H. B. Charlton, *Shakespearian Tragedy* (Cambridge: Cambridge University Press, 1968), 4, 18–24.

15. Hardin Craig, *An Interpretation of Shakespeare* (New York: Dryden Press, 1948), 38–41.

16. Wilson, ed., *Titus,* li–lix.

17. M. C. Bradbrook, *Shakespeare and Elizabethan Poetry* (London: Chatto

& Windus, 1951), 104–110, 112; *Themes and Conventions of Elizabethan Tragedy* (Cambridge: Cambridge University Press, 1935), 98–99.

18. Wolfgang H. Clemen, *The Development of Shakespeare's Imagery* (London: Methuen, 1951; 2nd ed., 1977), 21–29.

19. G. B. Harrison, *Shakespeare's Tragedies* (New York: Oxford University Press, 1952; Reprint rev., 1969), 30–46.

20. T. J. B. Spencer, "Shakespeare and the Elizabethan Romans," *ShS* 10 (1957), 27–38; Reprint, *Discussion of Shakespeare's Roman Plays,* ed. Maurice Charney (Boston: Heath, 1964) 1–15.

21. Eugene M. Waith, "The Metamorphosis of Violence in *Titus Andronicus ShS* 10 (1957), 39–49. In later essays, Waith traces the dramatic background of civil disorder in the play, demonstrating its structural and thematic importance, and studies the numerous ceremonies and rituals scattered through *Titus,* elucidating their significance. "*Titus Andronicus* and the Wounds of Civil War," *Literary Theory and Criticism Festschrift Presented to Rene Wellek in Honor of his Eightieth Birthday,* ed. Joseph P. Strelka (Bern: Lang, 1984) 1351–62; "The Ceremonies in *Titus Andronicus*" *Mirror up to Shakespeare Essays in Honor of G. R. Hibbard,* ed. J. C. Gray (Toronto: University of Toronto Press, 1984), 159–70. All three are reprinted in Eugene M. Waith, *Patterns and Perspectives in English Renaissance Drama* (Newark: University of Delaware Press, 1988), 41–54, 127–37, and 138–47 respectively. Michael Neill views ceremonial stage obsequies as pageantry with a "freight of social and political meanings" that dramatists relate to tragedy, as Shakespeare does in *Titus* "'Exeunt with a Dead March:' Funeral Pageantry on the Shakespearean Stage," *Pageantry in the Shakespearean Theater,* ed. David M. Bergeron (Athens: University of Georgia Press, 1985), 153–93, esp. 168–72.

22. Bernard Spivack, *Shakespeare and the Allegory of Evil* (New York: Columbia University Press, 1958), 379–86.

23. Helen Gardner, *The Business of Criticism* (Oxford: Oxford University Press, 1959), 41–46. Vyvyan finds that *Titus* exhibits Shakespearean ethical principles seen in his later tragedies, notably that revenge "imitates an unending death-sequence, until an act of creative mercy lifts the curse . . . building a play upon [such] an ethical theorem is pure Shakespeare." John Vyvyan, *The Shakespearean Ethic* (London: Chatto & Windus, 1959), 188–205.

24. Irving Ribner, *Patterns in Shakespearean Tragedy* (London: Methuen, 1960), 14–35.

25. Gordon Ross Smith, "The Credibility of Shakespeare's Aaron," *Literature and Psychology* 10 (1960), 11–13.

26. Alan Sommers, "'Wilderness of Tigers: 'Structure and Symbolism in *Titus Andronicus,*" *EIC* 10 (1960), 275–89.

27. Ernest William Talbert, *Elizabethan Drama and Shakespeare's Early Plays* (Chapel Hill: University of North Carolina Press, 1963; Reprint, New York: Gordian Press, 1973), 132–43; Judith M. Karr, "The Pleas in *Titus Andronicus,*" *SQ* 14 (1963), 278–79.

28. Robert Hapgood, "Shakespeare's Maimed Rites: The Early Tragedies," *Centennial Review* 9 (1965), 494–508.

29. Eldred Jones, *Othello's Countrymen* (London: Oxford University Press, 1965), 49–60.

30. A. C. Hamilton, *The Early Shakespeare* (San Marino, CA: Huntington Library, 1967), 63–89.

31. Eleanor Prosser, *Hamlet and Revenge* (Stanford, CA: Stanford University Press, 1967), 84–89.

32. Nicholas Brooke, *Shakespeare's Early Tragedies* (London: Methuen, 1968), 13–47.

33. John P. Cutts, "Shadow and Substance: Structural Unity in *Titus Andronicus*," *CompD* 2 (1968), 161–72.

34. Judah L. Stampfer, *The Tragic Engagement: A Study of Shakespeare's Classical Tragedies* (New York: Funk & Wagnalls, 1968), 22–58.

35. Jagannath Chakravorty, *The Idea of Revenge in Shakespeare* (Calcutta: Jadavpur University, 1969), 17–40.

36. Ronald Broude, "Roman and Goth in *Titus Andronicus*," *ShakS* 6 (1970), 27–34; "Four Forms of Vengeance in *Titus Andronicus*," *JEGP* 78 (1979), 494–507.

37. Andrew V. Ettin, "Shakespeare's First Roman Tragedy," *ELH* 37 (1970), 325–41.

38. Jack E. Reese, "The Formalization of Horror in *Titus Andronicus*," *SQ* 21 (1970), 77–84.

39. Jack Shadoian, "*Titus Andronicus*," *Discourse* 13 (1970), 152–75.

40. Reuben A. Brower, *Hero and Saint Shakespeare and the Graeco-Roman Heroic Tradition* (New York: Oxford University Press, 1971), 173–203.

41. James L. Calderwood, *Shakespearean Metadrama* (Minneapolis: University of Minnesota Press, 1971), 5, 18, 23–51.

42. John Arthos, *Shakespeare: The Early Writings* (London: Bowes; and Totowa, N.J.: Rowman and Littlefield, 1972), 241–49.

43. Leslie A. Fiedler, *The Stranger in Shakespeare* (New York: Stein and Day, 1972), 176–83.

44. Clifford Chalmers Huffman, "*Titus Andronicus:* Metamorphosis and Renewal," *MLR* 67 (1972), 730–41.

45. Ann Haaker, "*Non sine causa:* The Use of Emblematic Method and Iconology in the Thematic Structure of *Titus Andronicus*," *RORD* 13–14 (1972), 143–68.

46. Kenneth Muir, *Shakespeare's Tragic Sequence* (London: Hutchinson University Library, 1972; Reprint, New York: Harper, 1979), 20–25.

47. D. J. Palmer, "The Unspeakable in Pursuit of the Uneatable: Language and Action in *Titus Andronicus*," *CritQ* 14 (1972), 320–39.

48. William B. Toole III, "The Collision of Action and Character Patterns in *Titus Andronicus:* A Failure in Dramatic Strategy," *RenP 1971* (1972), 25–39.

49. William Leigh Godshalk, *Patterning in Shakespearean Drama* (The Hague: Mouton, 1973), 13–16, 23–41, 179–80.

50. Ruth Nevo, "Tragic Form in *Titus Andronicus*," *Pubs. of the Hebrew Univ., Jerusalem*, 25 (1973), 1–18.

51. Alan B. Rothenberg, "Infantile Fantasies in Shakespearean Metaphor," *Psychoanalytic Review* 60 (1973), 205–22.

52. Lawrence N. Danson, "The Device of Wonder: *Titus Andronicus* and Revenge Tragedies," *TSLL* 16 (1974): 27–43; Reprint, revised, in *Tragic Alphabet: Shakespeare's Drama of Language* (New Haven: Yale University Press, 1974), 1–21. Passages cited are from the book.

53. G. K. Hunter, "Shakespeare's Earliest Tragedies: *Titus Andronicus* and *Romeo and Juliet*, *ShS* 27 (1974), 1–9; Reprint in Hunter, *Dramatic Identities and Cultural Tradition*, 319–34. See above n. 8.

54. A. L. and M. K. Kistner, "The Senecan Background of Despair in *The Spanish Tragedy* and *Titus Andronicus*," *ShakS* 7 (1974), 1–9.

NOTES TO CHAPTER 2

55. Michael Payne, *Irony in Shakespeare's Roman Plays*, Elizabethan Studies 19 (Salzburg: Institut für Englische Sprache und Literatur, Universität Salzburg, 1974), vi–ix, 1–28.

56. Albert H. Tricomi, "The Aesthetics of Mutilation in *Titus Andronicus*," *ShS* 27 (1974), 11–19; "The Mutilated Garden in *Titus Andronicus*," *ShakS* 9 (1976), 89–105.

57. W. Gordon Zeeveld, *The Temper of Shakespeare's Thought* (New Haven: Yale University Press, 1974), 205–10.

58. Larry S. Champion, *Shakespeare's Tragic Perspective* (Athens: University of Georgia Press, 1976), 8–26.

59. Marco Mincoff, *Shakespeare: The First Steps* (Sofia: Bulgarian Academy of Sciences, 1976), 112–137, 210–13.

60. G. Wilson Knight, *Shakespeare's Dramatic Challenge* (London: Croom; New York: Barnes & Noble, 1977).

61. J. L. Styan, *The Shakespeare Revolution* (Cambridge: Cambridge University Press, 1977), passim, esp. 1–5, 34–36, 64–65, 69, 232–37.

62. Ann Thompson, "Philomel in *Titus Andronicus* and *Cymbeline*," *ShS* 31 (1978), 23–32.

63. David Willbern, "Rape and Revenge in *Titus Andronicus*," *ELR* 8 (1978), 159–82.

64. Richard T. Brucher, "'Tragedy, Laugh On:' Comic Violence in *Titus Andronicus*," *RenD* 10 (1979), 71–91.

65. Bertrand Evans, *Shakespeare's Tragic Practice* (Oxford: Clarendon Press, 1979), 1–21.

66. S. Clark Hulse, "Wresting the Alphabet: Oratory and Action in *Titus Andronicus*," *Criticism* 21 (1979), 106–18.

67. William W. E. Slights, "The Sacrificial Crisis in *Titus Andronicus*," *UTQ* 49 (1979), 18–32.

68. Huston Diehl, "The Iconography of Violence in English Renaissance Tragedy," *RenD* 11 (1980), 27–44.

69. Charles R. Forker, "*Titus Andronicus, Hamlet* and the Limits of Expressibility," *HamS* 2 (1980), 1–33; "The Green Underworld of Early Shakespearean Tragedy," *ShakS* 17 (1985), 25–47.

70. G. R. Hibbard, *The Making of Shakespeare's Dramatic Poetry* (Toronto: University of Toronto Press, 1981), 41–53.

71. Elliot H. Tokson, *The Popular Image of the Black Man in English Drama, 1550–1688* (Boston: Hall, 1982).

72. Grace Starry West, "Going by the Book: Classical Allusions in Shakespeare's *Titus Andronicus*," *SP* 79 (1982), 62–77.

73. A. R. Braunmuller, "Characterization through Language in the Early Plays of Shakespeare and His Contemporaries," *Shakespeare Man of the Theater*, ed. Kenneth Muir, Jay L. Halio, and D. J. Palmer (Newark: University of Delaware Press, 1983), 128–47; "Early Shakespearian Tragedy and its Contemporary Context: Cause and Emotion in *Titus Andronicus, Richard III*, and *The Rape of Lucrece*," *Shakespearian Tragedy*, ed. Malcolm Bradbury and David Palmer, (Stratford-Upon-Avon Studies 20) (London: Arnold, 1984), 97–128.

74. Mary Laughlin Fawcett, "Arms/Words/Tears: Language and the Body in *Titus Andronicus*," *ELS* 50 (1983), 261–77.

75. Robert S. Miola, *Shakespeare's Rome* (Cambridge: Cambridge University Press, 1983), 42–75, 236. Miola discusses Senecan influence on *Titus* in *Shake-*

speare and Classical Tragedy (Oxford: Clarendon Press, 1992), passim, esp. 13–32.

76. Maurice Charney, "Shakespeare's Aaron Between Marlowe's Tamburlaine and Barabas/Ithamore," read to the Marlowe Society meeting, December 1984; *Titus Andronicus* (Hemel Hempstead: Harvester Wheatsheaf, 1990), passim.

77. Jean E. Howard, *Shakespeare's Art of Orchestration: Stage Technique and Audience Response* (Urbana: University of Illinois Press, 1984), 2–8, 84–86, 152–55.

78. Michael Platt, *Rome and Romans According to Shakespeare,* rev. ed. (Lanham, MD: University Press of America, 1984), 289–97. Martha Tuck Rozett analyzes *Titus* in comparison to *The Spanish Tragedy.* "Titus' errors in judgment are inexplicable. They do not seem to result from inborn character traits, but to stem from violent and self-destructive impulses . . ." The crux of "both Titus' and Hieronimo's tragedies is their eventual inability to distinguish justice from revenge." *The Doctrine of Election and the Emergence of Elizabethan Tragedy* (Princeton: Princeton University Press, 1984), 193–200.

79. J. A. Bryant Jr., "Aaron and the Pattern of Shakespeare's Villains, *RenP 1984* (1985), 29–36.

80. Henry E. Jacobs, "The Banquet of Blood and the Masque of Death: Social Ritual and Ideology in English Revenge Tragedy," *RenP 1985* (1985), 39–50. Although Jacobs does not discuss Tamora's disguising in 5.2 as a form of either play or masque it has been designated by others to be analogous to such forms.

81. Paul A. Jorgensen, *William Shakespeare: The Tragedies* (Boston: Twayne, 1985), 18–26.

82. Richard Marienstras, *New perspectives on the Shakespearean world,* trans. Janet Lloyd (Cambridge: Cambridge University Press, 1985), 40–47.

83. Michael Neill, "'Exeunt with a Dead March:' Funeral Pageantry on the Shakespearean Stage," *Pageantry in the Shakespearean Theater,* ed. David M. Bergeron (Athens: University of Georgia Press, 1985), 162–63; 168–72.

84. Peter M. Sacks, *The English Elegy* (Baltimore: Johns Hopkins University Press, 1985), 1–3, 63–89.

85. J. L. Simmons, "Shakespeare's Treatment of Roman History," *William Shakespeare: His World, His Work, His Influence,* ed. John F. Andrews, 3 vols. (New York: Scribner's, 1985) I:473–88.

86. C. L. Barber and Richard P. Wheeler, *The Whole Journey: Shakespeare's Power of Development* (Berkeley: University of California Press, 1986), 4–5, 125–57.

87. Leonard Barkan, *The Gods Made Flesh: Metamorphosis & the Pursuit of Paganism* (New Haven: Yale University Press, 1986), 243–47.

88. James Black, "Shakespeare and the Comedy of Revenge," *Comparative Critical Approaches to Renaissance Comedy,* ed. Donald Beecher and Massimo Ciavolella (Ottawa: Dovehouse, 1986), 137–51.

89. Leonard Tennenhouse, *Power on Display: The politics of Shakespeare's genres* (New York: Methuen, 1986), 1–6, 102–12.

90. Anthony Gerard Barthelemy, *Black Face Maligned Race* (Baton Rouge: Louisiana State University Press, 1987), 91–103.

91. Jane S. Carducci, "Shakespeare's *Titus Andronicus:* An Experiment in Expression," *CahiersE* 31 (1987), 1–9.

92. Marjorie Garber, *Shakespeare's Ghost Writers* (London: Methuen, 1987), xiii, xiv, 22–25.

93. Jane Hiles, "A Margin for Error: Rhetorical Context in *Titus Andronicus*," *Style* 21 (1987), 62–75.

94. John W. Mahon, "'For now we sit to chat as well as eat:' conviviality and conflict in Shakespeare's meals," *"Fanned and Winnowed Opinions:" Shakespearean Essays Presented to Harold Jenkins*, ed. John W. Mahon and Thomas A. Pendleton (London: Methuen, 1987), 238–39.

95. Peter Mercer, *Hamlet and the Acting of Revenge* (Iowa City: University of Iowa Press, 1987), 256–59.

96. Douglas H. Parker, "Shakespeare's Use of Comic Conventions in *Titus Andronicus*," *UTQ* 56 (1987), 486–97.

97. Jean Richer, "Une Pièce Expérimentale: *Titus Andronicus* de Shakespeare," *Hommage a Claude Digeon* (Paris: *Belles Lettres*, 1987), 17–26.

98. Kristian Smidt, "Levels and Discontinuities in *Titus Andronicus*," *Multiple Worlds, Multiple Words: Essays in Honour of Irene Simon*, ed. Hena Maes-Jelinek, Pierre Michel, Paulette Michel-Michot (Liege: University of Liege, 1987), 283–93; Reprint Smidt, *Unconformities in Shakespeare's Tragedies* (New York: St. Martins Press, 1990).

99. Charles H. Frey, *Experiencing Shakespeare* (Columbia: University of Missouri Press, 1988), 112–21.

100. Maurice Hunt, "Compelling Art in *Titus Andronicus*," *SEL* 28 (1988), 197–218.

101. Mary Ellen Lamb, "Shakespeare's Lavinia: A Renaissance Rereading of Ovid's Philomela Myth," read at the Dec. 1988 MLA meeting.

102. John D. Cox, *Shakespeare and the Dramaturgy of Power* (Princeton: Princeton University Press, 1989), 171–78.

103. Douglas E. Green, "Interpreting 'her martyr'd signs': Gender and Tragedy in *Titus Andronicus*," *SQ* 40 (1989), 317–26. In "Staging the Evidence: Shakespeare's Theatrical Avengers," Green examines in *Titus* stage conventions substantiating the guilt of villains in revenge tragedy. *UC* 12 (1992), 29–40.

104. Gillian Murray Kendall, "'Lend me thy hand': Metaphor and Mayhem in *Titus Andronicus*," *SQ* 40 (1989), 299–316.

105. Vivian Thomas, *Shakespeare's Roman Worlds* (London: Routledge, 1989), 1–39.

106. Philip C. Kolin, "Performing Texts in *Titus Andronicus*," *BNYSS*, 7:3 (1989), 5–8.

107. Brian Gibbons, "The Human Body in *Titus Andronicus* and Other Early Shakespeare Plays," *SJ 1989*, 209–22.

108. Gen. 38, 6–30; 2 Sam. 13, 1–39, *Revised English Bible* (Oxford and Cambridge: Oxford and Cambridge University Presses, 1989), 32–33, 268–70.

109. Dorothea Kehler, "'That Ravenous Tiger Tamora': Constructing the Female Alien in *Titus Andronicus*," Read to the 1989 SAA meeting, *ShN* 203–4 (1989), 34.

110. Karen Cunningham, "'Scars Can Witness': Trials by Ordeal and Lavinia's Body in *Titus Andronicus*," *Women and Violence in Literature*, ed. Katherine Anne Ackley (New York: Garland, 1990), 139–62.

111. Emily C. Bartels, "Making More of the Moor: Aaron, Othello and Renaissance Refashionings of Race," *SQ* 41 (1990), 433–54, esp. 433–47.

112. Curt Breight, "'Your Company in hell:' Politics and Performance in *Titus Andronicus*," forthcoming.

113. Heather James, "Cultural disintegration in *Titus Andronicus*: mutilating Titus, Vergil and Rome," James Redmond, ed., *Violence in Drama* (Cambridge:

Cambridge University Press, 1991), 123–40. See also Jonas Barish, "Shakespear-ean violence: a preliminary survey," 101–10 in the Redmond volume.

114. Cynthia Marshall, "'I can interpret all her martyr'd signs': *Titus Androni-cus*, Feminism and the Limits of Interpretation," Carole Levin and Karen Robert-son, eds., *Sexuality and Politics in Renaissance Drama* (Lewiston, NY: Edwin Mellen Press, 1991), 193–209.

115. Marion Wynne-Davies, "'The Swallowing Womb': Consumed and Con-suming Women in *Titus Andronicus*" Valerie Wayne, ed., *The Matter of Differ-ence: Materialist Feminist Criticism of Shakespeare* (New York: Harvester Wheatsheaf, 1991), 129–51.

116. Jack D'Amico, *The Moor in English Renaissance Drama* (Tampa: Univer-sity of South Florida Press, 1991) 135–47. See also D'Amico, "Shakespeare's Rome: Politics and Theatre," *MLS* 12 (1992), 65–78.

117. Joyce Green MacDonald, "'The Force of Imagination': The Subject of Blackness in Shakespeare, Jonson, and Ravenscroft," *RenP*, 1991: 53–74.

118. Frederick A. de Armas, "Astraea's Fall: Senecan Images in Shakespeare's *Titus Andronicus* and Calderon's *La Vida es sueno*," Louise and Peter Fothergill-Payne, eds., *Parallel Lives: Spanish and English National Drama 1580–1680* (Lewisburg, PA: Bucknell University Press, 1991), 302–21.

119. Charles Wells, *The Wide Arch: Roman Values in Shakespeare* (New York: St. Martin's Press, 1992), 13–29.

120. Jonathan Bate, *Shakespeare and Ovid* (Oxford: Clarendon Press, 1993), passim esp. 101–73, 196–98, 215–16. Bate rejects the chapbook *History of Titus Andronicus* as the narrative source of Shakespeare's play, citing the opinions of Marco Mincoff, G. K. Hunter, and MacDonald P. Jackson only. Later he says that the play "lack[s] a direct source," that the order of derivation is play-ballad-chapbook" and that "*Titus* would then be Shakespeare's only 'sourceless' trag-edy,' Pp. 102 and n. 31; p. 240 n. 26.

121. Jonathan Dollimore and Alan Sinfield, eds., *Political Shakespeare* (Man-chester University Press; Ithaca: Cornell University Press, 1985).

122. See above, p. 64 and n. 41.

123. Chambers, "William Shakespeare: An Epilogue." *RES* 16 (1940), 385–401; Reprint rev. *Shakespearean Gleanings* (London: Oxford University Press, 1944), 35–51. The passages quoted are on 36 and 48.

124. Kehler, "That Ravenous Tiger," 6.

125. See the concluding segment of the chapter on Sources, Origins, Influences.

126. There are a number of scholarly accounts and evaluations of the new lines of criticism. Especially of interest are: Jean E. Howard and Marion F. O'Connor, eds., *Shakespeare Reproduced: The text in history and ideology* (New York: Methuen, 1987); Harry Berger, Jr., *Imaginary Audition: Shakespeare on Stage and Page* (Berkeley: University of California Press, 1989); Peter Erickson, *Rewrit-ing Shakespeare, Rewriting Ourselves* (Berkeley: University of California Press, 1991); Hugh Grady, *The Modernist Shakespeare: Critical Texts in a Material World* (Oxford: Clarendon Press, 1991).

Chapter 3. Revision in *Titus Andronicus*

1. Edward Ravenscroft, *Titus Andronicus, or the Rape of Lavinia* (London, 1687; Reprint, London: Cornmarket Press, 1969), "To the Reader," sig. A2.

2. Harold DeW. Fuller, "The Sources of *Titus Andronicus*," *PMLA* 16 (1901), 1–65.

3. T. M. Parrott, "Shakespeare's Revision of *Titus Andronicus*," *MLR* 14 (1919), 16–17, esp. 17; J. S. G. Bolton, "The Authentic Text of *Titus Andronicus*," *PMLA* 44 (1929), 765–88, esp. 772–75, 782; *Titus Andronicus:* Shakespeare at Thirty," *SP* 30 (1933), 208–24, esp. 219–24; John Cranford Adams, "Shakespeare's Revisions in *Titus Andronicus*," *SQ* 15 (1964), 177–190, esp. 177.

4. Joseph Quincy Adams, ed., *Shakespeare's Titus Andronicus: The First Quarto 1594, Reproduced in facsimile* (New York: Scribner's, 1936), sig. A3ᵛ.

5. J. C. Maxwell, ed., *Titus Andronicus*, in *The New Arden Shakespeare*, 3rd ed. (London: Methuen, 1961), 5, n. 35a, citing E. K. Chambers, ed., *Titus Andronicus* (London: Blackie, 1906).

6. W. W. Greg, "Alteration in Act I of 'Titus Andronicus,'" *MLR* 48 (1953), 439–40.

7. Bolton, "Authentic Text," 780–82; reiterated in "A Plea for 3½ Rejected Shakespearian Lines," *SQ* 23 (1972), 261–63. For an impression of a "property" tomb, see C. Walter Hodges' *Globe Restored*, 2nd ed., 1968, 64.

8. H. F. Brooks, cited in Maxwell ed., *Titus*, 5, n. 35.

9. Citations not otherwise identified are to Eugene M. Waith, ed., *Titus Andronicus*, in *The Oxford Shakespeare* (Oxford: Clarendon Press, 1984).

10. Greg, *The Shakespeare First Folio* (Oxford: Clarendon Press, 1955), 203.

11. Walker's note refers to 1.1.35–38 of McKerrow's Oxford Shakespeare *Titus*. For the facts concerning this edition that did not attain publication, although nine plays, including *Titus*, were set up in type and proof sheets pulled, see Stanley Wells, *Re-Editing Shakespeare for the Modern Reader* (Oxford: Clarendon Press, 1984), p. [v].

12. Adams, ed., *Titus*, sig. H2ʳ. Waith drops from his text the second of the two questions.

13. Waith, ed., *Titus*, App. E, "The False Start in 4.3," 211.

14. Greg, *First Folio*, 204.

15. John Dover Wilson, ed., *Titus Andronicus*, in *The New [Cambridge] Shakespeare* (Cambridge: Cambridge University Press), 143, n. 94–107.

16. Maxwell, ed., *Titus*, 94, n. 96–97.

17. Waith, ed., *Titus*, 211–12. The lines he excises correspond to 4.3.104–12 in Maxwell's text.

18. Stanley Wells, Gary Taylor, John Jowett, and William Montgomery, eds., *Complete Oxford Shakespeare* (Oxford: Clarendon Press, 1986), 171; *William Shakespeare: A Textual Companion* (Oxford: Clarendon Press, 1987), 209–16. The passage quoted is on p. 212, n. 4.3.93. The role of the Clown was probably acted by Will Kemp, whose performance as one of the "mad" men of Goteham in the play entitled *A Knacke to knowe a Knaue* (first presented according to Henslow on 10 June 1592) was apparently so widely appreciated that the title page of the printed version notes that it includes "*KEMPS applauded Merriments* of the men of Goteham, in receiving the King into Goteham." Kempe succeeded the legendary Richard Tarleton as the chief clown of the Queen's Men upon the latter's death in 1588 and had, by 1590, already won a considerable reputation as a comedian, when *An Almond for a Parrat*, probably by Nashe, was dedicated "To that most Comicall and conceited Caualeire Monsieur du Kempe, Jestmonger and Vice-gerent generall to the Ghost of Dicke Tarlton." Shortly thereafter he seems to have joined Strange's Men, and by 1594 he was a member of Strange's successor company, the Lord Chamberlain's. His name appears in stage directions

in *Romeo and Juliet* and *Much Ado*. Chambers, *Elizabethan Stage*, 4 vols. (Oxford: Clarendon Press, 1923), 2:325–27; G. R. Proudfoot, ed., *A Knack to Know a Knave*, MSR (Oxford: Oxford University Press, 1963).

19. Charlton Hinman, ed., *The First Folio of Shakespeare*, The Norton Facsimile (New York: Norton, 1968), 658–59.

20. Greg, *First Folio*, 204.

21. Hereward T. Price, "Mirror-Scenes in Shakespeare," *Joseph Q. Adams Memorial Studies*, ed. James G. McManaway, Giles E. Dawson, and Edwin E. Willoughby (Washington: Folger Shakespeare Library, 1948), pp. 101–13.

22. Taylor, *Textual Companion*, 16.

23. Wells, "Revision in Shakespeare's Plays," *Editing and Editors: A Retrospect*, ed. Richard Landon (New York: AMS Press, 1988), 67–97. The quoted passage is on p. 89.

24. Price, "Mirror-Scenes," 102.

25. Chambers, *William Shakespeare: A Study of Facts and Problems*, 2 vols. (Oxford: Clarendon Press, 1930) 1:316; Greg, *First Folio*, 204.

26. John Kerrigan, "Revision, Adaptation and the Fool in *King Lear*," *The Division of the Kingdoms: Shakespeare's Two Versions of King Lear*, ed. Gary Taylor and Michael Warren (Oxford: Clarendon Press, 1983), 195–245, esp. 204–5 and ns. 36–39.

27. Waith, ed., *Titus*, 11.

28. Wilson, ed., *Titus*, xxxvi.

29. Waith, ed., *Titus*, 96, n. 287–88.

30. Wells, *Re-Editing Shakespeare*, 89, 99, 101.

31. *OED* finds the terms *rape* and *rapine* equivalent in one of the senses; and see Holger Nørgaard, "Never Wrong But With Just Cause," *ES* 45 (1964), 137–41. Titus calls Chiron "Rapine" three times at 5.2.29, .83, .103. Clearly he thinks "rapine" means "rape," since at 5.2.103 he says:

Good Rapine, stab him; he is a ravisher.

32. Wilson, ed., *Titus*, 151, n. 61.

33. Brooks, in Maxwell, ed., *Titus*, 131–32.

34. Waith, ed., *Titus*, 179, n. 61.

35. Brooks, in Maxwell, ed., *Titus*, 132.

36. Greg, *First Folio*, 203. The presumably nine lines deleted may have been as many as sixteen if the deficiencies of I2ᵛ and I3ʳ were to be taken into account. This would amount to just short of half page of text. In addition to the speech prefixes centered on sig. I2ʳ, there are a few others centered, of which one is lightly leaded. These all occur in the first sheet. There are two on sig. A3ʳ, one on A3ᵛ and three on A4ʳ. This count includes accepting "*Marcus Andronicus with the Crowne*" as a speech tag, not as a stage direction. Greg offers the following comment: "It is possible that the printer had not yet decided what typographical style to adopt." He adds that in the same year, Danter, the printer of Q1 of *Titus*, had "centered and leaded the speaker's names throughout the first sheet of *Orlando Furioso*." *The Editorial Problem in Shakespeare*, 3rd ed. (Oxford: Clarendon Press, 1954), 117. Also there occur on sheets A and B, and on sig. D4ʳ and on sig. E2ʳ six instances of stage directions that serve, in addition, to identify speakers, and the immediately succeeding line of dialogue is not preceded by a speech prefix. These are: on sig. A4ʳ *(Enter a Captaine)*; on B1ᵛ *(Enter Lauinia)*; two on sig. B4ᵛ *(Titus two ſonnes ſpeakes*; and *Titus ſonne ſpeakes)*; on sig. D4ʳ

(Enter Aron with two of Titus ſonnes [Quintus and Martius]; and on sig. E2ʳ *(Enter Marcus* [to Lavinia] *from hunting)*. These do not clearly exhibit characteristics, such as those that are apparent on sig. I2ʳ, that would support a contention of revision. For a discussion of other textual changes in Q1 that were made in the course of printing, See Frank E. Haggard, *The Printing of Shakespeare's Titus Andronicus, 1594* (Ann Arbor: University Microfilms, 1979, Michigan diss. 1966), 142–48.

37. Waith concludes on the basis of a rare word test developed by Jackson that the scene is later than the main body of the text, "but not much later—approximately contemporary with" *Rom.* and *R2. Titus* ed., 10, 40–41.

38. Wells, "Revisionist Shakespeare," *Oxford Magazine* 24 (Sixth Week, Trinity Term, 1987), 10–13. See also Wells, "Revision in Shakespeare's Plays" (n. 23 above), and chap. 4, *Re-Editing Shakespeare*, 79–113.

39. Taylor, *"King Lear:* The Date and Authorship of the Folio Version," *Division of the Kingdoms*, 351–489. The passage cited is on 355. The other plays, in addition to *Lr.*, to which Taylor refers (430, n. 6), are *Ado, LLL, MND, MV, R2, Tro., Tit., Ham.,* and *Oth.* On the general subject of Shakespeare's revision of his own texts, see the several works noted above and Nevill Coghill, *Shakespeare's Professional Skills* (Cambridge: Cambridge University Press, 1964); E. A. J. Honigmann, *The Stability of Shakespeare's Text* (London: Arnold, 1965); Michael J. Warren, "Quarto and Folio *King Lear* and the Interpretation of Albany and Edgar," *Shakespeare: Pattern of Excelling Nature,* ed. David Bevington and Jay L. Halio (Newark: University of Delaware Press, 1978), 95–107; Taylor, "The War in *King Lear," ShS* 33 (1980), 27–34; Honigmann, "Shakespeare's Revised Plays: *King Lear* and *Othello," Library* 6:4 (1982), 142–73; Peter W. M. Blayney, *The Texts of King Lear and their Origins* (Cambridge: Cambridge University Press, 1982), Honigmann, "Shakespeare as a Reviser"; and Michael J. Warren, "Textual Problems, Editorial Assertions in Editions of Shakespeare," *Textual Criticism and Literary Interpretation,* editor Jerome J. McGann (Chicago: University of Chicago Press, 1985), 1–22 and 23–37, respectively; Steven Urkowitz, "Good News about 'Bad' Quartos," *"Bad" Shakespeare: Revaluations of the Shakespeare Canon,* ed. Maurice Charney (Cranbury, NJ: Associated University Press, 1988), 189–206.

40. Wells, "Revisionist Shakespeare," 10, 11, 13.

41. Kerrigan, "Revision, Adaptation," 195, 204–5, 217.

42. Brooks, in Maxwell, ed., *Titus,* 132 n. 2.

43. Greg, "Alteration in Act I," 439 n. 1. Wells, *Textual Companion,* 209. For the Act, see Chamers, *Elizabethan Stage,* 4:338–39.

44. Waith, ed., *Titus,* 153, n. 36.

45. Maxwell, ed., *Titus,* 91, n. 31a.

46. Gary Taylor concludes an essay on revision in ten of Shakespeare's works, which he and others had previously demonstrated, with the summary comment that while in the past editors believed that Shakespeare "did *not* revise his work, all future editions should be, and I believe will be, based on the recognition that he habitually did." "Revising Shakespeare," *TEXT 3* (1987), 285–304, esp. 303. Grace Ioppolo canvasses the opinions of many scholars regarding revision in *Titus* and concludes that "Shakespeare evidently made most of his revisions . . . sometime between the play's composition around 1590 and its first printing in 1594." This may be so, but there may be a doubt that it is, since she also says that the spurious concluding four lines of Q2 "signals that they [the F printers] used this quarto to typeset the play," which is manifestly not so. Jaggard used a

copy of Q3. (See chapter on Text). *Revising Shakespeare* (Cambridge MA: Harvard University Press, 1991), 108–9.

Chapter 4. The Text

N. B.: Citations in the essay and in the notes reading "First Folio," "Folio," "Fl," and "F" refer to Charlton Hinman, ed., *The First Folio of Shakespeare*, The Norton Facsimile (New York: Norton, 1968).

1. Joseph Quincy Adams, ed., *Shakespeare's Titus Andronicus The First Quarto 1594* (New York: Scribner's, 1936). Wells has observed that since "we know only one copy of Q1, the possibility that Q2 preserves readings from corrected formes not found in this copy is unusually open." Stanley Wells and Gary Taylor with John Jowett and William Montgomery, *William Shakespeare A Textual Companion* (Oxford: Clarendon Press, 1987), 209.

2. For a listing of the copies of Q3 see Metz, "How Many Copies of *Titus Andronicus* Q3 are Extant?" *Library*, Sixth Series 3:4 (Dec., 1981): 336–40.

3. Discussions of the rationale of editors' selection of Q1 as copy text for modern editions may be found in Eugene M. Waith, ed., *Titus*, in the single volume series of the Oxford Shakespeare (Oxford: Clarendon Press, 1984), 39–43; and in Stanley Wells, *Re-Editing Shakespeare for the Modern Reader* (Oxford: Clarendon Press, 1984), Chapter 4, esp. 79–82. The classic treatment is W. W. Greg's "The Rationale of Copy-Text," *SB* 3 (1950), 19–36; Rpt., *Collected Papers*, ed. J. C. Maxwell (Oxford: Oxford University Press, 1966), 374–91.

4. The import of the three and a-half lines has been disputed. See C. J. Sisson, *New Readings in Shakespeare*, 2 vols. (London: Dawson's, 1961), 2:134–35; and Joseph S. G. Bolton, "A plea for 3½ Shakespearian Lines," *SQ* 23 (1972), 261–63. For a comprehensive discussion of the characteristics of foul papers, see Greg, *The Shakespeare First Folio* (Oxford: Clarendon Press, 1955), 96–97; 106–42. Specific references to *Titus* are on 127, 128 (3), 130, 132, and 137.

5. Frank E. Haggard, *The Printing of Shakespeare's Titus Andronicus, 1594* (University of Kansas dissertation (Ann Arbor: University Microfilms, 1966), passim. Paul L. Cantrell and George Walton Williams study the individual contributions of two compositors (printer James Roberts's Compositors X and Y) to the setting of *Titus* Q2. They note that the two "did not combine to set their material in a normal pattern for two-compositor work in which each man serves a different press." Only one press was used and "Compositor Y seems to have been responsible for the bulk of the reprint . . . [with] X assisting him at unpredictable intervals." Compositor X appears to have been "called in to help while Y was distributing type from a forme that had already been printed." "Roberts' Compositors in *Titus Andronicus* Q2," *SB* 8 (1956), 27–38.

6. MacDonald P. Jackson, "The Year's Contributions to Shakespearian Studies 3. Editions and Textual Studies," *ShS* 38 (1985), 248.

7. Adams, ed., *Titus* 20. See also Greg, *First Folio*, 208, n. A.

8. Bolton, "The Authentic Text of *Titus Andronicus*," *PMLA* 44 (1929), 765–88. The passage quoted is on 768. He studied the play before Adams's facsimile of Q1 was published and had only reproductions of seven pages to work from (p. 766).

9. Hinman, ed., *First Folio. Titus* is on 647–68.

10. Hinman, "The Prentice Hand in the Tragedies of the Shakespeare First Folio: Compositor E," *SB* 9, (1957), 3–20; *The Printing and Proof-Reading of the*

First Folio of Shakespeare, 2 vols. (Oxford: Clarendon Press, 1963), 1: 200–26, 380–95; 2: passim (see index 2: 536), especially 2: 512–13. See also J. K. Walton, *The Quarto Copy for the First Folio of Shakespeare* (Dublin: Dublin University Press, 1971), 40, 68, 230, 241–42, 245–48.

11. Hinman, *Printing and Proof-Reading,* 1: 214–26, esp. 224.

12. Andrew S. Cairncross, "Compositors E and F of the Shakespeare First Folio," *PBSA* 66 (1972), 369–406.

13. T. H. Howard-Hill, *Compositors B and E in the Shakespeare First Folio and Some Recent Studies* (Columbia SC: By the Author, 1976), 65–68.

14. W. W. Greg, *The Editorial Problem in Shakespeare,* 3rd ed. (Oxford: Clarendon Press, 1967), 119.

15. Greg, *First Folio,* 207: "the company had been using as its prompt-book an annotated copy of Q2 and . . . they commissioned a scribe to correct a copy of Q3 in accordance with it for the use of the printer."

16. The act, scene, and line numbers refer to Waith's ed. in the Oxford Shakespeare series; the TLNs are Hinman's.

17. Bolton, "Authentic Text," 766.

18. Bolton, "Authentic Text," 778–80; Adams, ed., *Titus,* 24; R. B. McKerrow, "A Note on *Titus Andronicus,*" *Library* 15 (1934–35), 49–53.

19. Adams, ed., *Titus,* 24–25.

20. J. C. Maxwell, ed., *Titus,* in *The New Arden Shakespeare* (London: Methuen, 1953), xiii. The ornament at the end of *Titus* Fl is the satyr woodcut used throughout F. It exists in two states and is therefore bibliographically useful. See John W. Shroeder, *The Great Folio of 1623* (Hamden, CT: Shoe String Press, 1956), 71–72; Hinman, *Printing and Proof-Reading,* 1:21–24, 37, 179–80, 336, 340–41, 355–56 358 n.3, and Pl. II.

21. Waith, ed., *Titus,* 40–41; Wells, Taylor et al., *Textual Companion,* 209.

22. J. Dover Wilson, ed., *Titus,* in *The New (Cambridge) Shakespeare* (Cambridge: Cambridge University Press, 1948), 125 ns. 33–36; Maxwell, ed., *Titus,* 59, n. 36; Sisson, *New Readings,* 2:139; Greg, *First Folio,* 206–7; Waith, ed., *Titus,* 40–41; Wells, Taylor et al., *Works* (Oxford: Clarendon Press, 1986), 155, ll. 33–36; *Textual Companion,* 211, n. on ll. 3.1.34–35.

23. Waith, ed., *Titus,* 141, n. 280; Maxwell, ed., *Titus,* 69 n. 281; Sisson, *New Readings,* 2:140; Bolton, "Authentic Text," 771, n. 15; Wells, Taylor, *Textual Companion,* 212 n. on ll. 3.1.280–1.

24. Wilson, ed., *Titus,* 144, n. 5; Waith, ed., *Titus,* 165, n. 5; Wells, Taylor, *Works,* 163, l. 4.4.5.

25. Sylvan Barnet, ed., *Titus,* in *Complete Signet Classic Shakespeare* (New York: Harcourt, 1972), 308, n. 88; Gustav Cross, ed., *Titus,* in *Complete Pelican Shakespeare* (Baltimore: Penguin, 1969), 843, n. 88; Irving Ribner, ed., *Titus,* in *New Kittredge Shakespeares* (Waltham, MA: Blaisdell, 1969), 60, n. 88.

26. Frank Kermode, ed., *Titus,* in *Riverside Shakespeare* (Boston: Houghton-Mifflin, 1974), 978. n. 88; David Bevington, ed., *Works* (Glenview, IL: Scott, Foresman, 1980), 978, n. 90; Waith, ed., *Titus,* 149, n. 87.

27. Wilson, ed., *Titus,* 144, n. 24; Maxwell, ed., *Titus,* 96, n. 25; Sisson, *New Readings,* 2:142; Waith, ed., *Titus* 165, n. 25.

28. Thomas L. Berger, "Press Variants in Substantive Shakespearian Dramatic Quartos," *Library* 6, 10:3 (1988), 231–41, esp. 236.

29. Adams, ed., *Titus,* 18–19 and 19n.1.

30. The four corrected copies are nos. 1192, 1200, 1203, and 1206 in Henrietta C. Bartlett and Alfred W. Pollard's *Census of Shakespeare's Plays in Quarto,* rev.

ed. (New Haven: Yale University Press, 1939). For additional details about the copies, see Metz, "How Many Copies of . . . Q3 are Extant?" (n. 2 above).

31. The earlier state appears in Bartlett and Pollard no. 1204.

32. The "uncorrected" state is found in Bartlett and Pollard nos. 1191, 1193, and 1197. The insufficient printing of the final "d" occurs in no. 1191 and, more noticeably, in no. 1193.

33. The "corrected" state is in Bartlett and Pollard's no. 1194; and the less clearly corrected in no. 1205.

34. Giles E. Dawson notes that "There is good evidence that he [Shakespeare] seldom used capital letters for any purpose," and that the F1 compositor of the play under discussion [*H5*] "was much given to using capital initials for nouns," as was Compositor E. Hinman determines that the relevant part of *H5* was set by Compositor A, which raises the possibility that capitalizing initial letters at least for nouns may have been a printing-house requirement. Dawson, "Shakespeare's Handwriting," *ShS* 42 (1990), 119–28, esp. 123; Hinman, *Printing and Proof-Reading*, 2:18. In response to an inquiry, Dr. Dawson tells me privately that he is sure "The free use of capital letters . . . was an individual matter."

35. An example of a variant spelling excluded from the list is:

Q1 Conquerour
Q2 Conquerer
Q3 conquerer
F   Conqueror

(1.1.104; 126)

An example of a difference in punctuation occurs in line 1.1.114, TLN 136: F reads "O!"; Qq have no punctuation of any kind.

36. Q1, Q2 read *Saturinus*.

37. The addition of "withall" was apparently an effort to mend the verse in Q3, which had omitted the word "Coſen" that is in Q1 and Q2.

38. Each of the texts in this passage is different. See above, p. 130.

39. Q1 and Q2 read "miſerie."

40. No doubt altered as a consequence of *An Acte to Restrain Abuses of Players* of 1606. E. K. Chambers, *The Elizabethan Stage*, 4 vols. (Oxford: Clarendon Press, 1923), 4:338–39.

41. The significance of this variant has been subject of some, chiefly editorial, discussion. Sisson cites Pope's emendation to read "give it that accord," which, he says, "is plausible" and adds that the F reading "seems to me an improvisation." Maxwell adopts the Folio line, offers the opinion that Q "cannot be accepted as it stands," and cites in support of his choice Bertram L. Joseph's monograph on *Elizabethan Acting* (Oxford: Oxford University Press, 1961; second enlarged ed. 1964). Dover Wilson concurs. Kermode emends Q to read "to give['t] that," glosses "accord" as "agreement," but adds that the F1 line is "an attractive reading." Waith finds the line as in Qq "somewhat awkward and metrically defective" and that the F reading "makes excellent sense, since 'action' as a rhetorical term meant 'delivery.'" Wells agrees, saying "F seems better sense," and he follows F. *Textual Companion*, 213, n. on l. 5.2.18

42. Q1 reads "Tut"; the Edinburgh Q2 has "Tnt"; the Huntington Q2 has "Tut."

43. Q1, Q2 read "mo ſunnes."

44. Q1, Q2 have "made me blind." This does not imply that E consulted them.

45. Q1 has "and force you to commiseration," which Q2 emends to "Lending your kind commiſeration," followed by Q3.

46. Q1 reads "Then gratious," Q2 "Then noble."

47. Q1, Q2 read "I am the turned."

48. This is a reading from the second of four non-Shakespearean lines possibly composed by someone in James Roberts's printing house and added to the authentic text in Q2. There is no corresponding passage in Q1, and it is not included in Waith's ed.

49. Hinman, *First Folio,* xx–xxiv; *Printing and Proof-Reading,* 1:226–27, 285–91; 2:157–58.

50. Adams, ed., *Titus,* 14–15.

51. Not entirely doubtless, since Langbaine wrote "Essex" instead of "Sussex" as it is on the Q1 title-page.

52. There are sixty-three such notations on forty-four pages.

53. There are twenty-five notations on twenty pages. Letitia Yeandle has verified that the handwriting in the Bartlett and Pollard copy no. 1199 is Kemble's.

54. Wilson, ed., *Titus,* x–xii; Barnet, ed., *Titus,* 285.

55. Stamm points out that Lavinia exhibits a "readiness to neglect the claims of instinct, natural emotion, and common sense. She is ready to marry Saturninus because her father wills it so although she is betrothed to Bassianus, with whom she is clearly in love. When the new emperor suddenly shows his extraordinary interest in the captive Queen of Goths . . . [and asks Lavinia if she is displeased] she answers politely, patiently, and according to the highest ethical standards . . . [hers] is a proud answer, too, since it rejects both Saturninus' suspicion that she could feel jealousy and the idea that he could be as weak and foolish as to desert her for the sake of Tamora." R. Stamm, "The Alphabet of Speechless Complaint: A Study of the Mangled Daughter in *Titus Andronicus,* ES 55 (1974), 325–39, esp. 325–26.

56. Wilson, ed., *Titus,* xi.

57. Wilson, ed., *Titus,* 144, n. 27–38. Wilson also notes (146, n. 7) that "Rome" in l. 5.1.7 (Waith ed.) refers to Saturninus, which appears to be distinctly possible, but Maxwell rejects the inference (ed., *Tit.,* 101, n. 7) even though the next line reads "Let *him* make treble satisfaction" (emphasis added).

Chapter 5. Sources, Origins, Influences

1. For Farmer's comment, see James Boswell, ed., *Plays and Poems,* Malone's Third Variorum, 21 vols. (London: 1821), 21:381. For the "old catalogue," see Joseph Quincy Adams, ed., *Shakespeare's Titus Andronicus The First Quarto 1594* (New York: Scribners, 1936), 7–9. Eugene M. Waith considers the identification of the old catalog of Farmer's with that issued by Dicey in 1764 to be "very likely," p. 29.

2. J. O. Halliwell-Phillipps, *Memoranda on All's Well that Ends Well, The Two Gentlemen of Verona, Much Ado about Nothing, and on Titus Andronicus* (Brighton: 1879; Reprint, New York: AMS Press, 1973), 61–76, esp. 66, 71–73. The title of the chapbook cited on 73 is incomplete, and either the place of publication is variant or in error. The title page of the Folger copy reads London. For the full title see page 63. Geoffrey Bullough (*Narrative and Dramatic Sources of Shakespeare.* London: Routledge; and New York: Columbia University Press, 1957–75, 8 vols.) reprints both the *History* and the ballad (6:34–48), as does Waith in ed., *Titus* 195–207. The copy of the chapbook that Halliwell-Phillipps had is

probably the one that is now in the Folger Library. On its flyleaf is the following note, said in the Folger catalog to be by Halliwell-Phillips, presumably in his own hand: "The only copy I ever saw. It is probably the chap-book version of the prose tale of Titus Andronicus, which was popular in Shakespeare's time, but of which no [such early] copy is now known to exist." *Folger Shakespeare Library: Catalog of the Shakespeare Collection* (Boston: Hall, 1972), 626.

3. Bullough, *Sources,* 6:11.

4. J. C. Maxwell, "Shakespeare's Roman Plays: 1900–1956," *ShS* 10 (1957), 1–3. Hypotheses based on an assumed source relationship, or independent derivation, of the German and Dutch versions have gradually died out, since Chambers examined these propositions and concluded that the continental texts are "adaptation[s] of *Titus Andronicus* for continental travel." (*William Shakespeare,* I: 318–19). For the relationship among these versions, see T. W. Baldwin, *On the Literary Genetics of Shakespeare's Plays 1592–1594* (Urbana: University of Illinois Press, 1959), 430–44; and W. Braekman, *Shakespeare's Titus Andronicus: Its Relationship to the German Play of 1620 and to Jan Vos's Aran en Titus* (Ghent: Seminar of English and American Literature of the University of Ghent. 1969), passim.

5. Adams, ed., *Titus,* 7–9. On the basis of the records of Dicey's printing establishment, Adams is able to establish the publication date of the Folger copy of the chapbook as "in or after 1736 and before 1764." He notes that no earlier edition of the *History* "upon which presumably this late reprint was based has come down to us" and he also speculates that Danter's *SR* entrance, usually thought to represent the play, may have actually entered the chapbook. Greg offers the opinion that "Both [the *History* and the ballad] are, no doubt, reprints of much earlier originals." W. W. Greg, *Bibliography of the English Printed Drama to the Restoration,* 4 vols. (London: The Bibliographical Society, 1939; Reprint, 1970), I:xxv.

6. Bullough, *Sources,* 6:8–11. See also Wilhelm Dibelius, "Zur Stoffgeschichte des Titus Andronikus" *SJ* 48 (1912): 1–12; Frank Granger, "Shakespeare and the Legend of Andronicus," *TLS* 1 April 1920), 213; and subsequent correspondence with R. Warwick Bond, *TLS* 15, 29 April and 6, 13, and 27 May 1920, 239, 272, 284, 302–3, and 335 respectively.

7. Bullough, *Sources,* 6:13–15. There is no evidence that Bandello's novel is connected directly to *Titus.*

8. Ralph M. Sargent, "The Source of *Titus Andronicus*," *SP* 46 (1949): 167–83. The passage quoted is on p. 171.

9. Bullough, *Sources,* 6:55.

10. In the second line cited from the ballad, Percy reads *clad* for *glad.* In the play, Shakespeare, in three of the eight times he refers to the disguised Chiron, calls him *Rapine* instead of *Rape.* It would seem that he considered the terms synonymous. *OED* lends support by citing one definition common to both terms: the act of seizing or taking by force. *Rape* sb.[2]; *Rapine* sb.

11. Bullough, *Sources,* 6:7, 16, 34.

12. Kenneth Muir, *The Sources of Shakespeare's Plays* (London: Methuen, 1977; New Haven: Yale University Press, 1978), 22–23. In an earlier source study, Muir expressed similar views. See *Shakespeare's Sources I Comedies and Tragedies* (London: Methuen, 1957), 258. Emrys Jones, in a review of Muir's 1978 *Sources,* points out that Muir's purpose—"to ascertain the sources for the plots of the plays and to illustrate, in a necessarily selective way, how Shakespeare's general reading nourished his writing"—allows Muir "to pass over comparatively quickly those [plays] which don't" interest him. *Titus Andronicus* seems to have

been one of these. "A Compact Summary of Shakespeare's Sources," *SQ* 34:3 (1983), 358–59. In another book, Muir identifies Seneca's *Theyestes*, Ovid's tale of Philomela, and Marlowe's *Jew of Malta* as Shakespeare's models for *Titus*. The *History* is not mentioned. *Shakespeare's Tragic Sequence* (London: Hutchison, 1972; Reprint, New York: Harper, 1979), 20–25.

13. Emrys Jones, *The Origins of Shakespeare* (Oxford: Clarendon Press, 1977), v, 85–107; passages cited are on 85–87.

14. Maxwell, ed., *Titus* in *New Arden Shakespeare*, 3rd ed., 1961) xxviii. He reiterates this opinion in "Shakespeare's Roman Plays: 1900–1956," 2. Dover Wilson says that the *History* "is apparently a late reprint of the prose tale upon which the play was based," but he expresses this view before he had had an opportunity to read the *History*. J. Dover Wilson, ed., *Titus* in *New (Cambridge) Shakespeare.*; reprint, ed. 1968.

15. Sylvan Barnet, ed., *Titus* in *Complete Signet Classic Shakespeare* (New York: Harcourt, 1972), 284–89, esp. 288; Irving Ribner, ed., *Titus*, in *The Kittredge Shakespeares* (Waltham, MA: Blaisdell, 1969), xiii. See also his *Patterns in Shakespearean Tragedy* (London: Methuen; Totawa, NJ: Rowman and Littlefield, 1960), 16 n. 3; Frank Kermode, ed., *Titus*, in *The Riverside Shakespeare* (Boston: Houghton, 1974), 1019–22, esp. 1020; John Munro, ed., *Titus*, in *The London Shakespeare*, 6 vols. (London: Eyre & Spottiswoode, 1957; New York: Simon and Schuster, 1958). 5: 1–8, esp 6; Gustav Cross, ed., *Titus* in *The Pelican Shakespeare* (Reprint, rev. Baltimore: Penguin, 1969), 823–25; David Bevington, ed., *Works* (Glenville, IL: Scott, Foresman, 1980), 956–59, esp. 956; Waith, ed., *Titus*, 27–38, esp. 29–33. See also Waith's frequently cited essay, "The Metamorphosis of Violence in *Titus Andronicus*," *ShS* 10 (1957): 39–49; Stanley Wells, ed., *Titus*, in *The Oxford Shakespeare* (Oxford: Clarendon Press, 1986), 141.

16. T. J. B. Spencer. "Shakespeare and the Elizabethan Romans," *ShS* 10 (1957): 27–38; Baldwin, *On the Literary Genetics of Shakespeare's Plays*, 429; Horst Oppel. *Titus Andronicus: Studien zur dramengeschichtlichen Stellung von Shakespeares früher Tragödie* (Heidelberg: Quelle & Meyer, 1961), 11–13; W. Braekman, *Shakespeare's Titus Andronicus: Its Relationship to the German Play of 1620 and to Jan Vos's Aran en Titus* (Ghent: Blandijnberg, 1969), 36; Albert H. Tricomi, "The Aesthetics of Mutilation in 'Titus Andronicus,'" *ShS* 27 (1974): 11–19; Charles R. Forker, "*Titus Andronicus, Hamlet* and the Limits of Expressibility," *HamS* 2 (1980): 1–33; Grace Starry West, "Going by the Book: Classical Allusions in Shakespeare's *Titus Andronicus*," *SP* (1982): 62–77; J. L. Simmons, "Shakespeare's Treatment of Roman History," *William Shakespeare His World His Work His Influence*, ed. John F. Andrews, 3 vols. (New York: Scribner's, 1985), 2:473–88.

17. Before Adams's announcement of his finding of the prose *History*, many scholars studied *Titus* to identify its origins, which they considered to be chiefly in classical literature. H. R. D. Anders (*Shakespeare's Books* [Berlin: Reimer, 1904; Reprint, New York: AMS, 1965], passim codified and developed the findings of earlier critics. For subsequent comment see John W. Velz, *Shakespeare and the Classical Tradition A Critical Guide to Commentary, 1660–1960* (Minneapolis: University of Minnesota Press, 1968).

18. The grammar mentioned is William Lily's *Brevissima Institutio* (1570), which was widely used in Elizabethan grammar schools, probably including the school at Stratford-upon-Avon.

19. J. A. K. Thomson, *Shakespeare and the Classics* (London: Allen & Unwin, 1952), 51–58. Bullough adds that the rivalry between Saturninus and Bassia-

nus "recalls faintly that between the brothers in Seneca's *Thebans*." *Sources*, 6:26.

20. Maxwell, ed., *Titus*, says lines 2.1.71–72 echo a passage in *The Spanish Tragedy*. Dover Wilson, ed., *Titus*, notes two others at 1.1.449 and 2.3.8. See also W. Schrichx, "The Background and Context of Hamlet's Second Soliloquy," *MLR* 68 (1973), 241–55. Bullough thinks Tamora's disguising was "suggested" by Kyd's play-within-the-play, but he also notes the widespread Elizabethan "liking for disguisings." *Sources*, 6:23, 28.

21. John W. Cunliffe, *The Influence of Seneca on Elizabethan Tragedy* London, 1893, Reprint, Hamden, CT: Archon, 1965, 69–72, 80, 128; Howard Baker, *Induction to Tragedy* (Baton Rouge: Louisiana State University Press, 1939; Reprint, New York: Russell, 1965), passim. Passages quotes are on 154 and 173. Baker's work is, as he acknowledges, linked to that of Willard Farnham, *The Medieval Heritage of Elizabethan Tragedy* (Berkeley: University of California Press; London: Cambridge University Press, 1936; See Baker: Prefatory Note and 6, 155, 173, 200. See also Jørgen W. Hansen, "Two Notes on Seneca and *Titus Andronicus*," *Anglia* 93 (1975), 161–65.

22. Henry W. Wells, "Senecan Influence on Elizabethan Tragedy," *SAB* 19 (1944): 71–84.

23. Thomson, *Classics*, 48–152, 154. Waith adduces solid support for the influence of Ovid, "The Metamorphosis of Violence in *Titus Andronicus*," *ShS* 10 (1957): 39–49. Bullough notes that references in *Titus* to Lucrece seems to show that Shakespeare knew Ovid's *Fasti*. *Sources*, 6:28.

24. Thomson, *Classics*, 239. Earlier commentators, and recently Bullough, have pointed out that "The writing in the sand may come from the story of Io in *Met[amorphoses]* . . . where the woman transformed into a cow writes with her foot to let her father know who she is." *Sources*, 6:13. Velz notes further that "Bullough could have added that both Lavinia and Io have been ravished." Rev. of Bullough's vol. 6, *ShakS* 3 (1967), 261. See also Velz's essay on "The Ovidian Soliloquy in Shakespeare," *ShakS* 18 (1986), 4. J. G. McManaway cites evidence that writing in sand was a school exercise in Shakespeare's time and could have been the inspiration for Lavinia's means of identifying her attackers. "Writing in Sand in *Titus Andronicus* iv.i.," *RES* 9 (1958), 601–3. Both may have been in Shakespeare's mind when he composed the scene.

25. Baker, *Induction*, 129, 139. He does not mention as sources Seneca's *Troades* and *Thyestes*, which are accepted by other commentators. See Thomson, *Classics*, 52–3; Maxwell, ed., *Titus*, notes on 1.1.154, 2.3.93, 4.3.64; Bullough, *Sources*, 6:13, 58–71; Jones, *Origins*, 85–86, 107. For allusions to other classical authors, see Maxwell, ed., *Titus*, for Virgil's *Aeneid*, notes on 1.1.87–88 and 316–17, 2.3.21–24 and 93, 3.2.27–28, 4.1.105, 4.2.93–95, 4.3.49–50, 5.3.80–87; for his *Georgics*, 1.1.154; for Livy 5.3.36–38; for Horace 2.3.149, 4.2.20–21; for Homer 1.1.80; for Herodotus 1.1.177; for Cicero 4.1.14. Baker's count of the number of allusions to Virgil—and the number to other poets—may include a few of the many generalized references in *Titus* to classical gods, heroes, and stories. These might have had their origins in collections of classical myths and legends. See Thomson, *Classics*, 56–57.

26. Maxwell, ed., *Titus*, xxxii and n.3. Other scholars have suggested that "the barren detested vale . . . overcome with moss and baleful mistletoe" of 2.3.93–95 reflects the dark wood of yew, cypress, and holm in which Atreus slaughtered the sons of Thyestes.

27. Hunter in a notable essay and Waith in his summation of the classical

sources both assert the greater importance of Ovid without denying the less pervasive, yet important, influence of Seneca. G. K. Hunter, "Seneca and the Elizabethans: A Case Study in 'Influence,'" *ShS* 20 (1967): 17–26; Reprint, *Dramatic Identities and Cultural Tradition* (Liverpool: Liverpool University Press; New York: Barnes & Noble, 1978), 159–73; Waith, ed., *Titus*, 36–37.

28. Thomson, *Classics*, 57–58. See also the notes by Maxwell and Waith on the passages in *Titus*. For an ingenious suggestion concerning the origin of the phrase "in his tent" in *Titus* as a misreading of a phrase in Golding's Ovid—"too thentent" meaning "for the intent"—see Barbara A. Mowat, "Lavinia's Message: Shakespeare and Myth," *RenP 1981* (1982): 55–69.

29. Kittridge, ed., *Works*, 971–72; Robert Adger Law, "The Roman Background of *Titus Andronicus*," *SP* 11 (1943): 145–53.

30. Law does not mention the *History*, which contains the names Lavinia, Titus, and Marcus. Bullough also discusses possible origins of names, sometimes arriving at suggestions different from those put forth by Law. *Sources*, 6:10–11.

31. Law, "Roman Background," 148, 150.

32. Jones, *Origins*, 87–107; 110–18 and notes. Jones also discusses the gradual ascent to the climax of feeling in *Titus*, 3.1., in *Scenic Form in Shakespeare* (Oxford: Clarendon Press, 1971), 8–13; Wilson, ed., *Titus*, ix and note.

33. Leo Kirschbaum, "Some New Light on *The Jew of Malta*," *MLQ* 7 (1946): 53–56; Maurice Charney, "Shakespeare's Aaron Between Marlowe's Tamberline and Barabas/Ithamore," read to Marlowe Society Meeting, December 1984. Law also briefly discusses Aaron, whose name is certainly of biblical origin, perhaps inspired by Marlowe's use of the biblical name Barabas for a character whom Aaron in some particulars resembles. Aaron is descended from the Vice of the moral plays along with Richard III, Don John, and Iago as Bernard Spivack has demonstrated (discussed below).

34. Andrew W. Ettin, "Shakespeare's First Roman Tragedy," *ELH* 37 (1970), 325–41. See also F. P. Wilson, *Marlowe and the Early Shakespeare* (Oxford: Clarendon Press, 1953), 136 n.67; Nicholas Brooke, "Marlowe as Provacative Agent in Shakespeare's Early Plays," *ShS* 14 (1961), 34–44; M. C. Bradbrook, "Shakespeare's recollections of Marlowe," *Shakespeare's Styles: Essays in honour of Kenneth Muir*, ed. Philip Edwards, Inga-Stina Ewbank, and G. K. Hunter (Cambridge: Cambridge University Press, 1980), 191–204.

35. Nancy Lenz Harvey, "*Titus Andronicus* and 'The Shearmen and Taylor's Play,'" *RenQ* 22 (1969), 27–31; Armstrong, *ShS* 17 (1964), 191, thinks Shakespeare may have seen the Coventry plays "during his boyhood or his 'teens.'"

36. R. A. Foakes and R. T. Rickert, eds., *Henslowe's Diary* (Cambridge: Cambridge University Press, 1961), 17–21.

37. See E. A. J. Honigmann, *Shakespeare's Impact on His Contemporaries* (London: Macmillan; Totawa, NJ: Barnes & Noble, 1982), 56–66, 78–88; Gary Taylor, "The Canon and Chronology of Shakespeare's Plays," *William Shakespeare: A Textual Companion* (Oxford: Clarendon Press, 1987), 119, 122–23, 128, 138, 140.

38. W. W. Greg, ed., *Henslowe's Diary*, 2 vols. (London: Bullen, 1904, 1908), 2:155.

39. Chambers, *William Shakespeare*, 1: 319–20; 2:308–9; Adams, ed., *Titus*, 10. Earlier Chambers had speculated that Henslowe's *Jerusalem* refers to *Godfrey of Bulloigne* and the First Crusade, *The Elizabethan Stage*, 4 vols. (Oxford: Clarendon Press, 1923), 3: 340–41. Bullough suggests that it may have been the second of two plays on the life of the Emperor Titus. *Sources*, 6: 3–4, 6.

40. Wilson, ed., *Titus*, xl; Maxwell, ed., *Titus*, xxii; Kermode, ed., *Titus*, 1020; Waith, ed., *Titus*, 8; Wells, ed., *Titus*, *Works*, 141.

41. G. R. Proudfoot, "A Note on 'Titus and Vespasian,'" *N&Q* 213 (1968), 131.

42. Eric Sams, ed., *Shakespeare's Edmund Ironside* (London: Fourth Estate, 1985; Rpt. with rev. and expanded intro., Aldershot: Wildwood House, 1986), 38.

43. Sams, ed., *Edmund Ironside*, 21–22; E. B. Everitt, *The Young Shakespeare*, *Anglistica II* (Copenhagen: Rosenkilde, 1954), 50. Actually, the Archbishop was not "instructed" by the Privy Council to review play scripts, which they had no authority to do, but was merely "desired [to appoint] some fit person well learned in divinity" to do so. See Chambers, *Elizabethan Stage*, 4: 306.

44. Donald Foster, Rev. *SQ* 39 (1988), 120–23; and "Exchange," *SQ* 40 (1989), 253. E. A. J. Honigmann, in a review of Sams's ed. devoted chiefly to a discussion of the claims for Shakespearean authorship and for the manuscript as a Shakespearean holograph, says of Sams's contention for an early date that "Not one of the arguments for a date before 1590 seems at all compelling." "Fingerprinting Shakespeare," *New York Review of Books*, 34:2 (12 Feb. 1987), 23–26. Boswell, in a discussion of date in her Malone Society ed., citing "characteristics of the semi-Senecan school which flourished in the early nineties . . . the monotonous end-stopped verse, and the archaic vocabulary . . . the original absence of act and scene divisions," the use of the word *Braggadochios* "first found . . . in Spenser's *Faery Queen* (1590) . . . Latinized names . . . various Biblical allusions," and a reference to the betrayal of Jesus by Judas of which she says that "it is questionable whether it would have been written much after the accession of James," seems to indicate a range of possible dates from 1590 to 1603, although she does not explicitly say so. Eleanore Boswell, ed., *Edmond Ironside or War Hath Made All Friends*, MSR 1927, 1928, x–xi. Greg, seemingly following Boswell, simply notes "1590–1600?" Bentley, perhaps influenced by Greg or Boswell, tells us that the play was "apparently written 1590–1600." Taylor says that "Sams's dating is possible, but certainly not certain, and probably not probable." W. W. Greg, *Dramatic Documents from the Elizabethan Playhouses*, 2 vols. (Oxford: Clarendon Press, 1931), "Commentary," 256; Gerald Eades Bentley, *The Jacobean and Caroline Stage*, 7 vols. (Oxford: Clarendon Press, 1941–68), 2:581; Gary Taylor, "The Canon and Chronology of Shakespeare's Plays," *William Shakespeare: A Textual Companion*, by Stanley Wells and Gary Taylor with John Jowett and William Montgomery (Oxford: Clarendon Press, 1987), 138. Sams received some support for his theory on authorship from the late Eliot Slater, but M. W. A. Smith effectively exposes defects in the statistical bases underlying the claim. Slater, *TLS*, 18 March 1983, 268; reprint as App. VI in Slater's *The Problem of The Reign of King Edward III: A Statistical Approach* (Cambridge: Cambridge University Press, 1988), 257–63; Smith, *N&Q* 233 (1988), 447–49.

45. M. Mincoff, "The Source of Titus Andronicus," *N&Q* 216 (1971), 131–34; Metz, "'The History of Titus Andronicus' and Shakespeare's Play," *N&Q* 220 (1975), 163–66.

46. G. K. Hunter, "The 'Sources' of *Titus Andronicus*—Once Again," *N&Q* 228 (1983), 114–16.

47. Metz, "Titus Andronicus: Three Versions of the Story," *N&Q* 233 (1988), 451–55.

48. G. K. Hunter, "Sources and Meaning in *Titus Andronicus*," *Mirror up to Shakespeare: Essays in Honour of G. R. Hibbard*, ed. J. C. Gray (Toronto: University of Toronto Press, 1984), 171–88.

49. Stanley Wells, "Between then and now," *TLS*, 30 March 1984, 1390.

50. Waith, ed., *Titus*, 29–33.

51. As an Addendum to my response to Hunter's 1983 *N&Q* paper, I briefly discussed some of MacDonald Jackson's comments on the relationships among the three versions of the Titus story that he had offered in the course of his review of Waith's edition (*ShS* 38 [1985], 246–50). In a rejoinder to my Addendum (*N&Q* 234 [1989], 315–17), Jackson noted that I did not properly take into account two additional points that he had made, and, on rereading his review, I am inclined to agree that they should have been discussed. They are fine points in support of the play-ballad-history hypothesis of the origin of the Titus story, which I did not find persuasive. Nevertheless I concur in his call for a reexamination "of the primary material [bearing on the source of *Titus*] without prejudice [including a fair assessment of the] arguments of Mincoff, Hunter, and myself."

52. Bullough, for example, sums up a discussion of the character thus: "Aaron is not so much a Senecan villain as the antithesis of all Christian goodness," i.e. the Vice (*Sources*, 6:21).

53. Bernard Spivack, *Shakespeare and the Allegory of Evil* (New York: Columbia University Press, 1958), passim.

54. The term "hybrid" suggests a dichotomy of mixed origins, but Aaron, at least, if not the other Shakespearean personified Vices, is not a heterogeneous mixture of diverse elements of the villain and the Vice, but, on the manifestly vastly more significant theological example of Christ who was at the same time entirely man and entirely God, Aaron is totally a villain and totally the Vice.

55. Spivack, *Allegory of Evil*, passim, esp. 35–36, 43–44, 56–59, 357–58, and 379–87. For a recent survey of the Vice in the sixteenth century drama and Shakespeare's debt to the moral plays, see Alan C. Dessen, *Shakespeare and the Late Moral Plays* (Lincoln: University of Nebraska Press, 1986).

56. Thomson, *Classics*, 96–97; Bullough, *Sources*, 3:171, 235–37; 4:9–11; 7:19, 25–26, 36–39, 451–54.

57. Muir, *Sources*, 37, 168, 211–14.

58. Jones, *Origins*, 267–72.

59. Kistners, "Senecan Background," *ShakS* 7 (1974), 8.

60. J. W. Lever, *The Tragedy of State* (London: Methuen, 1971), 16 n. 9. For a discussion of "some of the newer ways of thinking about Shakespeare" see Maurice Charney, "Contemporary Issues in Shakespearean Interpretation," *William Shakespeare: His World, His Work, His Influence*, ed. John F. Andrews, 3 vols. (New York: Scribners, 1985), 3:889–911; and specifically in regard to *Titus*, see Charney, *Titus Andronicus* (Hemel Hempstead: Harvester Wheatsheaf, 1990), passim.

61. Charles and Michelle Martindale, *Shakespeare and the Uses of Antiquity* (London: Routledge, 1990), 29–44, esp. 29–30, 42–44.

62. Bruce R. Smith, *Ancient Scripts & Modern Experience on the English Stage 1500–1700* (Princeton: Princeton University Press, 1988), 240–46, 270–71.

63. Philip Edwards, "Thrusting Elysium into Hell: The Originality of *The Spanish Tragedy*," *Elizabethan Theatre XI* (Port Credit: Meany, 1990), 117–32.

64. Robert S. Miola, *Shakespeare and Classical Tragedy: The Influence of Seneca* (Oxford: Clarendon Press, 1992), 13, 18–19, 20–26, 28–30. Miola also studies *MND* under the rubric "Light Seneca," as distinguished from the tragedies that are designated "Heavy Seneca." In addition, he comments less extensively though nonetheless illuminatingly on Seneca and some two dozen other plays in the Shakespeare canon.

65. Adams, ed., *Titus*, 7–9.

66. The texts employed are, for the play, Q1 ed. Adams with line refs. to Waith, ed., *Titus;* and for the *History,* Bullough reprint (ref. n. 2 above), which preserves the spelling and punctuation of the original chapbook, with page refs. to Waith's reprint (ref. also n. 2 above).

67. Waith reprint in ed., *Titus,* 196–98.

68. Waith reprint in ed., *Titus,* 198.

69. Waith, ed., *Titus,* 32; and reprint 198–200.

70. Waith, reprint in ed., *Titus,* 200–1. The false accusation is made in the play by an anonymous letter planted by Aaron.

71. Waith reprint in ed., *Titus,* 201–3.

Chapter 6. Date of Composition

1. Eugene M. Waith, ed., *Ben Jonson: Bartholomew Fair* (New Haven: Yale University Press, 1963), 31.

2. R. A. Foakes and R. T. Rickert, eds., *Henslowe's Diary* (Cambridge: Cambridge University Press, 1961), 21, 280.

3. The particle "ne" as used by Henslowe apparently had various meanings. It probably meant "new" whenever it was used, but it was not limited to the first time a play was acted. It seems also to have meant that the play was new to the particular acting troupe named; or that it was the first performance under Henslowe's auspices. Foakes and Rickert observe, on the basis of the amount of the takings, that it meant that the play, whether new or revised, had been newly licensed or relicensed. *Diary,* xxx–xxxi.

4. G. R. Proudfoot, ed., *A Knack to Know a Knave,* MSR (Oxford: Oxford University Press, 1963), sig. F2ᵛ.

5. The prose *History* and the ballad are reprinted in Waith's ed., *Titus,* in the Oxford Shakespeare series (Oxford: Clarendon Press, 1984), 195–207. References to *Titus,* unless otherwise identified, are to Waith's edition. The *History* and the ballad are also reprinted by Bullough in *Narrative and Dramatic Sources of Shakespeare,* 8 vols. (London: Routledge; New York: Columbia University Press, 1961–75), 6: 34–48.

6. T. J. B. Spencer, "Shakespeare and the Elizabethan Romans," *ShS* 10 (1957), 27–38.

7. J. C. Maxwell, ed., *Titus,* in *New Arden* (London: Metheun, 1953; rev. ed., 1961), xxii, xxiv.

8. Peter Alexander, *Introductions to Shakespeare* (London: Collins; New York: Norton, 1964), 151.

9. E. K. Chambers, *William Shakespeare,* 2 vols. (Oxford: Clarendon Press, 1930), 1:319. The *History* relates that "the Senators, by the Emperor's mandate, assembled with joy, who chose with one consent Andronicus their general" but no senatorial welcome is mentioned. (Waith, ed., *Titus,* 198). Paul E. Bennett argues that the word "Goths" crept into *A Knack* in the course of a particularly bad memorial reconstruction of the play by some of Derby's men in place of the original word, which Bennett maintains was "Jews" because the reference to Titus in the passage is to Titus Vespasianus, not to Titus Andronicus. In support of this "admittedly conjectural explanation," he cites "three direct references to . . . Vespasian and one to a son . . . apparently Domitian;" and the seriously defective state of the 1594 text, which is so poor that "we cannot assume that a single word [of it] . . . actually occurred in the original." Since the posited original is not extant, Bennett's explanation is purely speculative. "Apparent Allusion to "Titus

Andronicus;" and "The word Goths in A Knack to Know a Knave," *N&Q* 200 (1955), 422–24, 462–63. David George picked up a casual observation of Bennett's (p. 462) that *Titus* was first performed in 1594 by a "mixed company of actors" from Derby's Pembroke's and Sussex's men and elaborated an argument in favor of this contention, but it has not attained acceptance. "Shakespeare and Pembroke's Men," *SQ* 32 (1981), 305–23.

10. Both parts of *Troublesome Reign* are reprinted in Bullough, *Narrative and Dramatic Sources*. The passage quoted is on 4:147. Other passages are on 4:99, 103, 117, 121, and 124.

11. Alexander, *Shakespeare's Life and Art* (London: Nisbet, 1939; Reprint, New York: New York University Press, 1967), 85.

12. Maxwell, ed., *Titus*, xxi.

13. H. Dugdale Sykes, *Sidelights on Shakespeare* (Stratford-upon-Avon: Shakespeare Head Press, 1919).

14. T. W. Baldwin, *On the Literary Genetics of Shakespeare's Plays* (Urbana: University of Illinois Press, 1959), 412–13; J. M. Robertson, *An Introduction to the Study of the Shakespeare Canon* (London: Routledge, 1924; Reprint, Westport, CT: Greenwood Press, 1970), 178.

15. Chambers cites Fleay's dating. *Elizabethan Stage*, 4 vols. (Oxford: Clarendon Press, 1923), 3:460.

16. Chambers, *Elizabethan Stage*, 3:395–96; 424–25.

17. John Dover Wilson, ed., *Titus*, in *New (Cambridge) Shakespeare* (Cambridge: Cambridge University Press, 1968 issue), xxxviii, xxxix, xl, xlv; Maxwell. ed., *Titus*, xxi, xxii, xxiv; Anselm Schlösser, "*Titus Andronicus*," *SJ* 104 (1968), 75–84. The quoted phrase is on p. 76.

18. Sylvan Barnet, ed., *Titus*, 1964; reprint, *Complete Signet Classic Shakespeare*, 1972, p. 289; Gustav Cross, ed., *Titus*, *Pelican Shakespeare*, 1967; rev. ed., 1969, p. 823; Frank Kermode, ed., *Titus*, *Riverside Shakespeare*, 1974, p. 1020; David Bevington, ed., *Works*, 1980, p. 956; J. J. M. Tobin, "Nomenclature and the Dating of *Titus Andronicus*," *N&Q* 229 (1984), 186–87.

19. Waith, ed., *Titus*, 4–11.

20. Chambers, *William Shakespeare*, 2:254.

21. E. A. J. Honigmann, *Shakespeare's Impact on his Contemporaries* (London: Macmillan; Totowa, NJ: Barnes & Noble, 1982); *Shakespeare: the 'lost years.'* (Manchester: Manchester University Press; Totowa, NJ: Barnes & Noble, 1985), both passim.

22. *'Lost years'*, 59–63, 128.

23. Stanley Wells and Gary Taylor with John Jowett and William Montgomery, eds., *William Shakespeare: A Textual Companion* (Oxford: Clarendon Press, 1987), 113–14.

24. Wells, ed., *Titus*, in *Oxford Complete Works* (Oxford: Clarendon Press, 1986), 141.

25. Honigmann, *'Lost years'*, 61.

Chapter 7. Stage History: 1970–1994

1. For the earlier production record and staging of *Titus Andronicus*, see Metz, "Stage History of *Titus Andronicus*," *SQ* 28 (1977), 154–69; and "The Early Staging of *Titus Andronicus*," *ShakS* 14 (1981), 99–109. Some productions regrettably not mentioned in the "Stage History" are those of the Bungalow Players of Denver (acted six times in 1928), the Norwich Players at the Maddermarket

Theatre under the direction of Nugent Monck (seven performances in 1931), and the Pasadena Playhouse troupe directed by Gilmore Brown (played four times in 1937). Marga Munkelt also notes a burlesque experiment by Klaus Schlette at Munich (1968) and a version in "50 dramatische Szenen" presented at Basel in 1969 by Hans Hollmann and Hermann Beil. Elizabeth Carnahan, "'Four Boards and a Passion'—at the Bungalow," *SAB* 4 (1929), 175–79; Nugent Monck, "The Maddermarket Theatre and the Playing of Shakespeare," *ShS* 12 (1959), 71–75; Franklin J. Hildy, *Shakespeare at the Maddermarket* (Ann Arbor: UMI Research Press), [193]; *Pasadena Playhouse Playbill*, 16 November 1937; Marga Munkelt, "*Titus Andronicus:* Metamorphoses of a Text in Production," *Shakespeare Text, Language, Criticism: Essays in Honour of Marvin Spevack*, ed., Bernhard Fabian and Kurt Tetzeli von Rosador (Hildesheim: Olms, 1987), 212–34. In a book included in a series entitled "Shakespeare in Performance," intended by its series editors to be selective, limited to "a small number of productions of a particular play . . . [that] are significant interpretations in their own right," Dessen discusses *Titus*. Although adhering to the general plan, he nevertheless occasionally alludes to a few less well-known productions, mentioning among others a 1956 presentation featuring "a group of young actors (that included Colleen Dewhurst as Tamora) put on . . . at the Shakespeare Theatre Workshop" in New York. It was pronounced "for the most part a bloody bore" by a New York *Times* reviewer who, however, had praise for Roscoe Browne's Aaron. Alan C. Dessen, *Titus Andronicus* (Manchester: Manchester University Press, 1989), [ii], 14.

2. Armin Arnold, *Friedrich Dürrenmatt* (New York: Ungar, 1972), 72–73, 94–99; Hans Schwab-Felisch, "Grusical: Shakespeare/Dürrenmatt *Titus Andronicus,* Düsseldorf," *ThH* 12:2 (Feb. 1971), 21. For an insightful appraisal of Dürrenmatt's adaptation, see Mark E. Cory, "Shakespeare and Dürrenmatt: From Tragedy to Tragicomedy," *CL* 32 (1980), 253–73.

3. *SQ* 27 (1976), 422, item 453; New York *Times,* 21 May 1975.

4. A. R. Braunmuller and William L. Stull, "Shakespeare in Los Angeles," *SQ* 29 (1978), 259–67.

5. Joseph H. Stodder in a personal letter to R. Thad Taylor of 21 July 1977.

6. Bernard Beckerman, "New Jersey Shakespeare Festival," *SQ* 29 (1978), 232–34.

7. Philadelphia *Inquirer,* 9 July 1977; New York *Daily News,* 12 July 1977.

8. Phyllis Zatlin-Boring, "*Titus Andronicus,*" *Shakespeare Around the Globe,* ed. Samuel L. Leiter (Westport, CT: Greenwood Press, 1985, 741–42. In addition to the Catalonian mounting of *Titus* there were other overseas productions in 1976–77, notably the first staging of the play in Greece, *SQ* 30 (1979), 591, items 2734–36 and 2738–40.

9. Ralph Berry, "Stratford Festival Canada," *SQ* 30 (1979), 167–75.

10. Berry, "Stratford Festival Canada," *SQ* 32 (1981), 176–80; Roger Warren, "Shakespeare in Performance, 1980," *ShS* 34 (1981), 149–60. Media reviewers were also favorably impressed. New York *Times,* 14 June 1980; *Wall Street Journal,* 18 July 1980.

11. I. Palffy, "Shakespeare in Hungary," *SQ* 30 (1979), 289–90.

12. Glasgow *Herald, Scotsman,* 3 July 1979.

13. Patricia Olsen, "Great Lakes Shakespeare Festival," *SQ* 32 (1981), 232–33; Cleveland *Press,* 29 August 1980.

14. Rhoda-Gale Pollack, "Shakespeare in Wisconsin," *SQ* 32 (1981), 236–38; Chicago *Tribune,* 14 August 1980.

15. Gareth Lloyd Evans, "Shakespeare in Stratford and London, 1981," *SQ*

33 (1982), 184–88; Stanley Wells, "Elizabethan doublets," *TLS*, 18 September 1981, 1071; Roger Warren, "Interpretations of Shakespearian Comedy, 1981," *ShS* 35 (1982), 142–44. See also Munkelt, "Metamorphoses of a Text," 214–21.

16. *SQ* 33 (1982), 733, item 3170.

17. Henning Rischbieter. "*Titus Andronicus* in Hamburg oder: Kann man geh-aufte Greuel spielen?" *ThH* 23:2 (1983), 7–9.

18. *SQ* 36 (1985), 900–1, item 3546.

19. Mel Gordon, "Kestutis Nakas: Serial Worker," *Drama Review* 29:1 (1985), 113–15. See also *Village Voice*, 9 and 30 August, 1983.

20. J. Fuzier, F. Laroque, and J. M. Maguin, "*Titus Andronicus*," *CahiersE* 23 (1984), 119–21. Gabriele Lavia staged *Tito Andronico* in Italian, trans. Allesandro Serpieri, presented by the Compagnia del Teatro Eliseo of Rome in repertory beginning 22 February 1983. *SQ* 38 (1987), 807, item 3889. Dessen notes a presentation in 1985 at Trinity College, University of Toronto, inspired in part by Olivier's conception. *Titus Andronicus*, 73–74.

21. Stanley Wells, "The canon in the can," *TLS*, 10 May 1985, p. 522. Mary Z. Maher, who "watch[ed] this . . . revenge tragedy being transformed into a television play," has published a detailed account of her observations. "The Production Design in the BBC's *Titus Andronicus*," *BNYSS* 4:1 (1986), 5–7; Reprint, rev., *Shakespeare on Television*, ed. J. C. Bulman and H. R. Coursen (Hanover, NH: University Press of New England, 1988), 144–50. See also Susan Willis, *The BBC Shakespeare Plays* (Chapel Hill: University of North Carolina Press, 1991), 292–313.

22. Munkelt, "Metamorphosis of a Text," 221–29; Wilhelm Hortmann. "Shakespeare in West Germany, 1985," *SQ* 37 (1986), 494; Peter von Becker, "Shakespearekasperl," *ThH* 26:3 (1985), 41–43; Müller's adaptation of the text is printed following von Becker's review, pp. 44–59. It was presented a second time at the Index Theatre, Manchester in October 1991. Niky Rathbone, "Professional Shakespeare Productions in the British Isles, January–December 1991" *ShS* 46 (1994), 191.

23. Personal letters of 30 August 1988 and 22 July and 5 September 1990. I wish to express my thanks to Professor Munkelt for responding to my inquiries and for supplying a copy of the audio tape; and to Professor John W. Velz for calling *Titus Androgynous* to my attention.

24. Details provided by Dr. Ernst Haüblein of the von Humboldt Gymnasium. I am happy to acknowledge my debt to him for his assistance.

25. Portland *Oregonian*, 20 June 1986; Eugene *Register-Guard*, 23 June 1986; Vancouver *Columbian* 29 June 1986. The Los Angeles *Globe* essayed its second *Titus* in 1986. One reviewer found it "not funny enough for burlesque, not sobering enough for tragedy." Los Angeles *Times*, 26 February 1986. Laszlo Gerold mounted a *Titus* as part of a Shakespeare festival of July–August, 1986, at Palic, Hungary, in which he emphasized visual elements; Michel Dubois staged the play at the Theatre du Chaillot, France, in 1987; Maciej Prus directed *Tytus Andronikus* in Polish, trans. Leon Ulrich, at the Stefan Jaracz Theatre, Lodz in September 1987, *SQ* 39 (1988), 823, items 4325, 4327, 4328; *SQ* 40 (1990), 602, item 1047; Rudolf Seitz presented the play in German, trans. Erich Fried, at the Würtember-gischen Landesbühne, Esslingen, in repertory beginning 1 April 1987, *SQ* 40 (1990), 836, item 4609.

26. Margaret M. Tocci, "*Titus Andronicus*," *BNYSS* 5:2 (1987), 10–11; Wilson, ed., *Titus*, xii, 1i, 1vi; Fairfax VA *Journal*, 5 December 1986; Washington *Post*, 28 November 1986; Washington *Times*, 28 November 1986. In a similarly light-

hearted vein, the Reduced Shakespeare Company (RSC) presented at the 1987 Edinburgh Festival "The Complete Works of Shakespeare (Abridged)," including *Titus*, in a "fast forward cooking-show version" of the Thyestean banquet, featuring a Julia Child-type character in a fright wig. The segment was entitled "Titus Andronicus's Roman Meals." Since the Edinburgh Festival, this RSC has performed its abridged Shakespeare throughout the U. K., in Dublin; Melbourne, Australia; Canada; and New York. When asked about their commitment to Shakespeare, one of the troupe responded: "Hey look, as long as Shakespeare keeps writing them, we'll keep doing them." Alfred Weiss, "The Edinburgh Festival, 1987," *SQ* 39 (1988), 79–89, esp. 83, 88; New York *Times,* 13 June 1991. The first Yugoslav Shakespeare Festival presented in Subotica in 1986 seven of the tragedies, including *Titus,* acted in Yugoslavia for the first time. *ShN* 198 (1988), 24.

27. Stanley Wells, "Shakespeare Performances in London and Stratford-upon-Avon, 1986–7," *ShS* 41 (1989), 159–81, esp. 178–81.

28. Alan C. Dessen, "Exploring the Script: Shakespearean Pay-offs in 1987," *SQ* 39 (1988), 217–26, esp. 222–25; "Exciting Shakespeare in 1988," *SQ* 40 (1989), 198–207, esp. 198, 199, 202–3; 207. The conception of the interaction between Lavinia and Marcus in 2.4 was earlier expounded by Charney. See discussion of his essay in the chapter on Criticism.

29. H. R. Woudhuysen, "Savage laughter," *TLS* 22 May 1987, p. 551.

30. Irving Wardle, *The Times,* 5 July 1988; Michael Ratcliffe, *The Observer,* 10 July 1988; Michael Billington, *The Guardian,* 6 July 1988. Brother Patrick Ellis, then President and Professor of English at La Salle University, noted that in the performance at The Pit "the foreshadowing was what stood out for me: germs of *Lear, Othello, Hamlet* . . . The title role was a virtuoso performance . . . Sonia Ritter was brilliant, especially in her long wordless scenes . . . and there was not a weak member of the deep cast. The whole event is a rarity." Personal letter of 29 June 1988.

31. Michael Mullin, "The Colorado Shakespeare Festival, 1988," *SQ* 40 (1989), 336–41, esp. 339–41; *Daily Camera,* 11 October 1988.

32. Dessen, "Exciting Shakespeare," 201–3; San Jose *Mercury-News,* 8 August 1988.

33. Idaho *Press Tribune,* 27 July 1988; Idaho *Statesman,* 27 July 1988.

34. Seymour Rudin, *"Titus Andronicus,"* *BNYSS* 6:4 (1988), 8–9.

35. C. E. McGee, "Shakespeare in Canada: The Stratford Season, 1989," *SQ* 41 (1990), 114–20, esp. 114–15. McGee also briefly comments on this production as part of an overview of the 1989 Stratford Festival, *BNYSS* 7:6 (1989), 12–13; Wallace Sterling, *"Titus Andronicus* and *The Comedy of Errors,"* *BNYSS* 7:6 (1989), 18; Windsor *Star,* 30 May 1989; Detroit *Free Press,* 31 May 1989.

36. Naomi Conn Liebler, "The New Jersey Shakespeare Festival *Titus Andronicus,"* *BNYSS* 7:5 (1989), 21–22. With the production of *Jn.* in the summer of 1990 this Festival became the twelfth theater to have produced the cycle of Shakespearean plays. Paul Barry, Artistic Director, stands alone as the only Shakespearean producer to have personally mounted and directed thirty-eight of the plays: the thirty-six of the First Folio, plus *Per.* and *TNK.* Newark, NJ *Star-Ledger,* 4 July 1989; Princeton, NJ *Packet* 6 July 1989; New York *Times,* 13 August 1989.

37. Dorothy and Wayne Cook, "New York Theatre Reviews: *Titus Andronicus,"* *BNYSS* 8:1 (1990), 9.

38. Frank Rich, New York *Times*, 21 August 1989; Clive Barnes, New York *Post*, 21 August 1989.

39. Personal letter of 28 September 1989; Festival announcement of the production.

40. Montgomery AL *Advertiser*, 6 August 1989, Alabama *Journal*, 8 August 1989; *Montgomery!* 15 August 1989. In addition to the four North American productions there was a fifth at Rome in the same year. Peter Stein directed a *Tito Andronico* in Italian, trans. Agostino Lombardo, adapted by Stein. Initial public performances began at Teatro Quirino on 1 December 1989, followed by a tour of major Italian theaters. *SQ* 41 (1990), 858–59, items 4225, 4240.

41. Interview with Rich Gilmore, *Daily Spectrum*, 1 July 1990.

42. *Daily Spectrum*, 5 July 1990; *Deseret News*, 5 July 1990; Provo *Daily Herald*, 12 July 1990; Salt Lake *Tribune*, 5 July 1990.

43. Alfred Weiss, "The Edinburgh International Festival, 1990," *SQ* 42 (1991), 471.

44. Gustave Ungerer, "An Unrecorded Elizabethan Performance of *Titus Andronicus*," *ShS* 14 (1961), 102–9. For the Longleat drawing, see the chapter on the Longleat Manuscript.

45. In his discussion of the "discovery space" in the Globe Theatre, Hosley notes that "the Globe tiring-house would have been equipped with two (or three) double-hung stage doors. (Probably there were three rather than two doors.)" Later he refers to "a presumptive third door," adding that the term "discovery space . . . may well designate the space behind a middle door in the tiring-house wall." Richard Hosley, "The Discovery-Space in Shakespeare's Globe," *ShS* 12 (1959), 35–46, esp. 35.

46. Hosley calculates that with both halves of the center floor open wide the "discovery-space" would have been no "deeper than 4 ft. or wider than 7 ft.;" and the "inner stage" as conceived of by other scholars measured "some 7 ft. or 8 ft. in depth and 20 ft. or more in width." "Discovery-Space," pp. 35, 46. Ulrich Suerbaum challenges the very conception of such a playing space however denominated, saying "There is no tangible evidence of its existence," and citing specifically its absence from the De Witt drawing. "A Theatre for Shakespeare: The Early History of the Inner Stage Myth," *Shakespeare: Text, Language, Criticism. Essays in Honour of Marvin Spevack*, ed. Bernhard Fabian and Kurt Tetzeli von Rosador (Hildesheim: Olms, 1987), 280–303.

47. Richard Hosley, "Shakespeare's Use of a Gallery over the Stage," *ShS* 10 (1957), 77–89. See also Hosley, "The Gallery over the Stage in the Public Playhouse of Shakespeare's Time," *SQ* 8 (1957), 15–31. De Witt's drawing of the Swan has been frequently reproduced, recently by R. A. Foakes. *Illustrations of the English Stage, 1580–1642* (Stanford: Stanford University Press, 1985), no. 26, p. 53.

48. "Shakespeare's Use," 86, n. 4.

49. "Shakespeare's Use," 78 and 87, n. 11.

50. Almost all modern editors add "above" or "aloft" to the stage direction at 5.2.8.1. A modicum of support for such an editorial assumption may be found in the German *Tragödie von Tito Andronico*, which Chambers determines to be "an adaptation of *Titus Andronicus* for Continental travel." *William Shakespeare*, 1:319. In Scene VII of the German text, Aetiopissa (Tamora) and her two sons go to Titus's "palace." She calls out to Titus and he appears. An accompanying stage direction reads: "Titus siehet von oben hinunter," which Cohn freely translates as "Titus Andronicus looking down," but Brenneke renders more precisely

as "Titus looks down from above," which strongly implies that Titus is on the gallery. Albert Cohn, *Shakespeare in Germany in the Sixteenth and Seventeenth Centuries* (London: Asher, 1865; Reprint, Wiesbaden: Sändig, 1967), 223–24; Ernest Brennecke, *Shakespeare in Germany 1590–1700* (Chicago: University of Chicago Press, 1964), 46.

51. Hosley notes that another location thought to be higher than the gallery and referred to as the "top" in two Shakespearean plays (*1H6* and *Tmp.*) may allude to "the 'hut' on top of the 'cover' over the stage;" but he rejects it because "the difficulty of visibility seems forbidding." He concludes that the expression "on the top" probably refers to the gallery. "Shakespeare's Use," 86, n. 8. Modern editors are divided as to the desirability of supplying a stage direction calling for Marcus, Lucius, young Lucius, and perhaps a guard to go up to the gallery.

52. John Cranford Adams, "Shakespeare's Revisions in *Titus Andronicus*," *SQ* 15 (1964), 177–90; Reprint, *Shakespeare Quarterly Vol. XV, 1964* (New York: AMS, 1969), 177–90.

53. Rudolf Stamm, "The Alphabet of Speechless Complaint," *ES* 55 (1974), 325–39. In a revised and more comprehensive analysis of theatrical notation to be found in the entire text of *Titus*, Stamm successfully elucidates the staging hints and cues, especially those in the dialogue. *Shakespeare's Theatrical Notation: Early Tragedies* (Bern: Franke, 1989), 29–77.

54. G. K. Hunter, "Flatcaps and Bluecoats: Visual Signals on the Elizabethan Stage," *E&S* 33 (1980), 16–47, esp. 17–21.

55. Hunter points out that the stage direction in F differs from Qq, that Marcus may have entered on the gallery at this point or may have been with the group "aloft" since the initial entrance and at this point merely stepped forward with the crown. The direction in F reads *Enter Marcus Andronicus aloft with the Crowne;* Qq omit *"Enter"* and *"aloft."* The possibility exists that F preserves a later and altered staging.

56. Wells notes that "a formal departure through a central door representing the 'gates' seems equally possible." Stanley Wells, *Re-editing Shakespeare for the Modern Reader* (Oxford: Clarendon Press), 87, n. 13.

57. Here Hunter cites one of the three references in F that is plural. The other two in F and all three in Qq read the singular: "Coffin."

58. "Flatcaps," 20–21.

59. The external evidence of the *Messalina* and *Faustus* drawings is not completely clear as to the exact location of the trap in the platform, but it seems that it may not have been precisely in the center of the stage. See Foakes, *Illustrations of the English Stage*, 81, 110. See also E. K. Chambers, *Elizabethan Stage*, 4 vols. (Oxford: Clarendon Press, 1923), 3:42, 89–90; Gerald Eades Bentley, *Jacobean and Caroline Stage*, 7 vols., (Oxford: Clarendon Press, 1941–68), 6:51, 281. C. Walter Hodges prints a series of drawings of substantial stage properties that may represent those that were used in staging Shakespeare's plays at the Globe. Included is a tomb that, judging by the human figures nearby, would have been approximately twelve feet in width and fifteen feet in height. *The Globe Restored* (London: Oxford University Press, 1968), 64.

60. There are stage directions in half a dozen Elizabethan, Jacobean, and Caroline plays that explicitly refer to three doors in the tiring-house facade. See Chambers, *Elizabethan Stage*, 3:78–87, 132n; Hosley, "Discovery-Space," 41–46; Bentley, *Jacobean and Caroline Stage*, 6:51; Clifford Leech and T. W. Craik, eds., *The Revels History of Drama in English*, 3 vols., (London: Methuen, 1975), 3:128.

61. Michael Hattaway, *Elizabethan Popular Theatre: Plays in Performance* (London: Routledge, 1982), 186–207.

62. Wells, *Re-Editing*, 75–125.

63. Line citations refer to Waith, ed., *Titus;* TLNs refer to Hinman's facsimile of F1.

64. Maxwell, ed., *Titus*, 8, 69 stage direction. Waith in his ed. adds that "Several Coffins . . would crowd the stage and require more 'extras' in an already large cast. The Q1 stage direction is probably right" (1.1.149.1).

65. *Re-Editing*, 91–92.

66. Only a minority of twentieth-century editors of *Titus* adopt Rowe's addition.

67. *Re-Editing*, 108–112.

68. *Re-Editing*, 63, 114–25. Wells notes (p. 70, n. 8) that in my paper on the early staging of *Titus* (*ShakS* 14 [1981], 99–109), I did not consider "the possible use of a trap" to represent the tomb of the Andronici. It is true that in the essay the trap was not discussed, but in preparing it I did consider the possibility; however, in view of Titus's lines about the family monument (1.1.350–51), which imply a substantial stage property, it seemed unlikely that the use of the stage trap was intended by the playwright. It is, of course, also true, as Wells observes, (p. 70) that the problem of the representation of the tomb may have been solved "in different ways according to the different locations in which they played."

Chapter 8. The Longleat Manuscript

1. E. K. Chambers, "The First Illustration to 'Shakespeare.'" *Library* 4:5 (1924–25), 326–30.

2. Peter Thomson, *Shakespeare's Theatre* (London: Routledge, 1983), 115. Some aspects of the discussion on the design of the sketch were earlier pointed out by J. Dover Wilson, "*Titus Andronicus* on the Stage in 1595," *ShS* 1 (1948), 17–22.

3. *William Shakespeare*, 2 vols. (Oxford: Clarendon Press, 1930), 1:313.

4. Joseph Quincy Adams, ed., *Titus Andronicus The First Quarto 1594* (New York: Scribner's 1936), 31–40. For a discussion of Canon Jackson's pencil jottings, see Metz, "*Titus Andronicus:* A Watermark in the Longleat Manuscript," *SQ* 36 (1985), 450–53.

5. Wilson, "*Titus Andronicus* on the Stage," 19–22.

6. Wilson, ed., *Titus* in *New Cambridge Shakespeare* (Cambridge: Cambridge University Press, 1948), 98–99. Neither the note nor the reproduction of the drawing are included in the paperback issue of his edition.

7. John Munro, "*Titus Andronicus*," *TLS*, 10 June 1949, 385.

8. Line numbers not otherwise identified refer to Eugene M. Waith, ed., *Titus* in *Oxford Shakespeare* (Oxford: Clarendon Press, 1984).

9. Wilson, *TLS*, 24 June 1949, 413; Munro, *TLS*, 1 July 1949, 429; and *London Shakespeare*, 6 vols. (London: Eyre & Spottiswood; New York: Simon and Schuster, 1957), 5:6–7.

10. Arthur J. Perrett, "*Titus Andronicus*," *TLS*, 1 July 1949, 429.

11. Thomas M. Parrott, "Further Observations on *Titus Andronicus*," *SQ* 1 (1950), 22–29.

12. J. C. Maxwell, ed., *Titus* in *New Arden Shakespeare* (London: Metheun, 1953, 3rd ed., 1961), xiv–xv.

13. W. Moelwyn Merchant, "Classical Costume in Shakespearean Productions," *ShS* 10 (1957), 71–76, and Pl. I:6; Horst Oppel. *Titus Andronicus Studien*

zur dramengeschichtlichen Stellung von Shakespeare früher Tragödie (Heidelberg: Quelle & Meyer, 1961), 111–16.

14. Martin R. Holmes, *Shakespeare and His Players* (New York: Scribner's, 1972), 150–53.

15. Frank Kermode, ed., *Titus* in *Riverside Shakespeare*, ed. G. Blakemore Evans (Boston: Houghton Mifflin, 1974), 1019–20, 1022, and Pls. 9 and 14.

16. Robert S. Miola. "*Titus Andronicus* and the Mythos of Shakespeare's Rome," *ShakS* 14 (1981), 85–98.

17. Waith, ed., *Titus*, 20–27. The skepticism of Adams, Greg, and Wilson is based on a perceived inferiority of Peacham's draftsmanship in the emblem books, but a comparison of the character and execution of his emblem drawings with the Longleat picture reveals them to be of about the same level of competence. All are mere illustrations. See John Horden, ed., *English Emblem Books*, Nos. 29, 30, 31, and 32 (Ilkley: Scolar, 1976). As to the puzzling form of the date, one explanation for the troublesome *g* is that it is misplaced. The scribe may have intended to write "Anno m°qg°q¹°."

18. R. A. Foakes, *Illustrations of the English Stage 1580–1642* (London: Scolar; Stanford: Stanford University Press, 1985), 48–51.

19. Parrott, op. cit., 22; Adams, ed., cit., 32; Wilson, "Stage," 19; Munro, *TLS,* 10 June 1949, 385; Maxwell, ed., cit., xv.

20. For some corroboration of the date as 1595, see Metz, "*Titus Andronicus:* A Watermark," 452–53.

21. For a discussion of simultaneous representation in connection with Elizabethan drama, see John B. Gleason, "The Dutch Humanist Origins of the De Witt Drawing of the Swan Theatre," *SQ* 32 (1981), 324–38, esp. 335–38.

22. Robert Speaight, *Shakespeare: The Man and his Achievement* (London: Dent, 1977), 139.

23. E.g., Adams, ed., *Titus,* 36.

24. Adams, ed., *Titus,* 37–38.

25. Wilson, "Stage," 19–20; and ed., *Titus,* 98; Munro, *TLS,* 10 June 1949, 385; Maxwell, ed., *Titus,* 1961, xiv.

26. Waith, ed., *Titus,* 20–27, esp. 24–26.

27. Ibid., 23 and ns. 1 and 2; and 25 and n. 1.

Chapter 9. Nashe's *Unfortunate Traveller* and *Titus Andronicus*

1. Eugene M. Waith, ed., *Titus* in *Oxford Shakespeare* (Oxford: Clarendon Press, 1984). References are to this edition.

2. R. B. McKerrow, ed., *Works of Thomas Nashe*, 5 vols. (London: Bullen, 1904–10), 2:292; Reprint with corrections and supplementary notes by F. P. Wilson, 5 vols. (Oxford: Blackwell, 1957). References are to the corrected edition.

3. John Dale Ebbs, "A Note on Nashe and Shakespeare," *MLN,* 66 (1951) 480–81.

4. Ernest C. York, "Shakespeare and Nashe," *N&Q,* 198 (1953), 370–71.

5. McKerrow, ed., *Nashe,* 1:200.

6. W. Schrichx, "*Titus Andronicus* and Thomas Nashe," *ES,* 50 (1969), 82–84.

7. R. A. L. Burnet, "Nashe and *Titus Andronicus* II, iii. 129–30"; *ELN,* 18 (1980), 98–99; Waith, ed., *Titus,* 5.1.140, 3.1.223; McKerrow, ed., 2:292, 247. The *History* is reprinted by Geoffrey Bullough, *Narrative and Dramatic Sources of*

Shakespeare, 8 vols. (London: Routledge; and New York, Columbia University Press, 1957–75), 6:34–44; and by Waith, ed., *Titus,* 195–203. The rape sequence is in Chapter V of the *History.*

8. Stanley Wells, Gary Taylor, John Jowett, and William Montgomery, eds., *Works* (Oxford: Clarendon Press, 1986), *JC* 3.2.13, 74.

9. McKerrow, ed., 2:296, 301, 310–11; Waith, ed., *Titus,* 1.1.9, 2.1.64, 5.1.87–144.

10. Waith, ed., *Titus,* 2.3.116; McKerrow, ed., 2:288, 293.

11. McKerrow, ed., 2:326, 294–95.

12. See chapter on Sources, Origins, Influences.

13. George R. Coffman, "A Note on Shakespeare and Nashe," *MLR,* 42 (1927), 317–19; J. Dover Wilson, ed., *1H4* (Cambridge: Cambridge University Press, 1946), 191–96; W. Schrickx, *Shakespeare's Early Contemporaries* (Antwerp: Nederlandsche Boekhandel, 1956), 210–11; A. Davenport, "Shakespeare and Nashe's *Pierce Penilesse,*" *N&Q,* 198 (1953), 371–74; Frank W. Bradbrook, "Thomas Nashe and Shakespeare," *N&Q,* 199 (1954), 470. See also G. Blakemore Evans, "Thomas Nashe and the 'Dram of Eale,'" *N&Q,* 198 (1953), 377–78.

14. Wilson, New Cambridge *2H6,* 1952, xxvii–xliii. In a section of an article on the *H4* plays entitled "Thomas Nashe and *Henry IV,*" Wilson summarizes the links between the plays and Nashe's writings, explains the difficulties, and concludes: "There, however, I must leave the matter, an unresolved, perhaps insoluble, puzzle." "The Origins and Development of Shakespeare's *Henry IV,*" *Library,* 4:26 (1945), 2–16; Ed., *Titus,* 1948, 118.

15. Chambers, *William Shakespeare,* 2 vols. (Oxford: Oxford University Press, 1930), 1:223.

16. G. R. Hibbard, *Thomas Nashe A Critical Introduction* (Cambridge, MA: Harvard University Press, 1962), 168; David Kaula, "The Low Style in Nashe's *The Unfortunate Traveller,*" *SEL,* 6 (1966), 43–57; Alexander Leggatt, "Artistic Coherence in *The Unfortunate Traveller,*" *SEL* 14 (1974), 30–46; Neil Rhodes, *Elizabethan Grotesque* (London: Routledge, 1980), 89–99. Rhodes is primarily interested in the possible influence of Nashe's comic and satiric writing on Shakespeare's comedies.

17. Jonathan V. Crewe, *Unredeemed Rhetoric: Thomas Nashe and the Scandal of Authorship* (Baltimore: Johns Hopkins University Press, 1982), 11, 107n.21, 112n.2; Jürgen Schäfer, *Documentation in the O. E. D.: Shakespeare and Nashe as test cases* (Oxford: Clarendon Press, 1980), 62; Charles Nicoll, *A Cup of News: The Life of Thomas Nashe* (London: Routledge, 1984), 21, 87.

18. McKerrow, ed., 3:175–76.

19. McKerrow, ed., 1:271.

20. McKerrow, ed., 5:110–13.

21. R. A. Foakes and R. T. Rickert, eds., *Henslowe's Diary* (Cambridge: Cambridge University Press, 1961), 21.

22. G. R. Proudfoot, ed., *A Knack to Know a Knave, MSR* (Oxford: Oxford University Press, 1964), 11.1488–95.

23. Chambers, *William Shakespeare,* 1:319.

24. Peter Alexander, *Introductions to Shakespeare* (London: Collins, 1964), 151.

25. Foakes and Rickert, *Diary,* 19.

26. E. K. Chambers, *Elizabethan Stage,* 4 vols. (Oxford: Oxford University Press, 1923) 3:460.

27. For additional details see the chapter on Date and Chronology.

28. Waith sums up his discussion succinctly [ed., *Titus*, 6.]: "it is . . . quite possible that Nashe remembered lines of this successful play *[Titus]* from earlier performances."

Chapter 10. Music in *Titus Andronicus*

1. J. M. Nosworthy, "Music and its Functions in the Romances of Shakespeare," *ShS* 11 (1958), 60–69, esp. 62–63.

2. F. W. Sternfeld, *Music in Shakespearean Tragedy* (London: Routledge; New York: Dover, 1963; 2nd imp. with corrections, 1967), 217–18; F. W. Sternfeld and C. E. Wilson, "Music in Shakespeare's Work," *William Shakespeare His World His Work His Influence*, 3 vols., ed. John F. Andrews (New York: Scribners, 1985), 2:417–24. Other students of music in Shakespeare offer brief comments on *Titus*. See Edward W. Naylor, *Shakespeare and Music* (London: 1896; rev. ed., London: Dent; New York: Dutton. 1931; Reprint, New York: Da Capo, 1965), 169–72, 175–77, 203; and Charles Cudworth in Phyllis Hartnoll, ed., *Shakespeare in Music* (London: Macmillan; New York: St. Martins Press, 1964), 57, 96.

3. John H. Long, *Shakespeare's Use of Music: The Histories and Tragedies* (Gainsville: University of Florida Press, 1971), 33–38.

4. W. W. Greg, *The Editorial Problem in Shakespeare* (Oxford: Clarendon Press, 1942; 3rd ed., corrected, 1954), 177.

5. Probably because most editors in this century use Q1 as their copy-text, they tend to admit only the stage directions of that quarto. See Dover Wilson, ed., *Titus*, 101; Maxwell, ed., *Titus*, 1961 issue, xvii; Cross, ed., *Titus*, 825; Barnet, ed., *Titus*, 289; Ribner, ed., *Titus*, xii; Kermode, ed., *Titus*, 1019; Bevington, ed., *Works* (Glenview, IL: Scott, Foresman, 1980), 990n; Waith, ed., *Titus*, 43; Stanley Wells and Gary Taylor et. al., eds., *Works* (Oxford: Clarendon Press, 1986), 171. Most editors do not mention or note only in passing the F1 stage directions for music. Waith briefly comments on the most significant of them, the call for hoboyes after 5.3.25, and only Wells and Taylor include it in their text, p. 169.

6. Long, *Shakespeare's Use*, 34–37. Wells, in his examination of the staging problems presented to an editor as a consequence of the "two basic texts" of *Titus*, discusses the stage directions for music. He says in part that Folio's "*Flourish . . .* simply duplicates the Quarto's *Sound Trumpets*." This may be so, but it is not necessarily the case. As Long indicates, the two musical passages can be different and it should also be noted that the expression "sound trumpets" does not without exception call for a blare of trumpets. Wells, *Re-editing Shakespeare for the Modern Reader* (Oxford: Clarendon Press, 1984), 90, 108.

7. Long, ibid., 34–37.

8. Hereward T. Price, "The Authorship of 'Titus Andronicus,'" *JEGP* 42 (1943):55–81. The passage cited occurs on 60–61.

9. Michael Hattaway, *Elizabethan Popular Theatre Plays in Performance* (London: Routledge, 1982), 190–92.

10. R. W. Ingram, "'Their noise be our instruction:' Listening to *Titus Andronicus* and *Coriolanus*," *Mirror up to Shakespeare Essays in Honour of G. R. Hibbard*, ed. J. C. Gray (Toronto: University of Toronto Press, 1984), 277–94, esp. 277–84.

11. Transcribed from a photocopy of Sig. ff3 of the "Perkins Folio," generously provided to me by Professor James L. Sanderson from among the papers assembled by the late Professor Matthew W. Black in preparation for the pro-

jected New Variorum edition of *Titus*. The alterations in the text appear to be in the same hand as that of Collier's *persona,* the Old Corrector.

12. Richard David, "Drams of Eale," *ShS* 10 (1957), 126–34, esp. 126–27.

13. David, *Shakespeare in the Theatre* (Cambridge: Cambridge University Press, 1978), 5.

14. Sally Beauman, *The Royal Shakespeare Company* (Oxford: Oxford University Press, 1982), 224–25. Daniel Scuro, in a review of the RSC 1955 production based in part on an interview with Brook reprinted by Francis Martin in the *Evening Standard* of 24 August 1955, makes some insightful comments in regard to the use of music. "*Titus Andronicus:* A Crimson Flushed Stage!" *Ohio State University Theatre Collection Bulletin* 17 (1970), 40–48, esp. 46. Bryan N. S. Gooch and David Thatcher comprehensively chronicle the use of various kinds of music in the plays of Shakespeare, including *Titus. A Shakespeare Music Catalog,* 5 vols. (Oxford: Clarendon Press, 1991), 3:1682–87. In their Preface (1:xiii) they make the point that "music is an indispensable part of any Shakespearean production."

15. Gerald Freedman, Introduction to *Titus,* ed. M. R. Ridley (London: Folio Society, 1970), 3–5; Douglas Watt, New York *Daily News,* 7 August 1967, 64; Mildred C. Kuner, "The New York Shakespeare Festival 1967," *SQ* 8 (1967), 414–15.

16. Alan C. Dessen, *Shakespeare in Performance: Titus Andronicus* (Manchester: Manchester University Press, 1989), 31; Julie Bookman, Vancouver *Columbian,* 23 June 1986; Bob Hicks, Portland *Oregonian,* 23 June 1986.

Bibliography

Adams, John Cranford. "Shakespeare's Revisions in *Titus Andronicus*." *SQ* 15 (1964): 177–90.

Adams, Joseph Q. *A Life of William Shakespeare*. Cambridge, MA: Riverside, 1923.

Alexander, Peter. *Shakespeare's Henry VI and Richard III*. Cambridge: Cambridge University Press, 1929.

Arthos, John. *Shakespeare: The Early Writings*. London: Bowes; and Totowa, NJ: Rowman and Littlefield, 1972.

Ashley, Leonard R. N. *Authorship and Evidence*. Geneva: Droz, 1968.

Baker, Howard. *Induction to Tragedy*. Baton Rouge: Louisiana State University Press, 1939. Reprint, New York: Russell, 1965.

Baldwin, T. W. *Shakespeare's Love's Labor's Won*. Carbondale: Southern Illinois University Press, 1957.

——————. *On the Literary Genetics of Shakespeare's Plays 1592–1594*. Urbana: University of Illinois Press, 1959.

Barber, C. L., and Richard P. Wheeler. *The Whole Journey: Shakespeare's Power of Development*. Berkeley: University of California Press, 1986.

Barkan, Leonard. *The Gods Made Flesh: Metamorphosis & the Pursuit of Paganism*. New Haven: Yale University Press, 1986.

Bartels, Emily C. "Making More of the Moor: Aaron, Othello and Renaissance Refashionings of Race." *SQ* 41 (1990): 433–54.

Barthelemy, Anthony Gerard. *Black Face Maligned Race*. Baton Rouge: Louisiana State University Press, 1987.

Bate, Jonathan. *Shakespeare and Ovid*. Oxford: Clarendon Press, 1993.

Black, James. "Shakespeare and the Comedy of Revenge," *Comparative Critical Approaches to Renaissance Comedy*. Edited by Donald Beecher and Massimo Ciavolella. Ottawa: Dovehouse, 1986, pp. 137–51.

Boas, Frederick S. *Shakespeare and his Predecessors*. London, 1896. Reprint, Gordian, 1968.

Bolton, J. S. G. "The Authentic Text of *Titus Andronicus*." *PMLA* 44 (1929): 765–88. "*Titus Andronicus*: Shakespeare at Thirty." *SP* 30 (1933): 208–24.

Bowers, Fredson. *Elizabethan Revenge Tragedy 1587–1642*. Princeton: Princeton University Press, 1940. Reprint, 1966.

Bradbrook, M. C. *Themes and Conventions of Elizabethan Tragedy*. Cambridge: Cambridge University Press, 1935. *Shakespeare and Elizabethan Poetry*. London: Chatto & Windus, 1951.

Braunmuller, A. R. "Characterization through Language in the Early Plays of Shakespeare and His Contemporaries." In *Shakespeare Man of the Theatre*, edited by Kenneth Muir, Jay L. Halio, and D. J. Palmer, 128–47. Newark: University of Delaware Press, 1983. "Early Shakespearean Tragedy and its Contemporary Context: Cause and Emotion in *Titus Andronicus, Richard III* and *The Rape of Lucrece.*" In *Shakespearean Tragedy,* edited by Malcolm Bradbury and David Palmer, 97–128. London: Arnold, 1984.

Brooke, Nicholas. "Marlowe as Provocative Agent in Shakespeare's Early Plays." *ShS* 14 (1961): 34–44.

Broude, Ronald. "Roman and Goth in *Titus Andronicus.*" *ShakS* 6 (1970): 27–34. "Four Forms of Vengeance in *Titus Andronicus.*" *JEGP* 78 (1979): 494–507.

Brower, Reuben A. *Hero and Saint Shakespeare and the Graeco-Roman Heroic Tradition.* New York: Oxford University Press, 1971.

Bryant, J. A., Jr. "Aaron and the Pattern of Shakespeare's Villains." *RenP 1984* (1985): 29–36.

Brucher, Richard T. "'Tragedy, Laugh On:' Comic Violence in *Titus Andronicus.*" *RenD* 10 (1979) 71–91.

Bullough, Geoffrey. *Narrative and Dramatic Sources of Shakespeare.* London: Routledge and Kegan Paul; New York: Columbia University Press, 1961–75. Vol. 6, 1966.

Calderwood, James L. *Shakespearean Metadrama.* Minneapolis: University of Minnesota Press, 1971.

Carducci, Jane S. "Shakespeare's *Titus Andronicus:* An Experiment in Expression." *CahiersE* 31 (1987): 1–9.

Chakravorty, Jagannath. *The Idea of Revenge in Shakespeare.* Calcutta: Jadavpur University Press, 1969.

Chambers, E. K. *William Shakespeare A Study of Facts and Problems.* 2 vols. Oxford: Clarendon Press, 1930. "William Shakespeare: An Epilogue." *RES* 16 (1940): 385–401. Reprint, rev. ed., *Shakespearean Gleanings.* London: Oxford University Press, 1944.

Champion, Larry S. *Shakespeare's Tragic Perspective.* Athens: University of Georgia Press, 1976.

Charlton, H. B. *Shakespearean Tragedy.* Cambridge: Cambridge University Press, 1948.

Charney, Maurice. *Titus Andronicus.* Hemel Hempstead: Harvester Wheatsheaf, 1990.

Clemen, Wolfgang H. *The Development of Shakespeare's Imagery.* London: Methuen, 1951. 2d ed., 1977.

Cokayne, Sir Aston. *A Chain of Golden Poems.* London, 1658.

Craig, Hardin. *An Interpretation of Shakespeare.* New York: Dryden Press, 1948.

Cross, Gustav, ed. *Titus Andronicus,* Alfred Harbage, gen. ed., Baltimore: Penguin, 1969.

Cunningham, Karen. "'Scars Can Witness': Trials by Ordeal and Lavinia's Body in *Titus Andronicus.*" In *Women and Violence in Literature,* edited by Katherine Anne Ackley, 139–62. New York: Garland, 1990.

Cutts, John P. "Shadow and Substance: Structural Unity in *Titus Andronicus.*" *CompD* 2 (1968): 161–72.

D'Amico, Jack. *The Moor in English Renaissance Drama.* University of South Florida Press, 1991.

Danson, Lawrence N. "The Device of Wonder." In *Tragic Alphabet: Shakespeare's Drama of Language,* New Haven: Yale University Press, 1974.

de Armas, Frederick A. "Astraea's Fall" Senecan Images in Shakespeare's *Titus Andronicus* and Calderon's *La Vida es sueño.*" In *Parallel Lives: Spanish and English National Drama, 1580–1680,* edited by Louise and Peter Fothergill-Payne, 302–21. Lewisburg, PA: Bucknell University Press, 1991.

Dessen, Alan C. *Shakespeare in Performance: Titus Andronicus.* Manchester: Manchester University Press, 1989. Julie Bookman. Vancouver *Columbian,* 23 June 1986. Bob Hicks. Portland *Oregonian,* 23 June 1986.

Diehl, Huston. "The Iconography of Violence in English Renaissance Tragedy." *RenD* 11 (1980): 27–44.

Dollimore, Johnathan, and Alan Sinfield, eds. *Political Shakespeare.* Manchester: Manchester University Press; Ithaca: Cornell University Press, 1985.

Eliot, T. S. *Seneca His Tenne Tragedies Translated into English.* London: Constable: New York: Knopf, 1927.

Ettin, Andrew V. "Shakespeare's First Roman Tragedy," *ELH* 37 (1970): 325–41.

Evans, Bertrand. *Shakespeare's Tragic Practice.* Oxford: Clarendon Press, 1979.

Farnham, Willard. *The Medieval Heritage of Elizabethan Tragedy.* Berkeley: University of California Press, 1936.

Fawcett, Mary Laughlin. "Arms/Words/Tears: Language and the Body in *Titus Andronicus. ELS* 50 (1983): 261–77.

Feuillerat, Albert. *The Composition of Shakespeare's Plays.* New Haven: Yale University Press, 1953.

Fiedler, Leslie A. *The Stranger In Shakespeare.* New York: Stein and Day, 1972.

Fleay, Frederick G. "On Metrical Tests as Applied to Dramatic Poetry. Part I. Shakspere." *NSST, 1874.* [1874]. *Shakespeare Manual.* London: 1876, 1878.

Forker, Charles R. "*Titus Andronicus, Hamlet* and the Limits of Expressibility." *HamS* 2 (1980): 1–33. "The Green Underworld of Early Shakespearean Tragedy." *ShakS* 17 (1985): 25–47.

Frey, Charles H. *Experiencing Shakespeare.* Columbia: University of Missouri Press, 1988.

Fripp, Edger I. *Shakespeare, Man and Artist.* 2 vols. London: Oxford University Press, 1938.

Fuller, Harold de Witt. "The Sources of *Titus Andronicus.*" *PMLA* 16 (1901): 1–65.

Garber, Marjorie. *Shakespeare's Ghost Writers.* London: Methuen, 1987.

Gardner, Helen. *The Business of Criticism.* Oxford: Oxford University Press, 1959.

Gibbons, Brian. "The Human Body in *Titus Andronicus* and Other Early Shakespeare Plays." *SJ 1989,* (1989), 209–22.

Godshalk, William Leigh. *Patterning in Shakespearean Drama.* The Hague: Mouton, 1973.

Gray, A. K. "Shakespeare and *Titus Andronicus.*" *SP* 25 (1928): 309.

Gray, Henry D. "Chronology of Shakespeare's Plays." *MLN* 49 (1931): 147–50.

Green, Douglas E. "Interpreting 'her martyr'd signs': Gender and Tragedy in *Titus Andronicus.*" *SQ* 40 (1989): 317–26. See also Green, "Staging the Evidence: Shakespeare's Theatrical Avengers." *UC* 12 (1992): 29–40.

Greg, W. W. *The Shakespeare First Folio.* Oxford: Clarendon Press, 1955. *The Editorial Problem in Shakespeare.* Oxford: Clarendon Press, 3d ed., 1954. "Alteration in Act I of 'Titus Andronicus.'" *MLR* 48 (1953): 439–40.

Grosart, Alexander B. "Was Robert Green Substantially the Author of *Titus Andronicus?*" *Englische Studien* 22 (1896): 389–435.

Haaker, Ann. "*Non sine causa:* The use of the Emblematic Method and Iconology in the Thematic Structure of *Titus Andronicus.*" *RORD* 13–14 (1972): 143–68.

Hamilton, A. C. *The Early Shakespeare.* San Marino: Huntington Library, 1967. See also his "*Titus Andronicus:* The Form of Shakespearean Tragedy." *SQ* 14 (1963): 201–13.

Hapgood, Robert. "Shakespeare's Maimed Rites: The Early Tragedies." *Centennial Review* 9 (1965): 494–508.

Harrison, G. B. *Shakespeare's Tragedies.* New York: Oxford University Press, 1952. Reprint, rev. ed., 1969.

Hibbard, G. R. *The Making of Shakespeare's Dramatic Poetry.* Toronto: University of Toronto Press, 1981.

Highet, Gilbert. *The Classical Tradition.* Oxford: Oxford University Press, 1949. Reprint, New York: Oxford University Press, 1957.

Hiles, Jane. "A Margin for Error: Rhetorical Context in *Titus Andronicus.*" *Style* 21 (1987): 62–75.

Hill, R. F. "The Composition of *Titus Andronicus.*" *ShS* 10 (1957): 60–70.

Hinman, Charlton. "The Prentice Hand in the Tragedies of the Shakespeare First Folio: Compositor E." *SB* 9 (1957): 3–20. *The Printing and Proof-Reading of the First Folio of Shakespeare.* 2 vols. Oxford: Clarendon Press, 1963.

Howard-Hill, T. H. *Compositors B and E in the Shakespeare First Folio and Some Recent Studies.* Columbia, SC: By the author, 1976.

Hubbard, F. G. "Repetition and Parallelism in the Earlier English Drama." *PMLA* 20 (1905): 360–79.

Huffman, Clifford Chalmers. "*Titus Andronicus:* Metamorphosis and Renewal." *MLR* 67 (1972): 730–41.

Hulse, S. Clark. "Wresting the Alphabet: Oratory and Action in *Titus Andronicus.*" *Criticism* 21 (1979): 106–18.

Hunt, Maurice. "Compelling Art In *Titus Andronicus.*" *SEL* 28 (1988): 197–218.

Hunter, G. K. *Dramatic Identities and Cultural Tradition: Studies in Shakespeare and His Contemporaries.* Liverpool: Liverpool University Press, 1978.

Jacobs, Henry E. "The Banquet of Blood and the Masque of Death: Social Ritual and Ideology in English Revenge Tragedy." *RenP 1985* (1985): 39–50.

James, Heather. "Cultural disintegration in Titus Andronicus: mutilating Titus, Virgil and Rome." In *Violence in Drama,* edited by James Redmond, 123–40. Cambridge: Cambridge University Press, 1991.

Jones, Eldred. *Othello's Countrymen.* London: Oxford University Press, 1965.

Jones, Emrys. *The Origins of Shakespeare.* Oxford: Clarendon Press, 1977.

Jorgenson, Paul A. *William Shakespeare: The Tragedies.* Boston: Twayne, 1985.

Karr, Judith M. "The pleas in *Titus Andronicus.*" *SQ* 14 (1963): 278–79.

Kendall, Gillian Murray. "'Lend me thy hand': Metaphor and Mayhem in *Titus Andronicus.*" *SQ* 40 (1989): 299–316.

Kistner, A. L. and M. K. Kistner. "The Senecan Background of Despair in *The Spanish Tragedy* and *Titus Andronicus*." *ShakS* 7 (1974): 1–9.

Knight, G. Wilson. *Shakespeare's Dramatic Challenge*. London: Croom; New York: Barnes & Noble, 1977.

Langbaine, Gerard. *An Account of the English Dramatics*. Oxford: 1691. Reprint, Los Angeles: UCLA, 1971.

Law, Robert A. "The Roman Background of *Titus Andronicus*." *SP* 40 (1943): 145–53.

Long, John H. *Shakespeare's Use of Music: The Histories and Tragedies*. Gainsville: University of Florida Press, 1971.

MacDonald, Joyce Green. "'The Force of Imagination': The Subject of Blackness in Shakespeare, Jonson and Ravenscroft." *RenP* (1991): 53–74.

Marienstras, Richard. *New Perspectives on the Shakespearean World*. Translated by Janet Lloyd. Cambridge: Cambridge University Press, 1985.

Marshall, Cynthia. "'I can interpret all her martyr'd signs': *Titus Andronicus*, Feminism and the limits of Interpretation." In *Sexuality and Politics in Renaissance Drama*, edited by Carole Levin and Karen Robertson, 193–209. Lewiston, NY: Edwin Mellen Press, 1991.

Maxwell, J. C., ed. *Titus Andronicus*. New Arden Shakespeare. London: Metheun, 1953. 3d rev. ed., 1961. "Peele and Shakespeare: A Stylometric Test." *JEGP* 49 (1950): 557–61.

McManaway, James G. "The Year's Contributions to Shakespearean Study 3. Textual Studies." *ShS* 3 (1950): 143–46.

Mincoff, Marco. *Shakespeare: The First Steps*. Sofia: Bulgarian Academy of Sciences, 1976.

Miola, Robert S. *Shakespeare's Rome*. Cambridge: Cambridge University Press, 1983. *Shakespeare and Classical Tragedy*. Oxford: Clarendon Press, 1992.

Mowat, Barbara A. "Lavinia's Message: Shakespeare and Myth." *RenP 1981* (1982): 55–69.

Muir, Kenneth. *Shakespeare's Tragic Sequence*. London: Hutchison University Library, 1972. Reprint, New York: Harper, 1979.

Neill, Michael. "'Exeunt with a Dead March:' Funeral Pageantry on the Shakespearean Stage." In *Pageantry in the Shakespearean Theatre*, edited by David M. Bergeron, 153–93. Athens: University of Georgia Press, 1985.

Neilson, William Allan, and Ashley Horace Thorndike. *The Facts about Shakespeare*. New York: Macmillan, 1914.

Nevo, Ruth. "Tragic Form in *Titus Andronicus*." *Publications of the Hebrew University, Jerusalem*, 25 (1973): 1–18.

Oppel, Horst. *Titus Andronicus: Studien zur dramengeschichtlichen Stellung von Shakespeares früher Tragödie*. Heidelberg: Quelle & Meyer, 1961.

Palmer, D. J. "The Unspeakable in Pursuit of the Uneatable: Language and Action in *Titus Andronicus*." *CritQ* 14 (1972): 320–39.

Parker, Douglas H. "Shakespeare's Use of Comic Conventions in *Titus Andronicus*." *UTQ* 56 (1987): 486–97.

Parrott, T. M. "Shakespeare's Revision of *Titus Andronicus*." *MLR* 14 (1919): 16–37.

Payne, Michael. *Irony in Shakespeare's Roman Plays*. Salzburg: Universität Salzburg, 1974.

Platt, Michael. *Rome and Romans According to Shakespeare.* Rev. ed., Lanham, MD: University Press of America, 1984.

Price, Hereward T. "The Authorship of *Titus Andronicus.*" *JEGP* 42 (1943): 55–81.

———. *Construction in Shakespeare.* Ann Arbor: University of Michigan Press, 1951.

———. "Mirror Scenes in Shakespeare." In *Joseph Quincy Adams Memorial Studies,* edited by James G. McManaway, Giles E. Dawson, and Edwin E. Willoughby, 1.1–13. Washington: Folger Sh. Library, 1948.

Ravenscroft, Edward. *Titus Andronicus, or the Rape of Lavinia.* London: 1687. Facsimile reprint, London: Cornmarket Press, 1969.

Reese, Jack E. "The Formalization of Horror in *Titus Andronicus.*" *SQ* 21 (1970); 77–84.

Ribner, Irving. *Patterns in Shakespearean Tragedy.* London: Metheun, 1960.

Robertson, J. M. *Did Shakespeare Write Titus Andronicus?* London: Watts, 1905. Rev. ed., *An Introduction to the Shakespeare Canon.* London: Routledge, 1924. Reprint, Westport, CT: Greenwood Press, 1970.

Rothenberg, Alan B. "Infantile Fantasies in Shakespearean Metaphor." *Psychoanalytic Review* 60 (1973): 205–22.

Root, Robert K. *Classical Mythology in Shakespeare.* New York: Holt, 1903.

Rozett, Martha Tuck. *The Doctrine of Election and the Emergence of Elizabethan Tragedy.* Princeton: Princeton University Press, 1984.

Sacks, Peter M. *The English Elegy.* Baltimore: Johns Hopkins University Press, 1985.

Sarrazin, G[regor]. "Wortechos bei Shakespeare," *SJ* 1:33 (1897): 121–65; *SJ* 2:34 (1898): 119–69.

Schoenbaum, S. *Internal Evidence and Elizabethan Dramatic Authorship.* Evanston, IL: Northwestern University Press, 1966.

Schlösser, Anselm. "*Titus Andronicus.*" *SJW* 104 (1968): 75–84.

Shadoian, Jack. "*Titus Andronicus.*" *Discourse* 13 (1970): 152–75.

Simmons, J. L. "Shakespeare's Treatment of Roman History." In *William Shakespeare: His World, His Work, His Influence,* edited by John F. Andrews, 2:473–88. 3 vols. New York: Scribner's, 1985.

Slights, William W. E. "The Sacrificial Crisis in *Titus Andronicus.*" *UTQ* 49 (1979): 18–32.

Smidt, Kristian. "Levels and Discontinuities in *Titus Andronicus.*" In *Multiple Worlds, Multiple Words: Essays in Honor of Irene Simon,* edited by Hena Mass Jelinek, Pierre Michel, and Paulette Michel-Michot, 283–93. Liege: Univ. of Liege, 1987. Reprint, Smidt, *Unconformities in Shakespeare's Tragedies,* New York: St. Martin's Press, 1990.

Smith, Gordon Ross. "The Credibility of Shakespeare's Aaron." *Literature and Psychology* 10 (1960): 11–13.

Sommers, Alan. "'Wilderness of Tigers: Structure and Synbolism in *Titus Andronicus.*" *EIC* 10 (1960): 275–89.

Spencer, T. J. B. "Shakespeare and the Elizabethan Romans." *ShS* 10 (1957): 27–38. Reprint, *Discussion of Shakespeare's Roman Plays,* edited by Maurice Charney. Boston: Heath, 1964.

Spivack, Bernard. *Shakespeare and the Allegory of Evil.* New York: Columbia University Press, 1958.

Stauffer, Donald A. *Shakespeare's World of Images.* New York: Norton, 1949.

Stampfer, Judah L. *The Tragic Engagement: A Study of Shakespeare's Classical Tragedies.* New York: Funk & Wagnalls, 1968.

Sternfeld, F. W. *Music in Shakespearean Tragedy.* London: Routledge. New York: Dover, 1963.

Styan, J. L. *The Shakespearean Revolution.* Cambridge: Cambridge University Press, 1977.

Talbert, Ernest William. *Elizabethan Drama and Shakespeare's Early Plays.* Chapel Hill: University of North Carolina Press, 1963. Reprint, New York: Gordian Press, 1973.

Tennenhouse, Leonard. *Power on Display: The Politics of Shakespeare's Genres.* New York: Metheun, 1986.

Thomas, Vivian. *Shakespeare's Roman Worlds.* London: Routledge, 1989.

Thompson, Ann. "Philomel in *Titus Andronicus* and *Cymbeline.*" *ShS* 31 (1978): 23–32.

Tillyard, E. M. W. *Shakespeare's History Plays.* Chatto & Windus, 1944.

Timberlake, Philip W. *The Feminine Ending in English Blank Verse.* Menasha, WI: Banta, 1931.

Tokson, Elliot H. *The Popular Image of the Black Man in English Drama, 1550– 1688.* Boston: Hall, 1982.

Toole, William B., III. "The Collision of Action and Character Patterns in *Titus Andronicus:* A Failure in Dramatic Strategy." *RenP 1971* (1972): 25–39.

Tricomi, Albert H. "The Aesthetics of Mutilation in *Titus Andronicus.*" *ShS* 27 (1974): 11–19. "The Mutilated Garden in *Titus Andronicus.*" *ShakS* 9 (1976): 89–105.

van Doren, Mark. *Shakespeare.* Holt, 1939. Reprint, Garden City, NY: Double- day, 1953.

Velz, John W. "Topoi in Ravenscroft's Indictment of Shakespeare's *Titus Androni- cus.*" *MP* 83 (1985): 45–50.

Vyvyan, John. *Patterns in Shakespearean Tragedy.* London: Chatto & Windus, 1959.

Waith, Eugene M., ed. *Titus Andronicus.* Oxford Shakespeare. Oxford: Clarendon Press, 1955.

Wells, Charles. *The Wide Arch: Roman Values in Shakespeare.* New York: St. Martin's Press, 1992.

Wells, Stanley, and Gary Taylor, gen. eds. *Complete Works.* Oxford Shakespeare. Oxford: Clarendon Press, 1986.

Wells, Stanley. *Re-Editing Shakespeare for the Modern Reader.* Oxford: Clarendon Press, 1984.

Wentersdorf, Karl P. "Shakespearean Chronology and the Metrical Tests." In *Shakespeare-Studien: Festschrift für Heinrich Mutschmann,* edited by Walther Fischer and Karl Wentersdorf, 161–93. Marburg: Elwert, 1951.

West, Grace Starry. "Going by the Book: Classical Allusions in Shakespeare's *Titus Andronicus.*" *SP* 79 (1982): 62–77.

Willbern, David. "Rape and Revenge in *Titus Andronicus.*" *ELR* 8 (1978): 159–82.

Wilson, J. Dover, ed. *Titus Andronicus. New [Cambridge]* Shakespeare. Cambridge: Cambridge University Press, 1948. Reissued 1967 including a brief but significant note on p. 1xv.

Wynne-Davies, Marion. "'The Swallowing Womb': Consumed and Consuming Women in *Titus Andronicus*." In *Materialistic Feminist Criticism of Shakespeare*, 129–51. New York: Harvester Wheatsheaf, 1991.

Index

Adams, Joseph Quincy, 125, 138, 143, 151, 164
Alexander, Peter, 27, 192, 193, 194
Arthos, John, 64, 65
Atkins, Robert, 13

Baildon, H. Bellyse, 12, 46, 47
Baker, G. F., 12, 46
Baker, Howard, 12, 46, 159, 160, 161
Baldwin, T. W., 31, 32, 158, 194
Barber, C. L. and Richard F. Wheeler, 89, 90
Barkan, Leonard, 90
Barnet, Sylvan, 31, 157, 195
Bartels, Emily C., 101, 102
Barthelemy, Anthony Gerard, 91, 92
Bartholomew Fair, 11
Bate, Jonathan, 107
Bayliss, Lilian, 13
Bedford, Brian, 13
Berger, Thomas, 138
Bevington, David, 31, 157, 195
Black, James, 90, 91
Black, Matthew W., 14
Boss, Frederick S., 46
Bolton, Edmund, 12
Bolton, J. S. G., 46, 48, 112, 150, 272
Bowers, Fredson, 46, 48
Bradbrook, M. C., 12, 52
Bradley, A. C., 12
Braekman, W., 32, 33, 158
Braunmuller, A. R., 82
Breight, Curt, 102, 103
Brooke, Nicholas, 59
Brooke, Peter, 13, 31
Brooks, H. F., 112, 117
Broude, Ronald, 60, 61
Brower, Reuben A., 63, 64
Brucher, Richard T., 76, 77
Bryant, Jr., J. A., 86
Bullough, Geoffrey, 151

Cairncross, Andrew S., 128
Calderwood, James L., 64
Capell, Edward, 20
Carducci, Jane S., 92
Chakraworty, Jagsnnath, 60, 61
Chambers, E. K., 27, 36, 37, 51, 115, 164, 192, 194
Champion, Larry S., 72, 73
Charlton, H. B., 12, 51
Charney, Maurice, 13, 84
Clemen, Wolfgang H., 12, 52
Cox, John D., 96, 97
Craig, Harding, 61
Cross, Gustav, 31, 36, 157, 165, 195
Cunningham, Karen, 100
Cutts, John P., 59, 60

Dollimore, Johnathan, 273
D'Amico, Jack, 105
Danson, Lawrence N., 69, 70
Dawson, Giles E., 13
de Armas, Frederick A., 106
Dessen, Alan C., 13
Diehl, Huston, 78

Edwards, Philip, 286
Eliot, T. S., 26, 47
Ettin, Andrew V., 62
Evans, Bertrand, 77

Farmer, Richard, 150
Fawcett, Mary Laughlin, 82, 83
Fiedler, Leslie A., 65
Fleay, Frederick Gard, 21, 22, 23, 41
Forker, Charles R., 79, 80, 158
Freedman, Gerald, 13
Frey, Charles H., 95
Fuller, DeW. Harold 111

Garber, Marjorie, 92
Gardner, Helen, 12, 54, 55
Gibbons, Brian, 99, 100

307

Godshalk, William Leigh, 67, 68
Gray, Henry, 26, 27
Green, Douglas E., 96, 97
Greg, W. W., 25, 36, 112, 113, 115, 117, 129, 164

Haaker, Ann, 65, 66
Haggard, Frank E., 272
Halliwell-Phillipps, J. O., 21, 37, 150
Hamilton, A. C., 58, 59
Hapgood, Robert, 57
Harbage, Alfred, 50
Harrison, G. B., 12, 53
Hastings, William T., 46, 49
Hattaway, Michael, 224
Haublein, Ernst, 13
Hibbard, G. R., 80, 81
Highet, Gilbert, 24
Hiles, Jane, 92, 93
Hinman, Charlton, 128, 143
History of Titus Andronicus, 9
Hodges, C. Walter, 9, 13
Honigmann, E. A. J., 196, 197
Hosley, Richard, 13
Howard, Jean E., 85, 86
Howard-Hill, Trevor A., 13
Huffman, Clifford Chalmers, 65
Hulse, S. Clark, 77, 78
Hunt, Maurice, 96
Hunter, G. K., 70, 167, 168, 169

Jackson, McD. P., 33, 34
Jacobs, Henry E., 86, 87
James, Heather, 103, 104
Jeronimo. See The Spanish Tragedy, 11
Johnson, Samuel, 21
Jones, Eldred, 57, 58
Jones, Emrys, 157, 162, 163, 171
Jonson, Ben, 11
Jorgenson, Paul A., 87

Kehler, Dorothea, 100, 101, 109
Kendall, Gillian Murray, 97
Kermode, Frank, 33, 36, 157, 195
Kerrigan, John, 115, 121
Kistner, A. L. and M. K., 70, 172
Kittredge, George Lyman, 28, 37, 161
Knight, Charles, 45
Knight, G. Wilson, 74
Kolin, Philip C., 99

Lamb, Mary Ellen, 96

Langbaine, Gerard, 11, 17, 19, 37
Law, Robert A., 24, 161
Lee, Sidney, 36
Long, William B., 13
Longleat drawing, 9

MacDonald, Joyce Green, 105, 106
Mahon, John W., 93
Malone, Edmund, 20, 21
Marienstras, Richard, 87, 88
Marshall, Cynthia, 104, 105
Maxwell, J. C., 31, 36, 38, 40, 46, 113, 114, 135, 136, 137, 138, 157, 192, 193, 194, 195
McKerrow, R. B., 130, 273
McManaway, James G., 31
Mercer, Peter, 93, 94
Mincoff, Marco, 73, 74, 166, 167, 265
Miola, Robert W., 83, 84, 286
Morton, A. Q., 34
Muir, Kenneth, 66, 156, 171
Munkelt, Marga, 13
Munro, John, 31, 157

Neill, Michael, 88
Neilson, William Allen, 26
Nevo, Ruth, 68, 69

Olivier, Laurence, 13
Oppel, Horst, 31, 158

Palmer, D. J., 66, 67
Papp, Joseph, 13
Parker, Douglas H., 94
Parrott, T. N., 26, 27
Payne, Michael, 71
Pollard, A. W., 36
Pope, Alexander, 19, 21
Price, Hereward T., 28, 29, 30, 31, 36, 46, 49, 115
Prosser, Eleanor, 59

Ravenscroft, Edward, 11, 17, 18, 19, 111
Reese, Jack E., 62, 63
Ribner, Irving, 55, 165
Richer, Jean, 94, 95
Robertson, J. M., 25, 27, 37, 41, 194
Root, Robert K., 24
Rothenberg, Alan B., 69, 70
Rozett, Martha Tuck, 271 n. 78

Sacks, Peter M., 88, 89
Saintsbury, George, 27
Sampley, Arthur M., 28
Sams, Eric, 165, 166
Sanderson, James A., 13
Schlosser, Anselm, 31, 195
Schoenbaum, Samuel, 31
Shadoian, Jack, 63
Simmons, J. L., 89
Simpson, Richard, 23, 24
Sinfield, Alan, 273
Sisson, C. J., 31, 136, 273
Slater, Eliot, 33, 34
Slights, William W. C., 78
Smidt, Kristian, 95
Smith, Bruce R., 172, 173
Smith, Gordon Ross, 55, 56
Sommers, Alan, 56
Spencer, T. J. B., 12, 53, 158
Spivack, Bernard, 12, 54, 170, 171
Stampfer, Judah L., 60
Stodder, Joseph H., 13
Styan, J. L., 74
Sykes, H. Dugdale, 194, 288

Talbert, Ernest William, 56, 57
Taylor, Gary, 13, 34, 35, 36, 41, 42, 116, 196
Tennenhouse, Leonard, 91
Theobald, Lewis, 20, 21
Thomas, Vivian, 98, 99
Thompson, Ann, 75
Thomson, J. A. K., 159, 160, 171

Thorndike, Ashley Horace, 26
Tillyard, E. M. W., 46, 50
Timberlake, Philip W., 27
Tobin, J. J. M., 195
Tocci, Margaret M., 207
Tokson, Elliot H., 81
Toole, William B. III, 67
Tricomi, Albert H., 71, 72

Velz, John W., 13
Vocabulary tests, 23, 24

Waith, Eugene M., 12, 33, 36, 53, 54, 113, 114, 116, 135, 136, 138, 157, 166, 169, 195, 196
Walker, Alice, 113
Warner, Deborah, 13
Wells, Charles, 106
Wells, Henry W., 160
Wells, Stanley, 13, 114, 119, 135, 136, 137, 157, 165, 169
West, Grace Starry, 81, 82
Wheeler, Richard P., 89, 90
Wlilbern, David, 75
Williams, Harcourt, 13
Wilson, J. Dover, 30, 36, 41, 45, 46, 52, 113, 115, 135, 138, 147, 194, 195
Wynne-Davies, Marion, 104, 105

Yates, Frances A., 51
Yeandle, Letitia, 13

Zeeveld, W. Gordon, 72